For Kourtney

ACKNOWLEDGMENTS

Many thanks to Emi Smith, Jenny Davidson, and Joshua Smith for their editing and production efforts that led to this completed book. I am especially thankful to Emi for giving me extra time to make this a labor of love rather than just another book. I absolutely enjoyed this subject and trust the end result reflects the attention that went into it.

Thanks to my wife, Jennifer, and our little ones, for your wonderful distractions. When the first edition was published in 2004, we had only two: Jeremiah and Kayleigh. By the time the second edition went to print in 2007, we had added two more to our family: Kaitlyn and Kourtney. Some day when you read this, know that you have filled my life with joy.

Much appreciation goes out to Eden Celeste for her beautiful character art featured on the cover and in several chapters—all of the hero and monster illustrations are hers. See her work at www.edenceleste.com. It seems like she can draw anything I can imagine and always surprises me with her work.

I am grateful to Reiner Prokein for allowing me to use his extraordinary artwork, which has made the examples in this book possible. His website, Reiner's Tilesets, is located at www.reinerstileset.de. I would not have even *attempted* to create a role-playing game for this book had Reiner not made his artwork available in the first place. The game artwork is all from Reiner.

ABOUT THE AUTHOR

Jonathan S. Harbour is a freelance writer, teacher, and indie game developer, who has been programming video games since the 1980s. His first video game system was an Atari 2600, which he disassembled on the floor of his room at age 9. He has written on languages and subjects that include C++, C#, Basic, Java, DirectX, Allegro, Lua, DarkBasic, XNA Game Studio, Pocket PC, Nintendo GBA, and game console hacking. He is the author of *Visual C# Game Programming for Teens*; *Beginning Java Game Programming, Third Edition*; *Beginning Game Programming, Third Edition*; *Multi-Threaded Game Engine Design*; and *Advanced 2D Game Development*. His next project is *The Complete XNA 4.0*, expected in early 2011. Visit his website at www.jharbour.com, which includes a blog and game development forum.

Contents

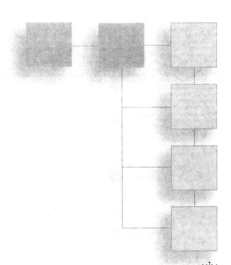

viii   Contents

INTRODUCTION

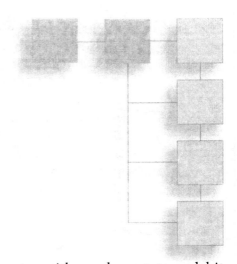

Imagine this: You create a new paladin character with random stats and hit points, receive your first quest, and begin exploring the game world. You stumble upon a skeleton warrior pacing near a pile of treasure. You attack the skeleton, and it hits you back! You roll 1D20 and score a critical hit! The 20-point die, plus dexterity, against the skeleton's armor class, nets a guaranteed hit. Your damage roll is 1D8 plus your strength and weapon modifier, which is 1D4, more than enough to kill the monster! It falls to the ground, a jumble of bones. Lying next to the unmoving skeleton is chain mail armor, which you pick up and equip, giving your character a huge boost in armor points. You also pick up 10 gold coins and gain 25 experience points. A magic key is also found, completing the first quest! Now you dream of finding a better sword. Off to the right, you spot a whole group of undead, the remains of a cursed Viking army, which surely have gear and gold you could use . . . and you head toward them to battle!

This is no fictional narrative. You *will* learn to build a game with *every* feature just described in detail! This book will teach you how to create your own fully functional role-playing game (RPG) using Visual Basic. You will learn step-by-step how to construct each part of the game engine using Windows Forms and GDI+, including a tiled scroller, game editors, and scripting. If you think role-playing games are fun to play, wait until you start working on your very own adventure! Constructing an RPG is more fun than playing one, because you are in complete control over the game world, and you can let your imagination loose to create adventures for others to enjoy. However, it is not easy! Just as your game character must gain experience and level up, so must you level up by reading each chapter to learn new skills!

Before you can get to the point where you are able to design an adventure and build an RPG with Visual Basic, you will need to learn the language. My goal with this book is to teach you just what you need to know in order to make this happen. You will learn what you need to know to construct an RPG. You might choose to use a product such as RPG Maker (on the PlayStation 2), rather than writing your own RPG with Visual Basic. That is certainly a good alternative, but wouldn't it be better to have complete control over how the game works? Certainly you can create many complete RPGs of your own design with RPG Maker in the time it takes to build just one RPG from scratch by doing all of your own programming. But in the end, you will have learned a promising skill—game programming! In addition, you will have complete creative control over how the game operates, and will be able to make many games from the same code and tools.

Pacing and Experience

This book reads like a hobby book, with no pressure and limited goals, because the primary purpose of this book is to help you to have fun learning about game programming. Typing in long source code listings out of a book is not fun, so I don't ask you to do that in this book. Instead, you will learn by studying the short examples in each chapter, and over time you will get the hang of it. There is no memorization required here, as I'm a firm believer that repetition and practice is the best way to learn, not theory and memorization. The Celtic Crusader game is built from one chapter to the next, with new features and gameplay elements added in each new chapter. You will learn to create this game completely from scratch in a very short amount of time.

The finished game in the last chapter includes all the source code to make your own RPG with the features described above, including combat with monsters and enemy NPCs; treasure and gold drops; creating items with the custom item editor; picking up item drops; managing inventory with drag-drop; equipping gear with buffs (stat modifiers) such as armor and weapons; creating NPCs with the character editor; rolling new player characters; saving the game; creating the game world with a custom level editor; and creating quests with the quest editor. Whew! That sounds like a lot of work, but we make all of this happen in the pages of this book, and you will have a playable, customizable RPG game system by the time you reach the last chapter! In fact, why don't you flip to the last chapter now to see what it looks like? I'll wait here for you to return.

Prerequisites

The goal of this book is to teach you how to create an RPG. You will benefit from a basic knowledge of Visual Basic in advance, because beyond Chapter 2 we don't spend any time explaining the Visual Basic language. Programming an RPG is a serious challenge, but if you pay attention and study the examples, you'll be able to do it! We cover the Basic language in Chapter 2, and Form programming in Chapter 3, so you can refer to those chapters any time you have a question about some of the code we're going over. Celtic Crusader is a large game, and it's very hard to program your own RPG! But I'll try to explain it one step at a time. All of the game editors are also covered in the book, but not in complete detail. So, we cover the key code for the editors but don't list all of the source code because that would take up 500 pages!

Visual Basic 2008 and the .NET Framework

This book supports Visual Basic 2008 and requires the .NET Framework 2.0 or later. Although the project files are slightly different, the code is absolutely the same for Visual Basic 2010 as well. If you have 2010 you will still be able to run all of the code in the book, but you will have to import the projects to the 2010 format. I have left the projects in the 2008 format so that more readers will be able to open the projects with either version. I recommend that you download the free version of Visual Basic Express Edition. You can find it at http://www.microsoft.com/express/Downloads/#2010-Visual-Basic. Since web links change frequently, I recommend you instead Google for "Visual Basic Express download." There are links to the 2008 version as well, but 2010 is now the officially supported current version so go ahead and use that version if you want. Just note that the 2008 projects will need to be imported when you open them in 2010. This should not pose a problem; it's just one additional step, and it allows us to support both versions of Visual Basic. One caveat: the LuaInterface library requires the .NET Framework 2.0, so when it comes to the script examples and the final game project in Chapter 20, you may need to create a *new* Visual Basic 2010 project and then import the sources to it, in order for LuaInterface to work correctly. As an option, an advanced reader may recompile LuaInterface with Visual Basic 2010 and then use the later .NET Framework. If you feel confused about this issue, please visit the author's web forum with any questions (www.jharbour.com).

Managed DirectX Goes Away?

This book *no longer* uses Managed DirectX. The first edition, published in 2004, used Visual Basic 6.0 with the DirectX 8 type library. The second edition, published in 2007, changed everything by switching to Visual Basic .NET 2005 and Managed DirectX. This third edition changes everything again by using Visual Basic .NET 2008 and. . . that's all. DirectX is not required because we are not using it any longer. Instead, this book has completely shifted to Windows Forms programming with the Windows GDI+ (Graphics Device Interface). I made this decision after so many readers contacted me with questions about Managed DirectX not working right on their PCs. It was very difficult, and further complicated by the fact that it doesn't work any longer with modern 64-bit Windows.

Contacting the Author

I maintain a website at http://www.jharbour.com, which has information about this book that you may find useful. This site also features an online forum where you can pose questions and keep up to date with the latest discussions about Visual Basic and Celtic Crusader with other programmers. If you have any problems working through this book, stop by the site to chat.

BOOK CONTENTS

The book is divided into three major parts.

"Part I, Building Blocks," includes eight chapters that form the foundation of the role-playing game that is developed in the book. These chapters cover subjects like Windows Forms, bitmaps, sprite animation, user input, collision detection, and similar core subjects.

"Part II, Game World," includes five chapters devoted to building the game engine components needed to manage and render the game world in which the player will live. The core of this game world is a tiled scroller and a level editor.

"Part III, Gameplay," includes seven chapters that develop all of the gameplay components of the role-playing game that make the game truly playable. This part offers additional game editors and classes that make it possible to fight monsters, pick up treasure, manage the player's inventory and equipped gear, gain experience and level up, talk with NPCs, and go on quests. The final game demo in the last chapter shows how the reader may build his own custom RPG using all of the tools and source code.

CONVENTIONS USED IN THIS BOOK

Source code is presented in fixed-width font for easy readability.

```
REM This is what source code will look like in the text
Public Sub Hello()
    Console.WriteLine("Hello World")
End Sub
```

The following styles are used in this book to highlight portions of text that are important.

Hint

Hints offer additional pointers on the current subject being covered.

Trick

Tricks offer guidance and suggestions on what to do or not do in a given situation.

COMPANION WEBSITE DOWNLOADS

You may download the companion website files from www.courseptr.com/downloads. Please note that you will be redirected to our Cengage Learning site.

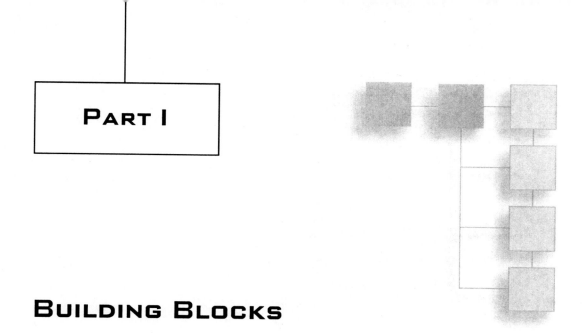

PART I

BUILDING BLOCKS

Welcome to the first part of the book, covering the fundamental building blocks needed to develop the game engine that will be used for the Celtic Crusader game.

- Chapter 1: Getting Started
- Chapter 2: Visual Basic Primer
- Chapter 3: Forms and Controls
- Chapter 4: Drawing with GDI+
- Chapter 5: Bitmaps: Our First Building Block
- Chapter 6: Sprites and Real-Time Animation
- Chapter 7: Collision Detection
- Chapter 8: Playing Sound Effects and Music

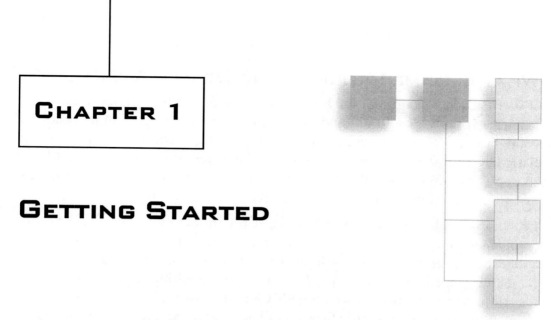

CHAPTER 1

GETTING STARTED

Welcome to the first chapter of *Visual Basic Game Programming for Teens, Third Edition*. This chapter gives you a little overview of what to expect in future chapters and helps set the pace at which we will delve into Visual Basic. The goal of the book is to take you step by step through the development of a role-playing game (RPG) called Celtic Crusader. First, we'll learn the core techniques in 2D game programming in order to fill our "toolbox" with tools—the classes and functions needed for most games, such as bitmaps and sprites. Next, we'll explore game design, work on some game editors, build the game world, and begin populating it with monsters, NPCs, and so on. In order to accomplish these goals, we have to start with the basics.

Here's what we'll cover in this chapter:

- What is game programming really all about?
- Get your feet wet first, ask questions later
- Let your creativity fly
- Creativity, talent, and hard work
- The sky's the limit
- Learning the tricks of the trade
- Taking a look at Celtic Crusader

What Is Game Programming Really All About?

Visual Basic is a good tool for beginners to use for writing games because the language is fairly easy to use and Form-based graphics programming produces good, fast results, which we need for a high-speed game loop. This book treats Basic like a professional game development language. What makes Visual Basic so popular in application development will be useful for our needs as well—we just won't be using any data flow diagrams or flowcharts here!

I spent quite a few years doing Visual Basic programming work for a variety of companies, and I enjoy using it, but I must admit that for every line of application code I have ever written, I was dreaming about game code. Now, no matter what I do day by day, I *love* game programming, and let me tell you, it's *still* a blast! I've been working with C++ most of the time for the last few years, using DirectX and other SDKs, so I have a good perspective on where and how Visual Basic fits into things. As a game development tool, it does a pretty good job in the hands of a good programmer. But, as is the case with even a more powerful language like C++, in the hands of a beginner, it simply will not meet its potential. What you'll need to do over the next few hundred pages is learn how to get the most out of the Basic language, and push it to its limits! We're not using DirectX here, but our gameplay goals are simple enough in the graphics department—we need a 2D scrolling game world with RPG fantasy characters and scenery. The "Visual" in Visual Basic allows us to *also* create some game editors as well—and that's something you *can't* do easily in C++ (I've tried!). Making a 2D RPG is feasible with just about any language and platform, but we're going to explore RPG creation with Basic.

Note

If you also like the C# language and want to learn even *more* role-playing game development tricks, then check out the sister book, *Visual C# Game Programming for Teens*, which will be available soon. Not simply a port of the Visual Basic projects to Visual C#, the C# book takes on a *whole new* sub-genre: *dungeons*! But it gets even better: the game you'll create in *this* book—an open world with towns, trees, and beaches—will *link up* with the *dungeon crawler* game in the C# book, so that when you enter a portal in the world, it will take you into a dungeon. The C# language is quite different from Visual Basic, but the .NET Framework and Forms code is the same. That book may also be a good stepping-stone toward getting into XNA Game Studio. See, there are so many great tools for us to use today!

However, you have to keep something in mind: This is a small book, and our goal is to create a role-playing game (RPG) with all the trimmings within these pages. If you feel that you are completely lost within the next few chapters, my advice is to pick up a Visual Basic primer to get up to speed, and then return to this book. Nothing in here is confusing, but a lot of information is presented at a fast pace, so you don't want to get left behind. If you are totally new to Visual Basic, then the next chapter will at least give you an overview of the language, with enough information to help you to understand the Celtic Crusader game.

Tip

Those familiar with the previous editions of this book will recall our use of Managed DirectX. In this new *Third Edition*, we are no longer using DirectX, because the Managed libraries are no longer supported by Microsoft, and there is no 64-bit version available (nor will there ever be one). We can achieve similar results with Windows Forms-based graphics programming using GDI+ (the modern graphics device interface for working with Form-based graphics). By *not* supporting DirectX any longer, we can devote those pages toward gameplay! In other words, the game will be more complete, more playable, and more fun, as a result—and *this time*, we have *game editors*! So even if you are more of a designer than a programmer, you will be able to build an RPG using the editors and the demo game without having to write much code.

Get Your Feet Wet First, Ask Questions Later

For every great game idea that someone has, a thousand more ideas are waiting to be thought up by a creative person. One thing I want you to do while reading this book is learn to think outside the box. I realize that is a cliché that you have heard many times, but it is an important concept because it helps you visualize the point very clearly. Most people, and many programmers for that matter, are unable to think beyond the experience of their collected memories. A very rare person is able to think about something completely foreign, the likes of which has never been thought of before. The phrase "thinking outside the box" can mean many things, depending on the context, but when I'm talking about writing a game, I mean you should think of ideas that are *above and beyond* what has already been done. The greatest game ideas have *not* all been taken already!

For every *Doom* there are a dozen more trend-setting game ideas waiting to be invented. Don't be discouraged, believing that the best ideas have been discovered already. That is what many gamers believed before real-time strategy games *took over* the game industry a few years ago. (If you don't believe me, just take a look at sales for *StarCraft* II!) What's the next great game genre? It hasn't been *invented* yet. That is your job!

Tip

Before you can let your creativity flow, you need a foundation in the basics of programming, so you aren't always bogged down, not knowing how to make your imagination come to life on the screen. Learn as much as you can so your ideas can be put into motion without losing your momentum while looking up basic programming issues. Get up to speed *quickly* so you can create games, and move beyond the learner stage.

Do you really think John Carmack, John Romero, and Adrian Carmack based *Doom* on their memories of *Pac-Man* back in 1993? It's entirely possible that *Doom* is older than you are (or at least older than you were before you could play games). Many of the current generation don't understand the hoopla over *Doom* because games were so different back then. In 1992, I was playing Sid Meier's *Civilization* on my PC, *Super Mario World* on my Super NES (which you might recognize as *Super Mario Advance 2* on the GBA, which is *already* obsolete now that we have the Nintendo DSi and 3DS), and *Dragon Crystal* on my Game Gear. The fact is, most people did *not* play games back then, unlike today, when almost everyone does! A game like *Doom* was unbelievable at the time, which is why people are still sharing fond memories about it today; that is why *Doom III* was created, and that is why David Kushner wrote the book *Masters of Doom*. *Doom* was so dramatically different from all the other games at the time that a whole new genre was created: the first-person shooter (FPS). FPS games dominate the game world today, unlike any other genre, partially because it consumed the virtual reality market, which was flagging at the time.

Do you want to create a game like *Doom* using Visual Basic? That goal is *absolutely* possible, but it would be a challenge. The Visual Basic compiler creates intermediate language (IL) code that looks exactly the same regardless of whether you're using Basic or C#, and then that IL code is compiled to an object file and linked into an executable file. That compiled Visual Basic game code *could* deliver a gaming experience like *Doom*. There are few third-party libraries available for Basic, like there are for C#—and even more so, C++. For example, most C++ games use helper libraries like Perlin (a texture generator), zlib (for reading Zip files), FMOD or libogg (for audio playback), and none of these are available for Basic. So, even though we could technically build a game like *Doom* in Basic, we would have to re-invent a lot of things on our own, or link up those C++ libraries through a complex interop library with .NET wrappers for each of the C++ functions we need. It's just a lot of work, and Basic is not often a favorite among professionals because of this reason. Why stop there? How about *Quake*? The first two *Quake* games were not extremely advanced beyond *Doom*. Oh, sure, they used matrix transformations and lighting and 3D models, but it would be no problem for your modern video card to handle brute force rendering *without* any optimization. But, again, it comes down to the language. So, we're not going to build a *Doom*-style game in Basic, but we *are* going to create an incredibly fun role-playing game engine!

What if we wanted to make a game like *World of Warcraft*? You could *definitely* create a smaller, less ambitious version of *WoW* using Basic and Managed DirectX (which is now obsolete—replaced by XNA Game Studio), but we can't do that kind of 3D rendering with Forms-based graphics. The most challenging aspect of the game is the server, and in the case of *WoW*, there is not a single server, or even a bunch of servers; there are *racks* and *racks* with hundreds of servers at several geographical locations around the *world*. So, while it is technically feasible to play *WoW* with your friend from Australia (by signing on to the same region), the odds are that bandwidth would be a challenge. The limitation has to do with latency, or lag, due to the number of jumps required to send a packet of data around the world. In a game like *WoW*, you need a fast Internet connection with very few latency problems in order for the gaming experience to be realistic.

I'm sure you've experienced the rare and humorous "slideshow effect" in some games where the server becomes overburdened and cannot keep up, so players do not receive server updates for several seconds until the server can catch up. This primarily happens when a number of players are connecting with high latency, causing the connections to lag. In sufficient numbers this causes the game to stutter or go into "slideshow mode." (The phrase comes from the frequent exclamation by gamers to the effect of, "I'm enjoying the slideshow of screenshots today!") Although Blizzard makes millions of dollars in player fees every month, the company *spends* millions on Internet bandwidth to make the game even possible.

On Programming Languages

So, what kind of hardware do you need to play a game built using Forms-based Visual Basic? Basically, we're talking about the same kind of gaming hardware needed to play just about any game currently on store shelves, but we can get by with lower-end PCs since we will not be invoking any 3D rendering devices. Consider the typical NHRA dragster. It can make usually only a few passes down the quarter mile before the engine needs to be rebuilt. It can do it in about *four seconds*, but only once. On the other hand, your average family sedan or minivan will take about 20 seconds to reach the 1,320-foot mark, and a sports car will do it in about 12 seconds. But what about ease of use, multipurpose functionality, fuel mileage, and so on? You can't exactly strap a child's car seat to a dragster to go to a doctor's appointment. Although you could potentially get there a lot faster, the darned car can barely turn left or right, let alone navigate in traffic. So, what if we use a more realistic racecar as an example: a *NASCAR car*. Here, we have a little more versatility, and the *power potential* is still stratospheric. But there are no headlights, taillights, or any modern conveniences such as air conditioning or *mufflers*. Do you know how loud a car sounds without mufflers? You don't even need a racing engine to deafen yourself. At any rate, a typical *NASCAR* vehicle is insanely fast, but very inflexible and error-prone, unable to withstand the abuses of stop-and-go city traffic.

The same might be said of C++; it is incredibly fast and powerful, but very fragile. I write a lot of C++ code. I have about 15 years of experience with the language. And even after all that, I still get stuck for hours at a time trying to figure out a syntax error in my C++ programs. This happens all the time! It's part of the understanding one must have with this language. But if you show it the proper respect, understand its power, and try not to get frustrated, then little by little you make progress, wrapping the lowest-level features of a game in a layer of protective classes, then another layer, and so on until you have a well-behaved program that is error free. Windows itself—yes, the operating system—was written in C++. When you work with the DirectX SDK using C++, you literally are working with the internals of the Windows OS, and can tinker with the Windows.h source code file.

Here's one that will blow your mind: Visual Basic was created with the C++ language! (Technically, we're talking about Visual Studio.) Weird, isn't it? I'm talking about the compiler, the editor, and so on. I've written about another game programming tool for beginners called DarkBASIC Professional, developed by The Game Creators (www.thegamecreators.com), and this tool (along with its DirectX game engine) was also created in C++. Even the latest version of Visual C++ was created with the *previous* version of Visual C++. That can kind of mess with your head if you think about it.

Building a modern first-person shooter (FPS) game requires a lot more than just rendering polygons. You have to write the code to load a BSP level, the code to load hierarchical meshes, the shader code to render meshes with lighting and special effects, the code to load and play sound effects and music, and that's just the technical side. You also have to consider the game's *design*, because a game that just looks cool is not all that great without a good story, and that's where the designer comes in. *Quake II* didn't have much of a design behind it, and actually it seems to me that id Software sort of tacked on the story after the game was nearly finished. But we're talking about a world famous game studio here, not "*<insert your name>* Studios."

Let Your Creativity Fly

The important thing to realize, though, is that thinking outside the box and coming up with something unprecedented is just the first step toward creating a new game. You must have the technical know-how to pull it off. In the field of video games, that means you must be a skilled programmer. If you are just getting started, then this book is perfect because Visual Basic allows you to practice some of your game ideas without getting too bogged down with a difficult programming language (such as C++). These languages have a tendency to suck away all of your time and leave your mind numb and unable to think creatively. Writing solid code has a tendency to do that to a person, which is why it is a huge help when you start with a not-too-difficult language, such as Basic.

Tip

You don't need to be a C++ programmer to write a killer game! All it takes is good artwork, a good story, and well-written code. You don't need to write *fancy* code with complex algorithms; you simply must follow through and *complete the game*. That is really what it's all about—and *that* is what game industry professionals are looking for in a candidate.

On Creativity, Talent, and Hard Work

I have seen some high-quality games created with DarkBASIC. After you have finished with this book, I encourage you to consider *DarkBASIC Pro Game Programming, Second Edition* (Course Technology, 2006). Once you have mastered the Basic language and written a few games with it, maybe then you will have some experience with which to support a study of C++. I've ported some games from Visual Basic to C++/DirectX, and then to DarkBASIC, and then Java. In fact, the tile scroller engine developed in this book was featured in that DarkBASIC book; see Chapter 15, "2D Game Worlds: Level Editing and Tile-Based Scrolling." And for the C++ code, see Chapter 10, "Scrolling the Background" in *Beginning Game Programming, Third Edition*. Source code is *very similar* among languages when you understand the *concepts* behind it. The tiled layer scrolling you'll learn about in this book formed the foundation of several games created in other languages, and now we will port it again from the Managed DirectX version from the previous edition to Windows Forms and GDI+ in this new edition. Remember, it's all about *concepts*!

What you want to strive for as a budding game programmer is an understanding of these *concepts*, and the best way to do that is to write games using your favorite language. Believe it or not, I got started in programming with Microsoft Basic, which came with most of the old computers at the dawn of the PC industry (on such systems as Apple II, Commodore PET, and IBM PC).

I have to say that technical programming language skills are about equal in importance to your creativity. I've known some very talented programmers who don't have an ounce of creativity in their bones, so they are not able to do anything unique and interesting without someone else giving them the ideas first. It's okay to be a person like that—really, really good at programming but not very creative—because you can always borrow ideas from other games and things like movies, and leave the ideas to a game designer or another person who needs your technical skills. It doesn't matter if you have the technical or creative bent, because you really need to learn everything you can. Think about your favorite subjects in school, or favorite movies, and always ask yourself this question: could I make a game out of *that*?

The Sky's the Limit

Did you know that you could write your own games for the Game Boy Advance? I'm talking about the GBA, the GBA SP, *and* the DS. Imagine seeing your own games running on the GBA. Would that be the coolest thing ever, or what? That's something you definitely *can* do once you have learned enough and mastered a few programming languages, as I have suggested in the previous few paragraphs. All console programming, such as that for the GBA, is done in C++. For more information on GBA and DS programming, you can download my free e-book, *Programming the Nintendo Game Boy Advance*, from my website at www.jharbour.com. This e-book is intermediate to advanced, assuming that you already know how to program in C++.

Did you know that you could also write your own games for the Xbox 360? Microsoft provides XNA Game Studio 4.0 for free, and it uses Visual C# 2010 Express as the compiler. For a small annual fee, you can upload your XNA games to a special "developer's" location on Xbox Live Arcade, which is called the Creator's Club, and then download the game to your Xbox 360 and see *your own code* running on a real 360. You can also sell your game on Xbox Live for a 70% royalty without a retail license agreement (the licensing is similar to web gaming sites).

You don't need to limit your creative juices to just what you *think* is possible. In fact, don't limit yourself at all, and don't assume that you *can't* do anything, even if you have tried and failed. If you can imagine something, no matter how out of this world it might seem, then it's possible to build it. That is what human imagination is all about. What Jules Verne imagined back in the late 1890s—ideas that were so crazy that everyone laughed at them—suddenly became a reality fewer than 70 years later. Imagine that—people riding around in horse carriages, on dirt or cobblestone roads, and some crazy writer suggests that people will walk on the moon. What a lunatic, right? If you lived in 1890, you probably would have thought he was crazy! It's easy for us to make fun of people when we later know better (something called *hindsight*), just as it is easy to criticize a small flaw in a complex automobile or computer. (It's *easy* to critique; it's *hard* to create. Why do you think there are so many blogs on the net today? Uncreative people tend to criticize what they are not able to create on their own.)

Jules Verne described the rocket ship that would blast off the Earth with an explosion of mighty power that would lift the huge rocket off the ground and propel men into space so they could land on the moon. Doesn't that sound familiar? If you have ever watched a video of the Apollo 11 mission, it is uncanny how Jules Verne described the launch 70 years before that time. Even today, boosters are launched into orbit using the same basic technology, although the rockets are a lot more powerful and more efficient than they were during the Apollo program (so much so that private companies are springing up with plans to usher in space tourism in the near future). What am I getting at here? Just this: don't *assume* that a wild idea is impossible before trying. I'm sure you've heard the story about how many failed light bulbs Thomas Edison built before finally getting one to work. I've found that one of the best ways to make a great game is to base it on one of my own favorite subjects—something with which I am intimately familiar! That makes it easy to build the game because no design doc is really needed.

Learn the Tricks of the Trade

The most technically skilled programmers are often those who copy the most creatively talented people in the world. From that perspective, people are still copying the work of John Carmack (of id Software), who continues to crank out unbelievable game engines. The vast majority of game developers are trying to keep up or succumb to Carmack's genius and end up paying to use his latest game engine. Carmack is one of the few who possesses both unmatched technical skill and incredible creative talent. Although he was born with the talent, he learned the technical skill purely from hard work, putting in an unbelievable number of hours at his keyboard, experimenting, tweaking, and trying new things, day after day, month after month, year after year. . . and he is still going at it.

If your whole purpose is just to have some fun while learning how to write your own game, and you have no real desire to become a master of it, that is perfectly okay! I am one of those people. I love writing games for the enjoyment of myself and others, and I don't really care whether my latest game is any good. If you are approaching game development from the standpoint of a hobby, the whole point is to have fun. If you want to get serious, attend a game-development college, and then get a job as a professional game developer, you'll probably take the subject a little more seriously. There are benefits to just treating this subject as a hobby: no deadlines or pressure, and the freedom to do whatever you want. Have you always wanted to create your very own role-playing game (or another type of game), and you've decided to learn how to do it on your own? That's great! In fact, that is largely the direction this book takes. If your goal is to do this for a living, then I wish you the very best; this book may be your first stepping-stone on the path toward that dream.

When I suggest you think outside the box, therefore, I'm advising that you try not to succumb to the "been there, done that" mentality of creating yet another mod (using a game engine like *Battlefield*), or another *Tetris* clone, or another version of *Breakout*. These terrific learning experiences are very common because these latter two types of games are easy to make and demonstrate important concepts in game programming. A game engine mod, on the other hand, is an entirely different issue; most mods require little or no programming. They are merely conversions with new 3D models and game levels to match a new theme (as is the case with *Desert Combat* [a *Battlefield 1942* mod] and *Counter-Strike* [a *Half-Life* mod]). Try to come up with some completely original game ideas and develop them; no matter how simple a game concept is, if it's a brand-new idea, then it will probably be interesting! Of course, the fun factor is entirely up to you, the game's designer and programmer.

Note

For good examples of indie games developed by a team of volunteers, check out *Starflight—The Lost Colony* at www.starflightgame.com, and *Aquaphobia: Mutant Brain Sponge Madness*, at www.aquaphobiagame.com.

TAKING A LOOK AT CELTIC CRUSADER

This book builds just one game to teach the subject of game programming and to give an overall picture of how the topics in each chapter are put to use in a real game. The alternatives are to forego a sample game altogether or to just use small example games or graphics demos to explain how a new subject can be put to use. Small demos and mini games provide good examples of individual subjects, but an entire game will give you a better grasp of the "big picture." This game we're going to build is based on a scrolling game world and animated sprites with pre-existing royalty-free artwork, courtesy of Reiner

Figure 1.1
Celtic Crusader is a game you create from scratch in this book.

Prokein (www.reinerstileset.de). Figure 1.1 shows the game as it will look when you are finished with it in this book's last chapter.

Building a Role-Playing Game

I chose to create a complete RPG for this book because no other subject digs deeper into the depths of game programming than a real RPG with all of the functionality you expect from this genre. Since I come from the old school of gaming, I am still fond of classics such as *Ultima VII: The Black Gate*. There's an open source engine called *Exult Ultima7 Engine* (shown in Figure 1.2) that uses the original *Ultima VII* artwork and data files and re-creates the gameplay, with

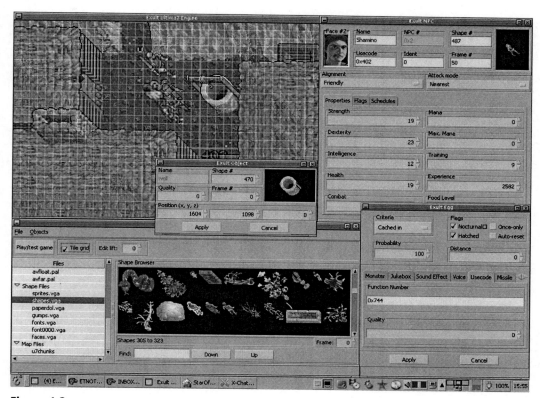

Figure 1.2
Exult Ultima7 Engine.

complete game editors included. Download and play it from http://exult.
sourceforge.net.

My second choice was a game based on *Star Trek*, but there are the obvious
copyright problems when using a TV show as the basis for a game. If you really
love some subject such as *Star Trek*, then I encourage you to go ahead and write
a game about that subject and then give it away to your friends. The learning
experience is enhanced when you are working on a game about a subject that
you really enjoy and that has a lot of texture, with a huge background story
surrounding it. The RPG we will build as an overall learning experience is called
Celtic Crusader and takes place in medieval Ireland, complete with ancient
Celtic history and myth as background material for our game. We'll be building
this game while learning important new skills in each new chapter.

The Story

"On the isle of Eire, Norse Vikings begin invading inland, while they have historically been content with coastal towns. They discover an ancient ruin in the region of Ulster. The ruin is the tomb of an evil warlord of ages past, which curses the Viking army. They wander the countryside as undead, attacking everyone and destroying everything they find. The game begins in the middle of this nightmare. Player must discover what happened via quests, and find a way to seal the tomb again, which will remove the undead curse and bring peace."

The story in Celtic Crusader does not include just fantasy creatures as you might find in some RPGs (vampires, skeletons, werewolves, giant snakes, giant spiders, dragons, and the like)—there will be some creatures like this to make the gameplay as fun and engaging as possible. But, we will also have human characters to fight against, such as the aforementioned Vikings, as well as non-player characters (NPCs) in towns and villages scattered across the isle. Figure 1.3 shows some of the monster sprites we have available for the game, courtesy of Reiner Prokein. While fantasy characters are a lot of fun to kill in most RPGs, and Celtic Crusader has a lot of creatures to fight, this game also features some human characters that your player will encounter.

N o t e

The artwork shown here for the Celtic Crusader game was created by Reiner "Tiles" Prokein, who makes them freely available with no strings attached. You may browse Reiner's sprites and tiles at www.reinerstileset.de.

Describing the Player's Character

The most robust RPGs usually allow the player to create a custom character to play, although in recent years this has taken a backseat to hack-and-slash games

Figure 1.3
Assortment of monster sprites available for our game.

like *Baldur's Gate* (which is okay because it introduces another type of gamer to the great fun had with an RPG and gives the type of person who would not normally play an RPG a glimpse into a bigger world).

This is just a glimpse at a larger game that you have an opportunity to create in this book! Of course, you can tweak and modify the game to suit your own imagination, and you will have the technical know-how after reading this book to do just that. We'll be going over the game engine for Celtic Crusader step by step, and will develop the game in each new chapter, but the complete game with quests and goals is up to you!

I am taking this game in a slightly different direction and following a real-world scenario, as you might find in the *Ultima* and *Legend of Zelda* series. There are a lot of human characters in Celtic Crusader (as you learn in the next few chapters), and the player can choose from several character classes. Good *non-player characters (NPCs)* also help the player to successfully complete the game's primary quest chain and sub-quests. In our game, we will allow the player to create a custom character based on several character classes, as shown in Figure 1.4. Some possible classes include:

Warrior	Strong melee fighter with powerful weapons and plate armor
Paladin	Balanced melee fighter who wears plate armor and heals himself
Hunter	Dexterous ranged fighter who wears leather armor
Mage	Powerful magic user who wears cloth and wields a staff

Figure 1.4
Some of the character class sprites available for our game.

Tip

You will be able to define your own character classes using the character editor in Chapter 14, "Creating The Character Editor."

Adventure Game or Dungeon Crawler?

Two types of classic RPGs exist in my opinion: adventure games and dungeon crawlers. The typical dungeon crawler is made up of a town where you can equip your character (purchase weapons, armor, and so on) using the treasure you find in the dungeon, which is usually made up of many levels and driving deep into the Earth, and is often portrayed as a gold mine that became infested with evil creatures. The standard of the genre is widely considered to be the classic game *Rogue*, shown in Figure 1.5. While you are killing bad guys (represented as little ASCII characters like #, %, and &), your experience is going up and you are finding gold. As your experience goes up, your skills go up as well, and this is reflected by your character's level. A level-20 warrior, for instance, can dispatch level-5 skeleton archers with the back of his hand, so to speak, while a level-18 fire dragon poses a serious threat! This type of game is typically very simple in concept, lacking any serious storyline or plot—hence the term *dungeon crawler* or *dungeon hack*. *Diablo* and *Dungeon Siege* epitomize this type of game, and that is the focus of the sister book, *Visual C# Game Programming for Teens*.

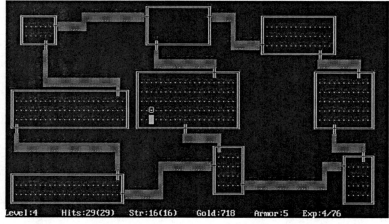

Figure 1.5
Rogue defined the RPG genre in the ancient days of computer gaming.

The other type of RPG, the adventure game, usually takes place on the surface rather than in a dungeon or underground mine and often involves a deeper storyline with quests to challenge the player. This game allows the player's character to gain experience, weapons, and special items, such as armor, amulets, magic rings, and so on. Although the main quest of an adventure RPG might be very difficult, sub-quests allow the player's character to reach a level sufficient to beat the game's main quest. Sub-quests offer plenty of opportunity for a creative game designer to insert fascinating stories and interactions with NPCs. *Ultima VII* is a good example of this type of game.

I must admit, the latter is my choice of RPG between the two types, because in an adventure RPG, you can create multiple towns across the countryside and allow the player to explore a vast world. The dungeon hack is a lot of fun, I'll admit, and both types of RPG have merit. I've chosen the adventure type of game for Celtic Crusader, but the game world can easily accommodate dungeons as well—see Chapter 13, "Using Portals to Expand the World," for information on how Celtic Crusader will be linked with the dungeon engine developed in C#.

We will be building a level editor just for this game, entirely from scratch. Since the editor will also be used to create the dungeon crawler game, this particular editor is built in C#. The other editors featured in upcoming chapters (character editor, item editor, and quest editor) are built with Basic.

Level Up!

This chapter introduced you to the main concepts you'll be learning about in the rest of the book from a high-level point of view. In the upcoming chapters, you will learn how to take the first step toward writing games with Visual Basic by creating your first Visual Basic project and delving into Forms-based GDI+ graphics programming. This chapter was short on details but long on ideas, presenting a glimpse of the Celtic Crusader game, an RPG that you create while following along with this book. The remaining chapters in Part I will give you a primer on the Basic language, and introduction to GDI+ graphics programming, and the foundational code that will be needed for the game.

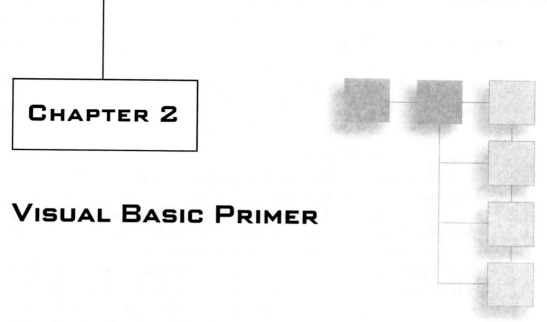

CHAPTER 2

VISUAL BASIC PRIMER

This chapter is a quick overview of Visual Basic: a little theory here, a little source code there, and a lot of new stuff throughout. Visual Basic is an exciting language, and it's a blast to use! As I'm sure you will find out soon enough, the learning curve for Visual Basic is a shallow one. You'll be up to speed and able to write your own programs from scratch in no time. I'll help you through the tough spots and introduce you to key topics and those parts of the language that you need to get things done. The rest is up to you! Software development is highly dependent upon one's creativity, so don your creative hat.

Here's what we'll cover in this chapter:

- What is Visual Basic?
- Writing your first Visual Basic program
- Variables of all types
- Branching/conditional statements
- Subroutines and functions
- Mathematical operators
- Relational operators
- Looping statements

- Arrays and structures
- Object-oriented programming

WHAT IS VISUAL BASIC?

Visual Basic is a graphical programming language and the top of the class in Rapid Application Development (RAD) tools for Windows. In fact, Visual Basic is the most popular Windows development tool with millions of users. The key to the success of *Visual* Basic is the fantastic and easy-to-learn *Basic* language that powers a drag-and-drop visual user interface design tool—called an IDE, or *integrated development environment*. Visual Basic shares a Windows Form engine with other .NET Framework languages so all of the source code that you write with Visual Basic *.NET* is compatible with Visual C# *.NET* and Visual C++ *.NET* (referring to what's called "managed code"). But what is a user interface? A graphical user interface, or GUI as it has come to be known, is a visual method of using software, primarily with a mouse. In the old days of UNIX and MS-DOS, computer users had to memorize complex commands, typed into a command prompt. Type a command, hit Enter, and the computer spews out some information (or more commonly, it would beep with a rude error message).

Windows replaced MS-DOS, just as Linux gradually replaced UNIX, and along with the "GUI way" came even more complexity–for the *programmer*, that is. Windows is not an easy operating system to program. Believe it or not, in the old days, Windows programmers had to use Microsoft C, which ran under MS-DOS! Talk about ironic. Not only was Windows difficult to program, the development tool didn't even run under Windows. As you can imagine, those were *not* the good old days for Microsoft developers. Most veteran Windows programmers have little fondness for the way things used to be. Visual Basic was really written to make Windows programming easier. The ability to drag controls onto a form and mold the controls to your liking using simple properties is a trademark feature of Visual Basic—which revolutionized the software industry.

We aren't going to get into too much of the technical side of the .NET Framework or anything like intermediate language issues in this book, but we do need to cover the fundamentals. Consider this chapter a quick reference on using the Basic language. If you already have some experience with Basic, you may want to skip this and the next chapter (covering forms and controls) and move on to Chapter 4, "Drawing with GDI+."

The .NET Framework

There are cases in which the complexity of software is just too much for a single person to grasp. System maintenance is becoming more important as software continues to evolve. Businesses depend on software for day-to-day work. The days of custom building monumental software systems are coming to an end, because such systems are impossible to maintain. The .NET Framework brings several languages and design tools together into a seamless whole so that people can focus on gathering the requirements for a system, building prototypes, and then completing their applications. The .NET Framework makes it possible to write huge Windows programs without needing a Windows API reference book handy. That is, essentially, the layman's definition of .NET!

Definition

The *.NET Framework* is the core architecture behind Visual Basic .NET and the other .NET languages, providing common runtime, compatible code libraries, and a fully integrated Windows API library.

Microsoft, as well as many other software companies, has tried in earnest to come up with a standard for code reuse, such as the Component Object Model (COM). Microsoft's COM pre-dates .NET. It allows developers to build custom user-interface controls and code component libraries that were reusable across many languages (such as Visual Basic and Borland Delphi—now owned by Embarcadero). The ability to write source code for a component using Visual Basic, and then reuse that component in Delphi was a significant step forward for software engineering. These two languages have very little in common! Visual Basic was originally based on the Basic language, while Delphi was based on Pascal. Many other products support COM as well, and this has only benefited their customers. The .NET Framework goes beyond COM by defining a standard collection of namespaces and classes for Windows development, and is similar to the C++ Standard Library.

Definition

The original Basic language stands for Beginner's All Purpose Symbolic Instruction Code. It was invented in 1964 by John Kemeny and Thomas Kurtz at Dartmouth College (New Hampshire) to make programming easier for non-engineers.

Windows Messages

The "engine" that works behind the scenes in a Visual Basic program interprets the Windows messaging system, which is how Windows tells your program when something happens to the user interface. The controls are part of the *form* and therefore have access to all of the messages that the operating system sends the program. For example, when you click a button on a form, Windows sends your program a special message that includes a header pointing to the form and the control that triggered the message. Visual Basic receives this special message from the operating system and routes it to the form containing the specific button that was clicked.

What happens at this point? The form engine—which is part of the runtime library (and also closely tied to the .NET Framework)—looks for a Click event for that button. If so, the event is called; otherwise, the message is discarded. From that point, it is up to you (the programmer) to decide what happens inside that event.

As you can imagine, there are thousands of messages streaming through the Windows operating system, which are being routed to operating system processes and running applications. Visual Basic handles all the details for you by breaking down the complexity into a number of events that are called automatically in your program through the common Windows Forms "engine" and .NET Framework. Visual Basic and Visual C# just tap into that engine.

WRITING YOUR FIRST VISUAL BASIC PROGRAM

If you are new to Visual Basic, then we'll get started right away by writing a simple program. If you're already familiar with the language, you may skip ahead. Visual Studio uses the concept of a "solution" to "solve programming problems." Most programs are written, after all, to process data in one way or another, and that data may not be in a suitable format that is useful. Visual Studio treats a project workspace as a solution, and the workspace (or solution) file even has an extension of .sln.

Visual Studio solutions can become quite complex. Not only can you have several Visual Basic projects in the solution, you can have Visual C# projects in the same solution as well! Isn't that amazing? In previous versions of Visual Studio, it was possible to create ActiveX components and share them between languages—in essence, these were Component Object Model (COM) objects, which is what Visual Studio 6.0 used for controls. That is no longer an issue with the .NET Framework. While you can still use COM and ActiveX, these technologies are now obsolete because it is possible to use .NET languages interchangeably.

Definition

Components are pieces of programs that are written in such a way that they can be used by more than one program. This is called "code reuse" and it is a very important concept that is at the core of Microsoft's .NET strategy.

Say Hello

Now it's time to get down to business. Are you tired of theory already? I'm not! This stuff is fun. But theory means nothing without practice. I've watched a lot of Jackie Chan movies, but I still don't know anything about Kung Fu. If you want to master something you have got to practice and start with the basics.

Start Visual Studio by opening Programs, Microsoft Visual Studio 2008, and then choose Microsoft Visual Studio 2008 from the list. The default Start Page should be the first thing that is displayed when Visual Studio starts running (shown in Figure 2.1). The Start Page shows all of the recent solutions that you have worked on (or it could be blank if this is the first time you have used it). There is a button on the Start Page called New Project that you will click in order to start a new project. If, for some reason, the Start Page does not show up by default when you run Visual Studio, just click the File menu at the top of the screen and select New, Project.

Using either method, the New Project dialog should appear. See Figure 2.2. Let's dissect this New Project dialog before going any further. On the left side of the dialog is a list of Project Types, which will look different depending on the version of Visual Studio you are using. The version shown here is from Visual Studio 2008 Professional. If you are using the free version, Visual Basic 2008

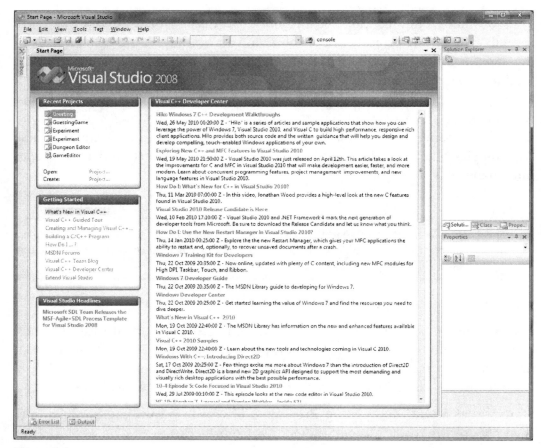

Figure 2.1
Start Page in Visual Studio 2008.

Express, then you will see only Visual Basic project types. On the right side of the dialog is the list of Templates for each project type.

You will notice that each language has its own set of icons for these templates, to make it easier to differentiate between them (usually when you have a large solution with multiple languages). Here is the list of templates for Visual Basic:

- Windows Forms Application
- Class Library

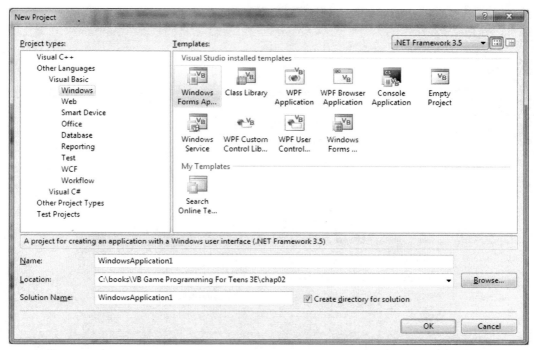

Figure 2.2
The Project Templates available in the New Project dialog.

- WPF Application
- WPF Browser Application
- Console Application
- Empty Project
- Windows Service
- WPF Custom Control Library
- WPF User Control Library
- Windows Forms Control Library

If you look at the top-right corner of the New Project dialog, you should see two small buttons that affect the layout of the items in the template list. You can switch between Large Icons and Small Icons by pressing either of these two

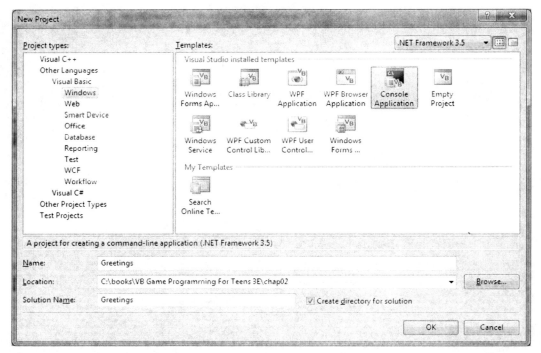

Figure 2.3
Choosing the Console Application project template.

buttons. The Small Icons view is sometimes more convenient because you can see more items in the list than you can when large icons are displayed. Regardless of the view you settle on, for this program you will want to select Console Application. Did you notice how the project name changed when you selected the Console Application template? The name was changed to ConsoleApplication1. Click on the Name field now and change the name of the program to Hello World or Greetings, as shown in Figure 2.3.

The next thing that you might want to do is select where the new project files will be stored on your hard drive. Select the folder by typing it into the Location field or locate an existing folder using the Browse button. You can store the project anywhere you like, although it makes sense to organize your projects under a main folder. You are now ready to create the new project by pressing the OK button.

Code Editor Window

When you click OK to close the New Project dialog, Visual Studio creates a new solution and a new project for you, as shown in Figure 2.4. Because this is a console application, there's no form or controls available in this program. What this means is that when you compile the program, you can run it from a Command Prompt. When you run the program from within Visual Studio, a new Command Prompt window automatically appears.

Now let's add some code to make this program actually do something useful. This program needs to display a line of text and then wait for the user to press Enter to continue. Add the following two lines of code inside Sub Main:

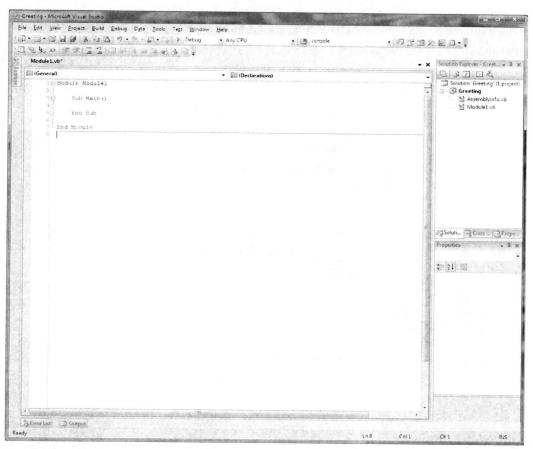

Figure 2.4
The new Console Application project is ready for your source code.

```
Console.WriteLine("Welcome to Visual Basic!")
Console.ReadLine()
```

It should be pretty obvious that the first line displays the message "Welcome to Visual Basic!", but what about the second line? ReadLine is a function that reads a line of characters from the keyboard and is ended with the Enter key.

Hint

You can start a program running in Visual Basic by pressing the F5 key.

So this means that you can type in a line of characters, and ReadLine will grab them out of the console. You can see what was typed in because ReadLine returns the characters as a string. In order to receive the string, you need to copy the value returned by ReadLine into a string variable.

Variables must be declared before they are used in Basic. To declare a new variable, you must use the Dim keyword, which is short for "dimension," referring to the process of reserving memory for the new variable. The process no longer even remotely resembles the Basic language of old (from which Visual Basic was based), but Dim has been around for a long time now. As I mentioned a moment ago, ReadLine returns a string. So this program needs a string variable. Declare the variable like this:

```
Dim name As String
```

How about that? You can create any variable you need using Dim. Here is the rest of the source code for the Greeting program. Type the lines in bold between the two existing lines of the program.

```
Console.WriteLine("Welcome to Visual Basic!")
Console.Write("Please type your name: ")
Dim name As String
name = Console.ReadLine()
Console.WriteLine("Hello, {0}!", name)
Console.WriteLine()
Console.WriteLine("Press Enter to quit...")
Console.ReadLine()
```

After you have made the changes to the source code, the program should look like Figure 2.5. (The new lines have been highlighted in the code editor window.)

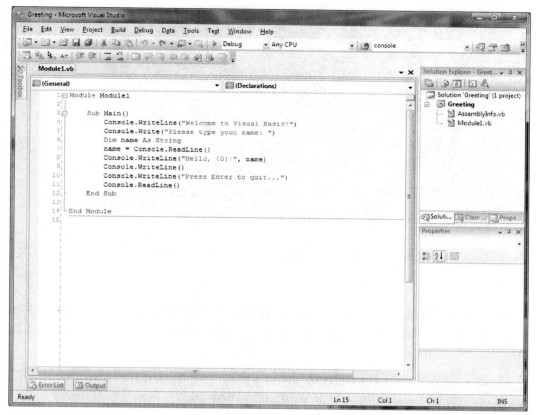

Figure 2.5
The new Greeting program in the Visual Basic editor.

After you type in the new code, save the project by clicking File, Save All (or click the Save All icon on the toolbar). Now go ahead and run the program by pressing F5. Figure 2.6 shows the output of the Greeting program.

There is one line of this program that displays the characters typed into the console (the user's name), and it looks kind of funny:

```
Console.WriteLine("Hello, {0}!'', name)
```

It's probably obvious to you what this line of code does from looking at the output, but how does it work? The curly braces surround a number that refers to the variable that follows. This is a feature of the WriteLine function. WriteLine

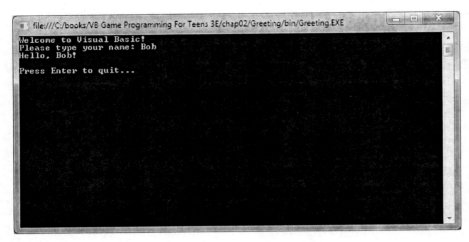

Figure 2.6
The Greeting program uses console input/output.

allows you to display the contents of variables in whatever order you want. Just separate each variable by a comma and then refer to them as {0}, {1}, {2}, and so on.

Congratulations, you have successfully run your first Visual Basic program! This program might be simple, but it helped to show you some key features of the Basic language and gave you some experience creating new projects and working with the editor. You can now close the Greeting program by selecting File, Close Solution.

Definition

Visual Basic is not a programming language! The *language* is Basic, just as C# (pronounced see-sharp) is a language, while its development environment is Visual C#. I know it's not common practice in many books and online references to address "Basic" without also the "Visual" part, but that is a trademarked product name, not a programming language. So, in this book we will refer more often to the Basic language (and the .NET Framework) when discussing programming issues, and Visual Basic when discussing the product.

VARIABLES OF ALL TYPES

Here's a simple question: What is a variable? A variable is something that can change, with the connotation that it can change unexpectedly. For example, weather forecasters often speak of variable winds and variable temperatures—meaning that the wind and temperature could change without warning. In the context of computers, however, variables only change when told and cannot do anything on their own.

In the old days when programmers used machine language and assembly language, they would create variables by grabbing a chunk of memory and then storing a number in the newly acquired spot. This was called *memory allocation*, which is a valid term in software today. Reserving a space in the computer's memory was a manual process, which required the programmer to keep track of exactly where that space was located by creating a pointer—which is where variables came from.

In order to make the task easier, programmers developed assembly languages that permitted the use of mnemonic words to replace the specific addresses of memory in which information is stored. Rather than keep track of the address in memory of a pointer, which in turn points to another address in memory where actual data is located, a mnemonic was used as the pointer. Mnemonics are easier to remember than physical addresses in memory; therefore, this greatly eased the job of writing programs.

Over time, these mnemonic words came to be known as variables. So, when you hear the word "variable," just remember that it is just a pointer to a location in memory in which some data is stored. Visual Basic keeps track of the type of data stored in that location and does all the hard work for you, but this process is essentially the same with all programming languages.

Using Variables

The `Dim` command is used to create new variables. The syntax of `Dim` looks like this:

```
Dim Variable_Name As Data_Type
```

Here's an example of a real `Dim` statement:

```
Dim Counter As Integer
```

This statement creates an `Integer` variable, which is capable of holding a number that has no decimal point.

Table 2.1 Variable Data Types

Data Type	Comment
Boolean	True or False
SByte	Tiny whole numbers (–128 to 127)
Byte	Tiny unsigned whole numbers (0 to 255)
Short	Small whole numbers (–32,768 to 32,767)
UShort	Small unsigned whole numbers (0 to 65,535)
Integer	Large whole numbers (+/– 2 billion)
UInteger	Large unsigned whole numbers (0 to 4 billion)
Long	Very large whole numbers
ULong	Very large unsigned whole numbers
Single	Small floating-point numbers
Decimal	Very large floating-point numbers
Double	High precision floating-point numbers
Date	A date such as Jan 1, 2010
Char	A single character
String	Any text made up of characters
Object	Any data type

Definition

A *variable* is an entity in a program, identified by name, that can store data based on its data type (such as Integer or String).

In addition to the Dim statement, there are two other ways to declare variables. The Public command causes a variable to be visible to other modules in the program, whereas the Private command prevents other modules from seeing a variable (and is the default when using Dim).

A data type is the attribute of a variable, which determines what kind of data it represents. There are many data types in Visual Basic, as shown in Table 2.1. I have rounded off the values in order to make them easier to comprehend. In my experience, the extreme range of a data type should not be an issue; just declare variables that are certain to be large enough to hold the value.

Definition

A *data type* represents the type of data stored in a variable. The data type tells Visual Basic how to handle the data.

In actual practice, don't be overly concerned about memory usage, just use the most obvious data type to handle the information it will need to remember. Most of the time, I use `Integer`, `Double`, or `String`, which keeps the code simple and gives programs plenty of room to breathe. If you feel comfortable using the more specific data types, by all means use them!

What's So Special about Strings?

The `String` data type is the most frequently used type in Visual Basic and deserves special recognition. Without strings, Visual Basic would be hobbled by difficult string-handling functions. The `String` data type is versatile in that it can contain up to two billion characters. Although it is definitely a possibility, I have never personally seen a two-gigabyte text file! Humorous as that may sound, a string could conceivably grow to that size, although I suspect that Windows would run out of memory before the string was filled to capacity. Most strings rarely exceed a few hundred characters. The `String` data type requires two bytes for each character (because Visual Basic strings use Unicode to store characters). To create a new `String`, simply use the `Dim` statement (or the affiliated `Public` or `Private` statements):

```
Dim FirstName As String
```

Simple string handling can be accomplished by setting a string equal to a value or another variable. There are two ways to combine strings: using the plus sign (+), or using the ampersand sign (&). Prior versions of Visual Basic required the ampersand when combining strings, but Visual Basic can use either.

```
Dim String1 As String = "This is String1"
Dim String2 As String = " and this is String2."
Dim String3 As String
String3 = String1 + String2
Console.WriteLine("String3 = {0}", String3);
```

The result of this snippet of code looks like this:

```
String3 = This is String1 and this is String2.
```

Tip

To make your Basic code more portable, I recommend using `Public` or `Private` rather than `Dim` to declare variables—that is how it's done in C#.

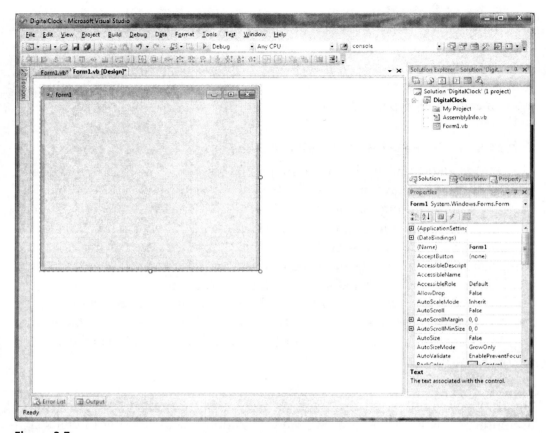

Figure 2.7
A new Windows Form project.

Telling Time

We're going to create a new Visual Basic project to display the current time by simulating a digital clock. First, create a new project as a Windows Forms Application, as shown in Figure 2.7. Set the Form1.Text property to "Digital Clock," as this will be how we identify the program in the Windows Taskbar and Task Manager.

Next, open the Toolbox and double-click the Timer control to add one to our form, as shown in Figure 2.8. The Timer control is located in the Components group in the Toolbox. The new Timer control is automatically named Timer1.

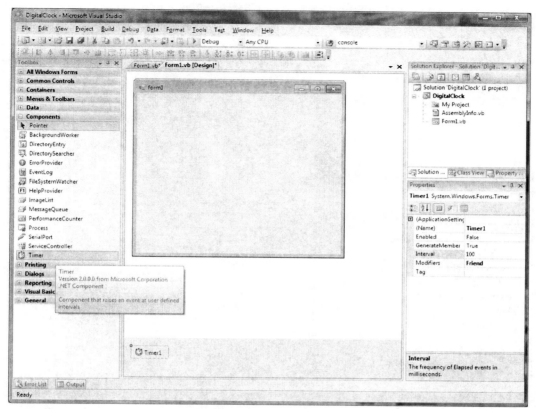

Figure 2.8
Adding a `Timer` to the project.

Next, take a look at the properties for the `Timer1` control. (If you don't see the Properties window, press Alt+Enter to bring it up.) Set the `Enabled` property to `True`, and `Interval` to `100`, as shown in Figure 2.9.

Label Control

Open the Toolbox again, and look in the Common Controls group for a control called `Label`—and double-click `Label` to add a new label to the form. New controls are automatically named, so this one will be called `Label1`. Set the following properties for `Label1`, after which the control will resemble the one in Figure 2.10.

Dock	Fill
Font	Arial, 48pt, style=Bold
ForeColor	Red
TextAlign	MiddleCenter

Figure 2.9
The Properties window is used to customize a control.

Timer Events

Next, double-click the Timer1 control (located below the Form window in the hidden form controls section). This will bring up the default event for the Timer1 control, called Timer1_Tick. Add the following code in the Timer1_Tick event function (noted in bold text):

```
Private Sub Timer1_Tick(ByVal sender As System.Object, _
    ByVal e As System.EventArgs) Handles Timer1.Tick
    REM get the time
    Dim time As String
    time = Format$(Now, "Long Time")
    REM display the time
    Label1.Text = time
End Sub
```

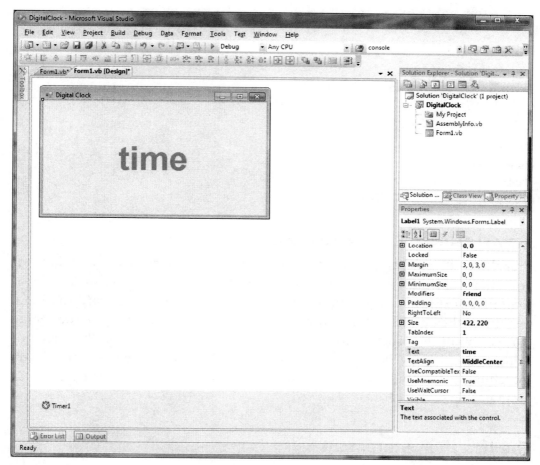

Figure 2.10
The form now contains a `Label` with a big red font.

Now you can run the program by pressing F5. Figure 2.11 shows the program running.

Hint

Basic does not support multi-line statements, unlike most other languages that ignore blank spaces and line spacing. To wrap a statement or function declaration to the next line, use the underscore character, _, at the end of a line.

Figure 2.11
The Digital Clock program.

BRANCHING/CONDITIONAL STATEMENTS

Branching statements are built into programming languages so that programmers can add logic to a program. Without branching (also known as *conditional*) statements, the program would only be able to forward the input directly to the output, without any processing. Although this may be something that you want the program to do (such as to display a text file on the screen or print a document), it is far more likely that you will need to actually do something with input data. Branching statements allow you to create complex program logic.

The If…Then Statement

The most common branching statement used in programming languages is the `If…Then` statement, which is often called the `If…Then…Else` statement. Here is the general syntax of the de-facto logic statement as it is used in Visual Basic:

```
If "condition is true" Then
    "perform commands based on true result"
Else
    "perform commands based on false result"
End If
```

Figure 2.12 is an example of an `If…Then…Else` statement and shows how input is tested for a true or false condition, whereupon program execution continues down the chosen path.

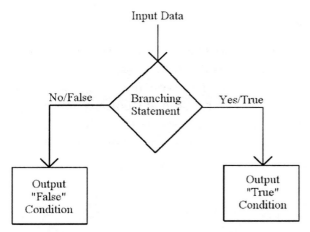

Figure 2.12
Illustration of a branching statement showing how program logic works.

Single-Line If...Then Statements

There is another format you can use with this branching statement, in which the `Else` and `End If` parts are not needed. Rather, you can code an `If...Then...Else` statement on a single line. Although this format is supported by Visual Basic, it is generally considered bad form, due to the lack of a closing statement—this is often a source of bugs in a program and difficult to track down. However, this form does save three lines of code. The real benefit to using this form is when you have to test many conditions in a row and you want to keep the code listing short. Of course, such situations beg for an alternate design altogether.

```
If "condition" Then "true statement" Else "false statement"
```

Using If...Then

How about a real example? Okay, here is how you might code the branching statement for a payroll program that calculates overtime pay.

```
If HoursWorked > 40 Then
    PayRate = 1.5
Else
    PayRate = 1.0
End If
```

The Select…Case Statement

There are times when the If…Then statement is just too unwieldy, particularly when a large number of conditions must be tested. In such circumstances, the Select…Case statement is a good alternative. In fact, you may feel free to use this branching statement instead of If…Then at any time; it's entirely up to you. Some prefer Select…Case because it is easier to add new cases to the condition in the future. I use it anytime there are more than two conditions to be tested. Here is the general format of the Select…Case statement:

```
Select Case "evaluation"
    Case value-1 [To value-2][, value-3]
        "perform condition-1 statements"
    Case value-1 [To value-2][, value-3]
        "perform condition-2 statements"
    Case value-1 [To value-2][, value-3]
        "perform condition-n statements"
    Case Else
        "perform alternate statements"
End Select
```

The Select…Case branching statement is versatile in that it is easy to add new cases (as you can see). It is also easier to read than in an If…Then statement when dealing with a lot of cases. To demonstrate how Select…Case works, let's rewrite the previous If…Then code as a Select…Case.

```
Select Case HoursWorked
    Case Is > 40
        Console.WriteLine("You worked over time.")
    Case Is = 40
        Console.WriteLine ("You worked regular time.")
    Case Else
        Console.WriteLine ("You worked part time.")
End Select
```

If you type that Select…Case statement into Visual Basic, you will notice that the editor adds the word Is before each condition. For example, if you type Case > 40, the editor will fill in Case Is > 40. This is simply the syntax required in Select…Case statements for Boolean evaluations. If you need only compare a range of values or a single value, the Is isn't needed. For example:

```
Select Case Mileage
```

```
    Case Is < 10
        Console.WriteLine ("The mileage is terrible.")
    Case 11, 12, 13, 14, 15
        Console.WriteLine ("The mileage is poor.")
    Case 16, 17, 18 To 20
        Console.WriteLine ("The mileage is average.")
    Case 21 To 30
        Console.WriteLine ("The mileage is good.")
    Case 31 To 50
        Console.WriteLine ("The mileage is great.")
    Case Is > 50
        Console.WriteLine ("The mileage is amazing!")
End Select
```

Guessing Game

We'll get some experience with conditional logic by making a simple but fun game. The Guessing Game project's form is shown in Figure 2.13. There are just three controls on the form, which I will let you add on your own without any help. If you use default names for the controls, then the label will be called Label1, the textbox will be TextBox1, and the button will be Button1. You may position the controls on the form as you wish.

We need two global variables declared just below the "Windows Form Designer generated code" section.

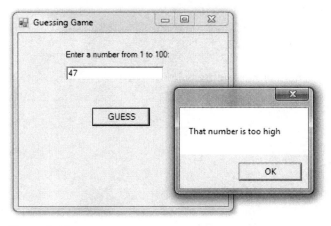

Figure 2.13
The Guessing Game form.

```
REM declare the number variable
Dim answer As Integer
Dim rand As Random
```

Next, the `Form_Load` function, which is the first thing that runs when a program starts up:

```
Private Sub Form1_Load(ByVal sender As Object, _
    ByVal e As System.EventArgs) Handles MyBase.Load

    rand = New Random()
    answer = rand.Next(1, 100)


End Sub
```

Lastly, the `Button1_Click` function. To automatically generate this function, double-click the `Button1` control on the form.

```
Private Sub Button1_Click(ByVal sender As System.Object, _
    ByVal e As System.EventArgs) Handles Button1.Click

    Dim num As Integer
    REM make sure the TextBox contains a number
    Try
        num = Integer.Parse(TextBox1.Text)
    Catch ex As Exception
        MessageBox.Show("Please enter a number between 1 and 100!")
        Exit Sub
    End Try

    REM make sure the number is between 1 and 10
    If num < 1 Or num > 100 Then
        MessageBox.Show("Please enter a number between 1 and 100!")
        Exit Sub
    End If
    REM check for high answer
    If num > answer Then
        MessageBox.Show("That number is too high")
    ElseIf num < answer Then
        MessageBox.Show("That number is too low")
    Else
        MessageBox.Show("That number is CORRECT!")
```

```
        End
    End If
End Sub
```

The conditional logic in this program tests the number entered into the textbox (when the button is pressed), and pops up a message box to tell the user whether the number is too low or too high. When the correct number is entered, then the program ends.

SUBROUTINES AND FUNCTIONS

Functions are important for breaking up a large program into smaller, more manageable pieces, leading to better code reuse and legibility. Functions are also important for creating program logic. Quite often, the conditional statements in a branching statement point to a function to keep the branching statement short. If each case in a branching statement includes a page of source code, it's easy to lose track of each case! Therefore, functions are essential parts of a programming language. A named *Sub* is a function that does not return a value, while a named *Function* does return a value.

Using Subs and Functions

Basic supports two types of subroutines: Sub and Function. Here is the syntax for a Sub:

```
[Public/Private] Sub SubName([Parameters])
End Sub
```

Here is an example of a Sub that does not have a parameter:

```
Private Sub PrintHello()
    Console.WriteLine("Hello!")
End Sub
```

Here is an example of a Sub that includes a String parameter:

```
Private Sub PrintHello(Name As String)
    Console.WriteLine("Hello, " + Name.ToString() + "!")
End Sub
```

Returning a Value

A Function is similar to a Sub, but a Function will return a value while a Sub does not. Here is the syntax for a Function:

```
[Public/Private] Function FunctionName([Parameters]) As DataType
End Function
```

Here is an example of a `Function` that does not have a parameter:

```
Private Function One() As Integer
     return 1
End Function
```

Strange as it may appear, this is a legal function! Do you see how the value is returned using the `return` statement? Note the `As Integer` part after the function name: this determines the type of value returned. Here is another example of a `Function`, this time with a parameter:

```
Private Function TimesTen(Num As Integer) As Integer
     return Num * 10
End Function
```

The `TimesTen` function is a little more interesting because you can have it return a value that is based on a parameter! The possibilities are utterly endless on what you can do with the power of subroutines. The return value of a function is determined by the data type of the function, which can be any data type that you use when creating variables, as well as custom data types that you create. Functions can also return an `Object`, which means that it can return any data type or even a user interface control (odd as that may sound).

MATHEMATICAL OPERATORS

Basic provides a good assortment of mathematical operators. These operators are built into the language. Using number conversion functions, such as `CInt()`, `CLng()`, and `CDbl()`—for integer, long, and double, respectively—we can convert any valid data type into a numeric variable for use in calculations using mathematical operations. (Remember, a `Long` integer is a whole number, while a `Double` precision floating point has a decimal point.)

Converting Data

Basic can perform number conversion on the fly using functions such as `CInt()`, based on the result of the operation. Technically, these numeric conversion functions are unique to Basic and not part of the .NET Framework, holdovers from Visual Basic 6.0 that are available via the Microsoft.VisualBasic namespace.

The other, and perhaps recommended way to convert data types is with the Convert class. `Convert.ToInt32()` and `Convert.ToDouble()` are common. In the code editor, typing `Convert.` will bring up the IntelliSense list of conversion functions available in the `Convert` class. For example:

```
Dim A As String = "10"
Dim B As Integer = CInt(A)
```

is equivalent to this:

```
Dim A As String = "10"
Dim B As Integer = Convert.ToInt32(A)
```

Since the `Convert` class is part of the .NET Framework, and therefore also likely to be used with the C# language, I recommend using it instead of the older intrinsic Basic conversion functions.

Addition and Subtraction

The plus sign and minus sign are used to add and subtract numbers. This includes variable assignment and formulas used in branching statements. Addition is commonly used to increment the value of a counter variable. For example:

```
Dim N As Integer = 0
N = N + 10
```

Note the use of an initializer for the variable, N. Although Visual Basic automatically sets numbers to zero upon initialization, it is sometimes convenient to include the explicit initializer. The second line, N = N + 10, is called a formula, because the variable is *receiving* the value of an addition operation. You could just as easily use a function to return a number that is assigned to the variable. For example:

```
Private Function Twelve() As Integer
    return 12
End Function

Dim N As Integer = 0
N = 10 + Twelve()
```

Visual Basic provides another way to add a number to a variable, called a *shortcut operator*, which looks like this: += and -=. Here is an example:

```
Dim N As Integer = 0
N += 10
```

Multiplication and Division

Multiplication was invented to make adding and subtracting easier, because it allows you to add or subtract many numbers quite easily. Like most programming languages, Visual Basic uses the asterisk (*) for multiplication. Here is an example:

```
Dim A As Integer = 9
Dim B As Integer = 6
Console.WriteLine("{0} times {1} = {2}", A, B, A * B)
```

Here is what the Console message looks like:

```
9 times 6 = 54
```

As you might have guessed, there is also a shortcut operator for multiplication, and I'll wager that you can guess what it looks like! If you guessed *=, then you are right!

```
Dim A As Integer = 12
A *= 12
```

How about a real-world example? The circumference of a circle is two times the radius times pi, or $C = 2\pi r$. Expressed in Visual Basic source code, here is how you can calculate it (note: the last line is a comment showing the result you should get by running this mini program):

```
Dim Radius As Integer = 10
Dim Circumference As Decimal
Circumference = 2 * System.Math.PI * Radius
Rem the answer is 62.8318530717959
```

Here is an example of integer division:

```
Dim A As Integer = 12
Dim B As Integer = 4
Dim C As Integer
C = A \ B
```

There are two ways to divide numbers in Visual Basic. First, standard division uses the forward slash character (/). This is below the question mark on a U.S. keyboard. Second, the backslash character (\), which is above the Enter key on a

Table 2.2 Division Characters

Char	Name	Description
/	Forward slash	Floating-point division (decimal remainder)
\	Backslash	Integer division (no remainder)

U.S. keyboard, is designed to return just an integer as an answer, dropping any remainder. Be sure to learn the difference between these characters, because the latter one doesn't work for floating-point numbers (such as Decimal, Single, and Double). Use Table 2.2 as a reference.

Here is another example of a division operation, this time using a floating-point number:

```
Dim A As Decimal = 973.65
Dim B As Decimal = 18.50
Dim C As Decimal
C = A / B
```

Trick

If you have a hard time remembering which division character to use, consider this analogy. The backslash is a downward slope that's quick and easy (using integers), whereas the forward slash is a hill that's difficult to climb (using decimals). You can also think of integers as a "downgrade" in precision, while thinking of floats as an "upgrade" in precision.

Modulus

After talking so much about remainders in floating-point and integer division, it is fitting that the next operator is the modulus, or Mod, operator. This works similarly to the other math operators, except there is no shortcut for modulus, because you must use the word *Mod*. Here is an example:

```
Dim A As Integer = 10
Dim B As Integer = 3
Dim C As Integer
C = A Mod B
```

The result of the last statement is that C = 1. Can you figure out why? When you divide 10 by 3, the answer is 3, but there is a remainder of 1. Mod ignores the answer and returns the remainder. Although this might not seem very useful to you at present, Mod is an extremely powerful math operator that can solve some uniquely difficult problems. One classic example is determining whether a number is an integer or float by looking at the remainder. You can perform that check using the following condition:

If **A Mod B = 0** Then

Here is a complete example:

```
If A Mod 2 = 0 Then
    Console.WriteLine("The variable is a whole number")
Else
    Console.WriteLine ("The variable is a floating-point number")
End If
```

Note

We'll use the modulus operator to make sprite animation possible in Chapter 6, "Sprites: The Key To 2D Games."

Math Quiz

The Math Quiz project demonstrates some of the math operators in the context of a little form-based quiz program. This program has a form with several Label controls, a TextBox, and two Buttons—see Figure 2.14 for the layout.

I will let you design the form on your own using this figure as a guide. Figure 2.15 shows the controls as they appear in the example. Note that the "+" and "=" signs are just Labels as well, and both Label2 and Label3 have their BorderStyle property set to Fixed3D to give them a beveled look (similar to a TextBox).

Here is the source code for the Math Quiz program, which should follow the "Windows Form Designer generated code" section in the source code listing.

```
Dim Answer As Integer
Private Sub Form1_Load(ByVal sender As System.Object, _
    ByVal e As System.EventArgs) Handles MyBase.Load
    REM seed the random number generator
    Randomize()
    REM initialize the game
    CreateMathProblem()
End Sub
```

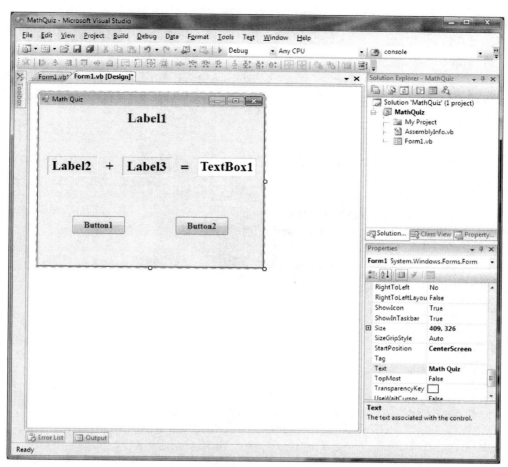

Figure 2.14
Control layout on the Math Quiz form.

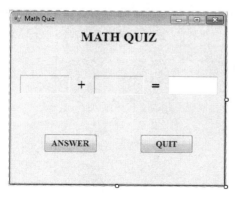

Figure 2.15
Finished form for the Math Quiz program.

```
Private Sub Button1_Click(ByVal sender As System.Object, _
    ByVal e As System.EventArgs) Handles Button1.Click
    REM make sure answer is a number
    If IsNumeric(TextBox1.Text) = False Then
        REM display error message
        MsgBox("Please enter a number.")
    Else
        REM check the answer
        If Val(TextBox1.Text) = Answer Then
            MsgBox("You got the answer right!", , "CORRECT")
        Else
            MsgBox("Oh no, you missed that one!", , "WRONG")
        End If
    End If
    REM create a new math problem
    CreateMathProblem()
    REM clear the answer field
    TextBox1.Text = ""
End Sub

Private Sub Button2_Click(ByVal sender As System.Object, _
    ByVal e As System.EventArgs) Handles Button2.Click
    REM quit button ends the program
    End
End Sub

Private Sub CreateMathProblem()
    Dim First As Integer
    Dim Second As Integer

    REM randomize the first field
    First = Int(Rnd() * 10)
    Label2.Text = First
    REM randomize the second field
    Second = Int(Rnd() * 10)
    Label3.Text = Second
    REM set the math operator and answer
    Select Case Int(Rnd() * 3)
        Case 0
```

```
            REM addition problem
            Label4.Text = "+"
            Answer = First + Second
        Case 1
            REM subtraction problem
            Label4.Text = "-"
            Answer = First - Second
        Case 2
            REM multiplication problem
            Label4.Text = "x"
            Answer = First * Second
    End Select
End Sub
```

Relational Operators

The human mind is capable of seeing the differences and relationships between individual things and groups of things, such as cars in a car lot. By simply driving past a car lot, you are probably able to tell at a glance what types of cars are being offered for sale, such as pickup trucks, compact cars, vans, and sport-utility vehicles.

Computer programs are not blessed with the ability to instantly come to a conclusion with limited information. Rather, computers must evaluate differences at a highly detailed and specific level. For instance, a human might look at two cars and claim that they are absolutely identical. But a computer might examine the same two cars and find that they are made of different components, built in different years, and even point out flaws in the paint. As a result, computers are able to examine things with great precision, something humans are incapable of doing.

Relational operators deal with how values compare to each other, or rather, how they relate to each other. Relational operators are usually found within formulas that result in a Boolean (true or false) value, and are based on simple rules, such as equal, not equal, greater than, and less than. The way that objects relate to each other is determined by their data types. Variables of the same data type can relate directly without any conversion needed. But variables of different data types require some form of conversion before they can be compared using a relational operator.

Table 2.3 Relational Operators

Operator	Description
=	Equal to
<>	Not equal to
<	Less than
>	Greater than
<=	Less than or equal to
>=	Greater than or equal to

The actual operators used to perform relational comparisons are covered next, with a description of how to use each one. Table 2.3 provides a quick reference.

Here is an example of a test for an equal condition:

```
If (A = B) Then
    Console.WriteLine("True")
Else
    Console.WriteLine ("False")
End If
```

Hint

Basic uses the single equal sign, =, to test for equality *and* for assigning values to variables. The C# language uses double equal signs, ==, for conditional tests and a single one for assignment. This can lead to serious bugs: be mindful of the difference if you intend to learn both Basic and C#.

LOOPING STATEMENTS

Looping is a way of repeating something to accomplish a task (such as summarizing or averaging some values) or to process a long list of information. For example, it requires a loop to load a text file and display it in a TextBox, because the program must load each byte of the text file in order. Another example of a repeating process is drawing a picture on the screen, one pixel at a time, as each pixel in the picture file (which might be saved as a JPG, GIF, BMP, or other format) is copied to the screen. Looping is the process of repeating or iterating through a series, from a starting point to a fixed ending point, or upon the completion of a condition. Suppose you have a list of names, as follows:

- Bob
- Jane
- Mary
- Steve

If you need to print out all this information, you could display each name separately, like this:

```
Console.WriteLine("Bob is #1")
Console.WriteLine ("Jane is #2")
Console.WriteLine ("Mary is #3")
Console.WriteLine ("Steve is #4")
```

That might work for small lists, but what about lists with hundreds, thousands, or millions of entries? Computer databases could easily have millions of records, after all, and there's no way you can process each one individually. Obviously, a looping command is needed! How might you iterate through a series of sequential numbers? First, you start with a variable that is set to one. Each time through the loop, you add one to the variable. At the end of the loop, the variable will equal some number. Here is the basic concept:

1. Start with a value.

2. Add one to the value.

3. Repeat until a condition is met.

The condition that needs to be met might be a Boolean formula, such as (Num > 100) or (A = B). The condition might also be that the counter variable has reached a certain number. This is what computer science calls a For Loop, odd as that may sound. The reason it is called For Loop is because something happens "for every pass through the loop."

For Loop

The Visual Basic For Loop looks like this:

```
For variable = start To finish
     repeating commands
Next variable
```

Do Loops

The Do Loop is another form of looping command built into Visual Basic. Whereas For Loops are adept at handling number sequences, Do Loops excel when it comes to relational looping, in which a process will repeatedly loop until some Boolean condition is satisfied. There are four variations of the Do Loop.

The first form of the Do Loop is the Do While...Loop. This version causes the enclosed commands to repeat as long as the condition is true. You can paraphrase it like this: "While the condition is true, continue repeating the commands." Because of this wording format, it's possible that the repeating commands might never execute if the condition is false from the start. Here is the format for this version of the Do Loop:

```
Do While condition
     repeating commands
Loop
```

The Do While...Loop command is more versatile than the For Loop because you can have multiple conditions applied to the loop through every iteration. For example:

```
Do While EndOfFile = False
     'process the file
Loop
```

The Do...Loop While command is the reverse of the Do While...Loop command. The format of the condition and the way this loop handles repetition are similar, but there is one difference.

Here is the format of the command:

```
Do
     repeating commands
Loop While condition
```

The third type of Do Loop is the Do Until...Loop command. This one is also similar to the other Do Loops, but this format differs from the Do While...Loop in that it continues to repeat *until* the condition is met, rather than *while* the condition is met. It is the negative version of the Do Loop that continues as long as the condition is false. Here is the general format of the Do Until...Loop command:

```
Do Until condition
     repeating commands
Loop
```

The fourth version of the Do Loop is Do...Loop Until. This is the late conditional form of the Do Until...Loop, in which the condition is checked at the end of the loop rather than at the beginning. Therefore, this loop is guaranteed to process the repeating commands at least once.

```
Do
     repeating commands
Loop Until condition
```

Here is an example:

```
Do
     'process the file
Loop Until FileOpen = False
```

ARRAYS

Looping commands really start to make sense when dealing with long lists of information, as the preceding section demonstrated. But what happens when you don't have a ListBox control handy to use as a container for the information? The answer is an *array*, which is a variable that has many elements. Suppose you have a variable called Age, declared as an Integer, which holds your age. What if you would like to keep track of the age of everyone in your family or your class? You could create many Age variables, as follows:

```
Dim Age1 As Integer
Dim Age2 As Integer
Dim Age3 As Integer
Dim Age4 As Integer
```

That is an inefficient way to handle all of the data, and there is an additional problem that arises when you add another variable to the list, such as Age8. When you do that, you have to go back and modify the program so that Age8 is used properly. Obviously, there must be a better way.

The answer is an array. This is how you would declare the Age array:

```
Dim Ages(8) As Integer
```

Doesn't that look a lot more efficient? Not only can you iterate through an array with a looping command, you can also add new elements to an array at will, and if your program is written properly, you won't have to rewrite anything to add more elements.

Let's devise a hypothetical situation to help illustrate. There are eight people in your class, and you want to write a program that displays all of their ages using only a few lines of code, because you are in a hurry to get it finished. First, you need to declare an array of names to go along with the Age array:

```
Dim Names(8) As String
```

You need to fill the array with some data. For the sake of simplicity, let's do it the hard way. Here is how you might load the Names and Ages arrays:

```
Names(0) = "Thomas"
Ages(0) = 32
Names(1) = "James"
Ages(1) = 20
Names(2) = "Percy"
Ages(2) = 24
Names(3) = "Gordon"
Ages(3) = 38
```

Now that the arrays have been filled with sample data, let's write a loop to quickly display the arrays:

```
Dim n As Integer
For n = 0 To 3
    Console.WriteLine("{0} is {1} years old.", Names(n), Ages(n))
Next
```

STRUCTURES

The preceding section demonstrated how to combine two arrays of related information in a display. That method did work, but it was inefficient. For one thing, what if the names and ages need to be sorted? Sorting one of the arrays would mess up the sequence of the other arrays. What happens if you need to keep track of several more pieces of information about each person in this hypothetical situation, such as height and weight? Things could become messy in a hurry with four arrays to deal with.

Hint

Pay close attention to this section because we'll be using both classes and structures in the Celtic Crusader game!

A structure combines several variables into a group, which is then handled as a single entity. The real power of a structure, then, is the ability to create an array of that structure, rather than multiple arrays for each variable. Sound interesting? It is that, and extremely useful as well. Here is the general format of a structure:

```
Structure struct_name
    variable1 As data_type
    variable2 As data_type
    variable3 As data_type
End Structure
```

Let's create a real structure based on the Names and Ages arrays created in the previous section. Here is how you might design the structure in order to incorporate the previous two arrays:

```
Structure Students
    Dim Name As String
    Dim Age As Integer
End Structure
```

As you can see, it looks very similar to the individual array declarations for Names and Ages, but I have made the variable names singular. One important point to note is that once inside a structure, variables are referred to as *methods*.

Once you have created the structure, you can declare an array variable of the structure like this:

```
Dim people(8) As Students
```

Filling a structure array differs a little from filling a simple variable array. How do you get to those variables (oops, I mean methods) after you have created the structure array? Well, for starters, take a look at the variable itself, called people. There you will find the clue to accessing the methods within. As with built-in objects in Visual Basic, such as System.Math, Visual Basic provides the IntelliSense drop-down list any time you type in the name of an object followed by a period.

If you have Visual Basic open, go ahead and create a new Console Application project, and type in the preceding structure definition so you can try this out. Now, move the cursor to the blank line under Sub Main() and type in:

```
people(0).
```

That's it, just `people(0)` followed by a period. Because you declared `people` to be a structure array, you should see the drop-down list showing the two methods in that structure. But wait, what are those other items in the drop-down list? `Equals`, `GetHashCode`, `GetType`, and `ToString` don't belong in there! After all, the structure just has two methods, `Name` and `Age`. Don't worry about those extra methods. They are just standard methods built in that Visual Basic adds to the structure definition for advanced use.

Okay, now you at least have an idea of how to access the methods inside a structure. So, let's fill in the names and ages in this structure array to see how it works:

```
people(0).Name = "Thomas"
people(0).Age = 32
people(1).Name = "James"
people(1).Age = 20
people(2).Name = "Percy"
people(2).Age = 24
people(3).Name = "Gordon"
people(3).Age = 38
```

See how the structure name (`people`) now references the array index (0 to 7) instead of the method names? It makes more sense to do it this way, and it's more logical. Now you can add more methods to the structure and reference them like you did with `Name` and `Age`. Let's print out the array so you can see how that looks with a looping command.

```
Dim n As Integer
For n = 0 To 7
    Console.WriteLine("{0} is {1} years old.", _
        people(n).Name, people(n).Age)
Next
```

OBJECT-ORIENTED PROGRAMMING

Object-oriented programming (OOP) is a large-scale concept, which is more of a methodology than a specific way of writing programs. Applicable to many different languages, including Visual Basic, OOP has been around for many years. If this is your first exposure to OOP (or to programming, for that matter), it may not be clear how useful it is to be able to reuse source code on later projects or even share source code between projects currently in development. Try to think in the abstract: How can I write this program in such a way that when I'm finished, I can use parts of it again in another project? That way of thinking is a step in the right direction. To accomplish something like that, you need to break down a problem into manageable pieces, and then write the source code for those individual pieces separately, linking them together at the end to form a whole program. If you are new to programming, you can learn how to write OOP code correctly from the start and avoid having to change your way of thinking later. Software evolves; it changes every year.

Encapsulation

Encapsulation is the process of pulling all the data, and source code that manipulates that data, inside a self-contained entity (which is easier to refer to as just an object). By keeping all the data inside the object, as well as all the subroutines and functions that work with the data, you prevent others from using the data incorrectly. In addition, encapsulation enables you to design the format of the data, as well as the processes, so that everything follows the object model—if properly designed, it's a blueprint for the system.

Suppose you have an apple tree in your backyard. You are a kindly neighbor; therefore, you offer free apples to anyone who comes by for a visit. Soon, however, your neighbors begin to help themselves to the apples without even bothering to knock on the door and say hello. They have ignored you completely and helped themselves to the goodies.

To prevent this, what you really need to do is add a layer of control between your neighbors and your apple tree—for instance, a fence with a locked gate. But ideally, you need to pass out the apples yourself. So you do just that; every time a neighbor stops by for an apple, you select a ripe and healthy apple and present it to your neighbor. The neighbor thanks you and goes on his way. You have interfered with the neighbor's ability to gain direct access to the source of the apples, but in doing so, you made sure the neighbor received only good apples, because you threw out any bad apples beforehand.

This analogy aptly describes encapsulation of data. You want other processes in the program to have access to certain information, but you want to make sure that those processes don't do something incorrect with the information, possibly

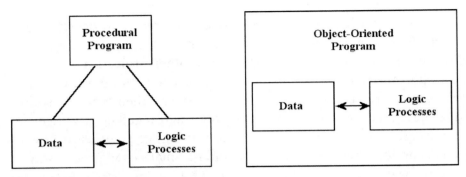

Figure 2.16
Procedural versus object-oriented.

causing a bug in the program. Does encapsulation limit or slow down a program? Not really. It takes the outside process just as much time to grab the information stored in a variable as it takes for your own custom process to provide the information to that outside process.

Let me give you an example to help clarify the matter. Figure 2.16 shows the difference between a procedural program (that exposes data and processes) and an object-oriented program (that protects data and processes).

Inheritance

Inheritance is another key component of an OOP program. Inheritance is the ability of one object to borrow things from another object. Inheritance is a play on words; it is more like cloning than receiving money from a departed loved one. I suspect reproduction and cloning sounded too biological, so the word inheritance was used instead. Regardless, the concept is that one object receives the attributes of another object. When the new object is used, it has a copy of the older object inside itself, which is very similar to the way genetics works. The parent passes down genes to offspring. See Figure 2.17.

Polymorphism

Polymorphism is the last of the three concepts that comprise an OOP program. Polymorphism as a word means "many shapes" and refers to the ability for the traits inside an object to change in response to different inputs or outputs.

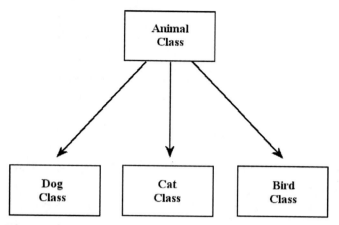

Figure 2.17
The Dog, Cat, and Bird classes all inherit data and processes from the Animal class.

Polymorphism is probably not as important to the overall OOP scheme as encapsulation and inheritance are, but it does play an important role in aiding the other two with multipurpose attributes that can accommodate many different situations. Polymorphism is arguably the least important of the three major traits of an object-oriented program, but it does provide a powerful and useful set of features that are difficult to do without once you have gotten used to them.

Properties

Without getting into too much detail at this point, I'd like to show you how to start using OOP. The true power of OOP comes from using classes. A *property* is a special type of function that behaves like a variable, so you can read and write data to a property as if it were a variable—when, in fact, it is a miniature class that protects its data. Properties can be a very powerful form of encapsulation, allowing you to hide variables and processes behind a simple interface. Here is an example property:

```
Dim decCirc As Decimal
Property Circumference() As Decimal
    Get
        Return decCirc
    End Get
    Set(ByVal value As Decimal)
```

```
            decCirc = value
      End Set
End Property
```

Note the use of the statements Get and Set—they allow a property to be accessed like a variable. Then, in your program, you can set the Circumference property like this:

```
Circumference = 100.0
```

Or you can retrieve the value of the Circumference property like so:

```
Dim circ as decimal = Circumference
```

Classes

Classes make object-oriented programming possible. A class is a source code blueprint for an object that is created at runtime (when the program is running). An object is a self-contained, functional component in a program, which accomplishes a single task, regardless of whether that task is simple or complex. A well-designed OOP program will utilize many different and versatile objects that work together to accomplish the goals of the program. The real power of this is that over time a programmer (or programming team) will be able to use these objects in more than one project. A professional programming shop will have an assortment of classes collected over time in a *class library*. The class library may be comprised of many smaller libraries of classes.

The Format of a Class

Classes can contain any information that you want and can generally be declared Friend or Public. Private classes can also be created, but their scope must fall within another class. Friend classes are visible only within the current namespace (in previous versions of Visual Basic that would have been *current project scope*). Generally, classes are created so that they can be used and reused in more than one application; therefore, classes are almost universally declared with Public scope. For all practical purposes, here is a sample class definition (with a single member variable) as you will see it most often:

```
Public Class MyClassName
      Private intVariable As Integer

      REM this is the constructor
```

```
Sub New()
    intVariable = 0
End Sub

REM this is a property
Property Variable() As Integer
    Get
        Return intVariable
    End Get
    Set(ByVal Value As Integer)
        intVariable = Value
    End Set
End Property
End Class
```

Class Variables

The first thing you will notice in the sample `MyClassName` class is the member variable called `intVariable`. Member variables can be declared with `Public`, `Private`, or `Protected` scope. You are already familiar with the first two; what, then, does `Protected` mean? `Protected` member variables are sort of in between `Public` and `Private`, accessible to descendant classes but not outside the class. `Private` member variables, on the other hand, are *not* visible to other classes (not even descendants). `Public` variables are visible all the time.

Class Constructor

The next thing you will notice in the sample `MyClassName` class is a constructor called `Sub New()`. Odd as it may appear, this is how constructors are created in Visual Basic, by overloading the `New` operator. Remember, when you create a new object, you use `New`, right? Well, `New` is just an operator, like +, -, and =. Visual Basic overloads the `New` operator to act as the constructor for the class. In case you are not familiar with the term, a *constructor* is a subroutine (method) that runs when the class is first instantiated (which means *created*).

Class Properties and Methods

The most common type of subroutine you will use in a class is a property, although you can add any `Sub` or `Function` that you want to a class, and it then becomes a member *method* of the class. I am a big fan of properties, and I am pleased that properties now play such a big role in Basic's OOP capabilities. You are free to use a property to do more than just provide access to a private variable. Anytime you need to return a value, for example, it is convenient to use a property, because properties are referenced just like variables in a class (and it's often difficult to tell the difference), but they afford us an opportunity to do error checking and protect the class variables.

Level Up!

If you were a newcomer to Visual Basic, I trust this chapter provided a good introduction to the language. You learned the basics of variables and data types, subroutines and functions, conditional statements, structures, classes, and many more key concepts. You may want to refer back to this chapter any time you run across code later on that you don't quite understand. Now, in the next chapter, we will be working even more with forms and controls by creating several even more challenging games.

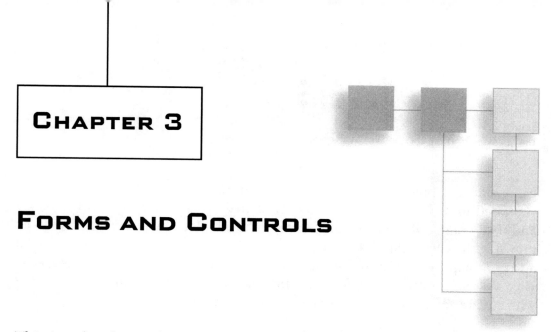

CHAPTER 3

FORMS AND CONTROLS

This is a hands-on chapter to explore forms and controls in more detail in Visual Basic. While the previous chapter was primarily a language reference, this one will lead directly into the graphics programming coming up in the *next* chapter. These are important topics that should be studied in order, especially if you are new to Basic or game programming.

Here's what we'll cover in this chapter:

- Dice War
- Block Buster
- Tic-Tac-Toe

DICE WAR

Our first example game in this chapter is Dice War, a game that simulates rolling of dice between two players and comparing scores—sort of a dice version of card-based *War*. There are three rounds during which the score of each player is accumulated, with the winner announced at the end of the third round. I have some personal affection for this game. Although simple in concept, it is a lot of fun and can be a programming challenge. I wrote my first Dice War game on my cousin's Commodore PET back in the 1980s and it was stored on cassette tape. Sadly, the computer and its tapes are long gone. A year later, I re-created the

Figure 3.1
The six sides of a die for the Dice War game.

game on an Apple IIgs in high school computer class—when the class was supposed to be learning about arrays or something, I'd finish the work quickly and then crank out my own game code in the lab. Back then, the dice had to be drawn with vector graphics, but in Visual Basic, we can use a PictureBox control and a bitmap for each of the six sides of the die. Figure 3.1 shows the images— what do you think, not bad for programmer art? I made each die side in GIMP with just rectangle and circle bevels and two-tone fills.

Hint

When a control such as PictureBox has a bitmap loaded via its Image property, that bitmap is stored in the form as a resource and the original bitmap file is no longer needed. Thus, it's possible to store *all* game art on a form in order to hide it from users, but the resulting exe file (and memory footprint) will be much larger.

Form Layout

Figure 3.2 shows the control layout on the Dice War form with all of the properties already set, which you may use as a reference when creating the form yourself. Note the Timer1 control in the hidden controls section of the form editor (below the form).

Trick

To make a PictureBox control resize itself to match the loaded Image, set its SizeMode property to AutoSize.

Figure 3.3 shows the form with named controls. For the Die1..Die6 PictureBox controls, there are bitmap files for the die face images available in the project folder. Just choose a bitmap file via the Image property and it will be loaded.

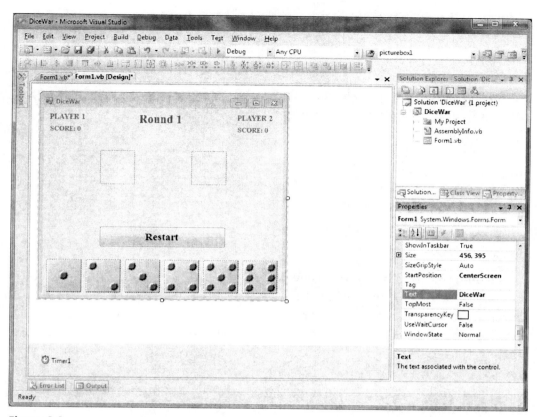

Figure 3.2
The control layout on the Dice War form.

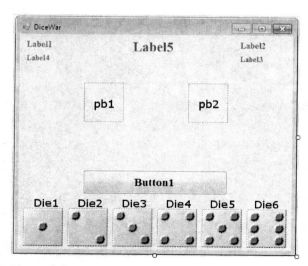

Figure 3.3
Named controls on the Dice War form.

Source

The following global variables are needed by the game, and should be located just below the "Windows Form Designer generated code" section.

```
Dim Player As Integer = 1
Dim Round As Integer = 1
Dim Roll1 As Integer = 1
Dim Roll2 As Integer = 3
Dim Rolls As Integer
Dim Score1 As Integer
Dim Score2 As Integer
Dim rand As Random
```

While building a game with Visual Basic, it's common to double-click some controls to have the function for the default event generated. I will present the source code in the most likely order that you'll need it as we go along. For instance, double-clicking the form itself generates the Form1_Load function.

```
Private Sub Form1_Load(ByVal sender As System.Object, _
    ByVal e As System.EventArgs) Handles MyBase.Load
    REM initialize the random number generator
    rand = New Random()
    REM draw initial dice images
    pb1.Image = Die6.Image
    pb2.Image = Die6.Image
End Sub
```

Now we will go over the code for the Button1 control, which will change depending on the state of the game—which player is rolling, etc. The Text property determines what happens when the button is clicked, causing either a game restart or a roll of the dice. The actual rolling animation is handled by the Timer1 event.

```
Private Sub Button1_Click(ByVal sender As System.Object, _
    ByVal e As System.EventArgs) Handles Button1.Click
    REM this event handles Restart as well as Roll
    If Button1.Text = "Restart" Then
        RestartGame()
    Else
        REM disable the Roll button
        Button1.Enabled = False
```

```
        REM start the rolling dice
        Timer1.Enabled = True
    End If
End Sub
```

Now, if you double-click the Timer1 control below the form, the default event for Timer is added to the source code in the same manner for visible form controls.

```
Private Sub Timer1_Tick(ByVal sender As System.Object, _
    ByVal e As System.EventArgs) Handles Timer1.Tick
    REM roll both dice
    RollDie1()
    RollDie2()
    REM increment the roll counter
    Rolls += 1
    REM stop after 30 rolls (3 seconds)
    If RollOver() Then
        REM reset roll counter
        Rolls = 0
        REM disable the rolling dice
        Timer1.Enabled = False
        REM disable the Roll button
        Button1.Enabled = True
        REM display the dice roll for this player
        DisplayRoll(Player)
        REM check for game over
        If GameOver() Then
            Button1.Text = "Restart"
            ShowWinner()
        Else
            REM not end of game, go to the next round
            Label5.Text = "Round " & Round
        End If
    End If
End Sub
```

That's the end of the control event functions, so now we can go over the helper functions called by the events. RestartGame() is called by Button1_Click at startup and whenever a game has ended (after three rounds). RollDie1() and RollDie2() are called by Timer1_Tick to get a random number (1 to 6) for each of the two dice—and this number is then used to draw the appropriate die image.

```
Private Sub RestartGame()
    REM reset the game settings
    Button1.Text = "Player 1 - Roll"
    Score1 = 0
    Score2 = 0
    Label4.Text = "SCORE: " & Score1
    Label3.Text = "SCORE: " & Score2
    Round = 1
    Label5.Text = "Round " & Round
    pb1.Image = Die6.Image
    pb2.Image = Die6.Image
End Sub

Private Sub RollDie1()
    REM generate random roll for die 1
    Roll1 = rand.Next(1, 6)
    REM display the corresponding image (die 1-6)
    Select Case Roll1
        Case 1
            pb1.Image = Die1.Image
        Case 2
            pb1.Image = Die2.Image
        Case 3
            pb1.Image = Die3.Image
        Case 4
            pb1.Image = Die4.Image
        Case 5
            pb1.Image = Die5.Image
        Case 6
            pb1.Image = Die6.Image
    End Select
End Sub

Private Sub RollDie2()
    REM generate random roll for die 2
    Roll2 = rand.Next(1, 6)
    REM display the corresponding image (die 1-6)
```

```
    Select Case Roll2
        Case 1
            pb2.Image = Die1.Image
        Case 2
            pb2.Image = Die2.Image
        Case 3
            pb2.Image = Die3.Image
        Case 4
            pb2.Image = Die4.Image
        Case 5
            pb2.Image = Die5.Image
        Case 6
            pb2.Image = Die6.Image
    End Select
End Sub
```

The RollOver() function is called by Timer1_Tick() to determine when it's time to stop rolling the dice and display the results. It's a small helper function that cleans up the code a bit. DisplayRoll() is called at the end of the dice rolling animation to notify the player of the result.

```
Private Function RollOver() As Boolean
    If Rolls > 30 Then
        RollOver = True
    Else
        RollOver = False
    End If
End Function


Private Sub DisplayRoll(ByVal PlayerNum As Integer)
    REM display total roll message depending on player
    Select Case PlayerNum
        Case 1
            REM give player 1's score
            MsgBox("Player 1, you rolled a " & CInt(Roll1 + Roll2) & ".")
            Score1 += Roll1 + Roll2
            Label4.Text = "SCORE: " & Score1
            REM reset for player 2
            Button1.Text = "Player 2 - Roll"
            Player = 2
```

```
        Case 2
            REM give player 2's score
            MsgBox("Player 2, you rolled a " & CInt(Roll1 + Roll2) & ".")
            Score2 += Roll1 + Roll2
            Label3.Text = "SCORE: " & Score2
            REM reset for player 1
            Button1.Text = "Player 1 - Roll"
            Player = 1
            REM player 2 marks end of each round
            Round += 1
        Case Else
            MsgBox("PlayerNum is invalid")
    End Select
End Sub
```

Finally, GameOver() is a helper that just determines when the third round has ended, while ShowWinner() displays the final results of the dice battle.

```
Private Function GameOver() As Boolean
    If Round > 3 Then
        GameOver = True
    Else
        GameOver = False
    End If
End Function

Private Sub ShowWinner()
    REM display the winner message
    If Score1 = Score2 Then
        MsgBox("This game is a draw!")
    ElseIf Score1 > Score2 Then
        MsgBox("Player 1 is the winner!")
    ElseIf Score2 > Score1 Then
        MsgBox("Player 2 is the winner!")
    End If
End Sub
```

Figure 3.4 shows the conclusion to a three-round game of Dice War, with player 2 winning 18 to 16! Do you know what would make this game even more interesting? How about a single-player mode against the computer?

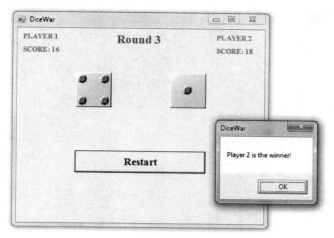

Figure 3.4
Named controls on the Dice War form.

BLOCK BUSTER

It's time to ratchet up the difficulty level a few notches! The last project was fun but still just a turn-based game. There's nothing quite like a *real-time* game to really experience exciting gameplay, because that requires a constant vigil over the controls and coordination without pause. It's a totally different experience when you go real-time! The game we'll create now is a simple version of the classic Atari *Breakout* ball-and-paddle game, which is really just a step above *Pong*, but a good example of a real-time game.

Form Layout

Figure 3.5 shows the layout of the Block Buster form. There are two labels at the top, Label1 to display the lives, and Label2 to display the score. There are four rows of colored blocks that are simply PictureBox controls with their BackColor property set to a color. You may use any color you wish for the blocks, so go ahead and design them however you want. The important thing (as far as the source code goes) is the name of the blocks. They are named Block1 to Block20, arranged in four rows and five columns. As long as there are 20 blocks with their names intact, the source code will work with the blocks, so you can move them

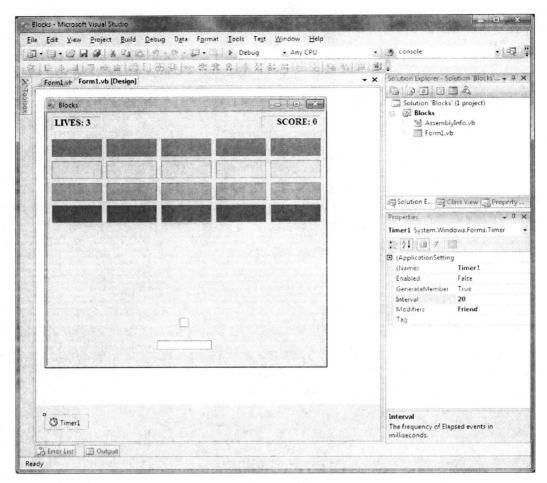

Figure 3.5
Layout of controls on the Block Buster form.

around if you wish. This game affords some design aspects if we want to take advantage of it!

Ball is another PictureBox control resized to 16x16 with a BackColor of White. The ball moves at a constant X,Y velocity until it hits the edge of the form or strikes the paddle or one of the blocks, at which point it changes direction. Likewise, Paddle is a PictureBox with a size of 96 × 24, and it moves left and right with the mouse cursor—so the game is entirely mouse controlled (see the Form1_MouseMove event).

Source

We'll go over the source code for the Block Buster game in the most common event order, starting with Form1_Load. Since this is a real-time game with constant movement, a timer is used to keep things moving.

```
Dim intSpeedX As Integer = 2
Dim intSpeedY As Integer = -2
Dim intScore As Integer
Dim intLives As Integer = 3
Dim intAllGone As Integer

Private Sub Form1_Load(ByVal sender As System.Object, _
    ByVal e As System.EventArgs) Handles MyBase.Load
    Timer1.Interval = 20
    Timer1.Enabled = True
End Sub
```

Next up is the Timer1_Tick function, which is called every time there is a timer tick. Since it was set to an Interval of 20, the timer will fire an event every 20 milliseconds (which is about 50 frames per second—or 50 Hz). A lot is happening in the timer function—in fact, all of the logic of the game happens here, including movement of the ball and checking for collisions. There are fewer comments this time; can you figure out what each portion of code is doing without comments?

```
Private Sub Timer1_Tick(ByVal sender As System.Object, _
    ByVal e As System.EventArgs) Handles Timer1.Tick
    AllGone = 0
    CheckCollisions()
    If AllGone = 1 Then
        Timer1.Enabled = False
        MsgBox("You finished the game!", , "CONGRATULATIONS")
    End If
    BallX += SpeedX
    If BallX < 3 Or BallX + Ball.Width > Me.Width - 5 Then
        SpeedX = -SpeedX
    End If

    BallY += SpeedY
    If BallY < 3 Then
        SpeedY = -SpeedY
    End If
```

```
      If BallY + Ball.Height > Me.Height - 5 Then
          Timer1.Enabled = False
          UpdateLives()
          BallX = 232
          BallY = 376
          SpeedX = 2
          SpeedY = -2
          If Lives < 1 Then
              MsgBox("You have lost the game.", , "OH NO!")
          Else
              MsgBox("You missed!", , "OH NO")
              Timer1.Enabled = True
          End If
      End If
  End Sub
```

The `Form1_MouseMove()` function responds to mouse movement over the form, so we can use this to move the paddle left or right based on the mouse's position.

```
Private Sub Form1_MouseMove(ByVal sender As Object, _
    ByVal e As System.Windows.Forms.MouseEventArgs) Handles MyBase.MouseMove
    Paddle.Left = e.X - Paddle.Width \ 2
End Sub
```

Since the ball (actually a small `PictureBox`) is smaller than the paddle and the blocks, we can perform simple collision detection to see if the ball is hitting anything. The `CheckCollision()` function looks at the dimensions of the passed `PictureBox` control; taking that and the ball's position on the form, it can be determined whether the ball is intersecting the passed `PictureBox`. Then it's just a matter of removing the block and adding points to the player's score.

```
Public Sub CheckCollisions()
    CheckCollision(Paddle, False)
    CheckCollision(Block1)
    CheckCollision(Block2)
    CheckCollision(Block3)
    CheckCollision(Block4)
    CheckCollision(Block5)
    CheckCollision(Block6)
    CheckCollision(Block7)
```

```
        CheckCollision(Block8)
        CheckCollision(Block9)
        CheckCollision(Block10)
        CheckCollision(Block11)
        CheckCollision(Block12)
        CheckCollision(Block13)
        CheckCollision(Block14)
        CheckCollision(Block15)
        CheckCollision(Block16)
        CheckCollision(Block17)
        CheckCollision(Block18)
        CheckCollision(Block19)
        CheckCollision(Block20)
End Sub

Public Sub CheckCollision(ByRef src As PictureBox, ByVal Hide As Boolean)
    If src.Visible = True Then
        If BallX > src.Location.X And _
            BallX < src.Location.X + src.Size.Width And _
            Ball.Location.Y > src.Location.Y And _
            Ball.Location.Y < src.Location.Y + src.Size.Height Then
            SpeedY = -SpeedY
            UpdateScore()
            If Hide Then
                src.Visible = False
            End If
        End If
        AllGone += 1
    End If
End Sub

REM declare the overloaded version of CheckCollision
Public Sub CheckCollision(ByVal src As PictureBox)
    REM call the original version
    CheckCollision(src, True)
End Sub
Public Sub UpdateScore()
    Score += 10
    Label2.Text = "SCORE: " & Score
End Sub
```

```
Public Sub UpdateLives()
    Lives -= 1
    Label1.Text = "LIVES: " & Lives
End Sub
```

Now we can see how useful a property can be in the source code for a real game. Following are several properties to illustrate the convenience afforded by this fascinating programming feature. We can just as easily use global variables directly in our functions, but use of a property instead of just a global variable is cleaner and allows for more control, not to mention error handling.

```
Public Property BallX() As Integer
    Get
        Return Ball.Left
    End Get
    Set(ByVal Value As Integer)
        Ball.Left = Value
    End Set
End Property

Public Property BallY() As Integer
    Get
        Return Ball.Top
    End Get
    Set(ByVal Value As Integer)
        Ball.Top = Value
    End Set
End Property

Public Property Lives() As Integer
    Get
        Return intLives
    End Get
    Set(ByVal Value As Integer)
        intLives = Value
    End Set
End Property

Public Property SpeedX() As Integer
    Get
        Return intSpeedX
```

```
        End Get
        Set(ByVal Value As Integer)
            intSpeedX = Value
        End Set
    End Property

    Public Property SpeedY() As Integer
        Get
            Return intSpeedY
        End Get
        Set(ByVal Value As Integer)
            intSpeedY = Value
        End Set
    End Property

    Public Property Score() As Integer
        Get
            Return intScore
        End Get
        Set(ByVal Value As Integer)
            intScore = Value
        End Set
    End Property

    Public Property AllGone() As Integer
        Get
            Return intAllGone
        End Get
        Set(ByVal Value As Integer)
            intAllGone = Value
        End Set
    End Property
```

TIC-TAC-TOE

Our last game example is a version of the classic game, Tic-Tac-Toe, also known as Naughts & Crosses. This game has a rudimentary playing board with blue Panel controls used as dividers for the nine squares, which are comprised of Button controls named Button1 to Button9. See Figure 3.6. There is no Timer control in this game because it is turn based. Create the form as shown with the nine buttons. The title control is Label1. The message control at the bottom

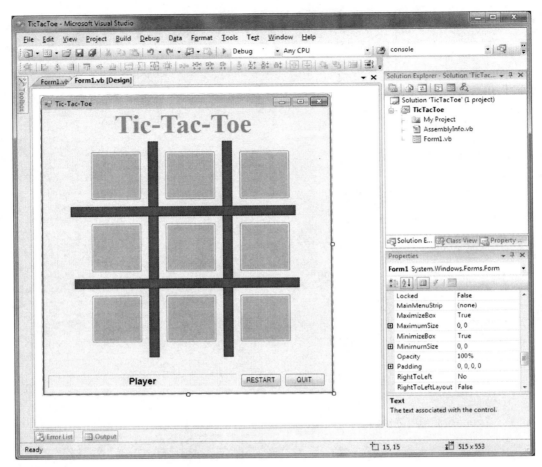

Figure 3.6
Layout of controls on the Tic-Tac-Toe form.

(which displays game states such as the current player) is called Label2. The button labeled "Restart" is Button10. The button labeled "Quit" is Button11. That should be all that's needed by the source code.

Button Events

We are going to use a little trick to cut down on the number of event functions in this game. Instead of generating an event for every one of the nine button click events, we're instead going to have them all use the same event function. This is done using the Property Events window (see Figure 3.7). Double-click the

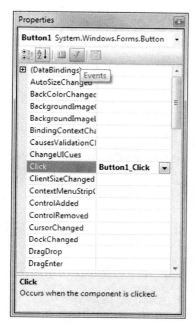

Figure 3.7
The list of control events in the Properties window.

first button, Button1, to generate the first event. Then go back to the form and select the remaining eight gameplay buttons, Button2 to Button9, and set their click events to Button1_Click.

Here is the source code for Button1_Click, which handles click events for all nine gameplay buttons. Note that all nine buttons are listed after the Handles keyword in the event definition. Now, the source code in this function is a bit different from usual. Instead of referring directly to Button1, Button2, etc., we instead use sender as the control. Since this function handles click events for *only* the controls listed, we needn't worry about any other controls generating this event and can respond to the event in a generic way. For our gameplay purposes, the Text property of the button is set to Token (which will be either "X" or "O" depending on the current player). Then that button is disabled so it can't be picked again, and CheckWinner() is called to test for three-in-a-row win conditions.

```
Private Sub Button1_Click(ByVal sender As System.Object, _
    ByVal e As System.EventArgs) Handles Button1.Click, _
```

```
        Button2.Click, Button3.Click, Button4.Click, Button5.Click, _
        Button6.Click, Button7.Click, Button8.Click, Button9.Click
        sender.Text = Token
        sender.Enabled = False
        CheckWinner()
End Sub
```

Source

Let's dig in to the rest of the source code now, first with two global variables and the `Form1_Load` function which calls `RestartGame()`.

```
Dim Token As Char
Dim Player As Integer
Dim Winner As Boolean

Private Sub Form1_Load(ByVal sender As System.Object, _
    ByVal e As System.EventArgs) Handles MyBase.Load
    RestartGame()
End Sub
```

Next up are the two event handlers for the Restart and Quit buttons.

```
Private Sub Button10_Click(ByVal sender As System.Object, _
    ByVal e As System.EventArgs) Handles Button10.Click
    REM restart button
    RestartGame()
End Sub

Private Sub Button11_Click(ByVal sender As System.Object, _
    ByVal e As System.EventArgs) Handles Button11.Click
    REM quit button
    End
End Sub
```

The `CheckWinner()` function goes through the rows, columns, and diagonals looking for matching Xs or Os to find a winner (if there is one). The helper function `TestThreeInARow()` performs the test on three squares at a time to see if there is a match. If no winner is found, then play continues to the next player. It does this by looking at the `Text` property of each `Button` control and simply checks whether the three are equal to each other, which means the player has chosen those three in a row.

```
Private Sub CheckWinner()
    REM check rows
    TestThreeInARow(Button1, Button2, Button3)
    TestThreeInARow(Button4, Button5, Button6)
    TestThreeInARow(Button7, Button8, Button9)
    REM check columns
    TestThreeInARow(Button1, Button4, Button7)
    TestThreeInARow(Button2, Button5, Button8)
    TestThreeInARow(Button3, Button6, Button9)
    REM check diagonals
    TestThreeInARow(Button1, Button5, Button9)
    TestThreeInARow(Button3, Button5, Button7)
    If Not Winner Then
        NextPlayer()
    End If
End Sub

Private Sub TestThreeInARow(ByRef one As Button, _
    ByRef two As Button, ByRef three As Button)
    If one.Text.Length + two.Text.Length + three.Text.Length > 0 _
        And one.Text = two.Text And two.Text = three.Text Then
        one.BackColor = Color.Yellow
        two.BackColor = Color.Yellow
        three.BackColor = Color.Yellow
        Winner = True
        DisplayWinner()
    End If
End Sub
```

Two helper functions help to keep the code clean and tidy: NextPlayer() goes to the next player by setting the Token and Player variables as appropriate; DisplayWinner() disables all of the buttons (to prevent any further moves) and displays the winner using Label2 on the bottom of the form.

```
Private Sub NextPlayer()
    If Player = 1 Then
        Token = "X"
        Player = 2
    ElseIf Player = 2 Then
        Token = "O"
        Player = 1
```

```
        End If
        Label2.Text = "Player " & Player & " : '" & Token & "'"
End Sub

Private Sub DisplayWinner()
        REM display winner message
        Label2.Text = "Player '" & Token & "' is the winner!"
        REM disable all the buttons
        Button1.Enabled = False
        Button2.Enabled = False
        Button3.Enabled = False
        Button4.Enabled = False
        Button5.Enabled = False
        Button6.Enabled = False
        Button7.Enabled = False
        Button8.Enabled = False
        Button9.Enabled = False
End Sub
```

Finally, RestartGame() resets the game's state, gameplay variables, and controls to the initial setting so the game can be played again.

```
Private Sub RestartGame()
        REM re-enable the buttons
        Button1.Enabled = True
        Button2.Enabled = True
        Button3.Enabled = True
        Button4.Enabled = True
        Button5.Enabled = True
        Button6.Enabled = True
        Button7.Enabled = True
        Button8.Enabled = True
        Button9.Enabled = True
        REM clear the button labels
        Button1.Text = ""
        Button2.Text = ""
        Button3.Text = ""
        Button4.Text = ""
        Button5.Text = ""
        Button6.Text = ""
        Button7.Text = ""
        Button8.Text = ""
        Button9.Text = ""
```

```
      REM set the button background colors
      Button1.BackColor = Color.LimeGreen
      Button2.BackColor = Color.LimeGreen
      Button3.BackColor = Color.LimeGreen
      Button4.BackColor = Color.LimeGreen
      Button5.BackColor = Color.LimeGreen
      Button6.BackColor = Color.LimeGreen
      Button7.BackColor = Color.LimeGreen
      Button8.BackColor = Color.LimeGreen
      Button9.BackColor = Color.LimeGreen
      REM set up the new game
      Winner = False
      Player = 2
      Token = "O"
      NextPlayer()
End Sub
```

Figure 3.8 shows the Tic-Tac-Toe game running with the first column of Xs giving victory to the X player!

Figure 3.8
The Tic-Tac-Toe game showing a winner.

LEVEL UP!

It's time to level up after learning so many new skills with Visual Basic forms and controls! In this chapter you have studied the intricacies of control programming (and a few special tricks) while building three complete games. As you were working on the games, I'm sure you saw some areas for improvement. After all, these games are kept on the simple side so they are easy to understand. But you are under no such limitation! So, why don't you see if you can add some new gameplay capabilities to these games to make them more interesting, and ultimately, more playable?

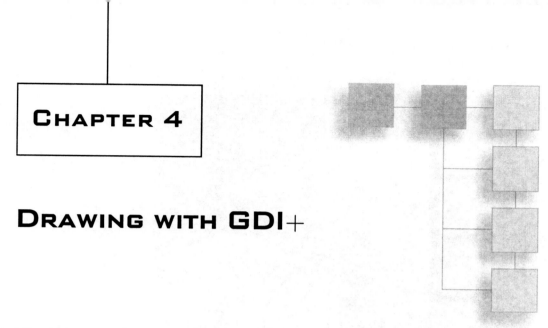

CHAPTER 4

DRAWING WITH GDI+

We are now on the verge of getting started on the Celtic Crusader RPG, which is the focus of most of this book! The first three chapters should have brought you up to speed on the basics of programming in Visual Basic and working with forms and controls. Now we will begin studying the graphics capabilities of the .NET Framework that will make it possible to build a complex game. Examples will no longer be tied to the form and its controls and their limitations, as far as game programming is concerned. Although future chapters will again use forms and controls for our game editors, graphics code will no longer be dependent on controls. The .NET Framework has abstracted classes around the Windows Graphics Device Interface (GDI) so that we can create drawing surfaces and render shapes onto them using classes such as Graphics and Bitmap in conjunction with a PictureBox control. We will just create what is needed at runtime. The examples will be hands on once again so that you will learn new techniques first by using them rather than learning about them.

Here's what we'll cover in this chapter:

- Drawing lines
- Drawing rectangles

Figure 4.1
Drawing lines with managed GDI+ objects.

DRAWING LINES

Lines and other vector shapes may not be very exciting but we are going to use line drawing as a starting point for learning about graphics programming with the .NET Framework and GDI+. The graphics code we'll go over here in a bit produces the result shown in Figure 4.1.

PictureBox Is Our Friend

For our purposes in this chapter, we will just look at the features specific to 2D graphics programming using the Image property of a PictureBox control. The PictureBox can be added to a form manually, but it's easier to use a global PictureBox control and just create it at runtime in the Form1_Load function. In fact, we will just configure the form in code as well so that no manual property editing is needed. Any property you see in the Properties window of the Form Designer can be modified in code—and it's easier to do that in code. So, in the globals section of `Public Class Form1`, let's add a new `PictureBox` control:

```
Public pb As PictureBox
Public rand As Random
```

In Form1_Load, we will create this new `PictureBox` and add it to the form. The `Parent` property is used to attach the control to `Form1` (referred to with the `Me` keyword—which is like the `this` keyword in C++: it refers to the current `Form`). `DockStyle.Fill` causes the `PictureBox` to fill the entire form, so that we can set the size of the form and the `PictureBox` will resize with it.

```
pb = New PictureBox()
pb.Parent = Me
pb.Dock = DockStyle.Fill
pb.BackColor = Color.Black
```

While we're working in Form1_Load, let's just go ahead and set the form's settings. Again, this is being done in code while it could also be done using the Properties window in the Form Designer.

```
REM set up the form
Me.Text = "Line Drawing Demo"
Me.FormBorderStyle = Windows.Forms.FormBorderStyle.FixedSingle
Me.MaximizeBox = False
Me.Size = New Point(600, 500)

REM create random generator
rand = New Random()
```

Surfaces and Devices

Back in the globals sections at the top of the code, we need two new objects: a `Bitmap` and a `Graphics` object.

```
Public surface As Bitmap
Public device As Graphics
```

The Bitmap represents a drawing surface and is really just a pointer to the data in memory. After drawing something using the Graphics object (onto a Picture-Box.Image), we then set the Bitmap variable (which is a pointer) equal to the PictureBox.Image, and that Bitmap can then be treated as an independent surface—which can be copied elsewhere, saved to a file, and other things. The Bitmap should be created with the same dimensions as the PictureBox control. This code goes in Form1_Load:

```
surface = New Bitmap(Me.Size.Width, Me.Size.Height)
pb.Image = surface
device = Graphics.FromImage(surface)
```

There are quite a few versions of the Graphics.DrawLine() function with various parameter variations that use Points, Single-, and Integer-based X,Y coordinates and drawing modes. I will use a pen defined with the desired color and line width. The drawLine() function creates a pen with a random color and random line size, and two random points for the line ends that fit inside the dimensions of the form. After calling DrawLine(), then the PictureBox.Image is refreshed.

```
Private Sub drawLine()
    REM make a random color
    Dim A As Integer = rand.Next(0, 255)
    Dim R As Integer = rand.Next(0, 255)
    Dim G As Integer = rand.Next(0, 255)
    Dim B As Integer = rand.Next(0, 255)
    Dim color As Color = color.FromArgb(A, R, G, B)
    REM make a pen
    Dim width As Integer = rand.Next(2, 8)
    Dim pen As New Pen(color, width)
    REM random line ends
    Dim x1 As Integer = rand.Next(1, Me.Size.Width)
    Dim y1 As Integer = rand.Next(1, Me.Size.Height)
    Dim x2 As Integer = rand.Next(1, Me.Size.Width)
    Dim y2 As Integer = rand.Next(1, Me.Size.Height)
    REM draw the line
    device.DrawLine(pen, x1, y1, x2, y2)
    REM refresh the drawing surface
    pb.Image = surface
End Sub
```

4D Programming with a Timer

We can even create a `Timer` in code without using the Form Designer. There is just one extra step to take and then the new `Timer` will work like usual—its variable must be declared using the `WithEvents` keyword:

```
Public WithEvents timer As Timer
```

We can then initialize the `Timer` object and set its properties in `Form1_Load`:

```
REM set up the timer
timer = New Timer()
timer.Interval = 20
timer.Enabled = True
```

When a new object is declared using `WithEvents`, then it is "visible" to the event handler system in Visual Basic, and can be used as an event trigger even when we write the function ourselves (rather than having Visual Basic generate it for us). Suffice it to say, we want the `drawLine()` function to run every 20 milliseconds, which is 50 frames per second (50 Hz).

```
Private Sub timer_Tick(ByVal sender As System.Object, _
    ByVal e As System.EventArgs) Handles timer.Tick
    drawLine()
End Sub
```

One final point: we must always free memory after we finish with objects created in heap memory. This is best done in the `FormClosed` event.

```
Private Sub Form1_FormClosed(ByVal sender As Object, _
    ByVal e As System.Windows.Forms.FormClosedEventArgs) _
    Handles Me.FormClosed
    device.Dispose()
    surface.Dispose()
    timer.Dispose()
End Sub
```

DRAWING RECTANGLES

Once we have the framework in place to draw lines, there are many other vector shapes that can be drawn with only a few minor changes in the code. One such shape is a rectangle, which we will look at next. Figure 4.2 shows the result.

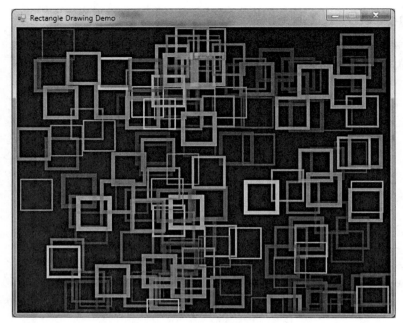

Figure 4.2
Drawing rectangles with managed GDI+ objects.

For reference, we'll go over the entire code listing (which is still quite short). First up are the global variables, Form1_Load, which initializes the program, and Form1_FormClosed, which frees memory.

```
Public pb As PictureBox
Public WithEvents timer As Timer
Public surface As Bitmap
Public device As Graphics
Public rand As Random

Private Sub Form1_Load(ByVal sender As System.Object, _
    ByVal e As System.EventArgs) Handles MyBase.Load
    REM set up the form
    Me.Text = "Rectangle Drawing Demo"
    Me.FormBorderStyle = Windows.Forms.FormBorderStyle.FixedSingle
    Me.MaximizeBox = False
    Me.Size = New Point(600, 500)
    REM create a new picturebox
```

```
        pb = New PictureBox()
        pb.Parent = Me
        pb.Dock = DockStyle.Fill
        pb.BackColor = Color.Black
        REM create graphics device
        surface = New Bitmap(Me.Size.Width, Me.Size.Height)
        pb.Image = surface
        device = Graphics.FromImage(surface)
        REM create random generator
        rand = New Random()
        REM set up the timer
        timer = New Timer()
        timer.Interval = 20
        timer.Enabled = True
    End Sub

    Private Sub Form1_FormClosed(ByVal sender As Object, _
        ByVal e As System.Windows.Forms.FormClosedEventArgs) _
        Handles Me.FormClosed
        device.Dispose()
        surface.Dispose()
        timer.Dispose()
    End Sub
```

Lastly, we have the `timer_Tick` event and the `drawRect()` function, which does the actual rasterizing of rectangle shapes. Again, there are several versions of the `Graphics.DrawRectangle()` function, and I have just chosen the easiest one, but there are others that let you use a `Point` for the coordinates instead of individual X and Y values.

```
    Private Sub timer_Tick(ByVal sender As System.Object, _
        ByVal e As System.EventArgs) _
        Handles timer.Tick
        drawRect()
    End Sub

    Private Sub drawRect()
        REM make a random color
        Dim A As Integer = rand.Next(0, 255)
        Dim R As Integer = rand.Next(0, 255)
        Dim G As Integer = rand.Next(0, 255)
        Dim B As Integer = rand.Next(0, 255)
        Dim color As Color = color.FromArgb(A, R, G, B)
```

```
      REM make pen out of color
      Dim width As Integer = rand.Next(2, 8)
      Dim pen As New Pen(color, width)
      REM random line ends
      Dim x As Integer = rand.Next(1, Me.Size.Width - 50)
      Dim y As Integer = rand.Next(1, Me.Size.Height - 50)
      Dim rect As New Rectangle(x, y, 50, 50)
      REM draw the rectangle
      device.DrawRectangle(pen, rect)
      REM refresh the drawing surface
      pb.Image = surface
End Sub
```

DRAWING TEXT

We will need to draw text onto the game screen using any desired font, and the Graphics class gives us this ability too via the DrawString() function. There are several versions of the function with various sets of parameters, but we will be using the simplest version that just needs a String (for the words we want to print out), a custom Font object, the color, and the coordinates. Figure 4.3 shows the result of this example program.

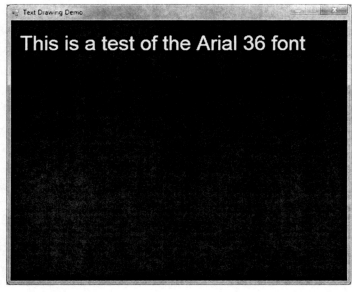

Figure 4.3
Printing text using a custom font and color.

```
Public pb As PictureBox
Public surface As Bitmap
Public device As Graphics
Public rand As New Random()


Private Sub Form1_FormClosed(ByVal sender As Object, _
    ByVal e As System.Windows.Forms.FormClosedEventArgs) _
    Handles Me.FormClosed
    device.Dispose()
    surface.Dispose()
End Sub

Private Sub Form1_Load(ByVal sender As System.Object, _
    ByVal e As System.EventArgs) Handles MyBase.Load
    REM set up the form
    Me.Text = "Text Drawing Demo"
    Me.FormBorderStyle = Windows.Forms.FormBorderStyle.FixedSingle
    Me.MaximizeBox = False
    Me.Size = New Point(600, 500)
    REM create a new picturebox
    pb = New PictureBox()
    pb.Parent = Me
    pb.Dock = DockStyle.Fill
    pb.BackColor = Color.Black
    REM create graphics device
    surface = New Bitmap(Me.Size.Width, Me.Size.Height)
    pb.Image = surface
    device = Graphics.FromImage(surface)

    REM make a new font
    Dim font As New Font("Arial", 36, FontStyle.Regular, GraphicsUnit.Pixel)
    REM draw the text
    device.DrawString("This is a test of the Arial 36 font", _
        font, Brushes.White, 10, 20)
    REM refresh the drawing surface
    pb.Image = surface
End Sub
```

There are other shapes in addition to lines, rectangles, and text that the Graphics class can draw. Now that you have a foundation, see if you can modify the program to use any of the following functions:

- DrawArc

- DrawBezier

- DrawCurve

- DrawEllipse

- DrawPie

- DrawPolygon

LEVEL UP!

This quick chapter gave us the ability to create a rendering system in code and bypass the Form Designer (by creating controls at runtime instead of design time). Using this technique, we created a PictureBox for use in rendering and a Timer to give our programs real time updating. The one really big topic missing from this chapter was left out intentionally—drawing bitmaps. After all, we need bitmaps to make an RPG like Celtic Crusader, so what gives? That sole subject is the focus of Chapter 5.

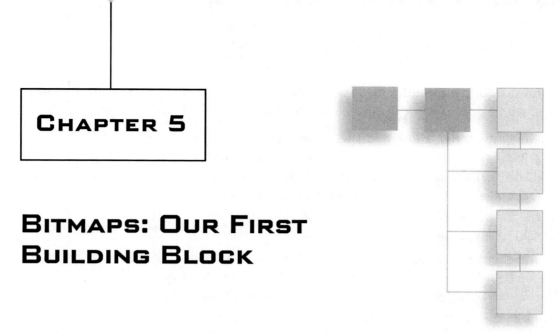

CHAPTER 5

BITMAPS: OUR FIRST BUILDING BLOCK

In Chapter 4, we learned how to tap into the `Graphics` class in the .NET Framework, which gives access to GDI+ graphics drawing capabilities above and beyond the forms and controls in Visual Basic. By using the `Bitmap` class and a `PictureBox`, we are able to create a rendering surface in code and draw onto it. Now that we have learned the basics of drawing with the `Graphics` class, we can begin to abstract away the "Visual" part of Visual Basic and focus on just a source code approach to game programming, and consider the Form—once the main focus of the program—as just another asset, like a bitmap or audio file.

Here's what we'll cover in this chapter:

- Loading a bitmap file
- Drawing a bitmap
- Rotating and flipping a bitmap
- Accessing bitmap pixels
- Creating a `Game` class

DISSECTING BITMAPS

Learning to draw a bitmap is the first step toward creating a 2D game like Celtic Crusader. When we have the ability to draw just one bitmap, then we can extend that to animation by drawing one frame after another in a timed sequence—and presto, sprite animation becomes a reality! We will focus on sprite animation in Chapter 5, and work on the basics of bitmap drawing now as a prerequisite.

Drawing on the code we learned about in the preceding chapter, a `Bitmap` object, a `PictureBox`, and a `Graphics` object work in tandem to represent a rendering device capable of drawing vector shapes and—as we will see next—bitmaps. Once again for reference, we have to declare the two variables:

```
Public surface As Bitmap
Public device As Graphics
```

and then, assuming we have a `PictureBox` control called `PictureBox1`, create the objects. The `PictureBox` control can be created at runtime (as we saw last chapter), but I've added it to the form manually this time.

```
surface = New Bitmap(Me.Size.Width, Me.Size.Height)
PictureBox1.Image = surface
device = Graphics.FromImage(surface)
```

So, we already knew this startup code, but—just to lay the groundwork—this is what is needed up front as a rendering device to draw a *bitmap*.

Loading a Bitmap File

We can load a bitmap in Basic by using the `Bitmap` class. But there is no `Bitmap.Load()` function (unfortunately!) so we have to use the constructor instead by passing the bitmap filename when the object is created.

```
Public bmp As Bitmap
bmp = New Bitmap("image.bmp")
```

Interestingly enough, in Basic we can create the object with this shorthand code:

```
Public bmp as New Bitmap("image.bmp")
```

The reason why I advise against doing this is because it breaks our ability to trap errors, and it is bad practice to create an object at the same time it is defined— better to create it inside a function like `Form1_Load` where we have more control over the result.

Definition

A *constructor* is a class function (also called a method) that runs when an object is first created. This is where class variables (also called properties) are initialized. A *destructor* is a class function that runs when the object is being destroyed: via `object.Dispose()` or `object = Nothing`.

Although both approaches work, and we can even pass a string rather than hard coding the filename, there is the very serious problem of error handling: if the file does not exist, an exception error will crash the program. Missing files are fairly common (usually due to their being in the wrong folder), and we want to display a friendly error message rather than allow the program to crash. The solution is to wrap the Bitmap loading code in a try...catch block. Here is an example:

```
Try
    bmp = New Bitmap(filename)
Catch ex As Exception
    MsgBox("Error loading file")
End Try
```

This code will *not crash* if the file is missing or if some other error occurs while reading the file. So, let's put it into a reusable function that returns a Bitmap if the file exists or Nothing (null) if it fails. One caveat: be sure to free memory used by the Bitmap when the program ends.

```
Public Function LoadBitmap(ByVal filename As String)
    Dim bmp As Bitmap
    Try
        bmp = New Bitmap(filename)
    Catch ex As Exception
        bmp = Nothing
    End Try
    Return bmp
End Function
```

If the file does not exist, then LoadBitmap() will return Nothing as the object pointer rather than crashing with an exception error. This is a very handy little function! And it demonstrates the power of code reuse and customization—whatever features we need that are not already in an SDK or library we can just write ourselves. One might even go so far as to write their own new Bitmap wrapper class (called something like CBitmap?) with a Load() function. You could easily do this yourself with just the small amount of code we have used so far.

Hint

To ensure that created objects are properly disposed of when the program ends, I recommend putting the Form1_FormClosed() function at the top of the source code, just below the variable declarations, where it will be quick and easy to write the code needed to free an object. Always write creation/deletion code together in pairs to avoid memory leaks!

Drawing a Bitmap

There are several versions of the Graphics.DrawImage() function; the alternate versions are called *overloaded functions* in "OOP speak." The simplest version of the function calls for just a Bitmap or Image parameter and then the X and Y position. For example, this line

```
device.DrawImage( bmp, 10, 10 )
```

will draw the bitmap bmp at pixel coordinates 10,10. Figure 5.1 shows an example.

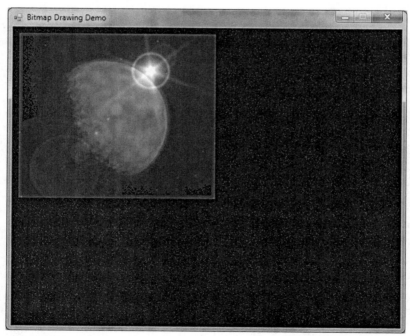

Figure 5.1
Drawing an image loaded from a bitmap file.

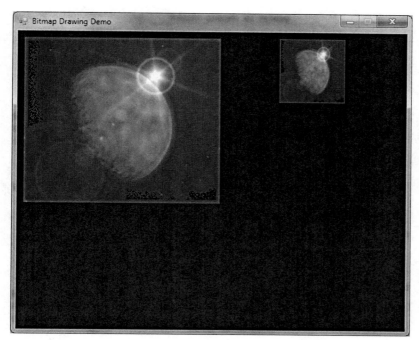

Figure 5.2
Drawing a scaled bitmap.

We can optionally use a `Point` with the X and Y coordinates combined into one object, or use floating-point `Single` variables. There are also *scaling* features that make it possible to resize the image. By passing additional width and height parameters, we can define a new target size for the image. Figure 5.2 shows another example with the addition of this line, which draws another copy of the planet bitmap scaled down to a smaller size.

```
device.DrawImage(planet, 400, 10, 64, 64)
```

Rotating and Flipping a Bitmap

The `Bitmap` class has some helper functions for manipulating the image and even its individual pixels. The `Bitmap.RotateFlip()` function will rotate a bitmap in 90-degree increments (90, 180, and 270 degrees), as well as flip the bitmap vertically, horizontally, or both. Here is an example that rotates the bitmap 90 degrees:

```
planet.RotateFlip(RotateFlipType.Rotate90FlipNone)
```

The `RotateFlipType` options are:

- `Rotate180FlipNone`
- `Rotate180FlipX`
- `Rotate180FlipXY`
- `Rotate180FlipY`
- `Rotate270FlipNone`
- `Rotate270FlipX`
- `Rotate270FlipXY`
- `Rotate270FlipY`
- `Rotate90FlipNone`
- `Rotate90FlipX`
- `Rotate90FlipXY`
- `Rotate90FlipY`
- `RotateNoneFlipX`
- `RotateNoneFlipXY`
- `RotateNoneFlipY`

The Bitmap Drawing Demo has several buttons on the form to let you explore rotating and flipping a bitmap in various ways, as you can see in Figure 5.3. In addition to calling `RotateFlip()`, we still need to draw the image again and refresh the `PictureBox` like usual:

```
planet.RotateFlip(RotateFlipType.Rotate180FlipNone)
device.DrawImage(planet, 10, 10)
PictureBox1.Image = surface
```

Accessing Bitmap Pixels

We can also examine and modify the pixel buffer of a bitmap directly using functions in the `Bitmap` class. The `Bitmap.GetPixel()` function retrieves the pixel of a bitmap at given X,Y coordinates, returning it as a `Color` variable. Likewise,

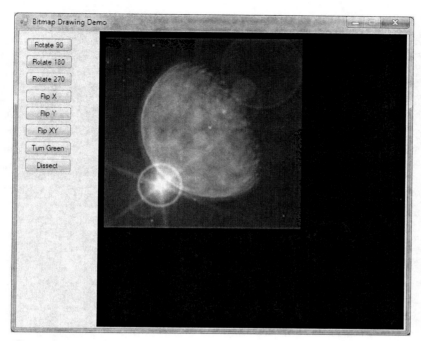

Figure 5.3
Rotating and flipping a bitmap.

the `Bitmap.SetPixel()` will change the color of a pixel at the given coordinates. The following example reads every pixel in the planet bitmap and changes it to green by setting the red and blue components of the color to zero, which leaves just the green color remaining. Figure 5.4 shows the Bitmap Drawing Demo with the pixels modified—not very interesting but it does a good job of showing what you can do with this capability.

```
For x = 0 To planet.Width - 1
    For y = 0 To planet.Height - 1
        Dim pixelColor As Color = planet.GetPixel(x, y)
        Dim newColor As Color = Color.FromArgb(0, pixelColor.G, 0)
        planet.SetPixel(x, y, newColor)
    Next
Next
```

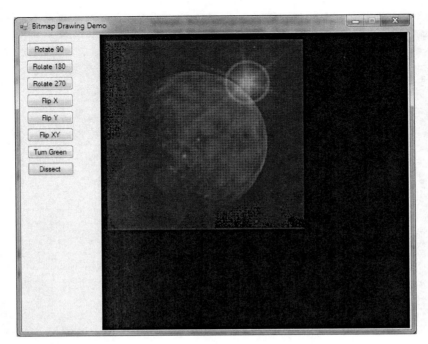

Figure 5.4
Modifying the color value of pixels in a bitmap.

CREATING A GAME CLASS

We have enough code now at this point to begin constructing a game framework for our future Basic projects. The purpose of a framework is to take care of repeating code. Any variables and functions that are needed regularly can be moved into a Game class as properties and methods where they will be both convenient and easily accessible. First, we'll create a new source code file called Game.vb, which will contain the source code for the Game class. Then, we'll copy this Game.vb file into the folder of any new project we create and add it to that project. Let's get started:

```
Public Class Game
    Private p_device As Graphics
    Private p_surface As Bitmap
    Private p_pb As PictureBox
    Private p_frm As Form
```

You might recognize the first three of these variables (oops—I mean, class *properties*) from previous examples. They have a p_ in front of their names so it's easy to tell at a glance that they are *private* variables in the class (as opposed to, say, parameters in a function). The fourth property, p_frm, is a reference to the main Form of a project, which will be set when the object is created.

Hint

A *class* is a blueprint written in source code for how an *object* should behave at runtime. Just as an object does not exist at compile time (i.e., when we're editing source code and building the project), a class does not exist during runtime. An object is created out of the class blueprint.

Game Class Constructor

The constructor is the first function that runs when a class is *instantiated* into an object. We can add parameters to the constructor in order to send information to the object at runtime—important things like the Form, or maybe a filename, or whatever you want.

Definition

Instantiation is the process of creating an object out of the blueprint specified in a class. When this happens, an object is *created* and the *constructor function* runs. Likewise, when the object is destroyed, the *destructor function* runs. These functions are defined in the class.

Here is the constructor for the Game class. This is just a starting point, as more code will be added in time. As you can see, this is not new code, it's just the code we've seen before to create the Graphics and Bitmap objects needed for rendering onto a PictureBox. Which, by the way, is created at runtime by this function and set to fill the entire form (Dock = DockStyle.Fill). To clarify what these objects are used for, the Graphics variable is called p_device—while not technically correct, it conveys the purpose adequately. To help illustrate when the constructor runs, a temporary message box pops up which you are welcome to remove after you get what it's doing.

```
Public Sub New(ByRef form As Form, ByVal width As Integer, ByVal height As Integer)
    MsgBox("Game class constructor")

    REM set form properties
    p_frm = form
```

```
    p_frm.FormBorderStyle = Windows.Forms.FormBorderStyle.FixedSingle
    p_frm.MaximizeBox = False
    p_frm.Size = New Point(width, height)

    REM create a picturebox
    p_pb = New PictureBox()
    p_pb.Parent = p_frm
    p_pb.Dock = DockStyle.Fill
    p_pb.BackColor = Color.Black

    REM create graphics device
    p_surface = New Bitmap(p_frm.Size.Width, p_frm.Size.Height)
    p_pb.Image = p_surface
    p_device = Graphics.FromImage(p_surface)
End Sub
```

Game Class Destructor

The *destructor* function is called automatically when the object is about to be deleted from memory (i.e., destroyed). In Basic, or, more specifically, in .NET, the name of the destructor is `Sub Finalize()`. The `Protected Overrides` part is very important: this allows any subclass (via inheritance—a key OOP feature) to also free memory used by its parent. There is also a message box that pops up from this function to illustrate when the object is being destroyed, and you may remove the `MsgBox()` function call if you wish.

```
Protected Overrides Sub Finalize()
    MsgBox("Game class destructor")
    REM free memory
    p_device.Dispose()
    p_surface.Dispose()
    p_pb.Dispose()
End Sub
```

Game Updates

We probably will not need an `Update()` function at this early stage but it's here as an option should you wish to use it to update the `PictureBox` any time drawing occurs on the "device." In due time, this function will be expanded to do quite a bit more than its meager one line of code currently shows. Also shown here is a `Property` called `Device`. A `Property` allows us to write code that looks like just a simple class property is being used (like p_device), when in fact a *function call* occurs.

```
Public Sub Update()
    REM refresh the drawing surface
    p_pb.Image = p_surface
End Sub

Public ReadOnly Property Device() As Graphics
    Get
        Return p_device
    End Get
End Property
End Class
```

So, for example, if we want to get the value returned by the Device property, we can do that like so:

```
Dim G as Graphics = game.Device
```

Note that I did not include parentheses at the end of Device. That's because it is not treated as a function, even though we are able to do something with the data before returning it. The key to a property is its Get and Set members. Since I did not want anyone to modify the p_device variable from outside the class, I have made the property read-only via the ReadOnly keyword—and as a result, there is no Set member, just a Get member. If I did want to make p_device writable, I would use a Set member that looks something like this:

```
Public ReadOnly Property Device() As Graphics
    Get
        Return p_device
    End Get
    Set(ByVal value As Graphics)
        p_device = value
    End Set
End Property
```

Properties are really helpful because they allow us to protect data in the class! Besides using ReadOnly, you can prevent changes to a variable by making sure value is in a valid range before allowing the change—so it's like a variable with benefits.

Framework Demo

The code in this Framework Demo program produces pretty much the same output as what we've seen earlier in the chapter (drawing a purple planet). The difference is, thanks to the new Game class, the source code is *much*, much shorter! Take a look.

```
Public Class Form1
    Public game As Game
    Public planet As Bitmap
    Private Sub Form1_Load(ByVal sender As Object, _
        ByVal e As System.EventArgs) Handles Me.Load
        REM set up the form
        Me.Text = "Bitmap Drawing Demo"

        REM create game object
        game = New Game(Me, 600, 500)

        REM load bitmap
        planet = LoadBitmap("planet.bmp")
        If planet Is Nothing Then
            MsgBox("Error loading planet.bmp")
            End
        End If

        REM draw the bitmap
        game.Device.DrawImage(planet, 10, 10)
        game.Device.DrawImage(planet, 400, 10, 100, 100)
    End Sub

    Public Function LoadBitmap(ByVal filename As String)
        Dim bmp As Bitmap
        Try
            bmp = New Bitmap(filename)
        Catch ex As Exception
            bmp = Nothing
        End Try
        Return bmp
    End Function
```

```
Private Sub Form1_FormClosed(ByVal sender As Object, _
    ByVal e As System.Windows.Forms.FormClosedEventArgs) _
    Handles Me.FormClosed
    REM delete game object
    game = Nothing
    planet = Nothing
End Sub
End Class
```

If we had moved the LoadBitmap() function into the Game class or into some new class for handling bitmaps, then this code would have been even shorter. That's a good thing—eliminating any reusable source code by moving it into a support file is like reducing a mathematical formula, rendering the new formula more *powerful* than it was before. Any code that does *not* have to be written increases your productivity as a programmer. So, look for every opportunity to cleanly and effectively recycle code, but don't reduce just for the sake of code reuse—make sure you keep variables and functions together that belong together and don't mish-mash them all together.

LEVEL UP!

That wraps up our basic bitmap loading, manipulating, and drawing needs. Most importantly, we have now learned enough about 2D graphics programming to begin working with sprites in the next chapter.

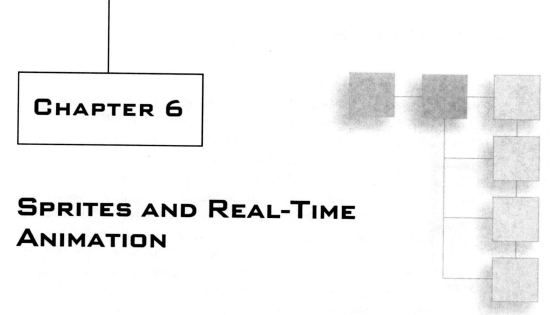

CHAPTER 6

SPRITES AND REAL-TIME ANIMATION

This chapter will show how to create a sprite using the code developed in Chapter 5 for working with bitmaps. We have a lot of ground to cover here, and we'll be going through it thoroughly because this is the foundation of the Celtic Crusader game. You will finish this chapter with a solid grasp of sprite programming knowledge, with the ability to load a sprite sheet and draw a sprite with timed animation. Because we want a sprite to draw transparently over any background image in a game, we'll also learn how to work with an alpha channel in a bitmap image to render an image with transparency. This chapter moves along at a pretty good clip, so you don't want to skip ahead or you might miss some important detail.

Here's what we'll cover in this chapter:

- What is a sprite?
- Sprite animation theory
- Creating a Sprite class
- Improving the Game class
- Separating Form and Module code
- Adding a real-time game loop
- Gameplay functions

WHAT IS A SPRITE?

The first question that often arises when the discussion of sprites comes up is, "What is a sprite?" To answer this question simply, a *sprite* is a small, transparent, animated game object that usually moves on the screen and interacts with other sprites. You might have trees or rocks or buildings in your game that don't move at all, but because those objects are loaded from a bitmap file when the game starts running, and drawn in the game separately from the background, it is reasonable to call them sprites. There are two basic types of sprites. One type of sprite is the "normal" sprite that I just described, which I refer to as a *dynamic sprite*. This type of sprite is often called an *actor* in game design theory. The other type of sprite might be called a *static sprite*; it is the sort that doesn't move or animate. A static sprite is used for scenery or objects that the player uses (such as items that might be picked up in the game world). This type of sprite is often called a *prop*.

Definition

A *sprite* is a small, transparent, animated game object that usually moves on the screen and interacts with other sprites. There are two types of sprites: actors and props.

I'm going to treat any game entity that is loaded and drawn separately from the background as a sprite. So, I might have a whole house, which normally would be considered part of the background, as a sprite. I use that concept in the sample program later in this chapter.

Figure 6.1 shows an example sprite of an Orc warrior. The sprite is really just the detailed pixels that you see at the center of the image, showing the Orc warrior

Transparent Background
(Alpha Channel)

Image Boundary
(Collision Rectangle)

Figure 6.1
The sprite boundary is a rectangle that encloses the sprite with transparent pixels.

holding a mace and shield. The sprite itself only takes up about half of the actual size of the sprite boundary because the computer only sees sprites in the shape of a rectangle. It is physically impossible to even store a sprite without the rectangular boundary because bitmap images are themselves rectangular. The real problem with a sprite is what to do about all the transparent pixels that should *not* be shown when the image is displayed on the screen (or rather, on the back buffer surface).

The amateur game programmer will try to draw a sprite using two loops that go through each pixel of the sprite's bitmap image, drawing only the solid pixels. Here is the pseudocode for how one might do this:

```
For Y = 1 To Sprite_Height
  For X = 1 to Sprite_Width
    If Pixel At X,Y Is Solid Then
      Draw Pixel At X,Y
    End If
  Next X
Next Y
```

This pseudocode algorithm goes through each pixel of the sprite image, checking for solid pixels, which are then drawn while transparent pixels are ignored. This draws a transparent sprite, but it runs so slowly that the game probably won't be playable (even on a top-of-the-line PC).

And yet, this is the *only* way to draw a transparent sprite! By one method or another, some process must check the pixels that are solid and render them. The key here is understanding how drawing works, because this very critical and time-consuming algorithm is quite old and has been built into the silicon of video cards for many years now. The process of copying a transparent image from one surface to another has been provided by video cards since Windows 3.1 first started supporting the concept of a "video accelerator." The process is called *bit block transfer* or just *blit* for short. Because this important process is handled by an extremely optimized and custom video chip, you don't need to worry about writing your own *blitter* for a game any longer. (Even older systems like the Nintendo Game Boy Advance have a hardware blitter.)

The video card uses *alpha blending* to draw textures with a translucent effect (which means you can see through them like a window) or with full

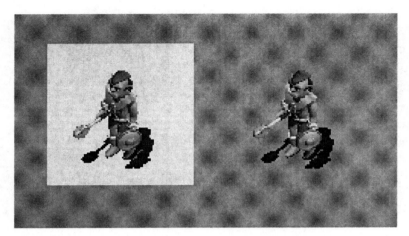

Figure 6.2
The sprite on the right is drawn without the transparent pixels.

transparency. Fifty-percent translucency means that half of the light rays are blocked and you can only see about half of the image. Zero-percent translucency is called *opaque*, which is completely solid. The opposite is 100-percent translucency, or fully transparent, which lets *all* light pass through. Figure 6.2 illustrates the difference between an opaque and transparent sprite background.

When an image needs to be drawn with transparency, we call the transparent color a *color key*, and the process of alpha blending causes that particular pixel color to be completely blended with the background. At the same time, no other pixels in the texture are affected by alpha blending, and the result is a transparent sprite. Color key transparency is not often used today.

Color key transparency is a pain. A better way to handle transparency is with an alpha channel and a file format that supports it (such as tga or png). (Note: bmp files do not support an alpha channel).

How Basic Handles Pathnames

A path is a complete description of a directory location. Consider a file with an absolute path, as in the following example:

C:\Program Files\Microsoft Visual Studio 8\Common7\IDE\devenv.exe

The filename is located at the end, "devenv.exe," while the path to this filename is everything else in front of the filename. The complete "path" to a file can be described in this absolute format.

The problem is, Visual Basic compiles programs into a subdirectory under your project directory called *bin*. Inside bin, depending on whether you're building the Debug or Release version of your program, there will be a folder called bin\Debug or bin\Release. You need to put all of your game's asset files (bitmaps, waves, etc.) inside this folder in order for it to run. You would not want to store your game's files inside the main folder of the project because when it runs (inside bin\Debug, for instance) it will not know where the files are located, and the program will crash.

You can hard-code the path into your game (like C:\Game), but this is a bad idea because then anyone who tries to play your game will have to create the exact same directory that you did when you created the game. Instead, put your artwork and other game resources inside bin\Debug while working on your game. When your game is finished and ready for release, then copy all of the files together into a new folder with the executable.

ANIMATING A SPRITE

After you have written a few games, you most likely find that many of the sprites in your games have similar behaviors, to the point of predictability. For instance, if you have sprites that just move around within the boundaries of the screen and wrap from one edge to the other, you can create a subroutine to produce this sprite behavior on call. Simply use that subroutine when you update the sprite's position. If you find that a lot of your sprites are doing other predictable movements, it is really helpful to create many different behavioral subroutines to control their actions.

This is just one simple example of a very primitive behavior (staying within the boundary of the screen), but you can create very complex behaviors by writing subroutines that cause sprites to react to other sprites or to the player, for instance, in different ways. You might have some behavior subroutines that cause a sprite to chase the player, or run away from the player, or attack the player. The possibilities are truly limited only by your imagination, and, generally, the most enjoyable games use movement patterns that the player can learn while playing. The Sprite Drawing Demo program in this chapter demonstrates sprite movement as well as animation, so you may refer to that program for an example of how the sprite movement code is used.

Sprite Animation Theory

Sprite animation goes back about three decades, when the first video game systems were being built for arcades. The earliest arcade games include classics such as *Asteroids* that used vector-based graphics rather than bitmap-based graphics. A *vector-based* graphics system uses lines connecting two points as the basis for all of the graphics on the screen. Although a rotating vector-based spaceship might not be considered a sprite by today's standards, it is basically the same thing. Any game object on the screen that uses more than one small image to represent itself might be considered a *sprite*. However, to be an *animated sprite*, the image must simulate a sequence of images that are cycled while the sprite is being displayed.

Animation is a fascinating subject because it brings life to a game and makes objects seem more realistic. An important concept to grasp at this point is that *every* frame of an animation sequence must be treated as a distinct image that is stored in a bitmap file; as an alternative, some animation might be created on the fly if a technique such as rotation or alpha cycling is used. (For instance, causing a sprite to fade in and out could be done at runtime.) In the past, professional game developers did not often use rotation of a sprite at runtime due to quality concerns, but we can do that today with pretty good results.

Animation is done with the use of a *sprite sheet*. A sprite sheet is a bitmap containing columns and rows of tiles, with each tile containing one frame of animation. It is not uncommon for a sprite with eight directions of movement to have 64 or more frames of animation just for one activity (such as walking, attacking, or dying).

Figure 6.3 shows a dragon sprite with 64 frames of animation. The dragon can move in any of eight directions of travel, and each direction has eight frames of animation. We'll learn to load this sprite sheet and then draw it transparently on the screen with animation later in this chapter. The source artwork (from Reiner Prokein) comes in individual bitmap files—so that 64-frame dragon sprite started out with 64 individual bitmap files.

Tip

This dragon sprite was provided courtesy of Reiner "Tiles" Prokein at www.reinerstileset.de. Most of the other sprite artwork in this book is also from Reiner's sprite collection, all of which includes a royalty-free license for personal or commercial use.

The trick to animating a sprite is keeping track of the current frame of animation along with the total animation frames in the animation sequence.

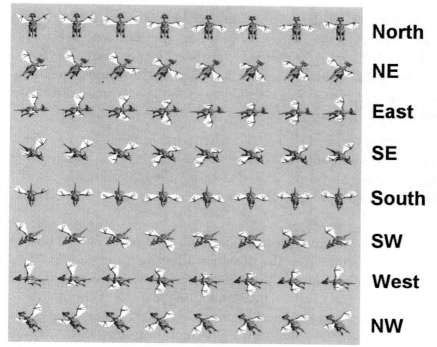

North

NE

East

SE

South

SW

West

NW

Figure 6.3
A dragon sprite sheet with an 8 × 8 layout of animation frames, courtesy of www.reinerstileset.de.

This dragon sprite is stored in a single, large bitmap image and was actually stored in 64 individual bitmaps before I converted it to a single bitmap using Pro Motion.

Trick

Cosmigo's Pro Motion is an excellent sprite animation editor available for download at www.cosmigo.com/promotion. All of the sprite sheets featured in this book were created using this tool.

After you have exported an animation sequence as a sprite sheet image, the trick is to get a handle on animating the sprite in source code. Storing all the frames of animation inside a single bitmap file makes it easier to use the animation in your program. However, it doesn't necessarily make it easier to set up; you have to deal with the animation looping around at a specific point, rather than looping through all 64 frames. Now we'll start to see where all of those odd properties and subroutines in the `Sprite` class will be used. I have animated the dragon sprite by passing a range to the `Animate` function that represents one of the four directions (up, down, left, right), which is determined by the user's keyboard input. Although the sprite sheet has frames for all eight directions, including diagonals, the example program in this chapter sticks to the four main directions to keep the code simpler.

To get the current frame, we need to find out where that frame is located inside the sprite sheet in the least amount of code possible. To get the Y position of a frame, you take the current frame and divide by the columns to get the appropriate row (and then multiply that by the frame height, or height of each tile).

To get the X position of the frame, perform that same division as before, but get the remainder (modulus result) from the division rather than the quotient, and then multiply by the sprite's width. At this point, the rest of the rectangle is set up using the sprite's width and height. The destination rectangle is configured to the sprite's current position, and then a call to the existing `Draw` subroutine takes care of business. Figure 6.4 shows the numbered columns and rows of a sprite sheet. Note that the numbering starts at 0 instead of 1. That is a little harder to follow when reading the code, but using a base of 0 makes the calculations *much* simpler. See if you can choose a frame number and calculate where it is located on the sprite sheet on your own!

Creating a Sprite Class

We could get by with a couple of reusable functions and a `Bitmap`. But, that would involve a lot of duplicated code that could very easily be put into a class. So, that is what we will do. There aren't very many classes in this book, in the interest of making source code easier to understand, but in some cases it's more difficult to *not* use a class—as is the case with sprite programming. I have some goals for our new `Sprite` class. First, it will be self contained, with the exception that it needs the rendering device in our `Game` class (`Game.Device`) for drawing. We can pass a reference to the game object to a sprite's constructor at runtime and that should take care of it. Second, the class should handle both drawing *and* animation with enough variation to support any needs we'll have in Celtic Crusader, with numerous properties to keep the code clean and tidy. This is a pretty good start, but we will make small

COLUMNS

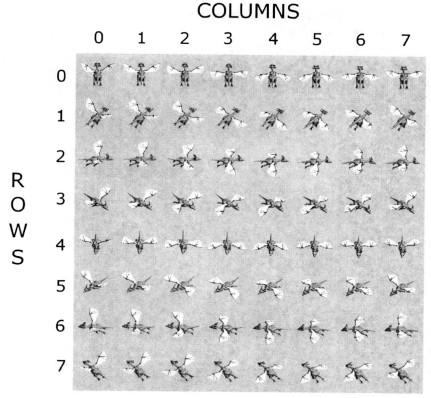

Figure 6.4
The numbered columns and rows of the dragon sprite sheet.

changes to Sprite over time to meet any new needs as the game begins to take shape.

```
Public Class Sprite
    Public Enum AnimateDir
        NONE = 0
        FORWARD = 1
        BACKWARD = -1
    End Enum
    Public Enum AnimateWrap
        WRAP = 0
        BOUNCE = 1
    End Enum
    Private p_game As Game
```

```
Private p_position As System.Drawing.PointF
Private p_size As System.Drawing.Size
Private p_bitmap As System.Drawing.Bitmap
Private p_alive As Boolean
Private p_columns As Integer
Private p_totalFrames As Integer
Private p_currentFrame As Integer
Private p_animationDir As AnimateDir
Private p_animationWrap As AnimateWrap
Private p_lastTime As Integer
Private p_animationRate As Integer
```

The constructor and destructor functions are next. The variables and references are initialized at this point. Although Basic does automatically initialize most variables to the most obvious value (Nothing or 0), it's good programming practice to set the initial values on our own.

```
Public Sub New(ByRef game As Game)
    REM keep reference to Game object
    p_game = game

    REM set core properties
    p_position = New PointF(0.0, 0.0)
    p_size = New Size(0, 0)
    p_bitmap = Nothing
    p_alive = True

    REM set animation to 1 frame by default
    p_columns = 1
    p_totalFrames = 1
    p_currentFrame = 0
    p_animationDir = AnimateDir.FORWARD
    p_animationWrap = AnimateWrap.WRAP
    p_lastTime = 0
    p_animationRate = 30
End Sub

Protected Overrides Sub Finalize()
    MyBase.Finalize()
End Sub
```

The Sprite class includes numerous properties to give access to its private variables. In most cases this is a direct Get/Set association with no real benefit to hiding the variables internally, but in some cases (such as AnimationRate) the values are manipulated.

```
Public Property Alive() As Boolean
    Get
        Return p_alive
    End Get
    Set(ByVal value As Boolean)
        p_alive = value
    End Set
End Property

Public Property Image() As System.Drawing.Bitmap
    Get
        Return p_bitmap
    End Get
    Set(ByVal value As Bitmap)
        p_bitmap = value
    End Set
End Property

Public Property Position() As System.Drawing.PointF
    Get
        Return p_position
    End Get
    Set(ByVal value As PointF)
        p_position = value
    End Set
End Property

REM optional way to change X position
Public Property X() As Single
    Get
        Return p_position.X
    End Get
    Set(ByVal value As Single)
        p_position.X = value
    End Set
End Property
```

```
REM optional way to change Y position
Public Property Y() As Single
    Get
        Return p_position.Y
    End Get
    Set(ByVal value As Single)
        p_position.Y = value
    End Set
End Property

Public Property Size() As System.Drawing.Size
    Get
        Return p_size
    End Get
    Set(ByVal value As System.Drawing.Size)
        p_size = value
    End Set
End Property

REM optional way to change size
Public Property Width() As Integer
    Get
        Return p_size.Width
    End Get
    Set(ByVal value As Integer)
        p_size.Width = value
    End Set
End Property

REM optional way to change size
Public Property Height() As Integer
    Get
        Return p_size.Height
    End Get
    Set(ByVal value As Integer)
        p_size.Height = value
    End Set
End Property
```

```
Public Property Columns() As Integer
    Get
        Return p_columns
    End Get
    Set(ByVal value As Integer)
        p_columns = value
    End Set
End Property

Public Property TotalFrames() As Integer
    Get
        Return p_totalFrames
    End Get
    Set(ByVal value As Integer)
        p_totalFrames = value
    End Set
End Property

Public Property AnimateDirection() As AnimateDir
    Get
        Return p_animationDir
    End Get
    Set(ByVal value As AnimateDir)
        p_animationDir = value
    End Set
End Property

Public Property AnimateWrapMode() As AnimateWrap
    Get
        Return p_animationWrap
    End Get
    Set(ByVal value As AnimateWrap)
        p_animationWrap = value
    End Set
End Property

Public Property AnimationRate() As Integer
    Get
        Return 1000 / p_animationRate
    End Get
```

```
        Set(ByVal value As Integer)
            If value = 0 Then value = 1
            p_animationRate = 1000 / value
        End Set
    End Property
```

Sprite animation is handled by the single `Animate()` function, which should be called from the gameplay functions `Game_Update()` or `Game_Draw()`. Animation timing is handled automatically in this function using a millisecond timer, so it can be called from the extremely fast-running `Game_Update()` without concern for animation speed being in sync with the drawing of the sprite. Without this built-in timing, the `Animate()` function would have to be called from `Game_Draw()`, which is timed at 60 Hz (or frames per second). Code such as this `Animate()` function really should be run from the fastest part of the game loop whenever possible, and only real drawing should take place in `Game_Draw()` due to timing considerations. If you were to put all of the gameplay code in `Game_Draw()` and hardly anything in `Game_Update()`, which is the fast running function, then the game would slow down quite a bit. We will also need the default `Animate()` function which defaults to animating the *whole* range of animation automatically.

```
    Public Sub Animate()
        Animate(0, p_totalFrames - 1)
    End Sub

    REM cycle the sprite's animation frame
    Public Sub Animate(ByVal startFrame As Integer, _
                    ByVal endFrame As Integer)
        REM do we even need to animate?
        If p_totalFrames > 0 Then

            REM check animation timing
            Dim time As Integer = My.Computer.Clock.TickCount()
            If time > p_lastTime + p_animationRate Then
                p_lastTime = time

                REM go to next frame
                p_currentFrame += p_animationDir

                If p_animationWrap = AnimateWrap.WRAP Then
                    REM need to wrap animation?
```

```
                    If p_currentFrame < startFrame Then
                        p_currentFrame = endFrame
                    ElseIf p_currentFrame > endFrame Then
                        p_currentFrame = startFrame
                    End If

                ElseIf p_animationWrap = AnimateWrap.BOUNCE Then
                    REM need to bounce animation?
                    If p_currentFrame < startFrame Then
                        p_currentFrame = startFrame
                        REM reverse direction
                        p_animationDir *= -1
                    ElseIf p_currentFrame > endFrame Then
                        p_currentFrame = endFrame
                        REM reverse direction
                        p_animationDir *= -1
                    End If
                End If
            End If
        End If
    End Sub
```

This single `Draw()` function can handle all of our sprite drawing needs, including animation! However, there is an optimization that can be made for sprites that do not animate (i.e., "props"): the modulus and division calculations being done in this function make sprite sheet animation possible, but this code can slow down a game if quite a few sprites are being drawn without any animation. The `Game.DrawBitmap()` function can be used in those cases, because it does not take up any processor cycles to calculate animation frames.

```
Public Sub Draw()
    Dim frame As New Rectangle
    frame.X = (p_currentFrame Mod p_columns) * p_size.Width
    frame.Y = (p_currentFrame \ p_columns) * p_size.Height
    frame.Width = p_size.Width
    frame.Height = p_size.Height
    p_game.Device.DrawImage(p_bitmap, Bounds(), frame, GraphicsUnit.Pixel)
End Sub
```

Oddly enough, even though we have not discussed the subject yet, this class already has collision detection included. We have a chapter dedicated to the subject: the very next chapter. So, let's just briefly take a look at this as-yet-unused code with plans to dig into it soon. There is one very useful function here called `Bounds()`, which returns a `Rectangle` representing the bounding box of the sprite at its current position on the screen. This is used both for drawing *and* collision testing. When drawing in the `Draw()` function, `Bounds()` is used to return the destination rectangle, which defines where the sprite is supposed to be drawn on the screen, and it can also specify scaling of the target image. The `IsColliding()` function below *also* uses `Bounds()`. One very handy function in the `Rectangle` class is `IntersectsWith()`. This function will return true if a passed rectangle is intersecting with it. In other words, if two sprites are touching, then we will know by using this function that is built in to the `Rectangle` class. We don't have to even write our own collision code! Nevertheless, we'll explore advanced collision techniques in the next chapter.

```
REM returns bounding rectangle around sprite
Public ReadOnly Property Bounds() As Rectangle
    Get
        Dim rect As Rectangle
        rect = New Rectangle(p_position.X, p_position.Y, _
                          p_size.Width, p_size.Height)
        Return rect
    End Get
End Property

Public Function IsColliding(ByRef other As Sprite) As Boolean
    REM test for bounding rectangle collision
    Dim collision As Boolean
    collision = Me.Bounds.IntersectsWith(other.Bounds)
    Return collision
End Function
End Class
```

SPRITE DRAWING DEMO

The Sprite Drawing Demo program shows how to use the new `Sprite` class, the improved `Game` class, and the new `Form`/`Module` code presented in this chapter to draw an animated sprite. The result is shown in Figure 6.5. The dragon sprite is actually comprised of animation frames that are each just 128×128 pixels in size, but I have enlarged the sprite sheet so the dragon is twice as large as

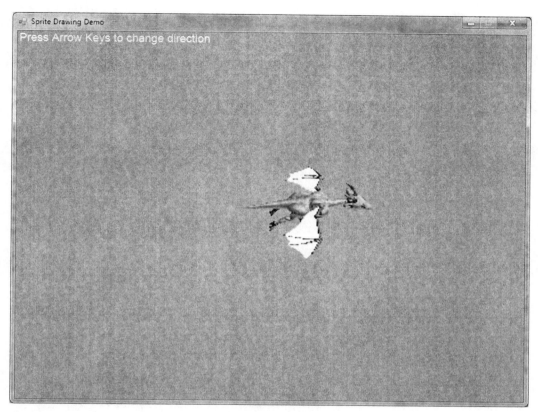

Figure 6.5
The user controls an animated dragon sprite in the Sprite Drawing Demo program.

normal. This isn't a great idea for a game, because we can resize the sprite at runtime (with the `Bitmap.DrawBitmap()` function), but it was a simple solution to make it appear bigger for the sake of illustration.

Improving the Game Class

It is completely possible to make a game within the source code file of the `Form`, without any support or helper code or external libraries. But, there will come a point where the complexity of the source code (in a single file) will exceed our ability to manage it effectively, and progress on the game will grind to a halt with new and frustrating bugs cropping up every time one is apparently fixed. Celtic Crusader is one such game. In previous editions of this book, there have been about a dozen Basic classes created for the game, such as `CSprite`, `CBitmapFont`,

CDirect3D, CKeyboard, and others. This worked at the time, but in trying to make the game's source code easier to use, these classes themselves added new complexity to what should have been an engaging exercise in gameplay programming. So, we're taking more of a structured programming approach this time, centralizing much of the code with most of it right inside the Form and only a few outside helper modules and classes.

We have already seen the early stages of a Game class, and have now added a new Sprite class to our game programming toolbox. In the next section we will build a real-time game loop with new gameplay function calls that will enable us to write code that runs extremely fast, and that is detached from Basic's event-driven Windows Forms architecture. The new and improved Game class still has the primary responsibility of creating the rendering device (i.e., our PictureBox/ Graphics/Bitmap concoction), but added to that is support for printing text in various fonts and loading and drawing bitmaps. At one point I had considered putting the game loop in the Game class, but it proved to be too complex and we're going for simple, fast, and practical instead of fancy—a Ford versus a Mercedes, if you will. Like Sprite, we may need to make changes to Game in the future. Don't think of any class as 100 percent complete right away! This is my best guess at this early stage, and I'm sure changes will be made later.

```
Public Class Game
    Private p_device As Graphics
    Private p_surface As Bitmap
    Private p_pb As PictureBox
    Private p_frm As Form
    Private p_font As Font
    Private p_gameOver As Boolean

    Protected Overrides Sub Finalize()
        p_device.Dispose()
        p_surface.Dispose()
        p_pb.Dispose()
        p_font.Dispose()
    End Sub

    Public Sub New(ByRef form As Form, ByVal width As Integer, _
            ByVal height As Integer)
        p_device = Nothing
```

```
        p_surface = Nothing
        p_pb = Nothing
        p_frm = Nothing
        p_font = Nothing
        p_gameOver = False

        REM set form properties
        p_frm = form
        p_frm.FormBorderStyle = Windows.Forms.FormBorderStyle.FixedSingle
        p_frm.MaximizeBox = False
        REM adjust size for window border
        p_frm.Size = New Point(width + 6, height + 28)

        REM create a picturebox
        p_pb = New PictureBox()
        p_pb.Parent = p_frm
        'p_pb.Dock = DockStyle.Fill
        p_pb.Location = New Point(0, 0)
        p_pb.Size = New Size(width, height)
        p_pb.BackColor = Color.Black

        REM create graphics device
        p_surface = New Bitmap(p_frm.Size.Width, p_frm.Size.Height)
        p_pb.Image = p_surface
        p_device = Graphics.FromImage(p_surface)

        REM set the default font
        SetFont("Arial", 18, FontStyle.Regular)
End Sub

Public ReadOnly Property Device() As Graphics
    Get
        Return p_device
    End Get
End Property

Public Sub Update()
    REM refresh the drawing surface
    p_pb.Image = p_surface
End Sub
```

We studied rudimentary text printing back in Chapter 4, "Drawing with GDI+," where we learned how to use the Font class to print text with any TrueType font, size, and color. Now, it's possible to use just the Font class and Graphics. DrawString() function for our text output needs, but I propose a simpler, more convenient approach. Instead of re-creating the font object in each game, let's add some text printing code to the Game class. This will handle *most* text output needs, while giving us the freedom to still create a custom font in the game if we want. Below is the new printing support in the Game class. You can now change the font using the SetFont() function and then use Print() to print text anywhere on the screen. A word of warning, though: changing the font several times per frame will slow down a game, so if you need more than one font, I recommend creating another one in your gameplay code and leave the built-in one at a fixed type and size.

```
REM ************************************************
REM font support with several Print variations
REM ************************************************
Public Sub SetFont(ByVal name As String, ByVal size As Integer, _
        ByVal style As FontStyle)
    p_font = New Font(name, size, style, GraphicsUnit.Pixel)
End Sub

Public Sub Print(ByVal x As Integer, ByVal y As Integer, _
        ByVal text As String, ByVal color As Brush)
    p_device.DrawString(text, p_font, color, x, y)
End Sub

Public Sub Print(ByVal x As Integer, ByVal y As Integer, _
        ByVal text As String)
    Print(x, y, text, Brushes.White)
End Sub

Public Sub Print(ByVal pos As Point, ByVal text As String, _
        ByVal color As Brush)
    Print(pos.X, pos.Y, text, color)
End Sub

Public Sub Print(ByVal pos As Point, ByVal text As String)
    Print(pos.X, pos.Y, text)
End Sub
```

Here is the new Bitmap support code with the old LoadBitmap() function and several versions of the DrawBitmap() function. When a function name is repeated, but has different parameters, we call that an *overloaded* function. Note: we are still inside the source code for the Game.vb file.

```
REM ************************************************
REM Bitmap support functions
REM ************************************************
Public Function LoadBitmap(ByVal filename As String)
    Dim bmp As Bitmap
    Try
        bmp = New Bitmap(filename)
    Catch ex As Exception
        bmp = Nothing
    End Try
    Return bmp
End Function


Public Sub DrawBitmap(ByRef bmp As Bitmap, ByVal x As Single, _
        ByVal y As Single)
    p_device.DrawImageUnscaled(bmp, x, y)
End Sub


Public Sub DrawBitmap(ByRef bmp As Bitmap, _
        ByVal x As Single, ByVal y As Single, _
        ByVal width As Integer, ByVal height As Integer)
    p_device.DrawImageUnscaled(bmp, x, y, width, height)
End Sub


Public Sub DrawBitmap(ByRef bmp As Bitmap, ByVal pos As Point)
    p_device.DrawImageUnscaled(bmp, pos)
End Sub


Public Sub DrawBitmap(ByRef bmp As Bitmap, ByVal pos As Point, _
        ByVal size As Size)
    p_device.DrawImageUnscaled(bmp, pos.X, pos.Y, size.Width, size.Height)
End Sub
End Class
```

Separating Form and Module Code

In order to make the architecture for this game framework work effectively, the different parts need to be able to talk to each other. One way is to pass references to the Form and Game object around to every function used in a game, but that becomes tedious very quickly. A much more elegant way is to use a module within the Form's source code file. A module is a programming construct, similar to a namespace, that allows for grouping of variables, classes, and structures together under one common, shared name. Think of a module like this: everything inside the module is treated as if it's found inside one long source code file.

Are you getting tired of all this talk about architectures, frameworks, and classes? I know how you feel, if that is the case. But, we have to set a solid framework for Celtic Crusader now or otherwise we'll have to make all kinds of changes later and that will slow down progress on the game. Our new Form source code will be quite short, because its job is now only to pass control to the Game class and to the main module. This code is found in the Form1.vb file in the project. Note that each of the events call only one function, and we haven't seen them before.

```
Public Class Form1
    Private Sub Form1_KeyDown(ByVal sender As Object, _
            ByVal e As System.Windows.Forms.KeyEventArgs) _
            Handles Me.KeyDown
        Game_KeyPressed(e.KeyCode)
    End Sub

    Private Sub Form1_Load(ByVal sender As System.Object, _
            ByVal e As System.EventArgs) Handles MyBase.Load
        Main()
    End Sub

    Private Sub Form1_FormClosed(ByVal sender As Object, _
            ByVal e As System.Windows.Forms.FormClosedEventArgs) _
            Handles Me.FormClosed
        Shutdown()
    End Sub
End Class
```

There is now a `Module` section of code in the `Form1.vb` source code file (right below the `Form1` class). Yes, it's okay to combine different modules and classes inside a single source code file! Although you can separate them, it's often easier to keep them together in cases like this. This is just an experiment to show you one way to go about creating a game loop. We could also just use a loop inside `Form1_Load` in the form's source code. Take your pick!

```
Public Module Module1
    Private p_gameOver As Boolean = False
    Private p_startTime As Integer = 0
    Private p_currentTime As Integer = 0

    Public game As Game
    Public dragonImage As Bitmap
    Public dragonSprite As Sprite
    Public grass As Bitmap

    Public frameCount As Integer = 0
    Public frameTimer As Integer = 0
    Public frameRate As Single = 0
    Public direction As Integer = 2
    Public velocity As PointF
```

Adding a Real-Time Game Loop

As you'll recall, in past chapters we used a `Timer` control to make things happen. In those cases, the `Timer` was sort of the *engine* for the program, causing something to happen automatically. Otherwise, the only thing we can do in our code is respond to events from the controls on a `Form`. The `Timer` control works pretty well for this, but we need to dig a bit deeper to get more performance out of our Basic code, and to do that we have to use our own timed loop. The function below is called `Main()`, which makes it somewhat resemble the `main()` function of a C++ program, or the `WinMain()` function of a Windows program. Before the `While` loop gets started, we create the game object and call `Game_Init()`, which is sort of the gameplay loading function where you can load game assets before the timed loop begins. After the loop exits, then the gameplay function `Game_End()` is called, followed by `End`.

```
    REM *******************************************
    REM real time game loop
```

```
REM ********************************************
Public Sub Main()
    game = New Game(Form1, 800, 600)
    REM load and initialize game assets
    Game_Init()
    While Not p_gameOver
        REM update timer
        p_currentTime = My.Computer.Clock.TickCount()

        REM let gameplay code update
        Game_Update(p_currentTime - p_startTime)

        REM refresh at 60 FPS
        If p_currentTime > p_startTime + 16 Then
            REM update timing
            p_startTime = p_currentTime
            REM let gameplay code draw
            Game_Draw()
            REM give the form some cycles
            Application.DoEvents()
            REM let the game object update
            game.Update()
        End If

        frameCount += 1
        If p_currentTime > frameTimer + 1000 Then
            frameTimer = p_currentTime
            frameRate = frameCount
            frameCount = 0
        End If
    End While
    REM free memory and shut down
    Game_End()
    End
End Sub
```

Calling the Shutdown() function from anywhere in the program causes it to end. No other code is needed besides setting p_gameOver to True, because that variable controls the real-time game loop, and when that ends, then two things will happen: 1) Game_End() is called, allowing the gameplay code to clean up; 2) End is called, which closes the program.

```
Public Sub Shutdown()
    p_gameOver = True
End Sub
```

Gameplay Functions

We're still in the source code module called `Module1` in the `Form1.vb` file at this point, continuing on into the gameplay functions. I call them by that name because the `Main()` function and everything else might be thought of as the game *engine* code, and now we're dealing with just gameplay. While the engine code seldom changes, the gameplay code changes frequently and certainly will be different from one game to the next. There is no rule that we must use these particular function names. XNA Game Studio gameplay functions are called `LoadContent()`, `Update()`, and `Draw()`. You are welcome to change them if you wish.

1. The first function called is `Game_Init()`, and this is where you can load game assets.

2. The `Game_Update()` function is called repeatedly in the untimed portion of the game loop, so it will be running code as fast as the processor can handle it.

3. The `Game_Draw()` function is called from the *timed* portion of the game loop, running at 60 FPS.

4. The `Game_End()` function is called after the game loop exits, allowing for cleanup code such as removing gameplay assets from memory.

5. The `Game_KeyPressed()` function is called from `Form1_KeyDown()`, and receives the code of any key being pressed. This is a bit of a workaround, when we could have just responded to the key press directly in `Form1_KeyDown()`, but we want the gameplay code to be kept together in one module. Eventually we'll have mouse input as well.

```
Public Sub Game_End()
    dragonImage = Nothing
    dragonSprite = Nothing
    grass = Nothing
End Sub
```

```
Public Function Game_Init() As Boolean
    Form1.Text = "Sprite Drawing Demo"
    grass = game.LoadBitmap("grass.bmp")
    dragonImage = game.LoadBitmap("dragon.png")
    dragonSprite = New Sprite(game)
    dragonSprite.Image = dragonImage
    dragonSprite.Width = 256
    dragonSprite.Height = 256
    dragonSprite.Columns = 8
    dragonSprite.TotalFrames = 64
    dragonSprite.AnimationRate = 20
    dragonSprite.X = 250
    dragonSprite.Y = 150
    Return True
End Function

REM not currently used
Public Sub Game_Update(ByVal time As Integer)
End Sub

Public Sub Game_Draw()
    REM draw background
    game.DrawBitmap(grass, 0, 0, 800, 600)

    REM move the dragon sprite
    Select Case direction
        Case 0 : velocity = New Point(0, -1)
        Case 2 : velocity = New Point(1, 0)
        Case 4 : velocity = New Point(0, 1)
        Case 6 : velocity = New Point(-1, 0)
    End Select
    dragonSprite.X += velocity.X
    dragonSprite.Y += velocity.Y

    REM animate and draw dragon sprite
    dragonSprite.Animate(direction * 8 + 1, direction * 8 + 7)
    dragonSprite.Draw()

    game.Print(0, 0, "Press Arrow Keys to change direction")
End Sub
```

```
Public Sub Game_KeyPressed(ByVal key As System.Windows.Forms.Keys)
    Select Case key
        Case Keys.Escape : Shutdown()
        Case Keys.Up : direction = 0
        Case Keys.Right : direction = 2
        Case Keys.Down : direction = 4
        Case Keys.Left : direction = 6
    End Select
End Sub
End Module
```

LEVEL UP!

The most remarkable accomplishment in this chapter is the creation of a robust `Sprite` class. Any time we need to give our sprites some new feature or behavior, it will be possible with this class. But no less significant is the start of a reusable game engine in Basic! From the new real-time game loop to the new sprite animation code to the new gameplay functions, it's been quite a romp in just a few pages! But we've set a foundation now for a truly robust engine for Celtic Crusader, and in a very short time we will begin discussing the design of the game and begin working on the editors.

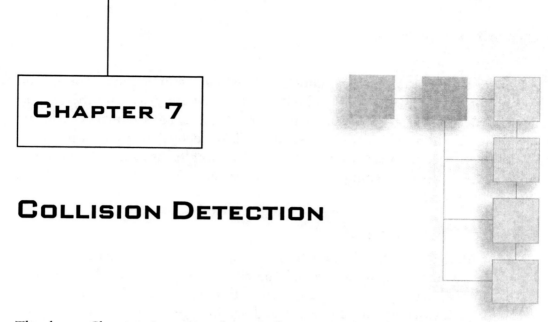

CHAPTER 7

COLLISION DETECTION

Thanks to Chapter 6, we can draw and animate sprites on the screen. In this chapter, we will make them more lifelike by giving them the ability to bump into each other. This is done using a technique called *collision detection*. A collision occurs when two sprites touch or overlap each other. To demonstrate this new concept, we will create a simple ball-and-paddle game like the old Atari game, *Breakout*. This is a higher-level technique than previous topics you have learned so far, which have focused more on just getting something up on the screen. This is a very direct way to test for collisions. Another technique, which is ultimately used in Celtic Crusader, is to calculate the distance between two sprites. Let's start with the simpler of the two in this chapter, and the distance approach down the road in the gameplay chapters.

Here's what we'll cover in this chapter:

- Reacting to solid objects
- Rectangle intersection
- Collision Demo program

REACTING TO SOLID OBJECTS

Collision detection is an important technique that you should learn. It is a requirement for every game ever made. I can't think of any game that does not need collision detection, because it is such an essential aspect of gameplay.

Without collisions, there is no action, goal, or purpose in a game. There is no way to interact with the game without collisions taking place. In other words, collision detection makes the sprites in a game come to life and makes the game believable. Not every situation in which collision detection occurs necessarily means that something is hit or destroyed. We can also use collision testing to prevent the player from going into certain areas (such as a lake or mountain area that is impassible).

Rectangle Intersection

Collision detection is pretty easy to do using the System.Drawing.Rectangle class. First, you will create a rectangle based on the position and size of one object, such as a sprite. Then you will need to create a similar rectangle for a second object. Once you have two rectangles, which represent the position and size of two objects, then you can test to see whether the rectangles are intersecting. We can do this with a function in the Rectangle class called IntersectsWith(). Figure 7.1 is an illustration showing the bounding rectangles of two sprites from the example program. In most cases, the image itself is used as the bounding rectangle, which includes the transparent pixels that usually surround an image.

In Chapter 6, when we first learned about sprite programming, and when we created the Sprite class, we added a function called IsColliding—but didn't use

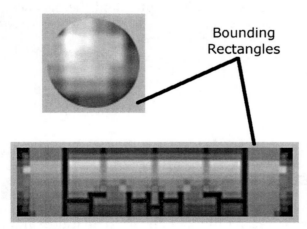

Figure 7.1
The dimensions of a sprite define its bounding rectangle.

it right away, as it was created in advance for our needs in *this* chapter! Here is the IsColliding() function:

```
Public Function IsColliding(ByRef other As Sprite) As Boolean
    REM test for bounding rectangle collision
    Dim collision As Boolean
    collision = Me.Bounds.IntersectsWith(other.Bounds)
    Return collision
End Function
```

Hint

You will get better results in your game if you make sure there is very little empty space around the edges of your sprite images, since the image is used as the bounding rectangle!

Let's dissect this function to determine what it does. First, notice that Collided-With returns a Boolean value (true or false). Notice also that there's only one Sprite passed by reference (ByRef). Thus, the entire sprite object in memory (with all of its properties and functions) is not copied to the function, only a reference to the sprite's location in memory (like a pointer). This function is small thanks in part to the Sprite.Bounds property, which returns a Rectangle representing a sprite's position and size as it appears on the screen. Thus, two rectangles are essentially created based on the position and size of each sprite, and then IntersectsWith() is used to see whether they are overlapping each other. Figure 7.2 shows an illustration of a collision taking place between two sprites.

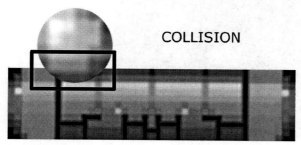

Figure 7.2
The two bounding rectangles have intersected.

Definition

"Collision" is a misnomer since nothing actually collides in a game unless we write code to make it happen. Sprites do not automatically bump into each other. That's yet another thing we have to deal with as game programmers!

COLLISION DEMO PROGRAM

To demonstrate sprite collision testing with our new function, I've put together a quick demo based on the old Atari game *Breakout*, and it's shown in Figure 7.3. Let me show you how to create this project. We'll reuse classes written previously to simplify the game and cut down on the amount of code that would otherwise be required. This game is *dramatically* different from the Blocks game back in Chapter 3, which was created using form controls to demonstrate how to work with a `PictureBox`! This new game is done entirely in graphics mode with real collision detection.

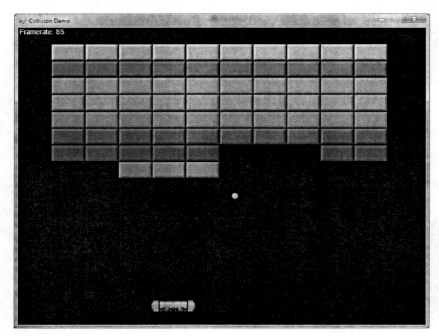

Figure 7.3
The Collision Demo program demonstrates bounding rectangle collision testing.

Sprite Class

Copy the `Sprite.vb` file from the Sprite Drawing Demo project in the previous chapter over to the new one so we don't have to re-list the source code over again in this chapter! Once copied, open up `Sprite.vb` to make some changes to it. It's almost impossible to foresee every property and function you'll need for a class ahead of time. Instead, these things tend to grow over time, accumulating new features as needed. Such is the case with our brand new `Sprite` class, christened just in the previous chapter. But, as is often the case, we already need to make some changes to it! We need to add properties to expose `Velocity` and `CurrentFrame`, and we need to add another function called `KeepInBounds()`! Our new project this chapter is called Collision Demo.

First, we will add a velocity value to the `Sprite` class. This will make it possible to set the speed for a sprite and then move it based on that speed.

```
Private p_velocity As System.Drawing.PointF
Public Property Velocity() As PointF
    Get
        Return p_velocity
    End Get
    Set(ByVal value As PointF)
        p_velocity = value
    End Set
End Property
```

Next up is the `CurrentFrame` property. We already have the `Sprite.p_current Frame` variable in the class, but need a way to access it so this property will fill that important need that was glossed over.

```
Public Property CurrentFrame() As Integer
    Get
        Return p_currentFrame
    End Get
    Set(ByVal value As Integer)
        p_currentFrame = value
    End Set
End Property
```

A new function will be added to the `Sprite` class: `KeepInBounds()`. This could easily be added to the program source rather than to the class, but it will be a helpful function in the long term and we need it for the example program.

```
Public Sub KeepInBounds(ByVal boundary As Rectangle)
    If p_position.X < boundary.Left Then
        p_velocity.X *= -1
        p_position.X = boundary.Left
    End If
    If p_position.X > boundary.Right Then
        p_velocity.X *= -1
        p_position.X = boundary.Right
    End If
    If p_position.Y < boundary.Top Then
        p_velocity.Y *= -1
        p_position.Y = boundary.Top
    End If
    If p_position.Y > boundary.Bottom Then
        p_velocity.Y *= -1
        p_position.Y = boundary.Bottom
    End If
End Sub
```

Game Class

I don't want to list the source code for Game.vb here again because it hasn't changed since Chapter 6, so just copy the file from your last project into the new one for this chapter. Here is just a sample of the class for reference.

```
Public Class Game
    Private p_device As Graphics
    Public p_surface As Bitmap
    Private p_pb As PictureBox
    ...
End Class
```

Form1 Class

Both the game loop and gameplay code are found in the Form source code file Form1.vb. When you create the new project, Form1 will be added automatically, so you can open the source code for it and enter this code. Add Game.vb and Sprite.vb to the project, grab the bitmap files, and watch it run.

```
Public Class Form1
    Private Sub Form1_Load(ByVal sender As System.Object, _
            ByVal e As System.EventArgs) Handles MyBase.Load
```

```
            Main()
        End Sub
        Private Sub Form1_FormClosed(ByVal sender As Object, _
                ByVal e As System.Windows.Forms.FormClosedEventArgs) _
                Handles Me.FormClosed
            Shutdown()
        End Sub
        Private Sub Form1_KeyDown(ByVal sender As Object, _
                ByVal e As System.Windows.Forms.KeyEventArgs) _
                Handles Me.KeyDown
            Game_KeyPressed(e.KeyCode)
        End Sub
        Private Sub Form1_KeyUp(ByVal sender As Object, _
                ByVal e As System.Windows.Forms.KeyEventArgs) _
                Handles Me.KeyUp
            Game_KeyReleased(e.KeyCode)
        End Sub
    End Class

Public Module Module1
    Public game As Game
    Public gameOver As Boolean = False
    Public startTime As Integer = 0
    REM framerate variables
    Public frameCount As Integer = 0
    Public frameTimer As Integer = 0
    Public frameRate As Integer = 0
    Public ballImage As Bitmap
    Public ball As Sprite
    Public Const PADDLE_SPEED As Integer = 6
    Public paddleImage As Bitmap
    Public paddle As Sprite
    Public blockImage As Bitmap
    Public blocks(10, 8) As Sprite
    Public score As Integer = 0

    Public Sub Main()
        game = New Game(Form1, 800, 600)
        Game_Init()
        While Not gameOver
```

```
                REM let gameplay code update
                Game_Update(0)
                REM let gameplay code draw
                Game_Draw()
                REM let the game object update
                game.Update()
                REM give the form some cycles
                Application.DoEvents()
                REM calculate framerate
                frameCount += 1
                If My.Computer.Clock.TickCount > frameTimer + 1000 Then
                    frameTimer = My.Computer.Clock.TickCount
                    frameRate = frameCount
                    frameCount = 0
                End If
            End While
            REM free memory and shut down
            Game_End()
            End
        End Sub

        Public Sub Game_End()
            ballImage = Nothing
            ball = Nothing
            paddleImage = Nothing
            paddle = Nothing
            blockImage = Nothing
            For y = 1 To 8
                For x = 1 To 10
                    blocks(x, y) = Nothing
                Next
            Next
        End Sub

        Public Function Game_Init() As Boolean
            Form1.Text = "Collision Demo"
            game.SetFont("Arial", 14, FontStyle.Regular)
            REM create ball sprite
            ballImage = Game.LoadBitmap("ball.png")
            ball = New Sprite(game)
```

```
        ball.Image = ballImage
        ball.Size = ballImage.Size
        ball.Position = New PointF(400, 300)
        ball.Velocity = New PointF(4.0, 2.5)
        REM create paddle sprite
        paddleImage = game.LoadBitmap("paddle.png")
        paddle = New Sprite(game)
        paddle.Image = paddleImage
        paddle.Size = paddleImage.Size
        paddle.Position = New PointF(350, 550)
        REM create blocks
        blockImage = Game.LoadBitmap("blocks.bmp")
        For y = 1 To 8
            For x = 1 To 10
                blocks(x, y) = New Sprite(game)
                blocks(x, y).Image = blockImage
                blocks(x, y).Alive = True
                blocks(x, y).Image = blockImage
                blocks(x, y).Columns = 4
                blocks(x, y).Width = 64
                blocks(x, y).Height = 32
                blocks(x, y).CurrentFrame = y - 1
                blocks(x, y).Position = New PointF( _
                    x * (64 + 2), y * (32 + 2))
            Next
        Next
        Return True
End Function


Public Sub Game_Update(ByVal time As Integer)
    ball.KeepInBounds(New Rectangle(0, 0, 800, 600))
    If paddle.X < 10 Then
        paddle.X = 10
    ElseIf paddle.X > 700 Then
        paddle.X = 700
    End If
    CheckCollisions()
End Sub
```

```
Public Sub Game_Draw()
    game.Device.Clear(Color.Black)
    REM move & draw the ball
    ball.X += ball.Velocity.X
    ball.Y += ball.Velocity.Y
    ball.Draw()
    REM move & draw the paddle
    paddle.X += paddle.Velocity.X
    paddle.Draw()
    DrawBlocks()
    game.Print(0, 0, "Framerate: " + frameRate.ToString(), _
        Brushes.White)
End Sub

Public Sub Game_KeyPressed(ByVal key As System.Windows.Forms.Keys)
    Select Case key
        Case Keys.Escape : Shutdown()
        Case Keys.Right
            paddle.Velocity = New PointF(PADDLE_SPEED, 0)
        Case Keys.Left
            paddle.Velocity = New PointF(-PADDLE_SPEED, 0)
    End Select
End Sub

Public Sub Game_KeyReleased(ByVal key As System.Windows.Forms.Keys)
    Select Case key
        Case Keys.Right
            paddle.Velocity = New PointF(0, 0)
        Case Keys.Left
            paddle.Velocity = New PointF(0, 0)
    End Select
End Sub

Private Sub CheckCollisions()
    Dim x As Integer
    Dim y As Integer
    REM test for collision with paddle
    If paddle.IsColliding(ball) Then
        ball.Velocity = New PointF(ball.Velocity.X, _
                ball.Velocity.Y * -1)
```

```
            End If
            REM test for collision with blocks
            For y = 1 To 8
                For x = 1 To 10
                    If blocks(x, y).Alive Then
                        If ball.IsColliding(blocks(x, y)) Then
                            score += 1
                            blocks(x, y).Alive = False
                            ball.Velocity = New PointF(ball.Velocity.X, _
                                    ball.Velocity.Y * -1)
                        End If
                    End If
                Next
            Next
        End Sub

    Private Sub DrawBlocks()
        For y As Integer = 1 To 8
            For x As Integer = 1 To 10
                If blocks(x, y).Alive Then
                    blocks(x, y).Draw()
                End If
            Next
        Next
    End Sub

    Public Sub Shutdown()
        gameOver = True
    End Sub
End Module
```

Level Up!

That's about all there is to sprite collision detection at this point. You learned about the basic collision between two sprites—or more accurately, between two rectangles—using the `Rectangle.IntersectsWith` method, which simplifies the collision code that you would otherwise have to write yourself. We will be using another form of collision detection later on when we are working with the game world, made up of a tile map, in which certain areas in the world will be impassible based on the tile values.

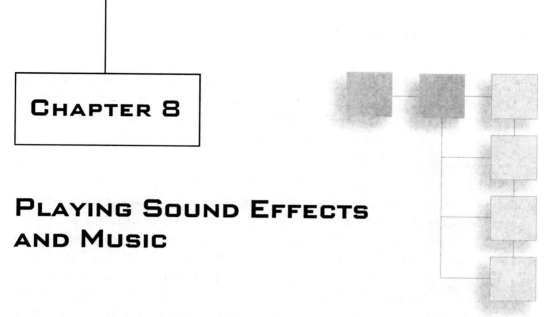

CHAPTER 8

PLAYING SOUND EFFECTS AND MUSIC

In years past, programming sound and music for games was an enormous task. Custom sound code was usually too difficult to write due to the conflicting standards among the various sound cards in the industry. Today, that is no longer a problem. Now a single, dominant hardware maker sets the PC audio standard and a single, dominant sound library sets the software standard. While some may argue the point, I believe that Creative Labs had the sound card market wrapped up with their Sound Blaster products, but today many motherboards include very capable audio hardware. This chapter is a quick jaunt through the basic audio features of Visual Basic, with demos to show how to play sound effects and music files in Visual Basic, including the versatile MP3 format.

Here's what we'll cover in this chapter:

- Playing wave files
- Playing wave resources
- Referencing the Media Player
- Playing MP3 and MIDI files

PROGRAMMING AUDIO

Audio is always a fun subject to explore because sound effects and music can influence our emotions so dramatically. Could you imagine playing a game like

153

Halo: Reach without audio? It would be a different experience entirely! What is a game without sound? Little more than a graphics demo, all but unplayable in my opinion (unless you're playing late at night and don't want anyone to know!). Sound is absolutely essential for the success of any game, in both the professional and indie market.

Even the simplest game needs some form of background music, or it is difficult for the player to remain interested. Remember this important rule of gaming: Any game without sound and music is just a technology demo. It is absolutely essential that you spend some of your development time on a game working on the music and sound effects. In fact, it is probably a good idea to do so during development. As the game takes shape, so should the sounds and music. Background music should reflect what is going on in the game and can even be used to invoke the emotions of the player. Consider a scene in which a beloved game character dies. Upbeat music would spoil the mood, whereas dark and menacing background music would engender feelings of remorse and sorrow (and perhaps even anger).

Keep this in mind when working on sections of a game and try to have a different background sequence for different circumstances. Victory should be rewarded with upbeat music, while menacing or dangerous situations should be accompanied by low-beat, low-tempo songs that reinforce the natural emotions that arise in such a circumstance. Later in this chapter, under the heading, "Using The Media Player Control," I'll show you how to use Windows Media Player to play an MP3 file in your game projects.

Ambient sound is a term that I borrowed from *ambient light*, which you might already understand. Just look at a light bulb in a light fixture on the ceiling. The light emitted by the bulb pretty much fills the room (unless you are in a very large room). When light permeates a room, it is said to be *ambient*; that is, the light does not seem to have a source. Contrast this idea with directional light and you get the idea behind ambient sound. *Ambient sound* refers to sound that appears to have no direction or source. Ambient sound is emitted by speakers uniformly, without any positional effects. This is the most common type of sound generated by most games (at least most older games—the tendency with modern games is to use positional sound).

Playing Wave Files

We can load and play a wave file using the class called System.Media.Sound-Player. This class has limited features but gets the job done for simple sound effects needs. First, we create an object:

```
Dim audio As System.Media.SoundPlayer
```

By adding System.Media to the list of imports, we can refer to just SoundPlayer.

```
audio = new SoundPlayer()
```

There are two overloads of the SoundPlayer() constructor, one to specify the audio file and another to specify a System.IO.Stream for loading the file. So, one way to load an audio clip is to pass the filename to the constructor:

```
audio = new SoundPlayer("sound.wav")
```

An option is to just use the default constructor and instead load the audio file manually. The SoundPlayer.SoundLocation property is used to specify the filename. Once set, we can use SoundPlayer.Load() to load the file.

```
audio.SoundLocation = "sound.wav"
audio.Load()
```

In either case, trapping errors is a good idea since a bad filename will generate an exception. We can write a LoadWave() function to trap errors and return a SoundPlayer object if loading succeeds.

Hint

If you have a very large wave file that may take a few seconds to load, use the SoundPlayer.LoadAsync() function and SoundPlayer.IsLoadCompleted() function to find out when loading has finished.

```
Public Function LoadWave(ByVal filename As String) As System.Media.SoundPlayer
    Dim sound As SoundPlayer = Nothing
    Try
        sound = New SoundPlayer()
        sound.SoundLocation = filename
        sound.Load()
    Catch ex As Exception
    End Try
    Return sound
End Function
```

Playing Wave Resources

We can play a wave file that has been added to the project as a resource using a class called `Microsoft.VisualBasic.Devices.Audio`. This class can play a wave from a file, from a byte buffer, from a stream, or from a resource. Since we can use `System.Media.SoundPlayer` to play waves from a file, we will just look at using the `Devices.Audio` class to play a wave that has been added to the project as a resource. One great advantage to using a resource file is that your game's asset files are compiled into the executable and are no longer exposed so that the user can access them. Let me show you how to add a resource file to the project.

First, open the Project menu and choose Add New Item. Choose the list of General items, and then Resources File, as shown in Figure 8.1.

Next, double click the `Resource1.resx` file to open the project's resources. Open the drop-down list of resource types and choose Audio, as shown in Figure 8.2.

Next, you can use the Add Resource drop-down list and choose a wave file to load, or you can just drag a wave file from Windows Explorer into the resource file asset pane, as shown in Figure 8.3.

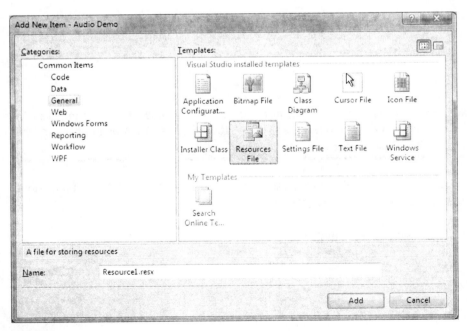

Figure 8.1
Adding a resource file to the project.

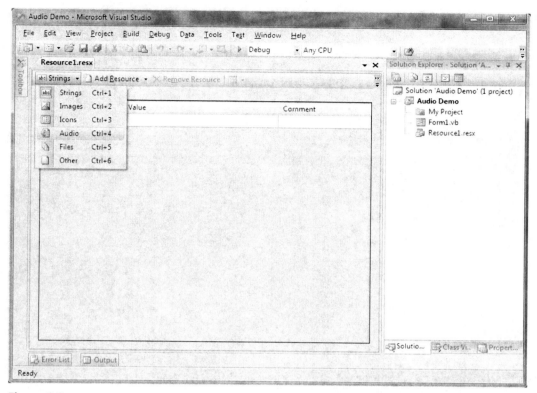

Figure 8.2
Selecting the Audio resources list.

To play an audio file from a resource, we can use the `Microsoft.VisualBasic.Devices.Audio` class.

```
Dim audioDevice As New Microsoft.VisualBasic.Devices.Audio
```

Or, by importing `Microsoft.VisualBasic`, we can refer to the class using just `Devices.Audio`. The `Play()` function has three overloads (plus the default), one of which accepts a resource. The second parameter is the `AudioPlayMode` enumeration with these options:

- `Background`
- `BackgroundLoop`
- `WaitToComplete`

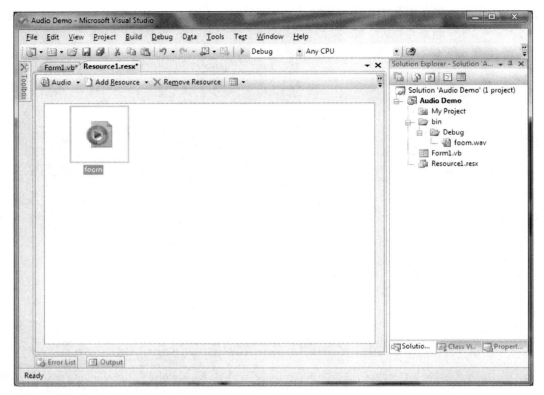

Figure 8.3
The foom.wav file has been added to the project as a resource.

So, based on our "foom" wave file added to the Resource1.resx file in our project, this is what the code to play the audio looks like:

```
audioDevice.Play(My.Resources.Resource1.foom, AudioPlayMode.Background)
```

The Audio Demo Program

The Audio Demo program demonstrates how to load wave files into memory and play them using System.Media.SoundPlayer. To demonstrate how sounds are automatically mixed, the program actually loads up another sound file as well. There are two buttons on the form; each plays one of the sound buffers. There is not much to this program other than the simple form. You will need to add two buttons to the form, simply called Button1 and Button2, as shown in Figure 8.4.

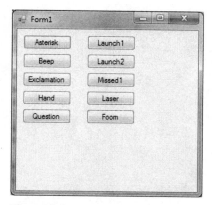

Figure 8.4
The Audio Demo program demonstrates how to play audio files.

```
Imports Microsoft.VisualBasic
Imports System.Media
Public Class Form1
    Dim audioDevice As Microsoft.VisualBasic.Devices.Audio
    Dim audio(4) As System.Media.SoundPlayer
    Public WithEvents button1 As Button
    Public WithEvents button2 As Button
    Public WithEvents button3 As Button
    Public WithEvents button4 As Button
    Public WithEvents button5 As Button
    Public WithEvents button6 As Button
    Public WithEvents button7 As Button
    Public WithEvents button8 As Button
    Public WithEvents button9 As Button
    Public WithEvents button10 As Button

    Private Sub Form1_Load(ByVal sender As System.Object, _
            ByVal e As System.EventArgs) Handles MyBase.Load
        Dim x = 10, y = 10
        REM create buttons used to play system sounds
        button1 = New Button()
        button1.Text = "Asterisk"
        button1.Location = New Point(x, y)
        button1.Parent = Me
        y += 30
```

```
button2 = New Button()
button2.Text = "Beep"
button2.Location = New Point(x, y)
button2.Parent = Me
y += 30
button3 = New Button()
button3.Text = "Exclamation"
button3.Location = New Point(x, y)
button3.Parent = Me
y += 30
button4 = New Button()
button4.Text = "Hand"
button4.Location = New Point(x, y)
button4.Parent = Me
y += 30
button5 = New Button()
button5.Text = "Question"
button5.Location = New Point(x, y)
button5.Parent = Me
y = 10
x += 100
REM create buttons used to play wave files
button6 = New Button()
button6.Text = "Launch1"
button6.Location = New Point(x, y)
button6.Parent = Me
y += 30
button7 = New Button()
button7.Text = "Launch2"
button7.Location = New Point(x, y)
button7.Parent = Me
y += 30
button8 = New Button()
button8.Text = "Missed1"
button8.Location = New Point(x, y)
button8.Parent = Me
y += 30
button9 = New Button()
button9.Text = "Laser"
button9.Location = New Point(x, y)
```

```
        button9.Parent = Me
        y += 30
        button10 = New Button()
        button10.Text = "Foom"
        button10.Location = New Point(x, y)
        button10.Parent = Me
        y += 30

        REM load audio file using constructor
        audio(0) = New SoundPlayer("launch1.wav")

        REM load audio file using Load function
        audio(1) = New SoundPlayer()
        audio(1).SoundLocation = "launch2.wav"
        audio(1).Load()

        REM load audio using our LoadWave function
        audio(2) = LoadWave("missed1.wav")
        audio(3) = LoadWave("laser.wav")

        REM create audio device
        audioDevice = New Devices.Audio()
    End Sub

    Public Function LoadWave(ByVal filename As String) _
            As System.Media.SoundPlayer
        Dim sound As SoundPlayer = Nothing
        Try
            sound = New SoundPlayer()
            sound.SoundLocation = filename
            sound.Load()
        Catch ex As Exception
        End Try
        Return sound
    End Function

    Private Sub button_clicked(ByVal sender As Object, _
            ByVal e As EventArgs) _
            Handles button1.Click, button2.Click, _
            button3.Click, button4.Click, button5.Click, _
```

```
                    button6.Click, button7.Click, button8.Click, _
                    button9.Click, button10.Click

            Dim button As Button = sender
            If button.Text = "Asterisk" Then
                REM play Asterisk sound
                SystemSounds.Asterisk.Play()
            ElseIf button.Text = "Beep" Then
                REM play Beep sound
                SystemSounds.Beep.Play()
            ElseIf button.Text = "Exclamation" Then
                REM play Exclamation sound
                SystemSounds.Exclamation.Play()
            ElseIf button.Text = "Hand" Then
                REM play Hand sound
                SystemSounds.Hand.Play()
            ElseIf button.Text = "Question" Then
                REM play Question sound
                SystemSounds.Question.Play()
            ElseIf button.Text = "Launch1" Then
                REM play loaded launch1.wav
                audio(0).Play()
            ElseIf button.Text = "Launch2" Then
                REM play loaded launch2.wav
                audio(1).Play()
            ElseIf button.Text = "Missed1" Then
                REM play loaded missed1.wav
                audio(2).Play()
            ElseIf button.Text = "Laser" Then
                REM play loaded laser.wav
                audio(3).Play()
            ElseIf button.Text = "Foom" Then
                REM player "foom" resource
                audioDevice.Play(My.Resources.Resource1.foom, AudioPlayMode.
Background)
            End If
        End Sub
    End Class
```

Using the Media Player Control

What if you want to use a more advanced audio file, such as an MP3, for your game's music? Although we don't have a library available for this, there is an alternative that works quite well that I'll introduce to you: the Windows Media Player control. You may be wondering: why would I want to use a Media Player control when we can already play audio files? Here's the reason: for simple music playback, `System.Media.SoundPlayer` and `Microsoft.VisualBasic.Devices.Audio` are preferred. But there is a drawback—they don't have very many options. Sure, you can play back an audio file, but that's about all you can do. Beyond that, the features are pretty slim. The Media Player control, on the other hand, is full of features, as the Media Player Demo program demonstrates.

So how does this work? Visual Basic has the ability to embed an object on a form, and this capability is called OLE (*Object Linking and Embedding*). You can, for instance, embed an Excel spreadsheet on a VB Form, and it will be fully functional! There are some obvious licensing issues when you embed a whole application onto a form, and usually applications that do this sort of thing just assume that the software (such as Excel) has already been preinstalled on the end user's PC. (The Excel control simply won't work unless Excel is already installed). But there are some Windows applications that are so common that we can pretty much count on them being available. One example is Windows Media Player, which is automatically installed on Windows systems today. Even if someone is still using an older version of Windows, odds are they have Windows Media Player installed because it is free.

Referencing the Media Player

I've included a project with this chapter called Media Player Demo, which demonstrates how to use an embedded Media Player object. The `Media Player` is not available as a .NET Component, so we have to add it from the list of COM/ActiveX components (see the COM tab in the Add Reference dialog box). See Figure 8.5—the ActiveX control is called Windows Media Player.

When the `Media Player` control is available to the project, you can drag it from the Toolbox to the form. The complete design of the form is shown in Figure 8.6. Note that the `Media Player` control is on the bottom of the form, and in the Properties window on the right, its `Visible` property has been set to false. This will allow us to

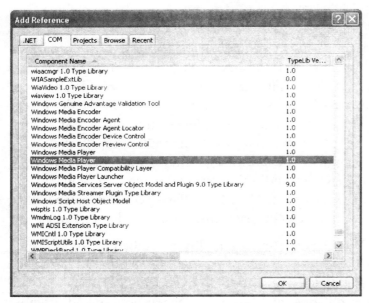

Figure 8.5
Adding a reference to the Windows Media Player control.

use the Media Player control in the program without it being visible, so our program will look as if it's a real media player, while in fact it is just using the features built into the control (namely, the ability to load and play any type of media file).

The Media Player Demo program lets you type in details for each media file, including a filename (which can be a local or remote media file streamed over the Internet, as shown in Figure 8.7).

Playing MP3 and MIDI Files

You can play any media file with the Windows Media Player control by setting its URL property equal to a filename (or a URL to a file on a website, for instance). This is deceptively simple, because there is really no "play" function at all. Once you set the URL property to a filename, playback will automatically start. Likewise, if you want to stop playback, set the URL to an empty string (""). The control can support the same media file formats supported by the full-blown Media Player, including MP3!

```
AxWindowsMediaPlayer1.URL = "symphony.rmi"
```

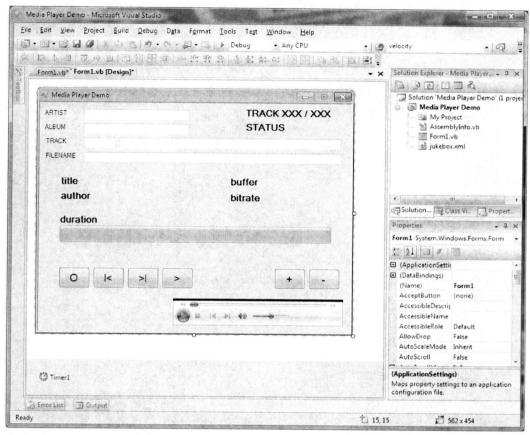

Figure 8.6
Adding the Windows Media Player control to the form.

The program has a media player-like interface and it keeps track of audio files in an XML database. If you have any MP3 music files (and who doesn't these days?) go ahead and copy a few to the project folder and add them to the program by clicking the "+" button and entering the filename and information. Then click the play button (">").

Since there is a form full of controls for this program, I will forego listing the source code here to save space, and instead encourage you to load the project and play around with it to learn how the Windows Media Player control works. It is extremely easy to use. Most of this program's source code is wrapped up in

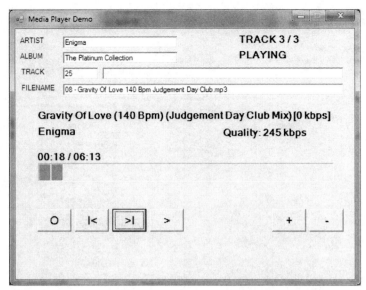

Figure 8.7
Media files can be played locally or streamed over the Internet.

just the user interface. To use the control in your own programs, just set its Visible property to false so it doesn't show up on the form!

LEVEL UP!

This chapter was a quick overview of Visual Basic audio support, giving you just enough information to add sound effects and music to your own games. By loading multiple sound files into memory and playing them at certain points in your game, you greatly enhance the gameplay experience. In a sense, you are the conductor of this orchestra by directing what happens in source code. You also learned how to use the Windows Media Player control for advanced audio file support such as MP3 files and streaming from a web URL. Just keep in mind that you cannot distribute copyrighted music.

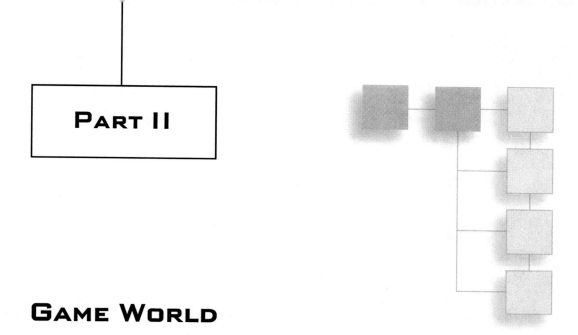

PART II

GAME WORLD

Welcome to the second part of the book, dedicated to designing and constructing the game world of Celtic Crusader. In these chapters you will learn how to create a game tool, a level editor for the game world. This subject falls under the banner of *tools programming*, and is one of the most highly sought-after skills in the game industry. After perusing the design of the game (i.e., the "big picture"), we will create a level editor and build one of the first regions of the game world. Once the first level is available, we will then learn how to load and draw it, and then chase that topic with a jaunt through sprite drawing once again. This part concludes with a chapter covering portals, an important concept that allows you to create a world much larger than available memory will allow.

- Chapter 9: Designing the Game of Celtic Crusader
- Chapter 10: Creating the Level Editor
- Chapter 11: Rendering a Game Level
- Chapter 12: Adding Objects to the World
- Chapter 13: Using Portals to Expand the World

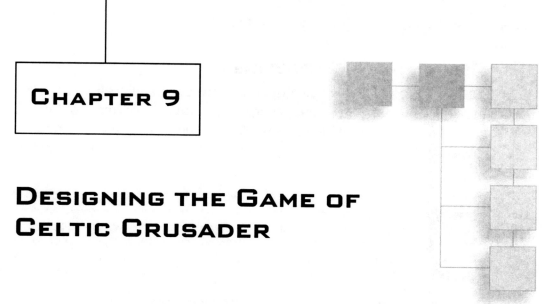

CHAPTER 9

DESIGNING THE GAME OF CELTIC CRUSADER

In this chapter, we will design the game world featured in Celtic Crusader. Designing a game is no simple task, and it should not be thrown together after the source code has been nearly completed. The design should direct what code gets written and what the game world looks like. I have written several successful game design documents, and they are very valuable to the development team on a game project. In this chapter we will merely design the game world and describe how the game will be played rather than creating an entire design doc. Here's what we'll cover in this chapter:

- The quest-based storyline
- Designing the RPG world
- The player's character (PC)
- The non-player characters (NPCs)
- Inventory and gold
- Weapons and armor
- Magic
- Communication
- Combat

THE QUEST-BASED STORYLINE

You can learn a lot about your subconscious motivations and creative impulses by designing a game with pencil and paper. I get so much enjoyment out of the design process that my enthusiasm gets the best of me and I want to jump into the code and start writing the game! At the same time, I enjoy drawing even though I have no talent.

Hint

For a complete discussion of how to design a role-playing game, see *Swords & Circuitry: A Designer's Guide to Computer Role-Playing Games* (Thomson Course PTR, 2002) by Neal and Jana Hallford. I also recommend *Character Development and Storytelling for Games* (Thomson Course PTR, 2004) by Lee Sheldon, if you are interested in learning how to create realistic storylines and characters for your games.

It's important to put as much on paper as possible before you start writing source code. It is good to get started on the artwork for a game while developing the design, because that helps you realize what is possible and somewhat helps with the creative process. If you start working on a game without any design at all, at worst it ends up being left unfinished, at best it is a clinical game (meaning it is functional but lacks substance).

Celtic Crusader is based in ninth-century Ireland, a country occupied by Norwegian Vikings, who ruled the seas at the time. The Vikings were not just barbarous raiders, although this game's story is about Viking occupation in Ireland and generally depicts Vikings as the bad guys. The Viking civilization was spread across a much wider area than even the Roman Empire, although it was not as strong and it was not based entirely on military conquest. The Vikings were explorers and traders who settled lands, such as Iceland and Greenland, that had never before been visited by humans. Although humans had migrated to North and South America before this time, the Vikings are also credited as being the first Europeans to discover and settle North America. (Actually, the Viking settlers in Greenland were the first Canadians.)

The storyline is usually not as important as the quests that move the story forward. Your character does not have a specific goal, because nothing in life is that clearly defined. Instead, the game develops while your character develops, mainly by fighting animals and fantasy creatures, as well as the occasional Viking raiding party. Your character's attributes determine how good he is in combat. (See "The Player's Character" section later in this chapter.) In Celtic Crusader, we're building both an adventure *and* a "hack-and-slash" game that may be compared with *Diablo* and *Baldur's Gate*. There are more complex adventure-based RPGs as well (such as *The Elder Scrolls* and *Might & Magic* series), and they tend to take a very long time to finish.

DESIGNING THE RPG WORLD

The game world in Celtic Crusader is based on the island country of Ireland. I chose this land because it has a rich mythology going back more than 2,000 years, providing a huge pool of possible plot elements for the storyline and sub-quests in a game. I thought of basing the game on ancient America, designing a game around the Mayan or Incan civilizations, but decided to go with Ireland because it is easier to write a story around an isolated community. That also makes it possible to set boundaries on the game map limiting the player's movement (as opposed to putting mountains or some sort of no-man's land at the boundary of a land-locked game world).

There is a lot to be said for a randomly generated world or a world based on a completely fictional land with no historical basis. It allows you (the game's designer) to let loose with your imagination to create a world that does not influence, nor is affected by, the "real world." Generating a random world is definitely possible, but I don't like the random factor because it prevents me from designing the game around real locations in the world. Celtic Crusader has characters that are from specific towns based on character class, and I want those towns to be real places on the map, not just generated locations in a random world. The goal is to build a game that has a lot of replay value by offering strong character development rather than anonymous random combat. The fact of the matter is most people love a good story. Giving your game a good story with believable characters makes it far more fun to play than a randomly generated world, even if the same characters appear in that fictional world. Even a great game franchise like *World of Warcraft* suffers from the animatronic-like affect of scripted, repeating events.

Map of the World

Figure 9.1 shows the map of the world in Celtic Crusader as a traditional hand-drawn illustration. This rough sketch represents Ireland in the ninth century, when the Vikings invaded England and Ireland from their empire in Norway, Denmark, and Sweden.

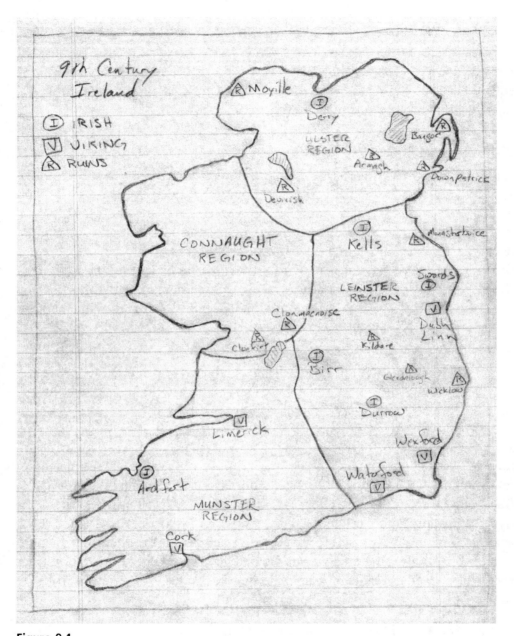

Figure 9.1
Hand-drawn illustration of the world in Celtic Crusader, based in Ireland.

This map shows Viking towns (a V inside a square), Irish towns (an I inside a circle), and ruins (an R inside a triangle), to give you an idea about how quests are based on the game world itself rather than by some random quest-generation system. In reality, I have taken some creative liberties with the true historical significance of the towns shown in this map. The Irish "towns" were, in reality, monasteries that the Vikings either did not discover or did not plunder for one reason or another. The ruins shown on the map are, in fact, monasteries that the Vikings had plundered by stealing all gold, silver, and valuables they could find. I thought the idea of a plundered monastery lent itself well to a ruin filled with evil creatures. The ruins in Celtic Crusader are based somewhat on historical fact, which I believe really helps with the story, with the idea being that the plundered monasteries, by becoming ruins, have been invaded by vile monsters that are not generally found elsewhere in the game.

The ruins are basically a training ground where the player's character gains experience, goes up in levels, and acquires gold to buy better equipment in the towns. The goal with this game engine is to have certain parts of the map load a new map via a portal, with the player inserted into a certain part of the new map. (We'll discuss issues like this when building the Level Editor in the next chapter.) However, I have found that this is a very difficult thing to do without causing the source code to grow in complexity (and I want to keep this game on the simple side). Therefore, the towns in the game world are represented on the map itself rather than as a *warp* type of system that enters and exits the towns. I really like this idea better because it keeps the suspension of disbelief going.

Definition

Suspension of disbelief is a term that describes one's immersion in a fictional setting. You may have experienced this while reading a good book or playing a good game: You lose track of the real world around you and become totally immersed in the fiction. This is a *very good thing* to strive for in your game designs, and you should strive to achieve it with every game. Anything that takes away the player's suspension of disbelief should be removed from the game. A clunky user interface, a difficult combat system, an overload of information on the screen—these all lead to ruining the player's feeling of total immersion.

By taking the hand-drawn map and scanning it into the computer, I have been able to clean it up and turn it into a digital version of this game's world. That world is shown in Figure 9.2.

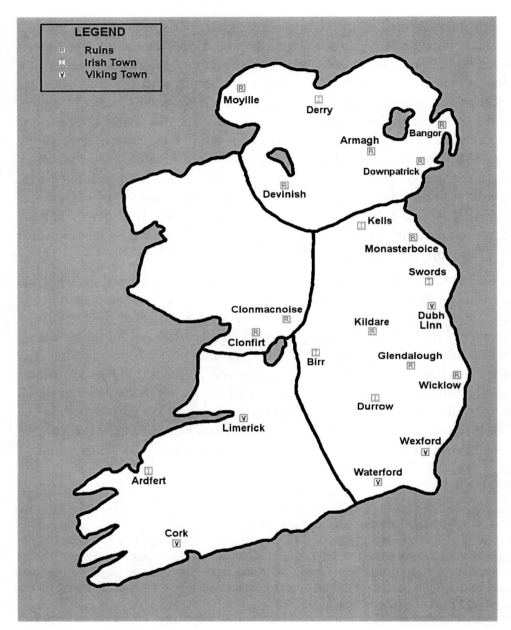

Figure 9.2
The hand-drawn map has been scanned and converted to a digital map.

My goal is to teach you how to create an RPG as well as a quest-driven game engine that you can customize to suit your own vision and imagination. I want to give you just enough to get the job done, while avoiding doing everything for you, so you are motivated to improve the game.

While you're working on a game like this, always consider ways to make whatever you're working on reusable. If you are constructing a player creation screen, think of ways to make the screen dynamic and flexible, without hard-coding anything specific. It is a good idea to keep things concrete and solidly built in the game, but not to the point where it's impossible to modify later. If you have buttons on the screen that the player needs to click with the mouse, make those buttons easy to move around—use constants at the top of the source code for that particular screen. Another option is to make everything in your game *skinnable*. You know, skins are all the rage in user interfaces today, and most music players for your PC support skinning. This is a process where the program controls can be repositioned and the images used to represent those controls can be modified—with some fantastic results. Why not take that excellent design methodology with you in the design of a game and make it totally customizable by storing skins and settings in files outside of the source code for the game? This excellent concept may be beyond the scope of this short book, but I want you to keep it in mind while you are working.

Figure 9.3 shows my admittedly crude mock-up for the scrolling game world. The player's sprite remains in the center of the screen at all times, with the world scrolling underfoot. With this design in mind, the map has to be laid out so there is room around the borders for the player to reach the edge of the map. In other words, when the player reaches the ocean, the map needs to have ocean squares going out a little so the player can walk right up to the seashore. The eight-way scrolling of the map is perfect for the sprites in this game, which have been rendered with animation in eight directions.

Regions

There are four provinces, or regions, in the version of Ireland represented in this game: Leinster, Munster, Connaught, and Ulster (see Figure 9.4). It is not crucial, but I have always found that a background story and historical depth make a game far more compelling for the player, greatly improving the sense of immersion in the game world. A game is not just backgrounds, sprites, and collision detection, and

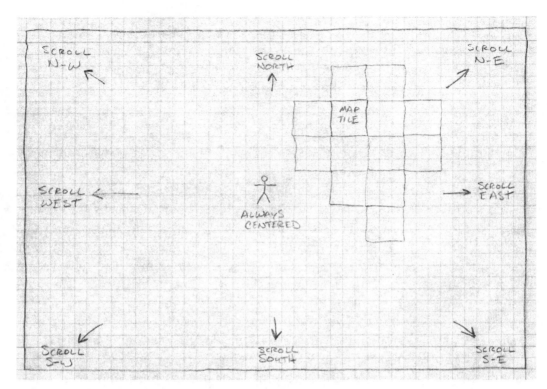

Figure 9.3
The player is centered on the screen within the scrolling game world.

players expect much more depth to an RPG than they expect from an arcade game. One aspect of the *Ultima* series that made it so popular is the wealth of historical information provided to the player within the game (usually through dialog with NPCs). You want to create the illusion that the player is just one person in a huge, populated world that goes on with or without him. At the start of the game, the player will begin in a town within one of these four regions—depending on the character class chosen—and the history of the region will be reflected in the people that the player will encounter early in the game.

Leinster Region

Leinster region, located on the east side of Ireland, is where most of the fighting takes place between the native Irish people (who are, admittedly, descended from Anglo-Saxons in the first place, never mind that the Celts are long gone. . .)

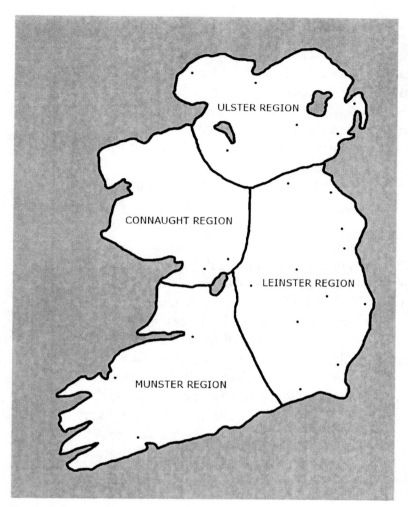

Figure 9.4
The four regions of the game world in Celtic Crusader.

and the Viking invaders who created three settlements: Dubh Linn, Wexford, and Waterford. Leinster borders all three of the other regions. The Irish monastery towns include Kells, Swords, Birr, and Durrow. There are also some ruins (pillaged monasteries) in this region: Monasterboice, Kildare, Glendalough, and Wicklow. This region produces the most axe-bearing warriors and sword-wielding paladins in the world.

Munster Region

The Munster region of Ireland, located in the southwest, is adjacent to Leinster and Connaught. Munster is the second strongest region of Viking occupation on Ireland with the two Viking settlements of Limerick and Cork. Although there are no ruins in this region at all, there is one Irish monastery town called Ardfert, which is famous for producing skilled archers (known by the character class scout), the likes of which fought against the Vikings during their initial invasion and occupation. The Vikings have never learned about the secret bow craft of Ardfert, so many patriotic archers are still trained there.

Ulster Region

Ulster region, located on the north side of Ireland, is the location for most of the island's religious artifacts; its inhabitants practice the ancient art of mastering the natural world. Ulster was devastated by the Vikings during their initial invasion, with many mages killed while trying to protect their monasteries. There were vast arrays of gold and silver artifacts given to the mages of Ulster as offerings throughout the generations. Despite mastery of the natural world, Ulster mages were peaceful in nature and abhorred violence of any kind, even in one's defense. As a result, the mages of Ulster were defenseless against an unknown enemy that brought brutality to the region, plundering the monasteries of Moyille, Devenish, Armagh, Downpatrick, and Bangor, leaving them in ruins. Only Derry remained unscathed by the plundering. The tenants of Derry, the last vestige of Celtic mages left alive, have been forced to abandon their prior unity with the natural world and focus their attention on combat in order to drive out the Viking invaders. Mages of Derry are masters of the staff in hand-to-hand combat and are able to wield some of the unseen forces of the world to aid them in battle.

Connaught Region

The Connaught region is located on the western side of Ireland. Connaught was once a vast grazing land for cows, sheep, and goats, with its wide open plains and plentiful feeding ranges. Connaught is not a widely settled region, though, and the Viking invasion rallied those few living in Connaught to the battle in defense of the land. The result is that forests have grown into Connaught from the south, and it is mainly a breeding ground for evil creatures and a hiding place for criminals. Two monasteries in southern Connaught—Clonmacnoise and Clonfert—were pillaged by the Vikings, who left them in ruins. The inhabitants of these two ruins are a constant nuisance to the hardworking citizens of Birr, located nearby in Leinster region.

THE PLAYER'S CHARACTER

One of the most enjoyable aspects of playing an RPG is creating your very own custom character to use in the game. This is why true RPGs have more depth and more replay value than games featuring a specific set of characters (as in the *Zelda* series). Because player character creation is so much a part of the experience, it's important to design the character creation screen with as much versatility as possible so the player can create his or her own persona for the game. Celtic Crusader is taking shape as an old-school RPG, and will eventually allow you to design your own character from scratch. The game should allow your character to interact within the confines of the main storyline of the game (as well as within the sub-quests). Figure 9.5 shows one possible

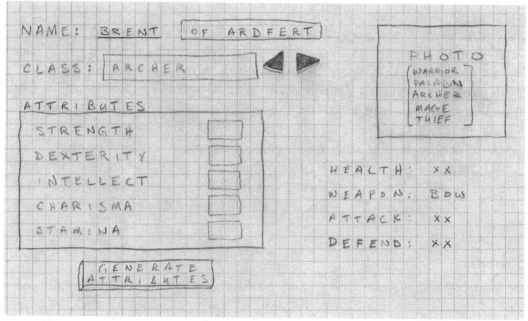

Figure 9.5
A rough-draft design for a possible character creation screen.

design for a character creation screen. This is a very crude drawing, but it should give you an idea of what you might do for your own character screen.

Hint

To see what the final character generation screen looks like, jump ahead to Chapter 20 to check it out! It's not exactly like the design, but comes close to it.

Character Attributes (Stats)

All characters in the game—including non-player characters and monsters—have the same set of attributes in order to make combat possible: strength, dexterity, stamina, intellect, and charisma.

Strength

Strength (STR) represents the character's ability to carry a weight and swing a weapon, and is generally good for the warrior and knight classes, which carry hand-to-hand combat weapons, such as axes and swords. The strength attribute is used to calculate the attack value for the character (meaning, the amount of damage the player inflicts on enemies with each swing of a weapon). Each time the character attacks, a dice roll (which is a random number in code) against the attack value determines whether the attack succeeds. If the attack is a hit, then the weapon's damage value is used to inflict damage against the opponent. Suppose your character has an attack value (ATT) of 12, which is calculated using the character's strength (mainly, although you may include dexterity in a custom calculation to make the game more interesting). Typical "attack rolls" are done with a D20 (a 20-sided die). In a Visual Basic program, you can simulate the roll of dice using the Random class. An attack value of 12 will go up against the other player's defense value to determine if any damage is dealt.

Dexterity

Dexterity (DEX) represents the agility of the character, the ability to manipulate objects (such as a weapon), and the skill with which the player uses his or her hands in general. A very low dexterity means the character is clumsy, while a very high dexterity means the character can manipulate complicated devices and perform fast, complex actions. Use of any weapon (such as a sword, a mace, or even a bow) is improved with a high dexterity, and a high skill might even allow the character to wield two weapons at once (dual wield).

Stamina

Stamina (STA) represents a character's endurance, or the ability to continue performing an activity for a long period of time. Stamina is also known as *constitution* in some RPGs. A very high stamina provides a character with the ability to engage in lengthy battles without rest, while a character with low stamina tires quickly (and likely falls in battle). Stamina affects the player's total number of hit points (HP).

Intellect

Intellect or Intelligence (INT) represents the character's ability to learn, remember things, and solve problems. The mage class requires a very high intellect, while relatively low intellect is common in melee combat classes that favor brute force over mental faculties. The intellect usually affects a player's ability to learn magic spells and perform spell-casting.

Charisma

Charisma represents the character's attractiveness and appearance, and generally affects how others respond to the character. A character with very high charisma attracts others, while one with very low charisma shuns others. Knights usually have very high charisma, reflecting their heroic stature, while Wizards often have a lower charisma since they are not as concerned with appearances.

Character Status

When the character is represented in the game with a sprite, you want the player to be able to view the information about his or her character by bringing up some sort of status screen, as is the norm with most RPGs. Figure 9.6 shows an example screen that I designed to show the player's stats in a sort of pop-up window over the game screen. The window shows information about the player such as attributes, equipment, health, gold, and so on.

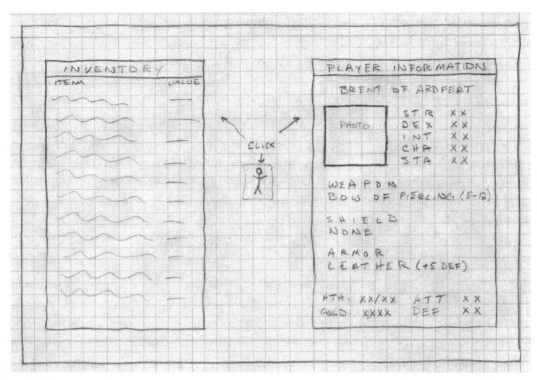

Figure 9.6
The design for the in-game player information screen.

Hint

Likewise, to see what the final inventory screen looks like, jump ahead to Chapter 18 and compare the final result with this early design!

This screen design also has one possible way of handling inventory management in the game. Since inventory is such a huge and complex issue, we'll be devoting two chapters to it in Part III. I've played games where inventory was so time consuming and required so much micro-management that it ruined my suspension of disbelief while playing the game. Realistically, if you are a soldier of one class or another, do you have the strength to carry 100 swords, shields, and suits of armor while also carrying 1,000 arrows and 250 rings? Some RPGs *are* that ridiculous. A limited form of inventory management is definitely needed. We will be creating an item editor in Chapter 17 and working an inventory manager into the game in Chapter 18.

I like how Peter Molyneux designed an intuitive inventory system for the game *Fable*. In *Fable*, your character can carry quite a lot of stuff, because there is a fascinating aspect of this game that allows you to become a trader, making money by buying and selling goods. But with respect to combat gear, the game automatically recognizes "suits" of related armor items so you can auto-equip all related items of armor at once. I could literally go on for pages describing this amazing game. One thing that caused me to fall off my seat with laughter was what happened to my character when I equipped him with a very heavy hammer weapon. The game accurately modeled the character *dragging* the hammer behind him, and he was barely able to swing it!

Character Classes

Each character class comes from a certain part of the world, where it is assumed that the raw materials and skills are available for that class. For instance, sword masters come from the Irish towns within the region of Leinster. There is no real reason for this historically, but I just like the idea of certain character classes coming from different parts of the world. Table 9.1 shows the character classes and their home regions. The two fighter classes—warrior and paladin—both originate in Leinster. In reality, a character might be born anywhere, but is located in one of the towns in a certain region when the character is created. In the context of the game, creating a character means simply that you, as the player, are finding and assuming the identity of someone in the fictional world (or rather, someone of whom you are taking control).

Table 9.1 Home Regions for Possible Character Classes

Character Class	Region
Warrior	Leinster
Paladin	Leinster
Hunter	Munster
Priest	Ulster

There are no towns in the region of Connaught (only two ruins), so no characters can originate from this region. This is generally going to be a chaotic region ruled by anarchy, populated with thieves, cutthroats, and evil creatures aplenty. The character attribute modifiers for each class are based on a fixed set of 15 points distributed among the attributes to reflect that class' strong and weak characteristics. If you add the modifiers together they equal 15, no matter the class, so there is no numerical advantage of one class over another. These base attributes are essential to defining each class. You should feel free to change this numerical basis for your own vision for this game. Just be sure to start off the base character classes with low "stats"—you don't want the player to become too strong early in the game.

Warrior Class

Warriors originate in the Leinster region due to the ongoing conflict with the Vikings, which have the strongest presence in all of Ireland. (There are three Viking settlements: Dubh Linn, Wexford, and Waterford.) It does make sense, if you think about it, because where there is the greatest conflict there is likely to be the most surplus of weapons available. A character in this region should be able to find a weapon and begin training—and there is the added possibility that a character was formerly an Irish patriot in a defeated and disbanded army.

Figure 9.7 shows an example of a concept drawing of a Viking warrior.

Warriors can wield any type of heavy weapon but are basically limited by the available artwork, meaning that the warrior in this game carries an axe. Warriors have the attribute modifiers detailed in Table 9.2.

Hint

For the final design of the game characters, including the final attribute modifiers with combat modifiers, refer to Chapter 14, "Creating the Character Editor."

Paladin Class

Paladins are holy warriors who pledge their loyalty to God and country, so to speak, although this has been fantasized in literature and fantasy gaming to mean that knights have certain magical capabilities (notably the ability to heal others). It is generally accepted that a knight in an RPG should always defend

Figure 9.7
An artist's concept drawing of a warrior (courtesy of Eden Celeste).

Table 9.2 Warrior Attribute Modifiers

Attribute	Modifier
Strength	+8
Dexterity	+3
Intellect	0
Charisma	0
Stamina	+4

good and fight against evil. You should never have an evil knight (otherwise, you should just create a character from another class), although it might be possible to have a "dark knight" who has become corrupted, which is an interesting story element.

Figure 9.8
An artist's concept drawing of a paladin (courtesy of Eden Celeste).

Figure 9.8 shows a concept drawing of a paladin. You can see from this single drawing that concept artwork is extremely valuable, as it helps to fully realize the potential of the game and gives the sprite artist an example of what the sprite should look like. When you have 100+ frames of animation for a sprite, you want to be sure that it is correct on the first frame because animation is very difficult to modify after the artist has completed the work.

In this game, I loosely define a paladin as a character wielding *any* type of weapon as long as he also has a shield. Paladins are well-rounded characters, with the character attribute modifiers in Table 9.3, with a strong emphasis on survivability due to a high stamina value. When we work on the character editor in Chapter 14, you will be able to define your own classes for the player, NPCs, and monsters, so consider these just common examples.

Table 9.3 Paladin Attribute Modifiers

Attribute	Modifier
Strength	+3
Dexterity	+3
Intellect	0
Charisma	+1
Stamina	+8

Hunter Class

Hunters are common in the land of Ireland since the bow is the most common hunting weapon in the world. However, the military-caliber archer is only found in one place: the forest-encroached Irish town of Ardfert, the only unscathed Irish settlement in the region of Munster. The craft of building bows and carving straight arrows may be found throughout the land, but the craft of building armor-piercing arrows and multi-string compound bows is now limited exclusively to Ardfert. The skilled archers of Ardfert are themselves as skilled in bowcraft as they are in warcraft, often recruited by Irish militia at the outlying towns and by rebel factions still fighting against the Vikings. Figure 9.9 shows a concept drawing of a hunter character. The attribute modifiers for the scout class are given in Table 9.4.

Priest Class

The priests of Ulster region were once peaceful caretakers of Ireland's monasteries, turning their attention to a mastery of the natural world, including the use of healing herbs and cultivating gardens. The invasion of the Vikings and subsequent pillaging of monasteries left many of the mages slaughtered, and those remaining fled to the few monasteries that were not discovered by the Vikings. Those who were left refocused their attention on righteous combat techniques, making the priests of Ulster skilled in hand-to-hand combat as well as in using holy attacks. In addition, priests still know the art of healing. Table 9.5 reveals the attribute modifiers for the priest class.

Figure 9.10 shows an artist's concept drawing of a priest character. What is the most significant thing that you notice about the concept drawings? They are

Figure 9.9
An artist's concept drawing of a hunter (courtesy of Eden Celeste).

Table 9.4 Hunter Attribute Modifiers

Attribute	Modifier
Strength	+2
Dexterity	+8
Intellect	0
Charisma	+1
Stamina	+4

hand-drawn, often in pencil, and scanned, rather than edited in a graphic editor program. Even if you have some fantastic character models already available for your game (that you plan to render into animated sprites), your game will still benefit greatly from hand-drawn concept renditions of each character.

Table 9.5 Priest Attribute Modifiers

Attribute	Modifier
Strength	0
Dexterity	+6
Intellect	+8
Charisma	0
Stamina	+1

Figure 9.10
An artist's concept drawing of a priest (courtesy of Eden Celeste).

NON-PLAYER CHARACTERS

Non-player characters (NPCs) represent everyone in the world other than the player's character (and the party in a game with more than one person playing, as in multiplayer games). NPCs are usually controlled by the game itself using a scripted or behavioral subroutine. Friendly NPCs might be common townsfolk walking around the towns, doing their work and conducting business. NPCs might also be enemies, hostile to the player's character, who attack the PC on sight. Most of the time, fantasy creatures and monsters are not called NPCs because they are just obstacles that the player must overcome to complete a quest, and they generally help build up the PC's experience to level and increase his skills.

The NPCs in Celtic Crusader should follow a simple predefined path in the towns and not venture outside the towns in which they are placed. This is accomplished by having them move around only within a limited range from their starting points. So, if the town of Durrow is located at a certain (X,Y) position on the map, then the game generates a certain number of NPCs and places them at the same location identified as that town (along with a small random value, so they aren't all bunched up). The NPCs then move about in random directions within a close proximity to their original starting points. In many cases, NPCs walk back and forth between two points on the map (a technique called "patrolling").

This rather simplistic behavior produces a surprisingly realistic town, and you can always insert some NPCs with more advanced behavior necessary to complete a certain quest. But most of the NPCs will simply move around in this manner and make themselves available to the player for dialogue. Each NPC is provided with a simple set of responses to dialogue in which the player can choose to engage (by walking up to an NPC and hitting a button). We will explore the dialogue when creating the character editor and quest editor.

WEAPONS AND ARMOR

The standard weapons are very weak in combat while the player is just getting started in the first few levels. This is balanced by the levels of creatures and enemy NPCs that the player encounters in the early stages. As the player increases in experience and goes up in levels, the foes are equally challenging to keep the player on edge all the time and to keep the good players from finishing the game too quickly. The player should be able to equip a standard weapon, shield, and armor and automatically swap gear when better items are found (which is not a significant part of the game, so it is not strongly emphasized).

Table 9.6 Standard Weapons by Class

Character Class	Standard Weapon
Warrior	Sword
Paladin	Axe & Shield
Hunter	Bow
Priest	Staff

Table 9.6 shows the standard weapons that may be used by each character class. We will create an item editor in Chapter 17 and work on an inventory system in Chapter 18.

Magic

Magic is a huge part of most RPGs and adds a lot to the character development aspects of a game. However, I have played many games that emphasize way too much magic, to the point of almost abandoning traditional weapons for offense and defense. In my opinion, magic should be downplayed as much as possible because it has the potential to ruin a story if over-emphasized. When there are hundreds of available magic spells that a character can learn, it tends to become the whole focus of the gameplay, and that's a shame! The game shouldn't be totally about character development and becoming the most powerful wizard in the world, although that is exactly what happens with some games.

One way to handle magic is by treating spells as animated projectile sprites with embedded damage modifiers that cause things to happen to the target. For instance, arrows fired by the scout do damage based on the scout's character attack value, which is affected by the quality of the character's bow and skill. Several factors determine the possible amount of damage that an arrow can inflict on an opponent, if the opponent doesn't block the attack. (A strong defense value causes the arrow to miss entirely in some attacks.)

The amount of magic that can be used in an RPG is greatly dependent upon the available artwork to render magic spells used as weapons (such as a fireball). It is better to start off with a limited magic system that allows the mage classes (which you might subclass into cleric, wizard, and so on) to heal themselves and others, as well as to enchant weapons. It is very common for magic in an RPG to grow in usage and depth as the game develops from one sequel to the next. Don't assume that you absolutely must get every single idea into the game on your first attempt. It's fun to leave room for growth, and players enjoy the new features of follow-up games in the series.

You might also consider the possibility of marketing a game as shareware, where you freely give away a limited version of the game (which may, for instance, just provide one character class), and then ask fans to pay for the full version, which would have a full assortment of magic spells and other important features.

COMMUNICATION

The communication system in the game is important, but not crucial to a hack-and-slash type of game. Granted, such games are popular and have a lot of fans, but I want to provide you with ample opportunity to customize and improve the game. I don't want to fix the game to a specific goal (such as defeating a certain boss character), although that is certainly a goal that might be put into the game as one way to win.

Dialogue in most games can take place at the bottom of the screen, where messages are printed out and where the player can choose what to say to the NPCs. Another way to handle dialogue is to display messages in balloon popups over the players, which is often done in controller-based console RPGs. A nice feature to add to the dialogue system is recorded voice acting, although if poorly presented, this can actually take away from the suspension of disbelief. (Always be careful not to do that!) It is sometimes better to just leave the player with his or her imagination, because many RPG fans regularly read fantasy books. We develop a way to communicate with NPCs in Chapter 15, "Dialogue: Talking with NPCs".

COMBAT

The combat in Celtic Crusader should take place in real time using the same scrolling map game engine used for walking around. The combat system is more challenging when programming NPCs to react realistically to the dynamic environment than to combat itself. The basis for combat is an engagement of weapons using a custom subset of animated sprite frames showing the swinging of a weapon or the shooting of an arrow.

When an attack takes place, the player's attack value (which is derived from the player's strength and character levels) is compared to the opponent's defense value (which is based on strength, shield, and armor), and the result is added to a randomly generated number. If the final result is positive, then the attack succeeded; otherwise, the attack missed. On a successful attack, the amount of damage done by the weapon is rolled (usually a range, such as 5 to 12), and that is how much damage the target takes. The damage reduces the health points of the player or NPC, and the target is killed if health drops below zero. We build a complete stats-based combat system in Chapter 16, "Fighting, Getting XP, and Leveling Up."

Level Up!

Although game design should be considerably more complete than the partial design provided in this chapter, I think you now have a good idea about how to get started with your own RPG design. This is such a rich and varied genre that a complete and detailed design is not entirely necessary, since we can just borrow from existing (and proven!) design concepts. Drawing what you think each screen should look like and brainstorming gameplay ideas ahead of time makes the game far more interesting when you start writing the source code that actually makes the game work. Without a solid design up front, you are destined to give up on the game before it is finished. In contrast, you will become more and more enthusiastic about the game as you complete the design of each part of the game, because the process opens your mind to the possibilities. This chapter explored just some of the primary aspects of the Celtic Crusader game, giving you a basic idea about how to design a game. Of *course* we can't create a completely fleshed-out game in just a book example, but all the pieces are falling into place already.

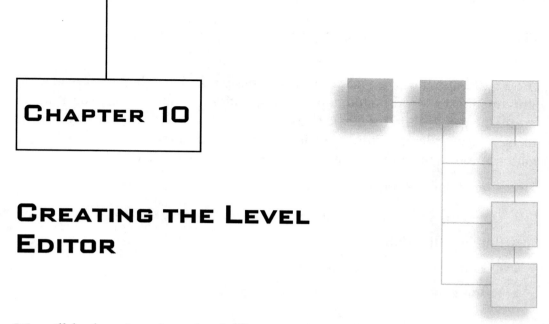

CHAPTER 10

CREATING THE LEVEL EDITOR

We will be learning about level editing in this chapter, which is a subset of a larger field called tools programming. A simple review of the employment statistics reveals this truth: tools programmers are among the highest paid people in the game industry, commanding salaries far greater than that of game designers, gameplay programmers, and even engine programmers. So, what does a tools programmer do? This is a high-demand skill set simply because it is not taught in schools, and few programmers have found a need to develop this particular type of skill in their daily activities. A "tool" in this context is any program or script that is needed during the game development process. Examples include Max and Maya scripts, file format converters, workflow pipeline programs, automated build scripts, and yes, even level editors.

We are going to focus on the level editing aspect of tools programming in this chapter. You will learn how to build a simple tilemap level editor. But first, I must disclaim something: we are going to use the C# language rather than Basic for this one. Most standalone tools are built with C#, so I want to give you a real-world experience using one of the "tools of the trade." That is not to say we could *not* build the editor in Basic—of course we could, as there are only cosmetic differences between C# and Basic. However, this editor will be useful for more than just one game genre.

The level or "game world" defines the rules of the game and presents the player with all of the obstacles that must be overcome to complete the game. Although the world is the most important aspect of a game, it is not always given the proper attention when a game is being designed. This chapter provides an introduction to world building, or more specifically, map editing. You learn to create the game world for Celtic Crusader, as well as levels for your own games, using a custom level editor. We will explore the features of this level editor to gain some insights and inspiration for creating our game levels.

Here's what we'll cover in this chapter:

- Designing our own level editor
- Building the editor
- Creating a new tilemap level
- Loading and saving level files

DESIGNING OUR OWN LEVEL EDITOR

We're going to build a custom level editor for Celtic Crusader so that we have full control over the tile format. The previous edition of this book used an off-the-shelf (so to speak) editor called Mappy (http://www.tilemap.co.uk). Mappy works well and has been used by many game studios for professional games, especially on handheld game systems like Nintendo GBA and DS. But, despite industry adoption and the popularity of Mappy, we will need our level editor this time to save tilemap data in such a way that it can be loaded into the game without too much effort. Previously, when using Mappy, we had to export tilemap data into a custom binary file and then write Basic code to load that binary data file, which was not easy!

So, let me explain the editor a bit. First of all, this is not a production editor yet. Since we're building it from scratch it will need to evolve to meet the needs of the game as the Celtic Crusader engine code takes shape. Nothing in this creative industry is ever finished, but we can make a solid effort to make the first iteration of the editor as useful as possible with the understanding that it will change over time to provide new features as needed. The first version of our editor must give us the ability to create and edit tilemaps using a fixed tile palette, and save the tilemap data using an .xml file. It is shown in Figure 10.1. An improved version of the editor with more features will be covered in Chapter 13. By presenting the editor in stages like this, you can see how it was developed from the earliest stage to a more complete version later in the book.

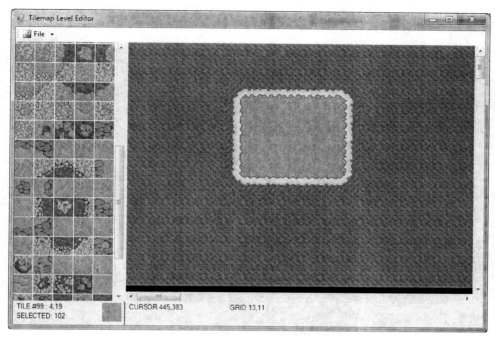

Figure 10.1
The Celtic Crusader level editor is coming along nicely.

Building the Editor

The tile palette is fixed for now with the tiles I plan to use in the game, but since the palette is a `PictureBox` with an associated `Graphics` and `Bitmap` object, we *can* modify it as needed—adding tiles, removing tiles, and so on. The tiles are fixed at 32 × 32 pixels since that is an assumption made for the game. There's no reason why we can't use a different tile size, since the source code can work with 32 × 32 or 64 × 64 or any other reasonable dimension as a variable just as well as a hard-coded pair of numbers.

The source code for the level editor is too long to list here, so I will instead recommend you open the editor project in the chapter's resource files (www. courseptr.com/downloads). In any event, the editor source code is a bit too much to cover in a single chapter, and this isn't a tool programming book either! The user interface has many complex controls such as splitters and panels to make the editor work correctly when the window is resized. We will not be

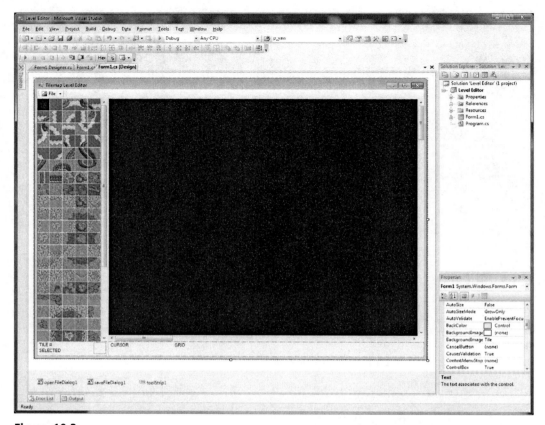

Figure 10.2
Editor GUI in the Form Designer of Visual Studio.

building the editor GUI here either, because that would be a daunting thing to explain step by step, if it's possible at all. I'll presume you have the project open while going over how it works. Figure 10.2 shows the editor in the form designer of Visual Studio.

On the left is the tile palette. This is the collection of source tiles used to create a game level, and each tile is 32 × 32 pixels in size. There is also a one-pixel border separating each tile in the palette. If you create your own palette or add to this one, be sure to maintain that one-pixel border between each tile because the editor (and the game!) counts on that space being there to work correctly. If you want to replace the palette image, just open up the PictureBox control's properties and choose a new image using its Image property. The height may be shorter or taller, but it's very important that you maintain the same width as the one currently in the editor! The current one has five tiles across. Just be sure any replacement palette image you want to use has the same five tiles in width and the replacement palette image should work fine!

Creating a New Tilemap Level

This early version of the editor does not know how to query the user for the filename when loading or saving a level file, so it just uses the same default filename when loading and saving. That filename is tilemap.xml, and it is located in Level Editor\bin\Debug. To create a new tilemap file, just rename tilemap.xml to a new filename and start up the editor to create a new tilemap.xml file automatically. Unfortunately, this is pretty typical of an early alpha version of a tool—it is functional but sorely lacking in usability features. The finished version in Chapter 13 has load/save dialogs that come up, among other useful features.

Loading and Saving Level Files

There is a single menu on the toolbar: File. This menu has several menu items under it:

- Save Editor Palette BMP (165 × 960)
- Save Tile Palette BMP (512 × 512)
- Save Level BMP (4096 × 4096)
- Load Tilemap XML
- Save Tilemap XML

Saving the Editor Palette

The first option, Save Editor Palette, saves the tile palette image (the tiles on the left side of the window) as a new bitmap file. The filename will be palette.bmp, and is shown in Figure 10.3. This file is useful if you want to edit the palette by replacing tiles or adding new tiles to it. If you want to do that, then the only way to import the new palette image is via the PictureBox control (the manual way). This shouldn't be much of a problem because the tile palette does not often change.

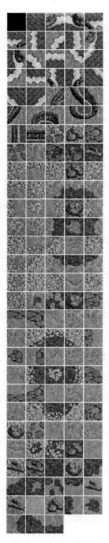

Figure 10.3
The editor's tile palette is saved to a bitmap file.

Saving the Tile Palette as a Texture

The second option, Save Tile Palette, exports the same tile palette image in a different format—a 512×512 bitmap file. This is useful in some cases because some game engines do not like bitmaps with odd dimensions. A Direct3D texture, for instance, works best with uniform dimensions like this and might

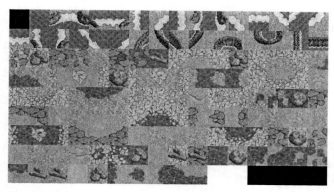

Figure 10.4
The editor's tile palette is saved to a bitmap file.

have difficulty loading a texture with a size of 165 × 960, which is the native size of the palette image. Figure 10.4 shows the exported texture file.

Saving the Whole Level as a Bitmap

The third option, Save Level, will export the entire tilemap as one huge bitmap! This is a pretty interesting option that lets you see the whole game level as one huge image, but I'm not sure if it's very useful in a game since it's so large. Beware, the file is 4096 × 4096 pixels—uncompressed it takes up 65 MB of memory!

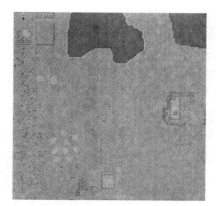

Figure 10.5
The complete tilemap is exported to a bitmap file.

Loading and Saving the Level

The tilemap level files are saved in .xml format. XML stands for Extensible Markup Language, and is similar to HTML (the language used for websites), in that it is a text format that you can open and read with a simple text editor. The following listing shows the first and last tiles in the tilemap.xml file saved by the level editor. Every tile is contained in a tag called "tiles," with an opening tag, <tiles>, and closing tag, "</tiles>". Within the tag are four properties: tile, value, x, and y.

```
<?xml version="1.0" standalone="yes"?>
<DocumentElement>
  <tiles>
    <tile>0</tile>
    <value>119</value>
    <x>0</x>
    <y>0</y>
  </tiles>
  .
  .
  .
  <tiles>
    <tile>16383</tile>
    <value>56</value>
    <x>127</x>
    <y>127</y>
  </tiles>
</DocumentElement>
```

As work continued on the level editor, I realized that the x and y values are completely unnecessary because the tile positions never change, and are based solely on the tile property. There are 128 × 128 tiles in a whole level, for a total of 16,384 tiles. That means there are also 16,384 <tiles> records in the .xml file. The value property is the key to the whole thing—that is the tile palette number, representing the image that should be shown for that tile.

LEVEL UP!

This chapter moved rather quickly through a brief tutorial on level design, which provided a working understanding of how a level editor should work to allow creating and editing game levels as tilemaps, before moving on to designing our own custom level editor for Celtic Crusader. The tilemap is the most important part of the game because it is the foundation—literally, it is *the world* on which our characters will walk. You can create a large, vast desert or a lush green world and populate it with vegetation and roads and even buildings. In the expanded version developed later, the editor will support collisions, portals, and additional data fields for each tile. But we have to start somewhere! It's my hope you will appreciate seeing the editor in this early state of development, and note the differences in the improved version.

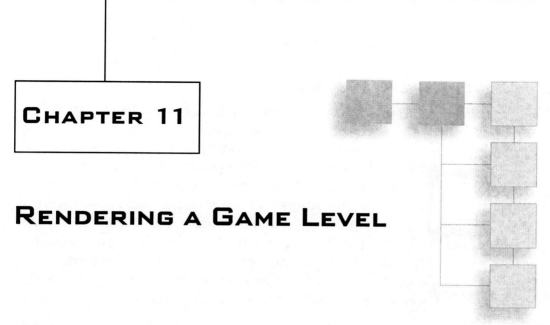

CHAPTER 11

RENDERING A GAME LEVEL

We're going to take our first steps into a new world in this chapter: we will be learning how to load a game level created with the custom level editor developed in Chapter 10. This editor gives us considerable leeway in how the game will play, and we will explore some of the gameplay possibilities related to the game world in this chapter. You will learn the techniques used in tile-based scrolling, gaining an understanding of how a scrolling display is created using a "partial-tile" buffered scrolling algorithm. We'll be using level data from our custom level editor program to construct the game world. By using a small surface about the same size as the screen, the tiles are drawn to the buffer in order to produce a smooth-scrolling game world. The resulting tile scrolling engine is the foundation for the Celtic Crusader game.

Here's what we'll cover in this chapter:

- Mapping the game world
- Loading and drawing the map/level file
- Introduction to tiled scrolling
- Scrolling a tiled game world
- Per-tile scrolling
- Per-pixel scrolling

MAPPING THE GAME WORLD

The first thing I discovered when attempting to create ninth-century Ireland using the level editor was that this game world has the potential of being *huge*. To manage the memory requirements of the game world, it should be divided up into many level files and linked together with portals. We'll learn more about portals in Chapter 13, "Using Portals to Expand the World." In the meantime, we'll focus on just rendering the tilemap for one level and begin to interact with the level. The goal is to put as much functionality into the rendering and interaction of one level as possible, because that very same functionality (such as preventing the characters from passing through solid objects) extends to any level. Getting one small portion of the game world up and running means that the *entire* game world can be rendered by the game engine based solely on the data files.

This is what we call *data-driven* programming—where the data describes what should happen, and the source code processes the data according to known rules. So, what we're doing here is applying professional software engineering methodology to our role-playing game engine. When you want to add a new feature to the game, and that feature is added to the engine based on properties in the level file, then suddenly *every* level you create has that feature. For example, let's consider collision tiles, because that is a feature we will be addressing shortly. The level editor lets us specify which tiles are collidable, and which tiles may be passed through. The collidable tiles should block the player from moving through them. Or, put differently: the *game* should prevent the player from moving through `collidable`—or let us say *solid*—tiles on the map. Any tile can be made solid by setting the property.

Tile-Based Ireland

Take a look at Figure 11.1, which shows the original map of ninth-century Ireland first introduced back in Chapter 9. As you may recall, this map was drawn by hand, scanned, and then cleaned up and enhanced. Why does the game need such a large game world? Actually, we don't need to re-create the entire land mass in the game, but having a good story up front helps with the gameplay since there are essentially endless places we can take the player in the game with such a large game world available. The gameplay we focus on just revolves around one area, but we could model any area of this game world using the level editor.

Figure 11.1
The original digitized and enhanced map of ninth-century Ireland.

The huge size of the game world in Celtic Crusader should be very encouraging to you, especially if you have a good imagination and you would like to create a massive RPG with a long, complex storyline and intense, varied character-development features. But this is just the beginning. By using portals, we could even open a "doorway" on the game world map into a dungeon, then after looting and pillaging (in classic RPG style), your character can return to the regular map again.

Trying to render the *entire* game world in one giant tile scroller tends to reduce the gameplay, and that was certainly the case with the game in the previous edition of this book. Now, we're taking an entirely different approach. Instead of editing one gigantic tilemap, we're going to create many smaller tilemaps with our own level

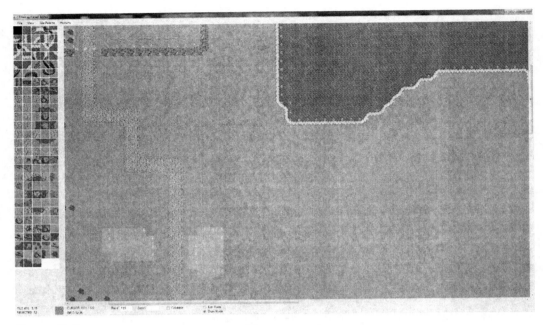

Figure 11.2
The level editor window is resizable for large widescreen displays.

editor. As you learned in the previous chapter, our tilemaps have a maximum size of 128 tiles across, and 128 tiles down, for a total *pixel* resolution of 4096 × 4096. Figure 11.2 shows the level editor enlarged so that more of this particular level is visible in the editor window. However, we don't have to *actually use* that full size for every map. By defining regions with the collidable property, we can limit the player's movements to a smaller area surrounded by trees or mountains or anything you want. Although the tilemap will remain fixed at 128 × 128, we can use much smaller areas, as well as combine several tilemaps (via portals) to create larger areas. The gameplay possibilities are endless!

Trick

I want to emphasize again that the game world truly has no limit when using level files with portal tiles. When a portal is entered, the game teleports the player to a new location. By using a portal *file* as well as the coordinates, we can even load up a new level file entirely and position the player at any location in that new file with the same technique. Furthermore, teleporting the player will be almost instantaneous. Which means, you could create a *huge* level with seamless edges by creating a strip of portal tiles along one edge so that when the player reaches that edge, the player continues to walk in the same direction. If the two level files are seamless in their edges, the player will never know they have just entered a new level file!

Loading and Drawing Level Files

Our custom level editor that was developed in Chapter 10 produces .xml files containing information about a game level. We can load the .xml file using .NET classes in the System.Xml namespace—so loading is not a problem. Rendering the level is where we'll focus most of our attention. First, let's just look at loading the data from a level file and render one screen full of tiles with it as a starting point. Until now, we have only seen game levels inside the editor, but now we'll be able to render the level with Basic code. To render a level, we need two things: 1) The tilemap data from the .xml file; and 2) The source tiles stored in a bitmap file. The level file describes the tile number that should be represented at each location in the game level. Here is the source code for the Level Viewer, shown in Figure 11.3. This example does not know how to scroll, but it's a good start.

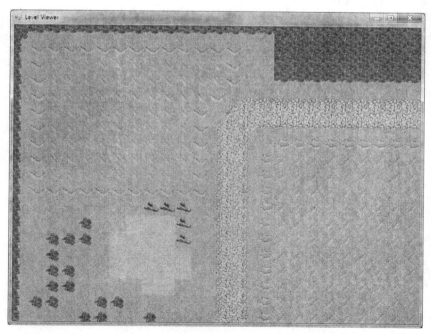

Figure 11.3
The Level Viewer demo displays just the upper-left corner of the game world.

```vbnet
Imports System.Xml
Public Class Form1
    Public Structure tilemapStruct
        Public tilenum As Integer
        Public data1 As String
        Public collidable As Boolean
    End Structure

    Const COLUMNS As Integer = 5
    Private bmpTiles As Bitmap
    Private bmpSurface As Bitmap
    Private pbSurface As PictureBox
    Private gfxSurface As Graphics
    Private fontArial As Font
    Private tilemap() As tilemapStruct

    Private Sub Form1_FormClosed(ByVal sender As Object, _
            ByVal e As System.Windows.Forms.FormClosedEventArgs) _
            Handles Me.FormClosed
        bmpSurface.Dispose()
        pbSurface.Dispose()
        gfxSurface.Dispose()
    End Sub

    Private Sub Form1_Load(ByVal sender As System.Object, _
            ByVal e As System.EventArgs) Handles MyBase.Load
        Me.Text = "Level Viewer"
        Me.Size = New Point(800 + 16, 600 + 38)
        REM create tilemap
        ReDim tilemap(128 * 128)
        REM set up level drawing surface
        bmpSurface = New Bitmap(800, 600)
        pbSurface = New PictureBox()
        pbSurface.Parent = Me
        pbSurface.BackColor = Color.Black
        pbSurface.Dock = DockStyle.Fill
        pbSurface.Image = bmpSurface
        gfxSurface = Graphics.FromImage(bmpSurface)
        REM create font
        fontArial = New Font("Arial Narrow", 8)
        REM load tiles bitmap
        bmpTiles = New Bitmap("palette.bmp")
```

```
        REM load the tilemap
        loadTilemapFile("tilemap.xml")
        drawTilemap()
    End Sub


    Private Sub loadTilemapFile(ByVal filename As String)
        Try
            Dim doc As XmlDocument = New XmlDocument()
            doc.Load(filename)
            Dim nodelist As XmlNodeList = doc.GetElementsByTagName("tiles")
            For Each node As XmlNode In nodelist
                Dim element As XmlElement = node
                Dim index As Integer = 0
                Dim value As Integer = 0
                Dim data1 As String = ""
                Dim collidable As Boolean = False
                REM read tile index #
                index = Convert.ToInt32( _
                    element.GetElementsByTagName("tile")(0).InnerText)
                REM read tilenum
                value = Convert.ToInt32( _
                    element.GetElementsByTagName("value")(0).InnerText)
                REM read data1
                data1 = Convert.ToString( _
                    element.GetElementsByTagName("data1")(0).InnerText)
                REM read collidable
                collidable = Convert.ToBoolean( _
                    element.GetElementsByTagName("collidable")(0).InnerText)
                tilemap(index).tilenum = value
                tilemap(index).data1 = data1
                tilemap(index).collidable = collidable
            Next
        Catch es As Exception
            MessageBox.Show(es.Message)
        End Try
    End Sub

    Private Sub drawTilemap()
        For x = 0 To 24
            For y = 0 To 18
                drawTileNumber(x, y, tilemap(y * 128 + x).tilenum)
```

```
            Next
        Next
    End Sub

    Public Sub drawTileNumber(ByVal x As Integer, ByVal y As Integer, _
            ByVal tile As Integer)
        REM draw tile
        Dim sx As Integer = (tile Mod COLUMNS) * 33
        Dim sy As Integer = (tile \ COLUMNS) * 33
        Dim src As New Rectangle(sx, sy, 32, 32)
        Dim dx As Integer = x * 32
        Dim dy As Integer = y * 32
        gfxSurface.DrawImage(bmpTiles, dx, dy, src, GraphicsUnit.Pixel)
        REM save changes
        pbSurface.Image = bmpSurface
    End Sub

    Private Sub Form1_KeyUp(ByVal sender As System.Object, _
            ByVal e As System.Windows.Forms.KeyEventArgs) _
            Handles MyBase.KeyUp
        If e.KeyCode = Keys.Escape Then End
    End Sub
End Class
```

Introduction to Tiled Scrolling

What is scrolling? In today's gaming world, where 3D is the focus of everyone's attention, it's not surprising to find gamers and programmers who have never heard of scrolling. What a shame! The heritage of modern games is a long and fascinating one that is still relevant today, even if it is not understood or appreciated. The console industry puts great effort and value into scrolling, particularly on handheld systems such as the Nintendo DS. *Scrolling* is the process of displaying a small window of a larger virtual game world. There are three basic ways to scroll the display:

▪ Loading a large tiled bitmap image

▪ Creating a large bitmap out of tiles at runtime

▪ Drawing tiles directly on the screen

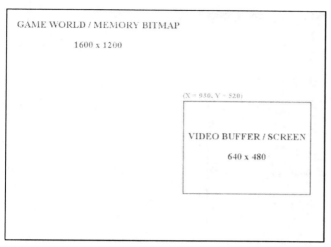

Figure 11.4
The scroll window shows a small part of a larger game world.

Figure 11.4 illustrates the concept of scrolling, which, in essence, involves the use of a large game world of which only a small portion is visible through the screen at a time.

The key to scrolling is having something in the virtual game world to display in the scroll window (or the screen). Also, I should point out that the entire screen need not be used as the scroll window. It is common to use the entire screen in scrolling-shooter games, but role-playing games (RPGs) often use a smaller window on the screen for scrolling, using the rest of the screen for gameplay (combat, inventory, and so on) and player/party information, as shown in Figure 11.5.

You could display one huge bitmap image in the virtual game world representing the current level of the game (or the *map*), and then copy a portion of that virtual world onto the screen. This is the simplest form of scrolling. Another method uses tiles to create the game world at runtime. Suppose we had a large bitmap file containing a pre-rendered image of the game world. You would then load up that large bitmap and copy a portion of it to the screen, and that portion would represent the current scroll position.

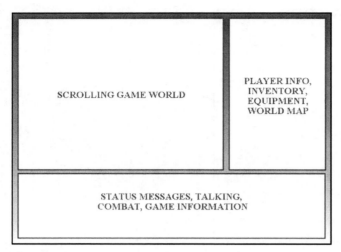

Figure 11.5
Some games use a smaller portion of the game screen for a scrolling window.

Constructing the Tiled Image

This theory of using a single large bitmap seems reasonable at first glance, but that method of scrolling has a very serious limitation. When you create a game world, the whole point is to interact with that game world. A single, large bitmap used to render the game world prevents you from actually tracking where the player is located on the map, as well as what other objects are on the map. In a tile-based game world, each tile is represented by a number, and that number has *meaning*. A tile containing a tree is *impassable*, whereas a tile of grass can be walked on. Of course, you could create a new array or some other method to keep track of the player, various enemies, and objects in the game world, but that requires a lot of extra work. There's a better way to do it. A high-speed scrolling arcade game automatically scrolls horizontally or vertically, displaying ground-, air-, or space-based terrain below the player's vehicle (usually represented by an airplane or spaceship). The point of such games is to keep the action moving so fast that the player doesn't have a chance to rest from one wave of enemies to the next.

Tile Buffer

Tiling is a process in which there really is no background, just an array of small images that make up the background as it is drawn. In other words, it is a virtual background and takes up very little memory compared to a full bitmapped background. You are already familiar with how tiling works after learning about the level editor, but you are probably wondering: How can I load tiles and make a scrolling game world out of a level file?

Most levels in a scrolling arcade game are quite large, comprised of thousands of tiles in one orientation or the other (usually just scrolling up and down—vertically—or left to right—horizontally). These types of games are called *shooters* for the most part, although the horizontally scrolling games are usually *platformers* (such as the original Mario games). Not only does your average Mario game have large scrolling levels, but those levels have parallax layers that make the background in the distance scroll by more slowly than the layer on which the player's character is walking.

When working on a new game, I find it helpful to start storing my tiles in a new image one by one as I need them, so that I can construct a new set of tiles for the game while I'm working on the game. This also helps to keep the tile numbers down to a smaller number. If you have a huge tile map with hundreds of tiles in it and you only need a few of them during the early stages of development, then you have to figure out where each tile must be drawn, and you have to work with a texture in memory.

Stepping Stones of the World

The process of drawing tiles to fill the game world reminds me of laying down stepping stones, and tiling is a perfect analogy for how this works. Basically, tiles of a larger pattern are laid down from left to right, top to bottom, in that order. The first row is added, one tile at a time, all the way across; then the next row down is filled in from left to right, and so on until the entire map is filled. A single large bitmap is just not used—that's amateur. Another possibility is that you could continue to use a single large bitmap, but *create* that bitmap at runtime, and fill it with tiles according to the map file and tile images. Although this solution would generate the game world on the fly, the resulting texture representing the game world would require several gigabytes of memory, which is not feasible.

Tile Rendering Theory

Now that you have a good understanding of what scrolling is and how we can edit tile maps and export them, let's take a look at the basic theory and code to actually draw a scrolling tile map on the screen. The problem with scrolling a large game world is that too much memory is required to create a texture in memory to contain an entire game world (even if you break the map into sections). You cannot create a single texture to hold the entire game world because most levels are far too large! It would consume so much memory that the program would not even run, and even if it did, that would be a *horrible* way to write a game. We're talking about old-school scrolling here, after all, from an era when video game systems had tiny amounts of memory—like 64kb! Surely we can figure out how *they* did it back then.

Let's examine a method of tile rendering that supports giant maps using very little memory. In fact, all the memory required for the tiled scroller developed here is a bitmap for the tiles and an array with all of the tile values, plus a screen-sized texture. (In other words, no more memory that would be needed for a background image.) A map comprised of several million tiles can be rendered by this tile engine and will require only a small memory footprint.

Figure 11.6 shows the game world with the scroll window superimposed, so you can see how the screen represents a portion of the game world. While viewing

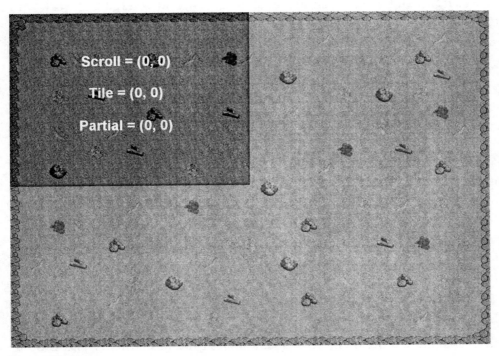

Figure 11.6
An example of a small game level.

this figure, imagine there is no image containing this game world map, just a virtual array of tile numbers. Those tiles are drawn *just* to the screen, based on what is visible in the darkened part of the figure. Do you see the rock border around the map? The border is helpful when you are developing a new tile scroller, because it shows the boundaries, allowing you to determine whether the scrolling view is being displayed at the correct location based on the scroll position. (In other words, it should stop scrolling when it reaches the edge of the "world," but should not skip any tiles.)

Now let's assume that you're using a screen resolution of 800 × 600, because this is a good resolution to use; it's relatively small so the screen updates quickly, but it is large enough to display a lot of details on the screen without crowding. We may even want to move up to 1024 × 768 at some point.

There is a simple calculation that gives you the tile number as well as the partial tile values relatively easily. Are you familiar with *modulus*? This is a mathematical operation that produces the *remainder* of a division operation. Let me give you a simple example:

$$10/5 = 2$$

This is simple enough to understand, right? What happens when you are using numbers that are not evenly divisible?

$$10/3 = 3.33333333$$

This is a problem, because the remainder is not an even number, and we're talking about pixels here. You can't deal with parts of a pixel! However, you can work with parts of a tile, because tiles are made up of many pixels. Thinking in terms of complete tiles here, let's take a look at that division again:

$$10/3 = 3, \text{ with a remainder of } 0.33333333$$

Let me now use numbers more relevant to the problem at hand:

$$800/64 = 12.5$$

This represents a calculation that returns the number of tiles that fit on a screen with a width of 800 pixels (assuming the tiles are 64 pixels wide). What does 12.5 tiles mean when you are writing a scroller? The .5 represents a *part* of a tile that must be drawn; hence, I call it *partial-tile scrolling*. Switching to 32×32 pixel tiles results in an evenly divisible screen, at least horizontally (32×32 results in 25 tiles across, 18.75 tiles down).

Here is where it gets really interesting! After you have drawn your tiles across the screen, and you want to fill in the remaining .5 of a tile, you can calculate the size of the tile like so:

$$64 \times 0.5 = 32$$

That is, 32 pixels of the partial tile must be drawn to handle the scrolling edge that was not lined up with a tile edge on the map. Rather than keeping track of the remainder at all, there is a simpler way to calculate the portion of the tile that must be drawn, in the measurement of pixels:

$$800 \text{ Mod } 64 = 32$$

Hint

The *modulus* operator ("Mod" in Basic) is similar to operators like multiply, divide, add, and subtract, but it simply returns the remainder of a division, which works great for our purposes here.

Try not to think of scrolling in *screen* terms, because the whole discussion revolves around the tile map in memory (the tile data itself). The tile data is expanded to full tiles when drawn to the screen, but until that happens, these tiles might be thought of as a huge virtual game world from which the scrolling window is drawn.

Try another problem so you get the hang of calculating partial tiles before we get into the source code. Suppose the scroll position is at (700,0) on the map, and the tiles are again 64×6432. Which would be the starting tile, and what is the value of the partial tile (in pixels)? To calculate first the tile position in the map data array, just drop the decimal part, which represents the remainder:

$$700/64 = 10.9375 \text{ (10 whole tiles plus a partial tile)}$$

Next, you *do* want to keep the remainder, and actually drop the tile position itself, because now you're interested in pixels.

700 Mod 64 = 60

To verify that this calculation is correct, you can do the following:

64 × 0.9375 = 60

The modulus operator greatly helps with this calculation by skipping that middle step. It simply provides the remainder value directly, giving the exact number of pixels that must be drawn from the partial tile to fill in the top and left edges of the screen. I have shown the calculation in Figure 11.7, which is based on 64 × 64-pixel tiles.

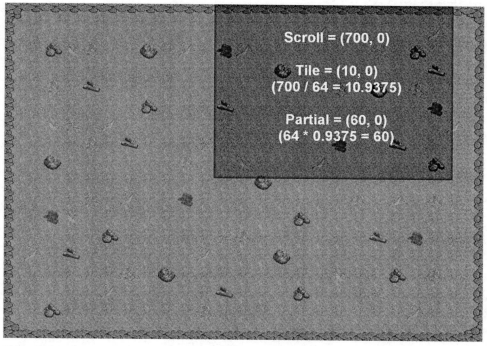

Figure 11.7
An example of how the partial tile calculation is performed at position (700,0).

Ready for another try at it? This time, calculate the tile numbers and partial-tile values for both the X and Y position of the scroll window at (372, 489). Below is the answer, but see if you can figure it out before looking. . . .

First the X value:

$$372/64 = 5.8125 \text{ (tile X = 5)}$$
$$64 \times 0.8125 = 52 \text{ (pixels)}$$

Now for the Y value:

$$489/64 = 7.640625 \text{ (tile Y = 7)}$$
$$64 \times 0.640625 = 41 \text{ (pixels)}$$

The same calculations are used for any size of tile, from 16×16 to 32×32 or any other size.

PER-TILE SCROLLING

Scrolling the level one tile at a time produces fairly good results, especially if you need extremely high performance in a very fast-paced game. Of course, a role-playing game is not a hectic, fast-paced scroller, but we do still need good performance. For an RPG, we need slower, more precise scrolling that is not possible with a full-tile scroller. What we need is sub-tile scrolling at a per-pixel rate. Let's learn the full-time method first, since that may come in handy for another game or two, and then we'll look at the sub-tile method.

Full Tile Scrolling

For the full tile-based scroller, we'll be keeping track of the scroll position as it relates to entire tiles with a width and height of 32×32, which is the effective scroll rate (since each tile is 32 pixels across). The Level Scroller demo shown in Figure 11.8 and listed below does let you move around and look at the whole level but only one step at a time. There is something appealing about this scroller. I like how precise it is, moving one whole tile at a time, and think this would work great for a turn-based war game or a *Civilization* type game. We'll peruse just the important code for the Level Scroller demo. The loadTilemapFile() function was already presented in the previous example, so we'll just skip any functions like this that have already been shown.

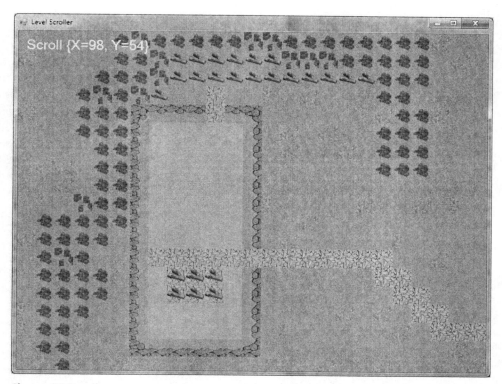

Figure 11.8
The Level Scroller demo scrolls the game world in one-tile increments.

```
Private Sub Form1_Load(ByVal sender As System.Object, _
        ByVal e As System.EventArgs) Handles MyBase.Load
    Me.Text = "Level Scroller"
    Me.Size = New Point(800 + 16, 600 + 38)
    REM create tilemap
    ReDim tilemap(128 * 128)
    REM set up level drawing surface
    bmpSurface = New Bitmap(800, 600)
    pbSurface = New PictureBox()
    pbSurface.Parent = Me
    pbSurface.BackColor = Color.Black
    pbSurface.Dock = DockStyle.Fill
    pbSurface.Image = bmpSurface
    gfxSurface = Graphics.FromImage(bmpSurface)
    REM create font
```

```
fontArial = New Font("Arial Bold", 18)
REM load the tilemap
bmpTiles = New Bitmap("palette.bmp")
loadTilemapFile("tilemap.xml")
drawTilemap()
End Sub
```

The drawTilemap() function assumes we have an 800 × 600 display (800/32 = 25 tiles across, and 600 / 32 = 19 tiles down).

```
Private Sub drawTilemap()
    Dim tilenum, sx, sy As Integer
    For x = 0 To 24
        For y = 0 To 18
            sx = scrollPos.X + x
            sy = scrollPos.Y + y
            tilenum = tilemap(sy * 128 + sx).tilenum
            drawTileNumber(x, y, tilenum)
        Next
    Next
End Sub
```

The drawTileNumber() function uses the modulus operator to draw a tile from the tile palette image (which looks like a vertical strip of five tiles across, shown in the previous chapter). This function does not handle partial-tile scrolling as discussed, but does use the same modulus operator for a similar purpose of drawing a tile out of a source image. The same function can be found in the level editor's source code.

```
Public Sub drawTileNumber(ByVal x As Integer, ByVal y As Integer, _
        ByVal tile As Integer)
    REM draw tile
    Dim sx As Integer = (tile Mod COLUMNS) * 33
    Dim sy As Integer = (tile \ COLUMNS) * 33
    Dim src As New Rectangle(sx, sy, 32, 32)
    Dim dx As Integer = x * 32
    Dim dy As Integer = y * 32
    gfxSurface.DrawImage(bmpTiles, dx, dy, src, GraphicsUnit.Pixel)

    REM save changes
    pbSurface.Image = bmpSurface
End Sub
```

The `Form1_KeyUp()` event is really the part of this program that causes things to happen. Based on user input, the tilemap is redrawn at a new scroll position. The `drawTilemap()` function does the work of filling in the window with tiles at the correct location of the tilemap.

```
    Private Sub Form1_KeyUp(ByVal sender As System.Object, _
            ByVal e As System.Windows.Forms.KeyEventArgs) _
            Handles MyBase.KeyUp
        Select Case (e.KeyCode)
            Case Keys.Escape
                End
            Case Keys.Up, Keys.W
                scrollPos.Y -= 1
                If scrollPos.Y < 0 Then scrollPos.Y = 0
                drawTilemap()
            Case Keys.Down, Keys.S
                scrollPos.Y += 1
                If scrollPos.Y > 127 - 18 Then scrollPos.Y = 127 - 18
                drawTilemap()
            Case Keys.Left, Keys.A
                scrollPos.X -= 1
                If scrollPos.X < 0 Then scrollPos.X = 0
                drawTilemap()
            Case Keys.Right, Keys.D
                scrollPos.X += 1
                If scrollPos.X > 127 - 24 Then scrollPos.X = 127 - 24
                drawTilemap()
        End Select
        Dim text As String = "Scroll " + scrollPos.ToString()
        gfxSurface.DrawString(text, fontArial, Brushes.White, 10, 10)
    End Sub
```

Full-Tile Smooth Scrolling

The preceding example showed how to scroll the level one tile per keypress, which would work for a turn-based game but is otherwise too slow. We'll now take a look at how to scroll while a key is pressed without requiring the user to hit the key repeatedly. The main difference between this and the preceding example is that a flag is used to track the key press and release states for the keys Up, Down, Left, and Right. As long as a key is being held, the map will continue

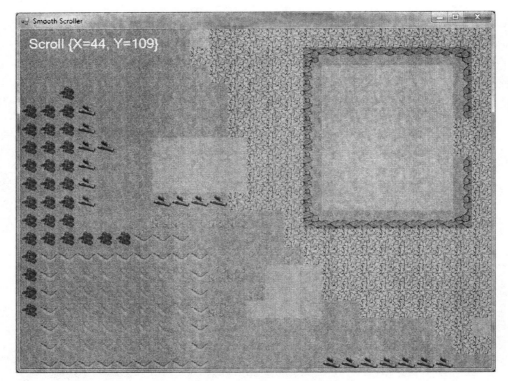

Figure 11.9
The Smooth Scroller demo scrolls the game world quickly and smoothly.

to scroll in that direction. The Smooth Scroller demo is shown in Figure 11.9. Its code follows. Since only a few changes have been made, only the modified code is shown.

```
Public Structure keyStates
    Public up, down, left, right As Boolean
End Structure

Const COLUMNS As Integer = 5
Private bmpTiles As Bitmap
Private bmpSurface As Bitmap
Private pbSurface As PictureBox
Private gfxSurface As Graphics
Private fontArial As Font
Private tilemap() As tilemapStruct
```

```
Private scrollPos As New PointF(0, 0)
Private oldScrollPos As New PointF(-1, -1)
Private keyState As keyStates
Private WithEvents timer1 As Timer

Private Sub Form1_Load(ByVal sender As System.Object, _
        ByVal e As System.EventArgs) Handles MyBase.Load
    Me.Text = "Smooth Scroller"
    Me.Size = New Point(800 + 16, 600 + 38)
    REM create tilemap
    ReDim tilemap(128 * 128)
    REM set up level drawing surface
    bmpSurface = New Bitmap(800, 600)
    pbSurface = New PictureBox()
    pbSurface.Parent = Me
    pbSurface.BackColor = Color.Black
    pbSurface.Dock = DockStyle.Fill
    pbSurface.Image = bmpSurface
    gfxSurface = Graphics.FromImage(bmpSurface)
    REM create font
    fontArial = New Font("Arial Bold", 18)
    REM load the tilemap
    bmpTiles = New Bitmap("palette.bmp")
    loadTilemapFile("tilemap.xml")
    REM start the timer
    timer1 = New Timer()
    timer1.Interval = 20
    timer1.Enabled = True
End Sub

Private Sub Form1_KeyDown(ByVal sender As Object, _
        ByVal e As System.Windows.Forms.KeyEventArgs) _
        Handles Me.KeyDown
    Select Case (e.KeyCode)
        Case Keys.Up, Keys.W : keyState.up = True
        Case Keys.Down, Keys.S : keyState.down = True
        Case Keys.Left, Keys.A : keyState.left = True
        Case Keys.Right, Keys.D : keyState.right = True
    End Select
End Sub
```

```
Private Sub Form1_KeyUp(ByVal sender As System.Object, _
        ByVal e As System.Windows.Forms.KeyEventArgs) _
        Handles MyBase.KeyUp
    Select Case (e.KeyCode)
        Case Keys.Escape : End
        Case Keys.Up, Keys.W : keyState.up = False
        Case Keys.Down, Keys.S : keyState.down = False
        Case Keys.Left, Keys.A : keyState.left = False
        Case Keys.Right, Keys.D : keyState.right = False
    End Select
End Sub
```

The "engine" behind this example is based on a Timer control called `timer1`, and the `timer1_tick()` function fires off regularly, which is what makes this a real-time program. Even if no scrolling is taking place, this function still causes the tilemap to redraw at a fast pace.

```
Private Sub timer1_tick() Handles timer1.Tick
    If keyState.up Then
        scrollPos.Y -= 1
        If scrollPos.Y < 0 Then scrollPos.Y = 0
    End If
    If keyState.down Then
        scrollPos.Y += 1
        If scrollPos.Y > 127 - 18 Then scrollPos.Y = 127 - 18
    End If
    If keyState.left Then
        scrollPos.X -= 1
        If scrollPos.X < 0 Then scrollPos.X = 0
    End If
    If keyState.right Then
        scrollPos.X += 1
        If scrollPos.X > 127 - 24 Then scrollPos.X = 127 - 24
    End If

    drawTilemap()

    Dim text As String = "Scroll " + scrollPos.ToString()
    gfxSurface.DrawString(text, fontArial, Brushes.White, 10, 10)
    End Sub
End Class
```

PER-PIXEL SCROLLING

Finally, we come to per-pixel, sub-tile scrolling. In the preceding example, the level was moved one tile at a time—that is, one whole row or column at a time. This is a good and fast way to move around the game world, and is the way I would recommend when you need to warp or jump from one location in the level to another very quickly. But for individual character movement in the game world, we need a slower, more precise form of scrolling, where only a few pixels at a time are shifted in the scroll direction. In order to accomplish this, we need a new feature—a scroll buffer. This buffer will be slightly larger than the screen, with a border around it equal to the size of the tiles. So, if our tiles are 32 × 32 pixels, then we need a 32-pixel border around the scroll buffer.

Sub-Tile Scrolling

The key to implementing a dynamic sub-tile scrolling engine is a third buffer in memory (so called because the screen and back buffer are the first two), upon which the tiles are drawn at the current scroll position. The word *dynamic* here refers to the way the tile engine draws what is needed at that particular point in the game world, while *sub-tile* refers to the way it draws full tiles and partial tiles to fill the borders. If you think about it, the tiles are 32 × 32 pixels in size so without the partial-tile capability, drawing tiles directly to the screen one portion at a time results in very jumpy scrolling, where the screen is only updated whenever complete tiles can be drawn (as was the case in the preceding example).

To make this technique work, we start with a `Point` variable called `scrollPos` to keep track of the scroll position. When drawing tiles directly, these variables give a precise position at which the tiles should start drawing in a left-to-right, top-to-bottom orientation. If the scroll position is at (500,500), what does this mean, exactly? It means that the tiles specified in the map should be drawn at the upper-left corner of the screen, *from* the position of the 500 × 500 point in the game world. Try to keep this concept in mind when you are working on scrolling, because the screen position is always the same: the scrolling view is rendered onto the screen at the upper left, 0 × 0. While the scroll position changes all the time, the destination location on the screen never changes. We're drawing one screen worth of the game world at a time, from any location in that game world. At the same time, we want to render the tiles that make up that portion of the game world *dynamically,* in order to keep the scroll engine efficient.

Drawing the Scroll Buffer

After you have filled the scroll buffer with tiles for the current scroll position within the game world, the next thing you must do is actually draw the scroll buffer to the screen. This is where things get a little interesting. The scroll buffer is filled only with complete tiles, but it is from here that the partial tiles are taken into account. This is interesting because the whole tiles were drawn onto the scroll buffer, but the partial tiles are handled when drawing the scroll buffer to the screen. The Point variable called `subtile` is given the result of the modulus calculation, and these values are then used as the upper-left corner of the scroll buffer that is copied to the screen.

Remember, the scrolling window is just the beginning. The rest of the game still has to be developed, and that includes a lot of animated sprites for the player's character, non-player characters (NPCs), plus buildings, animals, and any other objects that appear in the game. The bottom line is that the scroller needs to be as efficient as possible. (Yes, even with today's fast PCs, the scroller needs to be fast—never use the argument that PCs are fast to excuse poorly written code!).

Aligning Tiles to the Scroll Buffer

There is one factor that you must take into consideration while designing the screen layout of your game with a scrolling window. The size of the scrolling window must be evenly divisible by the size of the tiles, or you end up with a *floating overlap* at the uneven edge. This is an issue that I considered solving in the scrolling code itself. But it turns out that this is unnecessary because you can just change the destination rectangle when drawing the scroll buffer to the screen (something we'll explore later in this chapter with the "Scrolling Viewport" program).

If using a screen resolution of 800 × 600 with 32 × 32 tiles, your width is fine, but height doesn't quite line up evenly. Cut off the bottom of the scroll window at 576 (which is 18 tiles high), leaving the remaining 24 pixels unused at the bottom. This shouldn't be a problem because you can use that screen real estate for things like an in-game menu system, player status information, or perhaps in-game dialog (not to be confused with the discussion earlier about partial tiles.

We may want to limit the scrolling window to a portion of the screen as it makes more sense than displaying game information over the top of the scrolling window. This holds true unless we are doing something cool like drawing transparent windows over the top of the background. Two more options occur to me: we could just scale the buffer to fill the screen, or we could just draw the extra tile at the bottom and crop it.

Sub-Tile Scroll Buffering

Now we come to sub-tile scrolling, the type we need for a slow-paced RPG, in which a character walks around in the game world. This type of game requires a scroller with per-pixel granularity. In other words, scrolling at the pixel level rather than at the full tile level (which was 32 pixels at a time). I've called this method "sub-tile scroll buffering" because the game world needs to scroll slowly in any direction one pixel at a time. Some familiar techniques can be used again, but we need to modify the code quite a bit to support this more advanced form of scrolling.

To help you understand this technique better, I've created two examples. The first example (shown in Figure 11.10) just demonstrates how the scroll buffer works by

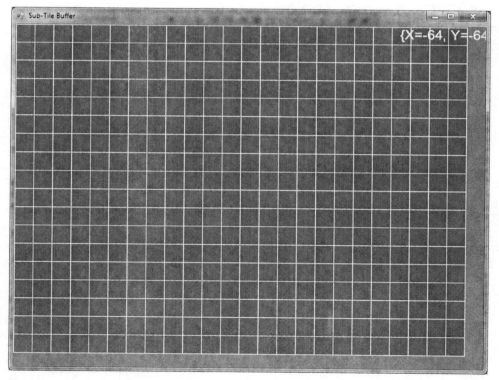

Figure 11.10
The key to dynamic sub-tile scrolling is the buffer border.

letting you move the scroll buffer around on the screen. The final example coming up in the next section demonstrates scrolling a game level with this technique. Again, only the key code is shown here for reference, not the complete code listing (with wasteful repeating of code). This project is called Sub-Tile Buffer Demo in the chapter's resources (www.courseptr.com/downloads).

```
Private Sub Form1_Load(ByVal sender As System.Object, _
        ByVal e As System.EventArgs) Handles MyBase.Load
    Me.Text = "Sub-Tile Buffer Demo"
    Me.Size = New Point(800 + 16, 600 + 38)
    REM set up level drawing surface
    bmpSurface = New Bitmap(800, 600)
    pbSurface = New PictureBox()
    pbSurface.Parent = Me
    pbSurface.BackColor = Color.Black
    pbSurface.Dock = DockStyle.Fill
    pbSurface.Image = bmpSurface
    gfxSurface = Graphics.FromImage(bmpSurface)
    REM create fonts
    fontArial12 = New Font("Arial", 12)
    fontArial18 = New Font("Arial", 18)
    REM create scroll buffer
    bmpScrollBuffer = New Bitmap(25 * 32 + 64, 19 * 32 + 64)
    gfxScrollBuffer = Graphics.FromImage(bmpScrollBuffer)
    REM fill buffer "border" area
    gfxScrollBuffer.FillRectangle(Brushes.Gray, _
        New Rectangle(0, 0, bmpScrollBuffer.Width, bmpScrollBuffer.Height))
    REM fill "screen" buffer area
    gfxScrollBuffer.FillRectangle(Brushes.BlueViolet, _
        New Rectangle(32, 32, 25 * 32, 19 * 32))

    For y = 0 To 18
        For x = 0 To 24
            gfxScrollBuffer.DrawRectangle(Pens.White, _
                32 + x * 32, 32 + y * 32, 32, 32)
        Next
    Next

    gfxScrollBuffer.DrawString("SCROLL BUFFER BORDER", fontArial12, _
        Brushes.White, 0, 0)
```

```
            REM get this thing running
            timer1 = New Timer()
            timer1.Interval = 16
            timer1.Enabled = True
        End Sub


        Private Sub timer1_tick() Handles timer1.Tick
            If keyState.down Then
                scrollPos.Y -= 2
                If scrollPos.Y < -64 Then scrollPos.Y = -64
            End If
            If keyState.up Then
                scrollPos.Y += 2
                If scrollPos.Y > 0 Then scrollPos.Y = 0
            End If
            If keyState.right Then
                scrollPos.X -= 2
                If scrollPos.X < -64 Then scrollPos.X = -64
            End If
            If keyState.left Then
                scrollPos.X += 2
                If scrollPos.X > 0 Then scrollPos.X = 0
            End If

            gfxSurface.DrawImage(bmpScrollBuffer, scrollPos)
            gfxSurface.DrawString(scrollPos.ToString(), fontArial18, _
                Brushes.White, 650, 0)
            pbSurface.Image = bmpSurface
        End Sub
```

Sub-Tile Smooth Scrolling

Now for the final example of the chapter—the sub-tile smooth scrolling. In the preceding example, you could see how the scroll buffer works with a border around the edges of the buffer to take into account the partial tiles. This produces smooth per-pixel scrolling in any direction. Figure 11.11 shows the example program that displays the right and bottom edges of the buffer so you can see how the sub-tile scroller works. (Note: there is a commented-out line of code that will render the scroll buffer smoothly without showing the partial tiles if you wish to see it, but this is more interesting as a learning experience with the tiles left in.)

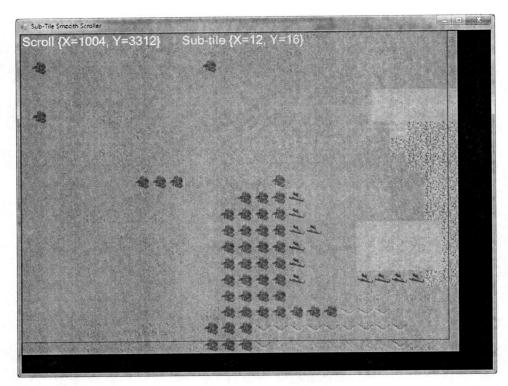

Figure 11.11
Smooth sub-tile scrolling is accomplished using an image buffer.

This tile scroller is now finished. We have data specific to each tile for use in gameplay (such as the `collidable` property), and a moving game world. However, there are optimizations that can still be made to this scroller—plus, we might want to create a reusable class to consolidate the code a bit. I think it would be nice if we could just call one function to load the tilemap, and another to draw it at any given position in the game level. This source code is found in the project called Sub-Tile Smooth Scroller in the chapter's resources.

```
Private Sub Form1_Load(ByVal sender As System.Object, _
        ByVal e As System.EventArgs) Handles MyBase.Load
    Me.Text = "Sub-Tile Smooth Scroller"
    Me.Size = New Point(900, 700)

    REM set up level drawing surface
    bmpSurface = New Bitmap(1024, 768)
```

```
        pbSurface = New PictureBox()
        pbSurface.Parent = Me
        pbSurface.BackColor = Color.Black
        pbSurface.Dock = DockStyle.Fill
        pbSurface.Image = bmpSurface
        gfxSurface = Graphics.FromImage(bmpSurface)

        REM create font
        fontArial = New Font("Arial Bold", 18)

        REM create tilemap
        ReDim tilemap(128 * 128)
        bmpTiles = New Bitmap("palette.bmp")
        loadTilemapFile("tilemap.xml")

        REM create scroll buffer
        bmpScrollBuffer = New Bitmap(25 * 32 + 32, 19 * 32 + 32)
        gfxScrollBuffer = Graphics.FromImage(bmpScrollBuffer)

        REM get this thing running
        timer1 = New Timer()
        timer1.Interval = 10
        timer1.Enabled = True
End Sub

Private Sub updateScrollBuffer()
        REM fill scroll buffer with tiles
        Dim tilenum, sx, sy As Integer
        For x = 0 To 25
            For y = 0 To 19
                sx = scrollPos.X \ 32 + x
                sy = scrollPos.Y \ 32 + y
                tilenum = tilemap(sy * 128 + sx).tilenum
                drawTileNumber(x, y, tilenum)
            Next
        Next
End Sub

Public Sub drawScrollBuffer()
        REM fill the scroll buffer only when moving
```

```
        If scrollPos <> oldScrollPos Then
            updateScrollBuffer()
            oldScrollPos = scrollPos
        End If

        REM calculate sub-tile size
        subtile.X = scrollPos.X Mod 32
        subtile.Y = scrollPos.Y Mod 32

        REM create the source rect
        REM Note that this example shows the edges of the scroll buffer
        REM but for production, use the commented-out line instead
        Dim source As New Rectangle(subtile.X, subtile.Y, _
            bmpScrollBuffer.Width, bmpScrollBuffer.Height)
        'Dim source As New Rectangle(subtile.X, subtile.Y, 800, 600)

        REM draw the scroll viewport
        gfxSurface.DrawImage(bmpScrollBuffer, 1, 1, source, GraphicsUnit.Pixel)
    End Sub

    Private Sub timer1_tick() Handles timer1.Tick
        REM respond to user input
        Dim steps As Integer = 4
        If keyState.up Then
            scrollPos.Y -= steps
            If scrollPos.Y < 0 Then scrollPos.Y = 0
        End If
        If keyState.down Then
            scrollPos.Y += steps
            If scrollPos.Y > (127 - 19) * 32 Then
                scrollPos.Y = (127 - 19) * 32
            End If
        End If
        If keyState.left Then
            scrollPos.X -= steps
            If scrollPos.X < 0 Then scrollPos.X = 0
        End If
        If keyState.right Then
            scrollPos.X += steps
            If scrollPos.X > (127 - 25) * 32 Then
```

```
                scrollPos.X = (127 - 25) * 32
            End If
        End If

        gfxSurface.Clear(Color.Black)

        drawScrollBuffer()

        gfxSurface.DrawString("Scroll " + scrollPos.ToString(), _
            fontArial, Brushes.White, 0, 0)
        gfxSurface.DrawString("Sub-tile " + subtile.ToString(), _
            fontArial, Brushes.White, 300, 0)

        gfxSurface.DrawRectangle(Pens.Blue, 0, 0, 801, 601)
        gfxSurface.DrawRectangle(Pens.Blue, 1, 1, 801, 601)
        pbSurface.Image = bmpSurface
    End Sub
End Class
```

LEVEL UP!

Wow, that was a ton of great information and some killer source code! This gives us enough information to begin working on the game world of Celtic Crusader! I don't know about you, but after this long wait, it feels good to have reached this point. Now that we have a level editor and a working level renderer, we can begin working on gameplay. Although the tilemap is drawing, we aren't using any of the extended data fields (such as collidable), which is the topic of the next two chapters!

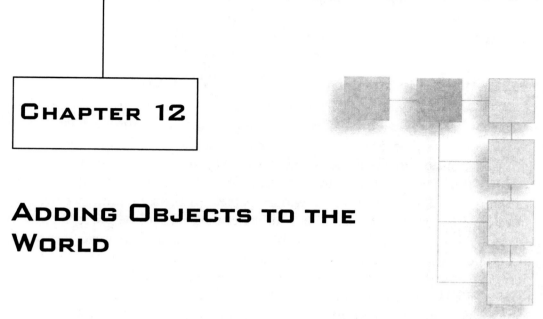

CHAPTER 12

ADDING OBJECTS TO THE WORLD

In this chapter we will learn how to add objects to the game world in such a way that they will show up when the viewport scrolls. This will require some coding trickery that goes a bit beyond the usual fare that we've needed so far, so if your experience with the Basic language is somewhat on the light side, you will want to pay close attention to the explanations here. We will go back to using the Game class that was first introduced back in Chapter 5, "Bitmaps: Our First Building Block", which handles most of the "framework" code needed for a game that has been put on hold while building the level editor and testing out game levels. But now we can return to the Game class, as well as the Sprite class from Chapter 6, "Sprites and Real-Time Animation".

Here's what we'll cover in this chapter:

- Adding scenery to the game world
- A new game loop
- Level class
- Adding trees
- Adding an animated character

ADDING SCENERY TO THE GAME WORLD

Our game level editor works great for creating tilemaps, and it has support for additional data fields and a collision property. But, there comes a point when you need more than just the tilemap data to make a real game—you need interactive objects in the game world as well. So, the first thing we're going to learn in this chapter is how to add some scenery objects, using the tilemap scrolling code developed in the previous chapter. At the same time, we need to address performance. The scrolling code takes up 100% of the processor when the scroll buffer is being refilled continuously. Even if you move the scroll position one pixel, the entire buffer is rebuilt. That is consuming huge amounts of processor time! It might not even be noticeable on a typical multi-core system today, but a laptop user would definitely notice because that tends to use up the battery very quickly. In addition to adding scenery, we'll work on a new core game loop that is more efficient.

A New Game Loop

If you open up the Sub-Tile Smooth Scroller project from the previous chapter, watch it run while looking at your processor's performance in Task Manager. To open Task Manager, you can right-click the Windows toolbar and choose Start Task Manager, or you can press Ctrl+Alt+Delete to bring up the switch user screen to find Task Manager. Figure 12.1 shows Task Manager while the aforementioned demo is running. Note how one of the cores is pretty much maxed out while the others are idle—that's because the program is running in just one thread, and it's pushing the processor pretty hard for such a seemingly simple graphics demo.

The reason for this processor abuse is the use of a timer for rendering. For reference, here is a cropped version of the timer1_tick() function from Chapter 11.

```
Private Sub timer1_tick() Handles timer1.Tick
    REM respond to user input
    Dim steps As Integer = 4
    ...

    REM refresh window
    pbSurface.Image = bmpSurface
End Sub
```

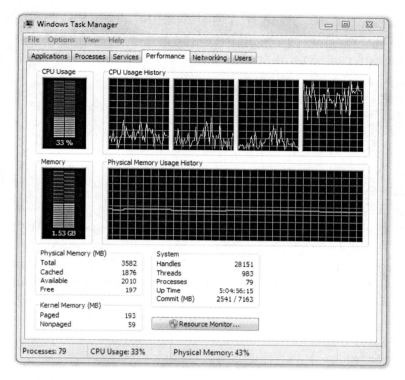

Figure 12.1
Observing processor utilization in Task Manager.

The `timer` event began firing when the `timer1` object was created via this code in `Form1_Load`:

```
REM get this thing running
timer1 = New Timer()
timer1.Interval = 10
timer1.Enabled = True
```

The `Timer` class was never really intended to be used as the engine for a high-speed game loop! Timers are more often used to fire off signals at regular intervals for hardware devices, to monitor a database for changes, that sort of thing. It does not have very good *granularity*, which means precision at high speed. So, we need to replace the timer with our own real-time loop. I've got just the thing—a `While` loop. But, Visual Basic programs are graphical and forms-based, so we can't just make a loop and do what we want, because that will freeze up the form. Fortunately, there's a function that will do all of the events: Application.DoEvents(). This code can be added to the end of Form1_Load so it's the last thing that runs after everything has been loaded for the game:

```
Dim gameover as Boolean = False
While Not gameover
    doUpdate()
End While
```

Modifying Game.vb

Somewhere in that doUpdate() function, we have to call Application.DoEvents() so the form can be refreshed. If we call it every frame, that will also be wasteful because Application.DoEvents() processes the event messages for form controls (like the Timer as well as for drawing the controls). If we call it every frame, then our game loop will be even more limited than it was with the timer! No, we need to learn just when and where to use this function and that calls for a knowledge of frame-rate timing.

```
Public Function FrameRate() As Integer
    Static count As Integer = 0
    Static lastTime As Integer = 0
    Static frames As Integer = 0
    REM calculate core frame rate
    Dim ticks As Integer = Environment.TickCount()
    count += 1
    If ticks > lastTime + 1000 Then
        lastTime = ticks
        frames = count
        count = 0
    End If
    Return frames
End Function
```

Do you recall the Game class from way back in Chapter 5? We will be using the Game class again in this chapter. The Game class is a good home for the FrameRate() function. While we're at it, let's add two more helper functions that we need for calculating random numbers (which is good for simulating the rolling of dice—absolutely essential when rolling new RPG characters!).

```
Private p_random As Random
```

```
Public Function Random(ByVal max As Integer)
    Return Random(0, max)
End Function

Public Function Random(ByVal min As Integer, ByVal max As Integer)
    Return p_random.Next(min, max)
End Function
```

A New Game Loop

Now that those dependencies are added, let's take a look at the new doUpdate() function, which is called from within the main While loop that will drive our game. I'll stick with just the bare minimum for now, leaving out any code specific to one example or another, and just show you a skeleton version of the function.

```
Private Sub doUpdate()
    Dim frameRate As Integer = game.FrameRate()
    Dim ticks As Integer = Environment.TickCount()
    Static drawLast As Integer = 0
    If ticks > drawLast + 16 Then
        drawLast = ticks
        game.Print(0, 0, "Frame rate " + frameRate.ToString())
        game.Update()
        Application.DoEvents()
    Else
        Threading.Thread.Sleep(1)
    End If
End Sub
```

Resolutions

One problem with a game based on Windows Forms and GDI+ is the lack of a fullscreen mode. Although we could extend the resolution of the game window to any desired size, it would be scaled necessarily to that target resolution, not rendered with higher detail. We could, for example, run the game at 1600 × 1200 by scaling the output of 800 x 600 by a factor of two. This would work, and the result might look pretty good since it's an even factor (odd factors tend to produce bad results when scaling graphics).

This bare minimum version of doUpdate() handles its own timing and is more action packed than it at first appears. First, we need to get the frame rate from the Game class, and this needs to happen *before* the If statement, because it needs to run as fast as possible. Everything within the If statement block of code is *slowed down* code for rendering. Anything we need to draw in the game goes inside that If block.

```
If ticks > drawLast + 16 Then
```

The If statement will be true once every 16 milliseconds. Where does that value come from? That is approximately 60 frames per second—a desirable goal for a game.

1 second = 1000 ms

delay = 1000 ms / 60 fps

delay = 16.66667 ms

Truncating the decimal part gives our code a few free frames per second, causing the actual frame rate to clock in at around 64 fps, but that depends on the processor—it might be less than 60 on some systems. The point is, we need this uber-vital code in the game loop to keep slow stuff from bottlenecking the whole game! That's exactly what was happening in Chapter 11's demos, which had no time-limiting code.

So, we first get the current system timer value in milliseconds with Environment. TickCount(), which will be some large millisecond number like 3828394918. That doesn't matter. What matters is *how many milliseconds* transpire from one frame to the next. Keeping track of that tick value in the drawLast variable allows our code to use it for comparison in the next frame. If at least 16 ms have gone by since the last time drawLast was set, then it's time to draw!

The real frame rate of a game is not the 60 fps draw rate, it's the rate at which the game is updated every frame. That includes any math and physics calculations, collision detection (which can be *very* time consuming!), A.I. for enemy movements, and so on. If we tried to do all of these things inside the 60 fps game loop, it would immediately drop to below that desired refresh rate, all the while many frames are going to waste *outside* the If statement.

Now to address the processor throttling: In Chapter 11, one thread would max out one processor core just to draw the tilemap, which seems silly for such a simple 2D graphic. The problem was not the drawing code but the timer. We'll correct that now. If 16 ms have not transpired so that it's time to draw, then we tell the current thread to sleep for 1 ms. This has the effect of allowing the processor core to rest if the game is idling for that short time period. 16 ms is an extremely small amount of time in human terms, but for the computer it's enough time to read a whole book! The Else statement in the code below kicks in if 16 ms have *not yet* transpired.

```
Else
    Threading.Thread.Sleep(1)
End If
```

New Level Class

The tilemap scrolling code has reached a level of critical mass where it's no longer possible to manage it all with global variables and functions—it's time to move all of this code into a class. This will clean up the main source code file for our projects significantly! The new Level class will have quite a few private variables, public properties, and public functions. All of the complex code will be hidden and the scroller will function in a turn-key fashion: simply load up a level file, and then call Update() and Draw() regularly. You will recognize all of the variables and functions present in the previous chapter's example projects, but now they are packaged nicely into the Level.vb file. There is *no new code* here— this is all just the same code we've already seen, organized into a class.

```
Imports System.Xml
Public Class Level
    Public Structure tilemapStruct
        Public tilenum As Integer
        Public data1 As String
        Public collidable As Boolean
    End Structure

    Private p_game As Game
    Private p_mapSize As New Point(0, 0)
    Private p_windowSize As New Point(0, 0)
    Private p_tileSize As Integer
    Private p_bmpTiles As Bitmap
    Private p_columns As Integer
    Private p_bmpScrollBuffer As Bitmap
    Private p_gfxScrollBuffer As Graphics
```

```
        Private p_tilemap() As tilemapStruct
        Private p_scrollPos As New PointF(0, 0)
        Private p_subtile As New PointF(0, 0)
        Private p_oldScrollPos As New PointF(-1, -1)

        Public Property ScrollPos() As PointF
            Get
                Return p_scrollPos
            End Get
            Set(ByVal value As PointF)
                REM save new scroll position
                p_scrollPos = value
            End Set
        End Property

        Public Sub New(ByRef gameObject As Game, ByVal width As Integer, _
                ByVal height As Integer, ByVal tileSize As Integer)
            p_game = gameObject
            p_windowSize = New Point(width, height)
            p_mapSize = New Point(width * tileSize, height * tileSize)
            p_tileSize = tileSize
            REM create scroll buffer
            p_bmpScrollBuffer = New Bitmap(p_mapSize.X + p_tileSize, _
                p_mapSize.Y + p_tileSize)
            p_gfxScrollBuffer = Graphics.FromImage(p_bmpScrollBuffer)
            REM create tilemap
            ReDim p_tilemap(128 * 128)
        End Sub

        Public Function loadTilemap(ByVal filename As String) As Boolean
            Try
                Dim doc As XmlDocument = New XmlDocument()
                doc.Load(filename)
                Dim nodelist As XmlNodeList = doc.GetElementsByTagName("tiles")
                For Each node As XmlNode In nodelist
                    Dim element As XmlElement = node
                    Dim index As Integer = 0
                    Dim value As Integer = 0
                    Dim data1 As String = ""
                    Dim collidable As Boolean = False
                    REM read tile index #
```

```vbnet
                    Dim data As String
                    data = element.GetElementsByTagName("tile")(0).InnerText
                    index = Convert.ToInt32(data)
                    REM read tilenum
                    data = element.GetElementsByTagName("value")(0).InnerText
                    value = Convert.ToInt32(data)
                    REM read data1
                    data = element.GetElementsByTagName("data1")(0).InnerText
                    data1 = Convert.ToString(data)
                    REM read collidable
                    data = element.GetElementsByTagName("collidable")(0)._
                        InnerText
                    collidable = Convert.ToBoolean(data)
                    p_tilemap(index).tilenum = value
                    p_tilemap(index).data1 = data1
                    p_tilemap(index).collidable = collidable
                Next
        Catch es As Exception
            MessageBox.Show(es.Message)
            Return False
        End Try
        Return True
    End Function

    Public Function loadPalette(ByVal filename As String, _
            ByVal columns As Integer) As Boolean
        p_columns = columns
        Try
            p_bmpTiles = New Bitmap(filename)
        Catch ex As Exception
            Return False
        End Try
        Return True
    End Function

    Public Sub Update()
        REM fill the scroll buffer only when moving
        If p_scrollPos <> p_oldScrollPos Then
            p_oldScrollPos = p_scrollPos
            REM validate X range
            If p_scrollPos.X < 0 Then p_scrollPos.X = 0
```

```
            If p_scrollPos.X > (127 - p_windowSize.X) * p_tileSize Then
                p_scrollPos.X = (127 - p_windowSize.X) * p_tileSize
            End If
            REM validate Y range
            If p_scrollPos.Y < 0 Then p_scrollPos.Y = 0
            If p_scrollPos.Y > (127 - p_windowSize.Y) * p_tileSize Then
                p_scrollPos.Y = (127 - p_windowSize.Y) * p_tileSize
            End If
            REM calculate sub-tile size
            p_subtile.X = p_scrollPos.X Mod p_tileSize
            p_subtile.Y = p_scrollPos.Y Mod p_tileSize
            REM fill scroll buffer with tiles
            Dim tilenum, sx, sy As Integer
            For x = 0 To p_windowSize.X
                For y = 0 To p_windowSize.Y
                    sx = p_scrollPos.X \ p_tileSize + x
                    sy = p_scrollPos.Y \ p_tileSize + y
                    tilenum = p_tilemap(sy * 128 + sx).tilenum
                    drawTileNumber(x, y, tilenum)
                Next
            Next
        End If
    End Sub

    Public Sub drawTileNumber(ByVal x As Integer, _
            ByVal y As Integer, ByVal tile As Integer)
        Dim sx As Integer = (tile Mod p_columns) * (p_tileSize + 1)
        Dim sy As Integer = (tile \ p_columns) * (p_tileSize + 1)
        Dim src As New Rectangle(sx, sy, p_tileSize, p_tileSize)
        Dim dx As Integer = x * p_tileSize
        Dim dy As Integer = y * p_tileSize
        p_gfxScrollBuffer.DrawImage(p_bmpTiles, dx, dy, src, _
            GraphicsUnit.Pixel)
    End Sub

    Public Sub Draw(ByVal rect As Rectangle)
        Draw(rect.X, rect.Y, rect.Width, rect.Height)
    End Sub

    Public Sub Draw(ByVal width As Integer, ByVal height As Integer)
        Draw(0, 0, width, height)
```

```
        End Sub

    Public Sub Draw(ByVal x As Integer, ByVal y As Integer, _
            ByVal width As Integer, ByVal height As Integer)
        REM draw the scroll viewport
        Dim source As New Rectangle(p_subtile.X, p_subtile.Y, _
            width, height)
        p_game.Device.DrawImage(p_bmpScrollBuffer, x, y, source, _
            GraphicsUnit.Pixel)
    End Sub
End Class
```

Adding Trees

The first example project in this chapter will add random trees to the game level—or, at least, make it *seem* that trees have been added. Actually, the trees are just drawn over the top of the tilemap scroller at a specific location meant to *appear* to be in the level. The first step to adding interactive objects to the game world involves moving them realistically with the scroller, and drawing those objects that are in view while not drawing any object that is outside the current viewport (which is the scroll position in the level plus the width and height of the window). First, we need to make some improvements to the Sprite class, then we'll get to the random trees afterward.

Modifying Sprite.vb

It turns out that we need to make some new improvements to the Sprite class introduced back in Chapter 6, "Sprites and Real-Time Animation". The changes are needed not because of a lack of foresight back then, but because of changing needs as work on Celtic Crusader progresses. Expect future needs and the changes they will require—versatility is important in software development! First, we need to gain access to the animation system in the Sprite class. It was originally designed with a very useful Animate() function, but I want to be able to set the starting frame of animation to a random value for the random trees example, and presently there is no way to specifically set the sprite frame. Here's a new property to do that:

```
Public Property CurrentFrame() As Integer
    Get
```

```
        Return p_currentFrame
    End Get
    Set(ByVal value As Integer)
        p_currentFrame = value
    End Set
End Property
```

Next, we need a new `Draw()` function. Adding a second version of the function will *overload* Draw in the class, giving it more features, but we must be careful not to disrupt any existing code in the process. Specifically, I need to be able to draw a *copy* of a sprite, based on its current animation frame, to any location on the screen, without *changing* the sprite's position. That calls for a new `Draw()` function that accepts screen coordinates. For reference, here is the existing `Draw()` function:

```
REM draw sprite frame at current position
Public Sub Draw()
    Dim frame As New Rectangle
    frame.X = (p_currentFrame Mod p_columns) * p_size.Width
    frame.Y = (p_currentFrame \ p_columns) * p_size.Height
    frame.Width = p_size.Width
    frame.Height = p_size.Height
    p_game.Device.DrawImage(p_bitmap, Bounds(), frame, GraphicsUnit.Pixel)
End Sub
```

And here is the new overloaded function:

```
REM draw sprite at specified position without changing original position
Public Sub Draw(ByVal x As Integer, ByVal y As Integer)
    REM source image
    Dim frame As New Rectangle
    frame.X = (p_currentFrame Mod p_columns) * p_size.Width
    frame.Y = (p_currentFrame \ p_columns) * p_size.Height
    frame.Width = p_size.Width
    frame.Height = p_size.Height
    REM target location
    Dim target As New Rectangle(x, y, p_size.Width, p_size.Height)
    REM draw sprite
    p_game.Device.DrawImage(p_bitmap, target, frame, GraphicsUnit.Pixel)
End Sub
```

Adding the Trees

Now that we have a new Level class and modified versions of the Game and Sprite classes, we can finally go over a new example involving interactive objects in the game world. In this example, the objects won't exactly be interactive—yet! The random trees will be visible and will seem to scroll with the tiles. The Random Tree Demo program includes optimizations to the game loop, with the addition of the game level renderer (via the Level class), and a linked list of tree sprites that are scattered randomly around the upper-left corner of the game level (so we don't have to move very far to see them all—but it is very easy to scatter the trees throughout the entire level). The source image for the tree scenery objects is shown in Figure 12.2. The images used in the demo are each 64 × 64 pixels in size.

Figure 12.2
The tree sprite sheet has 32 unique trees and bushes that can be used for scenery. Courtesy of Reiner Prokein.

Figure 12.3
Random trees are added to the game world.

Figure 12.3 shows the Random Trees demo program running. Note the frame rate value! As you can see in the source code listing below, the trees are only randomly placed within the first 1000 pixels, in both the horizontal and vertical directions. Feel free to experiment with the code, extending the range of the trees to the entire level if you wish. Just be mindful of the *number* of objects being added. Although only the visible tree sprites are drawn, the entire list is looked at every frame, which can slow down the program quite a bit if there are too many objects. Why don't you perform a little experiment? See how many trees you can add before the frame rate drops too low to be playable?

```
Public Class Form1
    Public Structure keyStates
        Public up, down, left, right As Boolean
    End Structure
```

```
Private game As Game
Private level As Level
Private keyState As keyStates
Private gameover As Boolean = False
Private treeImage As Bitmap
Private tree As Sprite
Private trees As List(Of Sprite)
Private treesVisible As Integer = 0

Private Sub Form1_Load(ByVal sender As System.Object, _
    ByVal e As System.EventArgs) Handles MyBase.Load
    Me.Text = "Random Tree Demo"
    REM create game object
    game = New Game(Me, 800, 600)
    REM create tilemap
    level = New Level(game, 25, 19, 32)
    level.loadTilemap("tilemap.xml")
    level.loadPalette("palette.bmp", 5)
    REM load trees
    treeImage = game.LoadBitmap("trees64.png")
    trees = New List(Of Sprite)
    For n = 0 To 100
        Dim tree As New Sprite(game)
        tree.Image = treeImage
        tree.Columns = 4
        tree.TotalFrames = 32
        tree.CurrentFrame = game.Random(31)
        tree.Size = New Point(64, 64)
        tree.Position = New PointF(game.Random(1000), game.Random(1000))
        trees.Add(tree)
    Next n
    REM game loop
    While Not gameover
        doUpdate()
    End While
End Sub

Private Sub Form1_KeyDown(ByVal sender As Object, _
    ByVal e As System.Windows.Forms.KeyEventArgs) Handles Me.KeyDown
    Select Case (e.KeyCode)
```

```
                Case Keys.Up, Keys.W : keyState.up = True
                Case Keys.Down, Keys.S : keyState.down = True
                Case Keys.Left, Keys.A : keyState.left = True
                Case Keys.Right, Keys.D : keyState.right = True
            End Select
        End Sub

        Private Sub Form1_KeyUp(ByVal sender As System.Object, ByVal e As System.
Windows.Forms.KeyEventArgs) Handles MyBase.KeyUp
            Select Case (e.KeyCode)
                Case Keys.Escape : End
                Case Keys.Up, Keys.W : keyState.up = False
                Case Keys.Down, Keys.S : keyState.down = False
                Case Keys.Left, Keys.A : keyState.left = False
                Case Keys.Right, Keys.D : keyState.right = False
            End Select
        End Sub

        Private Sub DrawTrees()
            Dim sx As Integer
            Dim sy As Integer
            treesVisible = 0
            For Each tree As Sprite In trees
                sx = level.ScrollPos.X
                sy = level.ScrollPos.Y
                If tree.X > sx And tree.X < sx + 23 * 32 _
                And tree.Y > sy And tree.Y < sy + 17 * 32 Then
                    Dim rx As Integer = Math.Abs(sx - tree.X)
                    Dim ry As Integer = Math.Abs(sy - tree.Y)
                    tree.Draw(rx, ry)
                    treesVisible += 1
                End If
            Next
        End Sub

        Private Sub doUpdate()
            REM respond to user input
            Dim steps As Integer = 8
            Dim pos As PointF = level.ScrollPos
            If keyState.up Then pos.Y -= steps
```

```
        If keyState.down Then pos.Y += steps
        If keyState.left Then pos.X -= steps
        If keyState.right Then pos.X += steps
        level.ScrollPos = pos
        REM refresh level renderer
        level.Update()
        REM get the untimed core frame rate
        Dim frameRate As Integer = game.FrameRate()
        REM drawing code should be limited to 60 fps
        Dim ticks As Integer = Environment.TickCount()
        Static drawLast As Integer = 0
        If ticks > drawLast + 16 Then '1000/60 = 16 ms
            drawLast = ticks
            REM draw the tilemap
            level.Draw(0, 0, 800, 600)
            REM draw the trees in view
            drawTrees()
            REM print da stats
            game.Print(0, 0, "Scroll " + level.ScrollPos.ToString())
            game.Print(250, 0, "Frame rate " + frameRate.ToString())
            game.Print(500, 0, "Visible trees " + treesVisible.ToString() + "/
100")
            REM refresh window
            game.Update()
            Application.DoEvents()
        Else
            REM throttle the cpu
            Threading.Thread.Sleep(1)
        End If
    End Sub
End Class
```

ADDING AN ANIMATED CHARACTER

Random trees are pretty interesting, but what is not all that fascinating any more is a scrolling game world without any characters in it. We're a little ahead of that subject at this point, which will not be covered until Chapter 14, "Creating the Character Editor". But, we do need an animated character to walk around and appear to begin interacting with the game world. Figure 12.4 shows the sprite sheet used for the character.

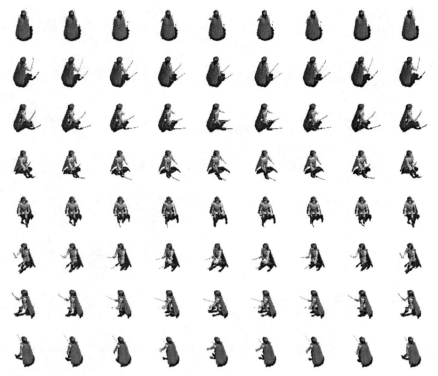

Figure 12.4
This sprite sheet is used for the animated walking character in the demo.

There are nine frames for each animation set and eight directions for a total of 72 frames of animation. Since the diagonal directions require two key presses (such as Up and Left), the diagonals are handled first, and then the four cardinal directions are handled with Else statements. The core code for this demo is in the doUpdate() function again, as it was in the previous demo. First, we draw the level that has the effect of also erasing the window, which saves processor cycles normally needed to clear the screen. Next, the trees are drawn if they are found within the current scroll region of the level. Finally, the hero character sprite is drawn. There is no sprite z-buffering in this demo—that is, no priority drawing of some sprites over the top of others, something that will need to be addressed in a fully featured game. Figure 12.5 shows the Walk About demo in action.

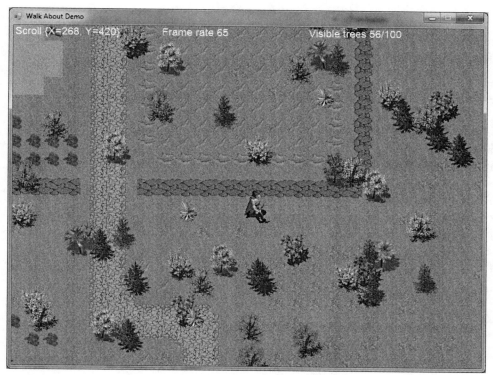

Figure 12.5
An animated character now walks in the direction that the scroller is moving.

Exaggerated Dimensions

The characters in the game are clearly out of scale with the environment. In some cases the player is taller than a full-size tree! This is fairly common in games of this type, drawing attention to the important items on the screen by highlighting them in some way. The characters will have to be somewhat larger than their surroundings so they're visible! If the game screen were rendered with all objects to scale, then characters would be only a few pixels tall compared to a tree. The game screen is a *representation* of the real world—or, at least, of some other world, anyway.

Regarding the tree artwork in this chapter: the trees are just a representation of any environment object you want in your game world. Just change the image and draw houses, signs, rocks, walls, or anything else you can imagine! Think of the trees as just placeholders for any object!

Since this program is very similar to the previous one, only the important code is shown here, not the complete listing. Refer to the chapter's resources for the complete Walk About demo.

```
Private game As Game
Private level As Level
Private keyState As keyStates
Private gameover As Boolean = False
Private treeImage As Bitmap
Private tree As Sprite
Private trees As List(Of Sprite)
Private treesVisible As Integer = 0
Private hero As Sprite
Private heroDir As Integer = 0

Private Sub Form1_Load(ByVal sender As System.Object, _
        ByVal e As System.EventArgs) Handles MyBase.Load
    Me.Text = "Walk About Demo"
    REM create game object
    game = New Game(Me, 800, 600)
    REM create tilemap
    level = New Level(game, 25, 19, 32)
    level.loadTilemap("tilemap.xml")
    level.loadPalette("palette.bmp", 5)
    REM load hero
    hero = New Sprite(game)
    hero.Image = game.LoadBitmap("hero_sword_walk.png")
    hero.Columns = 9
    hero.TotalFrames = 9 * 8
    hero.Size = New Point(96, 96)
    hero.Position = New Point(400 - 32, 300 - 32)
    hero.AnimateWrapMode = Sprite.AnimateWrap.WRAP
    hero.AnimationRate = 20
    REM load trees
    treeImage = game.LoadBitmap("trees64.png")
    trees = New List(Of Sprite)
    For n = 0 To 100
        Dim tree As New Sprite(game)
        tree.Image = treeImage
        tree.Columns = 4
        tree.TotalFrames = 32
```

```
            tree.CurrentFrame = game.Random(31)
            tree.Size = New Point(64, 64)
            tree.Position = New PointF(game.Random(1000), game.Random(1000))
            trees.Add(tree)
        Next n
        REM game loop
        While Not gameover
            doUpdate()
        End While
    End Sub


Private Sub doUpdate()
    REM move the tilemap scroll position
    Dim steps As Integer = 4
    Dim pos As PointF = level.ScrollPos
    If keyState.up Then pos.Y -= steps
    If keyState.down Then pos.Y += steps
    If keyState.left Then pos.X -= steps
    If keyState.right Then pos.X += steps
    level.ScrollPos = pos
    REM orient the player in the right direction
    If keyState.up And keyState.right Then
        heroDir = 1
    ElseIf keyState.right And keyState.down Then
        heroDir = 3
    ElseIf keyState.down And keyState.left Then
        heroDir = 5
    ElseIf keyState.left And keyState.up Then
        heroDir = 7
    ElseIf keyState.up Then
        heroDir = 0
    ElseIf keyState.right Then
        heroDir = 2
    ElseIf keyState.down Then
        heroDir = 4
    ElseIf keyState.left Then
        heroDir = 6
    Else
        heroDir = -1
```

```
    End If

    REM refresh level renderer
    level.Update()
    REM get the untimed core frame rate
    Dim frameRate As Integer = game.FrameRate()
    REM drawing code should be limited to 60 fps
    Dim ticks As Integer = Environment.TickCount()
    Static drawLast As Integer = 0
    If ticks > drawLast + 16 Then
        drawLast = ticks
        REM draw the tilemap
        level.Draw(0, 0, 800, 600)
        REM draw the trees in view
        DrawTrees()
        REM draw the hero
        Dim startFrame As Integer = heroDir * 9
        Dim endFrame As Integer = startFrame + 8
        If heroDir > -1 Then
            hero.Animate(startFrame, endFrame)
        End If
        hero.Draw()
        REM print da stats
        game.Print(0, 0, "Scroll " + level.ScrollPos.ToString())
        game.Print(250, 0, "Frame rate " + frameRate.ToString())
        game.Print(500, 0, "Visible trees " + _
            treesVisible.ToString() + "/100")
        REM refresh window
        game.Update()
        Application.DoEvents()
    Else
        REM throttle the cpu
        Threading.Thread.Sleep(1)
    End If
End Sub
```

There is one limitation to this first attempt at adding a playable character—due to the way in which the scroller works, we can't move the character all the way into the corner of the game world. The character sprite is fixed to the center of the screen. This will be remedied in the next chapter with some clever code!

LEVEL UP!

We have made quite a bit of positive progress in this chapter with some key features needed for a full-blown RPG. Although a few trees and an animated character don't seem like much to go on so far, we have laid the foundation for the interactive aspects of the game with the meager code in this chapter. Soon, we will be tapping into the data fields of the level data and positioning objects in the game world based on data entered in the level editor, which really makes for the start of a solid data-driven game. This is really the core of the game that will be expanded upon even further in the next chapter.

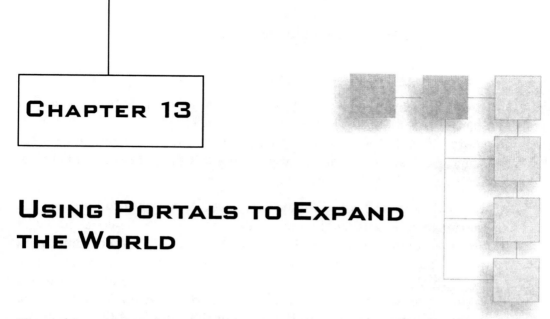

CHAPTER 13

USING PORTALS TO EXPAND THE WORLD

Up to this point, we have learned quite a bit about creating a game world, and we just started to interact with the game world in the previous chapter. We need to bump it up a notch now by adding to both the editor and the game project the ability to create and use *portals*. A portal is an opening that connects two worlds or allows someone to cross over from one area into another. In terms of a tiled game world, we need a portal that will teleport the player to another location on the map, as well as specify a position on a *different* level file entirely. Once the code to teleport to a new location on a map is understood, adding the ability to teleport to a new level is just a matter of loading that new level file with the Level class and then setting the scroll position to the target X,Y position. Fortunately, a new version of the level editor is available with fields for portals built in to the tile structure which we will examine in this chapter.

Here's what we'll cover in this chapter:

- Updating the level editor
- Level class modifications
- Teleporting to another dimension
- Looking for tile collisions
- Adding Lua support to the game

UPDATING THE LEVEL EDITOR

It's time for an update to the level editor to accommodate new features needed for this chapter. The editor project is available in the chapter's resource files with the full source code, but we won't be going over the sources here due to space concerns, and because the editor is being written in C#, for reasons stated back in Chapter 10, "Creating the Level Editor."

The file extension for level editor files is now .level. Although the content is still pure XML, a custom extension gives our editor more of a professional edge and helps with identifying level files in a directory full of other game files. Unfortunately, due to the many new fields in the new editor, it is no longer compatible with old level files from the previous version of the editor. If this was a production editor used to make games and an update was made to it, then of course we would want to provide an importer for the older level file format. But since this is a pre-alpha work in progress, that's not something you want to spend time doing with pre-release software—and an internal tool at that.

Perusing New Editor Features

Figure 13.1 shows the new version of the editor enhanced for the needs of this chapter. Note that the lonely "Data1" field and "Collidable" checkbox are no longer at the bottom of the form, but in the lower-left corner with some new fields. Also, the tile palette on the left has been shrunk a bit—it now affords a smaller selection area, but that is no problem due to the scrollbar.

I recall mentioning back in Chapter 10 that the early editor was already sufficient for making a tiled game world with collision, portals, and even item drops, through creative use of the single Data1 field. While that is true, there's no need to limit our tile data to just one shared field when we can use any number of fields—maybe even a whole secondary form filled with possible data for each tile! The .xml file format can handle it, and even 100 pieces of data for each tile would not lead to much slower load times. But, the fact is, we don't need that many fields. The four generic data fields store strings so you can put any data you want there—whole numbers, decimal numbers, text descriptions, etc. You could use one as a searchable item name field and then add an item to

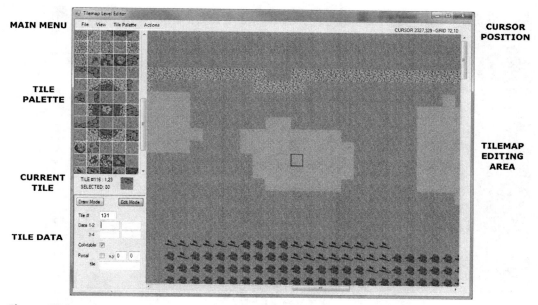

Figure 13.1
The new level editor has a cleaner user interface.

the game world at that tile location, or even something as exotic as a script function name. Here are the data fields for each tile:

- Tile palette number
- Data 1
- Data 2
- Data 3
- Data 4
- Collidable
- Portal
- Portal X
- Portal Y
- Portal file

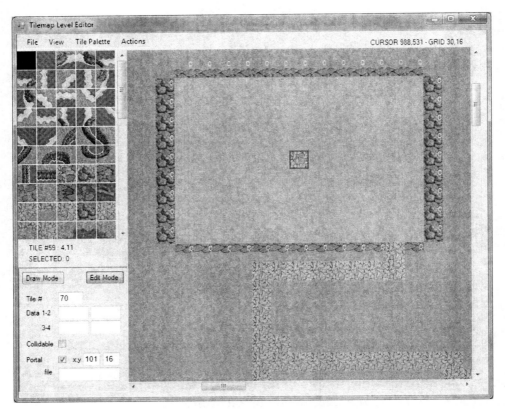

Figure 13.2
Creating a portal using the new tile data fields.

Creating a Portal

A portal is a doorway to another dimension. Or, in the case of our editor here, a new x,y location on the map. Or on another map file! Let's start with a series of portals on a single map first, and then look at how to portal to another world. Take a look at the data for the highlighted tile in Figure 13.2. The Portal flag is checked, while the x and y fields are set to coordinates (101,16).

The location (101,16) is on the right side of the map, shown in Figure 13.3. What we want to do is have the game jump to that location when our character walks into the portal tile. Nearby, the target location is another portal tile.

In case you are wondering why the two portals aren't linked directly together, that is something you can play with if you want, but if you point one portal to a

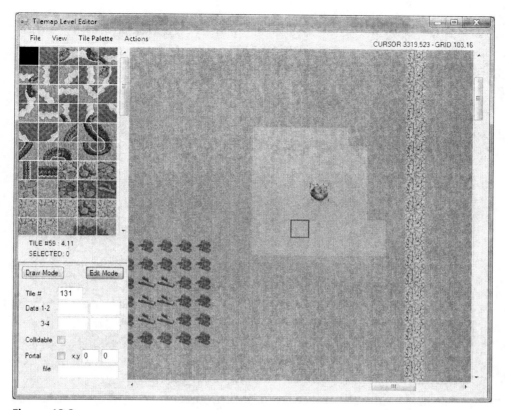

Figure 13.3
The target location of the first portal on the map is (103,16).

tile that contains *another* portal, then your character will teleport twice. Unless you want that kind of behavior, don't link portal squares directly—have one drop off the player nearby but not directly on another portal. Or, go ahead and do it and see for yourself what happens! In our example, you must press Space to trigger a portal, but if you use automatic teleporting then the player could be teleported repeatedly, possibly even getting stuck in a portal loop.

It's a Data-Driven Game World

In the previous chapter, we learned how to create a list of tree sprites and draw them in the game world, so that when the player moves around the trees come into view within the scrolling viewport. That works well when you want to scatter random environment items like bushes, houses, coffee shops, software stores, and, well, anything you want. We can also use the level editor to position objects at a specific location, which is more useful than using randomness, especially when you need to count on a certain thing being at a certain location. For instance, you might have a quest that has the player find a certain landmark where nearby a treasure is buried.

The data fields are numbered 1 to 4, and can contain *any* type of data—numbers or strings. If we used these fields to position an item, we could use them like so:

Data 1: Item number

Data 2: Position x

Data 3: Position y

Data 4: Script function

The item number would be out of the game item database, or it could be the number or *name* of a sprite. The x,y position of the item is next in Data 2 and 3. The fourth one is a bit interesting. What is a script function? This goes a bit beyond the scope of this book, but if we wanted to *really* make this level editor and game engine interesting, we could add Lua script support to the game. Lua is an interpreted programming language—meaning, Lua source code is not compiled, it is simply stored in a text file and treated as text, and yet the Lua interpreter will *run* our script code at runtime. The ramifications for scripting are enormous. Imagine being able to edit a script *without restarting the game.* Yes, that's possible: edit the script, save it, then load and execute the script with the Lua interpreter. Like I said, this gets a bit complicated but it adds a tremendous amount of design freedom to the game, which is otherwise bound by its data and engine. We will add Lua scripting support to the game in the next section.

Now we need to look at some Basic code to make this all work. Among other things, we have some work to do in the `loadTilemap()` function now because of the new fields.

Level Class Modifications

We need to make a few new changes to the `Level` class (`Level.vb`) to accommodate the changes required for this chapter. First, the new data fields need to be added to the `tilemapStruct` structure, and then we need to add a function to return tile data at a specified index in the tilemap so that the player's character sprite can interact with the level. In other words, we need to find out where the portals are and let the character get teleported! Here is the new `Level` class with an expanded `tilemapStruct` and `loadTilemap()` function. There is also a new set of `getTile()` functions, a `GridPos` property used as an alternative to `ScrollPos`.

```
Imports System.Xml
Public Class Level
    Public Structure tilemapStruct
        Public tilenum As Integer
        Public data1 As String
        Public data2 As String
        Public data3 As String
        Public data4 As String
        Public collidable As Boolean
        Public portal As Boolean
        Public portalx As Integer
        Public portaly As Integer
        Public portalfile As String
    End Structure
    Private p_game As Game
    Private p_mapSize As New Point(0, 0)
    Private p_windowSize As New Point(0, 0)
    Private p_tileSize As Integer
    Private p_bmpTiles As Bitmap
    Private p_columns As Integer
    Private p_bmpScrollBuffer As Bitmap
    Private p_gfxScrollBuffer As Graphics
    Private p_tilemap() As tilemapStruct
    Private p_scrollPos As New PointF(0, 0)
    Private p_subtile As New PointF(0, 0)
    Private p_oldScrollPos As New PointF(-1, -1)

    Public Function getTile(ByVal p As PointF) As tilemapStruct
        Return getTile(p.Y * 128 + p.X)
    End Function

    Public Function getTile(ByVal pixelx As Integer, _
            ByVal pixely As Integer) As tilemapStruct
```

```
        Return getTile(pixely * 128 + pixelx)
End Function

Public Function getTile(ByVal index As Integer) As tilemapStruct
        Return p_tilemap(index)
End Function

REM get/set scroll position by whole tile position
Public Property GridPos() As Point
    Get
            Dim x As Integer = p_scrollPos.X / p_tileSize
            Dim y As Integer = p_scrollPos.Y / p_tileSize
            Return New Point(x, y)
    End Get
    Set(ByVal value As Point)
            Dim x As Single = value.X * p_tileSize
            Dim y As Single = value.Y * p_tileSize
            p_scrollPos = New PointF(x, y)
    End Set
End Property

REM get/set scroll position by pixel position
Public Property ScrollPos() As PointF
    Get
            Return p_scrollPos
    End Get
    Set(ByVal value As PointF)
        REM save new scroll position
        p_scrollPos = value
    End Set
End Property

Public Sub New(ByRef gameObject As Game, ByVal width As Integer, _
        ByVal height As Integer, ByVal tileSize As Integer)
    p_game = gameObject
    p_windowSize = New Point(width, height)
    p_mapSize = New Point(width * tileSize, height * tileSize)
    p_tileSize = tileSize
    REM create scroll buffer
    p_bmpScrollBuffer = New Bitmap(p_mapSize.X + p_tileSize, _
```

```
                p_mapSize.Y + p_tileSize)
        p_gfxScrollBuffer = Graphics.FromImage(p_bmpScrollBuffer)
        REM create tilemap
        ReDim p_tilemap(128 * 128)
    End Sub


    Public Function loadTilemap(ByVal filename As String) As Boolean
        Try
            Dim doc As XmlDocument = New XmlDocument()
            doc.Load(filename)
            Dim nodelist As XmlNodeList = doc.GetElementsByTagName("tiles")
            For Each node As XmlNode In nodelist
                Dim element As XmlElement = node
                Dim index As Integer = 0
                Dim ts As tilemapStruct
                Dim data As String

                REM read data fields from xml
                Data = element.GetElementsByTagName("tile")(0).InnerText
                index = Convert.ToInt32(data)
                data = element.GetElementsByTagName("value")(0).InnerText
                ts.tilenum = Convert.ToInt32(data)
                data = element.GetElementsByTagName("data1")(0).InnerText
                ts.data1 = Convert.ToString(data)
                data = element.GetElementsByTagName("data2")(0).InnerText
                ts.data2 = Convert.ToString(data)
                data = element.GetElementsByTagName("data3")(0).InnerText
                ts.data3 = Convert.ToString(data)
                data = element.GetElementsByTagName("data4")(0).InnerText
                ts.data4 = Convert.ToString(data)
                data = element.GetElementsByTagName("collidable")(0).InnerText
                ts.collidable = Convert.ToBoolean(data)
                data = element.GetElementsByTagName("portal")(0).InnerText
                ts.portal = Convert.ToBoolean(data)
                data = element.GetElementsByTagName("portalx")(0).InnerText
                ts.portalx = Convert.ToInt32(data)
                data = element.GetElementsByTagName("portaly")(0).InnerText
                ts.portaly = Convert.ToInt32(data)
                data = element.GetElementsByTagName("portalfile")(0).InnerText
                ts.portalfile = Convert.ToString(data)
```

```
                REM store data in tilemap
                p_tilemap(index) = ts
            Next
        Catch es As Exception
            MessageBox.Show(es.Message)
            Return False
        End Try
        Return True
    End Function

    Public Function loadPalette(ByVal filename As String, _
            ByVal columns As Integer) As Boolean
        p_columns = columns
        Try
            p_bmpTiles = New Bitmap(filename)
        Catch ex As Exception
            Return False
        End Try
        Return True
    End Function

    Public Sub Update()
        REM fill the scroll buffer only when moving
        If p_scrollPos <> p_oldScrollPos Then
            p_oldScrollPos = p_scrollPos
            REM validate X range
            If p_scrollPos.X < 0 Then p_scrollPos.X = 0
            If p_scrollPos.X > (127 - p_windowSize.X) * p_tileSize Then
                p_scrollPos.X = (127 - p_windowSize.X) * p_tileSize
            End If
            REM validate Y range
            If p_scrollPos.Y < 0 Then p_scrollPos.Y = 0
            If p_scrollPos.Y > (127 - p_windowSize.Y) * p_tileSize Then
                p_scrollPos.Y = (127 - p_windowSize.Y) * p_tileSize
            End If
            REM calculate sub-tile size
            p_subtile.X = p_scrollPos.X Mod p_tileSize
            p_subtile.Y = p_scrollPos.Y Mod p_tileSize
            REM fill scroll buffer with tiles
```

```
            Dim tilenum, sx, sy As Integer
            For x = 0 To p_windowSize.X
                For y = 0 To p_windowSize.Y
                    sx = p_scrollPos.X \ p_tileSize + x
                    sy = p_scrollPos.Y \ p_tileSize + y
                    tilenum = p_tilemap(sy * 128 + sx).tilenum
                    drawTileNumber(x, y, tilenum)
                Next
            Next
        End If
    End Sub

    Public Sub drawTileNumber(ByVal x As Integer, ByVal y As Integer, _
            ByVal tile As Integer)
        Dim sx As Integer = (tile Mod p_columns) * (p_tileSize + 1)
        Dim sy As Integer = (tile \ p_columns) * (p_tileSize + 1)
        Dim src As New Rectangle(sx, sy, p_tileSize, p_tileSize)
        Dim dx As Integer = x * p_tileSize
        Dim dy As Integer = y * p_tileSize
        p_gfxScrollBuffer.DrawImage(p_bmpTiles, dx, dy, src, _
            GraphicsUnit.Pixel)
    End Sub

    Public Sub Draw(ByVal rect As Rectangle)
        Draw(rect.X, rect.Y, rect.Width, rect.Height)
    End Sub

    Public Sub Draw(ByVal width As Integer, ByVal height As Integer)
        Draw(0, 0, width, height)
    End Sub

    Public Sub Draw(ByVal x As Integer, ByVal y As Integer, _
            ByVal width As Integer, ByVal height As Integer)
        REM draw the scroll viewport
        Dim source As New Rectangle(p_subtile.X, p_subtile.Y, _
            width, height)
        p_game.Device.DrawImage(p_bmpScrollBuffer, x, y, source, _
            GraphicsUnit.Pixel)
    End Sub
End Class
```

Figure 13.4
Isolating the player sprite's "foot" contact with the ground.

Teleporting to Another Dimension

The first thing we need to do to get portals working is to isolate the portion of the character sprite that is actually on the "ground," so to speak. By default, the player sprite (which is called hero in our code) is positioned on the screen in the upper-left corner. Since the sprite is 96 × 96 pixels in size, there's a lot of area taken up by the sprite that is much larger than the 32 × 32 tiles. If we use the upper-left corner, then the player will be interacting with tiles on the ground from a position above and to the left of his or her head! That definitely won't work. So, we need to adjust the position used to determine what tile the player is walking on—we need to isolate the player's feet. Figure 13.4 shows the collision boxes for the player sprite. The blue box represents the entire character's collision box, while the small red box (and red dot) represent the walking collision box.

The small red collision box, and the red dot at its center, is what we actually want to use as a center point to determine which tile the sprite is "walking on." Thus, when the player walks onto a portal tile, it will accurately look as if the sprite's feet touched the tile before the teleport occurred. The Portal Demo program looks at that coordinate as a position relative to the scroll position and then retrieves the data for the tile at that location. Figure 13.5 shows information about the portal tile the player is standing on—note the message in the upper-left corner of the window.

In the game, it's up to you how the portals will work. You can make them automatically teleport the player just by merely walking on the tile, or you can require the player to take some action—perhaps using an item to trigger the portal. In our program, the Space key is the trigger. When the portal is

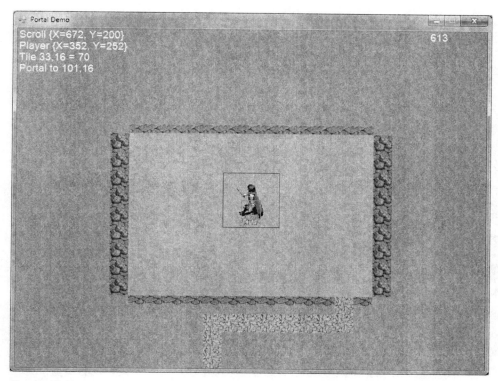

Figure 13.5
Detecting when the player walks on a portal tile.

engaged, the player is teleported to the target coordinate (101,16), as shown in Figure 13.6.

Trick

Getting tired of the same old ground tiles in every example? Replace them! You are encouraged to use a different set of ground tiles or add news ones to this collection. I am only using these same tiles for consistency. You may replace the tiles in the level editor and in the game. The only requirement is that your tile palette image be oriented like the one presented in the book and that the tiles remain at 32 × 32 pixels in size. Otherwise, some coding changes will be needed.

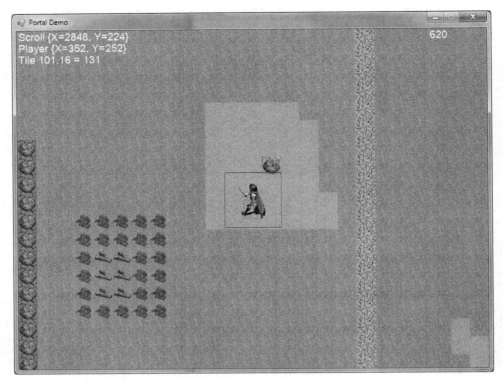

Figure 13.6
The portal has sent the player across the map!

Looking for Tile Collisions

The Portal Demo program also looks for the Collidable property in tiles and reports on the screen when a collidable tile is identified. Figure 13.7 shows the message that is printed when the player walks over a collidable tile. Although the sprite doesn't respond to collidable tiles yet in this example, we can use this information to enable collision response in the next major revision to the game.

Hint

This quick example is not quite polished yet, so expect to see some jittery sprites and timing problems. The point is to get these features to work first, and then make them work *great* afterward!

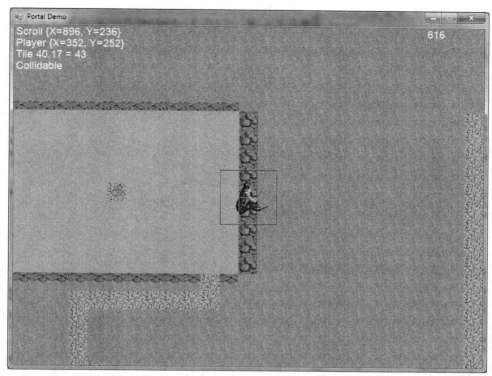

Figure 13.7
Detecting collidable tiles.

Portal Demo Program

Here is the source code for the Portal Demo program.

```
Public Class Form1
    Public Structure keyStates
        Public up, down, left, right As Boolean
    End Structure
    Private game As Game
    Private level As Level
    Private keyState As keyStates
    Private gameover As Boolean = False
    Private hero As Sprite
    Private heroDir As Integer = 0
    Private portalFlag As Boolean = False
    Private portalTarget As Point
```

```
Private Sub Form1_Load(ByVal sender As System.Object, _
    ByVal e As System.EventArgs) Handles MyBase.Load
    Me.Text = "Portal Demo"
    REM create game object
    game = New Game(Me, 800, 600)
    REM create tilemap
    level = New Level(game, 25, 19, 32)
    level.loadTilemap("portals.level")
    level.loadPalette("palette.bmp", 5)
    REM load hero
    hero = New Sprite(game)
    hero.Image = game.LoadBitmap("hero_sword_walk.png")
    hero.Columns = 9
    hero.TotalFrames = 9 * 8
    hero.Size = New Point(96, 96)
    hero.Position = New Point(400 - 48, 300 - 48)
    hero.AnimateWrapMode = Sprite.AnimateWrap.WRAP
    hero.AnimationRate = 20
    REM game loop
    While Not gameover
        doUpdate()
    End While
End Sub

Private Sub Form1_KeyDown(ByVal sender As Object, _
        ByVal e As System.Windows.Forms.KeyEventArgs) _
        Handles Me.KeyDown
    Select Case (e.KeyCode)
        Case Keys.Up, Keys.W : keyState.up = True
        Case Keys.Down, Keys.S : keyState.down = True
        Case Keys.Left, Keys.A : keyState.left = True
        Case Keys.Right, Keys.D : keyState.right = True
    End Select
End Sub

Private Sub Form1_KeyUp(ByVal sender As System.Object, _
        ByVal e As System.Windows.Forms.KeyEventArgs) _
        Handles MyBase.KeyUp
    Select Case (e.KeyCode)
        Case Keys.Escape : End
```

```
                Case Keys.Up, Keys.W : keyState.up = False
                Case Keys.Down, Keys.S : keyState.down = False
                Case Keys.Left, Keys.A : keyState.left = False
                Case Keys.Right, Keys.D : keyState.right = False
                Case Keys.Space
                    If portalFlag Then
                        level.GridPos = portalTarget
                    End If
            End Select
    End Sub


    Private Sub doUpdate()
        REM move the tilemap scroll position
        Dim steps As Integer = 8
        Dim pos As PointF = level.ScrollPos

        REM up key movement
        If keyState.up Then
            If hero.Y > 300 - 48 Then
                hero.Y -= steps
            Else
                pos.Y -= steps
                If pos.Y <= 0 Then
                    hero.Y -= steps
                End If
            End If
        REM down key movement
        ElseIf keyState.down Then
            If hero.Y < 300 - 48 Then
                hero.Y += steps
            Else
                pos.Y += steps
                If pos.Y >= (127 - 19) * 32 Then
                    hero.Y += steps
                End If
            End If
        End If
        REM left key movement
        If keyState.left Then
            If hero.X > 400 - 48 Then
```

```
                    hero.X -= steps
             Else
                    pos.X -= steps
                    If pos.X <= 0 Then
                            hero.X -= steps
                    End If
             End If
      REM right key movement
      ElseIf keyState.right Then
             If hero.X < 400 - 48 Then
                    hero.X += steps
             Else
                    pos.X += steps
                    If pos.X >= (127 - 25) * 32 Then
                            hero.X += steps
                    End If
             End If
      End If

      REM update scroller position
      level.ScrollPos = pos
      level.Update()

      REM limit player sprite to the screen boundary
      If hero.X < -32 Then
             hero.X = -32
      ElseIf hero.X > 800 - 65 Then
             hero.X = 800 - 65
      End If
      If hero.Y < -48 Then
             hero.Y = -48
      ElseIf hero.Y > 600 - 81 Then
             hero.Y = 600 - 81
      End If

      REM orient the player in the right direction
      If keyState.up And keyState.right Then
             heroDir = 1
      ElseIf keyState.right And keyState.down Then
             heroDir = 3
```

```
ElseIf keyState.down And keyState.left Then
    heroDir = 5
ElseIf keyState.left And keyState.up Then
    heroDir = 7
ElseIf keyState.up Then
    heroDir = 0
ElseIf keyState.right Then
    heroDir = 2
ElseIf keyState.down Then
    heroDir = 4
ElseIf keyState.left Then
    heroDir = 6
Else
    heroDir = -1
End If

REM get the untimed core frame rate
Dim frameRate As Integer = game.FrameRate()
REM drawing code should be limited to 60 fps
Dim ticks As Integer = Environment.TickCount()
Static drawLast As Integer = 0
If ticks > drawLast + 16 Then '1000/16 = ~60
    drawLast = ticks
    REM draw the tilemap
    level.Draw(0, 0, 800, 600)
    REM draw the hero
    Dim startFrame As Integer = heroDir * 9
    Dim endFrame As Integer = startFrame + 8
    If heroDir > -1 Then
        hero.Animate(startFrame, endFrame)
    End If
    hero.Draw()
    REM print stats
    game.Print(700, 0, frameRate.ToString())
    Dim y As Integer = 0
    game.Print(0, y, "Scroll " + level.ScrollPos.ToString())
    y += 20
    game.Print(0, y, "Player " + hero.Position.ToString())
    y += 20
    Dim feet As Point = HeroFeet()
```

```
                Dim tilex As Integer = (level.ScrollPos.X + feet.X) / 32
                Dim tiley As Integer = (level.ScrollPos.Y + feet.Y) / 32
                Dim ts As Level.tilemapStruct
                ts = level.getTile(tilex, tiley)
                game.Print(0, y, "Tile " + tilex.ToString() + "," + _
                    tiley.ToString() + " = " + ts.tilenum.ToString())
                y += 20
                If ts.collidable Then
                    game.Print(0, y, "Collidable")
                    y += 20
                End If
                If ts.portal Then
                    game.Print(0, y, "Portal to " + ts.portalx.ToString() + _
                        "," + ts.portaly.ToString())
                    portalFlag = True
                    portalTarget = New Point(ts.portalx - feet.X / 32, _
                        ts.portaly - feet.Y / 32)
                    y += 20
                Else
                    portalFlag = False
                End If

                REM highlight collision areas around player
                game.Device.DrawRectangle(Pens.Blue, hero.Bounds())
                game.Device.DrawRectangle(Pens.Red, feet.X + 16 - 1, _
                    feet.Y + 16 - 1, 2, 2)
                game.Device.DrawRectangle(Pens.Red, feet.X, feet.Y, 32, 32)

                REM refresh window
                game.Update()
                Application.DoEvents()
            Else
                REM throttle the cpu
                Threading.Thread.Sleep(1)
            End If
        End Sub

    REM return bottom center position of hero sprite where feet are touching
        ground
    Private Function HeroFeet() As Point
```

```
        Return New Point(hero.X + 32, hero.Y + 32 + 16)
    End Function
End Class
```

ADDING LUA SCRIPTING SUPPORT TO THE GAME

When you combine the versatility that a data-driven game engine affords, along with a custom level editor, you already have a great combination for making a great game. But when you add script support to the mix, things get even *more* interesting! We have progressed to the point in both the game and the level editor where, sure, we could get by with the excellent tools and code already in hand, but I want to raise the cool factor even higher with the addition of scripting support.

Now, let me disclaim something first: Yes, scripting is cool and adds incredible power to a game project, but it requires a lot of extra effort to make it work effectively.

The cool factor is that we can call Basic functions from within our Lua scripts! Likewise, we can call Lua functions from our Basic code—interpreted Lua functions!

But what about all of the global variables in a Lua source code file? The variables are automatically handled by the Lua engine when a script file is loaded. I'm not going to delve into a full-blown tutorial on the Lua language. Instead, we're just going to use it and learn more about Lua as needed. After this brief introduction, we will not be using Lua until the final game in Chapter 20. If you're really fascinated about Lua and want to dig into scripting right away, you may skip ahead to that chapter to see how it works in the finished game engine.

Hint

There is one really big drawback to Lua: once you have "seen the light," you may never go back to writing a game purely with a compiled language like Basic or C# again! Lua is so compelling that you'll wonder how in the world you ever got anything done before you discovered it.

Installing LuaInterface

The key to adding Lua support to our Visual Basic code is an open-source project called LuaInterface, hosted at the LuaForge website here: http://luaforge.

net/projects/luainterface/. The sources for LuaInterface are housed in a Google Code Subversion (SVN) repository at http://code.google.com/p/luainterface/, currently with support for Visual Basic 2008. I have included a project with this chapter that has the pre-compiled version of LuaInterface ready to use.

Definition

Lua is the Portuguese word for "Moon." The official spelling is LUA, with all caps, but I prefer to spell it without all caps because that leads the reader to assume it's an acronym rather than a word.

Testing LuaInterface

After compiling the LuaInterface project, you'll get a file called LuaInterface. dll—that's all you need. Copy this file to any project that needs Lua support and you'll be all set. (Note also that this dll must be distributed with your game's exe file.) Whether you compiled it yourself or just copied it from the chapter resource files, create a new Visual Basic project. Then, open the Project menu and select Add Reference. Locate the LuaInterface.dll file and select it, as shown in Figure 13.8.

Nothing will seem to change in the project. To verify that the component has been added, open Project, Properties, and bring up the References tab, where

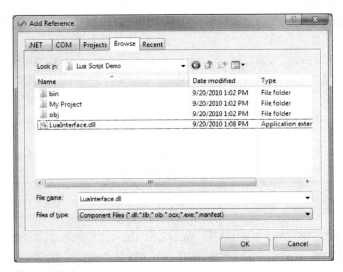

Figure 13.8
Adding the LuaInterface.dll file to the project.

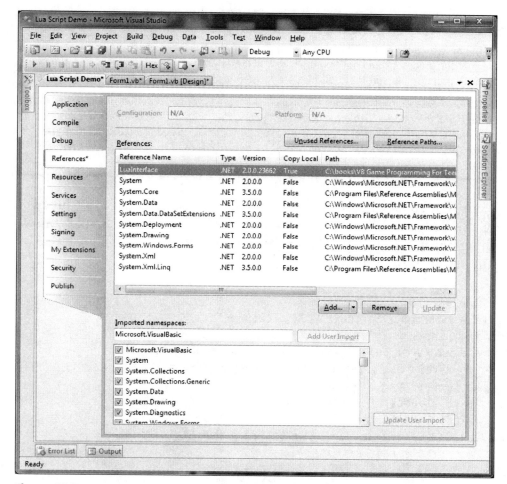

Figure 13.9
List of referenced components available for this project.

you should see the component among the others available to your project. See Figure 13.9.

Double click the default form to bring up the code window. At the top, type Imports. When you hit space, a list of namespaces should appear, including LuaInterface. If you don't see LuaInterface among those listed, then something went wrong when the component was added to the project as a reference, and you'll need to figure that out first before proceeding.

Hint

If you get an error such as this one below when running the Lua Script Demo program, that simply means that the program could not find the lua51.dll file, which is required in order for LuaInterface. dll to work properly. Be sure both dll files are located in the .\bin\Debug folder of your project.

An unhandled exception of type 'System.InvalidOperationException' occurred in Lua Script Demo. exe. Additional information: An error occurred creating the form. See Exception.InnerException for details. The error is: Could not load file or assembly 'lua51, Version=0.0.0.0, Culture=neutral, PublicKeyToken=1e1fb15b02227b8a' or one of its dependencies. The system cannot find the file specified.

Here is our first short example Basic program that loads a Lua script file. The form for this program has a `TextBox` control, which is used as a simple console for printing out text from both the Lua script and our Basic code. Figure 13.10 shows the result of the program.

```
Imports LuaInterface
Public Class Form1
    Private WithEvents TextBox1 As New TextBox()
    Public lua As Lua
    Private Sub Form1_Load(ByVal sender As System.Object, _
            ByVal e As System.EventArgs) Handles MyBase.Load
        Me.Text = "Lua Script Demo"
        TextBox1.Dock = DockStyle.Fill
        TextBox1.Multiline = True
        TextBox1.Font = New Font("System", 14, FontStyle.Regular)
        Me.Controls.Add(TextBox1)
```

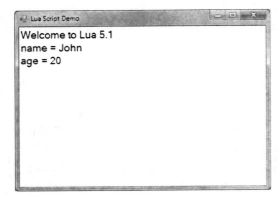

Figure 13.10
We now have Lua script language support for our game.

```
        REM create lua object
        lua = New Lua()

        REM link a Basic function to Lua
        lua.RegisterFunction("DoPrint", Me, Me.GetType().GetMethod
          ("DoPrint"))

        REM load lua script file
        lua.DoFile("script.lua")

        REM get globals from lua
        Dim name As String = lua("name")
        Dim age As Double = lua("age")
        DoPrint("name = " + name)
        DoPrint("age = " + age.ToString())
    End Sub

    Public Sub DoPrint(ByVal text As String)
        TextBox1.Text += text + vbCrLf
    End Sub
End Class
```

Hint

The LuaInterface.dll requires the .NET Framework 2.0, not the later versions such as 3.5. If you are using Visual Basic 2010, it will default to the later version of the .NET Framework. To get LuaInterface to work with your Visual Basic 2010 project, you will need to switch to .NET 2.0. If this is too difficult to figure out, then another option is to just create a new Visual Basic 2010 project and copy the source code into it rather than converting the 2008 project that comes with the book to 2010.

First, the TextBox control is created and added to the form with the Multiline property set to true so the control acts like a console rather than an entry field.

Next, the LuaInterface.Lua object is created. That object, called lua, is then used to register a Basic function called DoPrint(), which is defined as a normal Basic Sub (note that it must be declared with *Public* scope in order for Lua to see it!). Next, lua.DoFile() is called to load the script code in the script.lua file. This file must be located in the .\bin\Debug folder where the executable file is created at compile time. So, we can think of a script file like any game asset file, equivalent to a bitmap file or an audio file.

When DoFile() is called, that not only opens the script file, it also executes the code. This is one of the two ways to open a script file. The second way is to use LoadFile() instead, which simply loads the script into memory, registers the functions and globals, but does not start executing statements yet.

After the script has been loaded and run, then we can tap into the lua object to retrieve globals from the lua object, as well as call functions in the script code. In this example, we just grab two globals (name and age) and print out their values. This demonstrates that Lua can see our Basic function and call it, and that we can tap into the globals, which is the *most important* thing!

Here is the script.lua file for this project:

```
--This is my first Lua Script!
--create some globals
name = "John"
age = 20
--call a function in the Basic code
DoPrint( "Welcome to " .. _VERSION )
```

Hint

Do you see that odd-looking pair of dots in the last line of the script file? The double dot is Lua's way of attaching strings together (while Basic and most other languages use the plus (+) operator).

Sharing Tile Data with Lua

What's next? We have a Lua linkage in our Basic project, so we should give Lua more control over our game data. I want to be able to scroll the game world to any location with a function call, as well as read the data for any tile on the tilemap, including the tile under the player's current position, for obvious reasons. Once those things are done, then it will be possible to add Lua functions to the tilemap via our level editor. At that point, the game engine becomes less of a factor for gameplay code. Any variable in the Basic program can be sent to the Lua code as a global, and vice versa! This level of cooperation along with the runtime interpretation of Lua script makes it an extremely valuable addition to our project. We will use these advanced features of Lua in the final game project in Chapter 20!

Level Up!

This chapter saw some dramatic improvements to both the level editor and the Celtic Crusader game code, with the addition of code to detect collidable tiles, and code to make portals active, allowing us to teleport the player to a new location. Although the level editor provides the "portalfile" field to enable teleporting to a position in a *different* level file, we will reserve that feature for later. Finally, by adding Lua scripting support to the engine we will be able to do some remarkable things in script code that will free up some of the requirements on our Basic program.

Believe it or not, we now have a game world that is suitable as an environment for the Celtic Crusader game! That means we can shift focus from the game world and level editing over to a new subject—people and monsters!

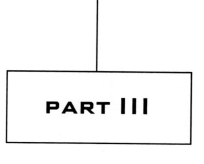

PART III

GAMEPLAY

This final part focuses purely on the gameplay perspective—creating the various parts of our Celtic Crusader game that bring it to life. Up to this point, we have been so focused on just getting something up on the screen and working as it should, we haven't had much time to explore gameplay. Now we have a game world and all of the engine-level features we need for the game. This part starts with a chapter on creating a character editor and using custom character files in the game. Chapters 15 and 16 then expand on characters by exploring a dialogue system, NPCs, and the combat side of the game. Chapters 17 and 18 develop an inventory system, making it possible to loot treasure and items. Finally, in the last two chapters, a quest system is developed and the finishing touches are made to the game.

- Chapter 14: Creating the Character Editor
- Chapter 15: Dialogue: Talking with NPCs
- Chapter 16: Fighting, Getting XP, and Leveling Up
- Chapter 17: Creating the Item Editor
- Chapter 18: Looting Treasure and Managing Inventory
- Chapter 19: Creating the Quest Editor
- Chapter 20: So You Want to Be a Hero?

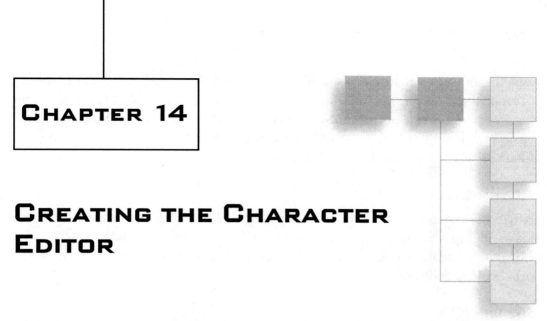

CHAPTER 14

CREATING THE CHARACTER EDITOR

This chapter covers character creation using a custom new editor tool, and discusses the usual attributes associated with an RPG based on character race, class, and so on. You will learn how to take the designs of the character classes and make use of them in the game by applying the player character's attributes to the combat system and other aspects of any traditional RPG, such as gaining experience and leveling up. Some of these issues will be dealt with in more detail in upcoming chapters, whereas the foundation is laid here for working with character data.

Here's what we'll cover in this chapter:

- Character classes and attributes
- Gaining experience and leveling up
- Base character classes
- Enemy and monster classes
- Loading character files in the game
- Character artwork

CHARACTER CLASSES AND ATTRIBUTES

All of the previous chapters have focused on the difficult task of getting a fully animated player to walk around in a scrolling game world. Both the animation and the movement should be semi-realistic, and tile-collision detection should prevent the player from walking through solid and impassable tiles (which still requires some work but is coming together), and using portals. Now that these basic problems have been solved, we can get into the game's design and the nuances of combat and NPC interaction.

Attributes

Attributes determine what a character is capable of doing in the game, whether it's swinging a sword, firing arrows, or defending against attacks from others. The player attributes are the most important part of the character creation process that follows.

Strength (STR)

Strength represents the character's ability to carry weight and deal damage with a melee weapon. It is generally good for the warrior and paladin classes, which use melee weapons. Strength is used to calculate the attack damage for the character if a hit is successful (see "Dexterity" for details on the "to hit" factor). First, the player has to *hit* the target before damage is calculated. So, even an enormous amount of STR will rarely come into play if dexterity is too low. Therefore, both of these attributes are crucial for a melee fighter! STR is of little use to a priest (who favors intellect) and is of minor import to a hunter (who relies more on dexterity).

Dexterity (DEX)

Dexterity represents the agility of a character, the skillful use of one's hands. This affects the ability to wield melee weapons and shields effectively to block and parry attacks and to hit accurately with a ranged weapon such as a bow. Low DEX leads to a somewhat clumsy character, while high DEX means the character can perform complex actions (perhaps wielding two weapons). Dexterity determines the defense and the chance to hit factors in combat. See Chapter 16, "Fighting, Getting XP, and Leveling Up," for more details on combat calculations. The "chance to hit" value is rolled against the defender's defense value to determine if an attack is successful. Thus, it is of little use for a level 1 character to attack someone who is level 20, because he will not be able to land hits, let alone do any damage.

Stamina (STA)

Stamina represents a character's endurance, the ability to continue performing an activity for a long period of time, and it is used directly in the calculation of hit points (health). High STA provides a character with the ability to engage in lengthy battles without rest, while low STA causes a character to get tired quickly and fall in battle. Although every class benefits from stamina, it is more vital for the melee characters since they engage in "in your face" combat. Although a low STA will lead a hunter or priest to fall just as quickly, they aren't likely to take as many hits since they attack at range.

Intellect (INT)

Intellect represents the character's ability to learn, remember things, and solve problems. A very high INT is required by the `priest` class, while relatively low INT is common in fighters where brute force is more important than mental faculties. Also, INT affects the amount of experience gained for performing actions such as defeating enemies and completing quests, so a character with high INT will level up more quickly. This is important for the ranged classes since they usually have fewer battles.

Charisma (CHA)

Charisma represents the character's attractiveness, which affects how others respond to the character. High CHA attracts people, while low CHA repels them—although in the violent world of Celtic Crusader, a "pretty boy" is of little use even to the ladies. In the converse, low CHA also represents the ugliness of a monster such as an undead zombie. CHA does not represent just a character or monster's scariness, but is more related to personality and physical attractiveness. In other words, it is possible for a dangerous creature (such as a dragon) to be beautiful.

Hit Points

Hit points, or HP, represent the amount of health a character has. HP is calculated initially (at level 1) by adding a D8 roll to the character's stamina. Then, each time the character levels, additional HP is added with another die roll. Thus, it is entirely possible to create a weakling of a warrior (by consistently rolling badly) who has less HP than even a priest. It's all left to chance, which is what makes RPGs so universally compelling. Purists will play with their rolled stats, while less serious players will re-roll their character until they get the points that they want. Generally, the class modifiers make up for bad initial rolls.

Gaining Experience and Leveling Up

One of the most rewarding aspects of an RPG is gaining experience by performing actions in the game (usually combat) and leveling up your character. When you start the game, the character is also just starting out as a level 1 with no experience. This reflects the player's own skill level with the game itself, and that is the appeal of an RPG: *You*, the player, gain experience with the game while your character gains experience at the same time in the virtual world. You grow together and become a seamless "person."

Both you and your character improve as you play the game, so you transfer some of your own identity to the character, and in some cases, younger players even assume some of the identity of their inspiring hero. This fascinating give-and-take relationship can really draw someone into your game if you design it well! Like I have said, cut back on the magic and let players really get in the game world and experience some good, solid combat to make the whole experience feel more real, and less detached. You want to do everything possible to suspend the players' disbelief that they are in a game—you want to bring them into your game world by doing things that cause them to invest emotionally in their characters.

The most common way to gain experience is through combat with monsters and enemy characters. We will study combat in detail in Chapter 16, "Fighting, Getting XP, and Leveling Up," and quests in Chapter 19, "Creating the Quest Editor." These are the only two ways to get experience and level up. Since there are a lot of calculations involved in the chance to hit, armor class, melee attack, ranged attack, spell attack, and other factors, I will reserve Chapter 16 for a discussion of the details.

The Base Character Classes

The standard, or base, classes can be used for the player as well as for the non-player characters (NPCs). You should feel free to create as many classes as you want to make your game world diversified and interesting. The classes I have described here are just the usual classes you find in an RPG, which you might consider the stock classes. Each class also has subclasses, or specialties within that class. For instance, Paladins are really just a subclass of the Knight, which may include Teutonic Knight, Crusader, and so on.

When you are designing a game, you can make it as historically accurate or as fictional as you want; don't feel compelled to make every class realistic or historically based. You might make up a fictional type of Knight subclass, such as a Dark Knight or Gothic Knight, with some dark magic abilities. However, I want to encourage you to shy away from overdoing the magic system in a game. Many RPGs have character classes that might be thought of as wizards on steroids, because the whole game boils down to upgrading spells and magic, with little emphasis on "realistic" combat.

You would be surprised by how effective an RPG can be with just a *few* magic abilities. You can really go overboard with the hocus pocus, and that tends to trivialize a well-designed storyline and render interesting characters into fireball targets. No warrior should be able to do *any* magic whatsoever. Think about it: The warriors are basically barbarians—massive, hulking fighters who use brute force to bash skulls on the battlefield (think Arnold Schwarzenegger in the *Conan* movies). This type of character can become civilized and educated, but so many games blur the line here and allow any class to develop magical abilities. (I'm just pointing out some obvious design concerns with characters. If you really want a world of magic, then go ahead and create magical characters; that sounds like a really fun game, as a matter of fact!) If you are designing a traditional RPG, then be realistic with your classes and keep the magic reasonable. Think about *The Lord of the Rings*; these stories are a source of inspiration for every RPG ever made. Everything since J.R.R. Tolkien has been derivative!

The character editor tool has the ability to apply modifiers to the basic stats, but this is a manual process. If you add new classes to the `cboClass` list in the editor, then you'll have to make changes to the modifiers manually in the code (hint: look for the code in `cboClass_SelectedIndexChanged()`).

One design consideration that we might use is the concept of class modifiers. Say you have a set of stock classes like those listed in the upcoming tables. Instead of re-creating a class from scratch using similar values, you can create a subclass based on the parent class—and modify the attributes by a small amount to produce the new class with custom attributes.

Say, for instance, that you want to create a new type of Warrior called the Berserker, which is an extremely stupid and ugly character with immense strength and stamina. Sounds a little bit scary, doesn't it? By setting the base class of the Berserker to Warrior, you can then modify the base class at any time and the Berserker automatically is changed along with the base class (Warrior). This works great for balancing the gameplay without requiring that you modify *every single* subclass that you have used in the game. Since our character class system in Celtic Crusader will be based on classes, we can easily subclass the base character classes to create new types of characters in this manner.

Hint

It goes without saying that female characters are fun to play with in an RPG. Unfortunately, we have no female equivalents to the four player characters represented in Celtic Crusader. Yes, there are some female NPCs available in the artwork from Reiner Prokein, but not for the primary character classes. If you have artwork available, I encourage you to add a gender property to the character editor. Gender is not extremely important to the gameplay, as it turns out.

Tables 14.1 to 14.4 present my idea of a character class structure that is programmed into the editor. Since this only applies to the editor, and not to any game source code, you may modify the editor to use your own preferred values and classes.

To keep your game character classes balanced, it's important to use a standard total for all modifiers so that they all add up to the same amount. I have based the following class modifiers on a total of 15 points. In testing the game, it seemed that values much lower made the hero characters less impressive (compared to, say, a peasant), while values much higher resulted in unusually powerful characters. If you want a character to have one very high attribute, then that will have to be balanced with an equally low value for another. Note also that monsters need not follow this standard—go ahead and use whatever factors you want to create unique foes. The goal of this point modifier system is to create player characters that are based on the same fixed number of attribute points.

Hint

The character class modifiers should add up to a total of 15 points. The points can be applied to any of the attributes. These mod values are then added to 2D6 rolls to come up with the total attribute values.

Warrior Class

The warrior class represents the strongest melee fighter who deals enormous crushing blows against his opponents, but who is not especially accurate at lower levels. Warriors are like home run hitters, in that they tend to knock it out of the park or strike out. In gameplay, a low-level warrior will miss a lot but then do massive damage when he does land a blow, which usually takes out most lower-level creatures. At higher levels, warriors gain an appreciable amount of DEX that compensates for the initial low starting value. Since the warrior is a rage-filled barbarian, he has low INT and CHA because these attributes are not important. Warriors can wear chain or plate armor, and have abilities like rage and berserk that boost his attributes during combat. Drawing from inspiration such as Tolkien, one might look to Gimli.

Table 14.1	Warrior Attributes	
Attribute	**Roll**	**Modifiers (+15)**
Strength	2D6	+8
Dexterity	2D6	+3
Stamina	2D6	+4
Intellect	2D6	0
Charisma	2D6	0
Hit Points	1D8	+STA

Paladin Class

The paladin is a balanced melee fighter with massive survivability. Classically, a paladin was a melee fighter with some healing abilities, making him a cross between warrior and priest. If you want to follow this traditional view of the paladin class, you may do so. I have taken a simpler approach to the paladin, making him slightly less damaging than the warrior but able to take more damage. While the single point in CHA might seem like a waste, it reflects the nature of the paladin as an attractive, heroic knight. He has abilities that give a temporary boost to his weapons and armor points. Paladins can wear chain or

Table 14.2 Paladin Attributes

Attribute	Roll	Modifiers (+15)
Strength	2D6	+3
Dexterity	2D6	+3
Stamina	2D6	+8
Intellect	2D6	0
Charisma	2D6	+1
Hit Points	1D8	+STA

plate armor, preferring the most brightly polished pieces of gear they can find. Drawing from popular inspiration, one might look to the Tolkien characters Baromir or Eomer.

Hunter Class

The hunter is a ranged class with no melee combat ability, but capable of dealing massive damage with a bow. Hunters are fast on their feet, wear light leather armor, and usually have many different types of arrows for their favorite bow. Hunters have a high DEX to improve ranged chance to hit, with less use for traits like STR and INT. Abilities revolve around ranged attack modifiers that improve accuracy (chance to hit). A good example from which to draw inspiration is the Tolkien character Legolas.

Table 14.3 Hunter Attributes

Attribute	Roll	Modifiers (+15)
Strength	2D6	+2
Dexterity	2D6	+8
Stamina	2D6	+4
Intellect	2D6	0
Charisma	2D6	+1
Hit Points	1D8	+STA

Priest Class

The `priest` class represents a holy man of the cloth who has been forced to fight the rampaging undead horde that has been destroying everything in its path. A priest is unlike a traditional magic user, both unwilling and unable to call on the evil powers required to conjure magic known to traditional wizards and mages (whom he would consider opponents). A priest uses holy power to fight evil, undead creatures, never to attack other human beings. His abilities include healing and exorcism. A loose example from Tolkien's universe might be Arwen.

Table 14.4 Priest Attributes

Attribute	Roll	Modifiers (+15)
Strength	2D6	0
Dexterity	2D6	+6
Stamina	2D6	+1
Intellect	2D6	+8
Charisma	2D6	0
Hit Points	1D8	+STA

Peasants as Quest-Giving NPCs

In addition to these player character classes, you might want to create base classes for some of the regular people in the world, like townsfolk, peasants, farmers, and so on. These non-combat NPCs might all just share the same character class (with weak combat skills, poor experience, and so on). We will need NPCs like this for the quest system coming up later. (See Table 14.5.) NPCs do not need to follow the same modifier rules reserved for player character classes (which, again, should be thought of as heroes). Note that NPCs and monsters generally have more HP than their levels imply to improve gameplay by increasing the difficulty early on—which makes the player eager to level up quickly.

Table 14.5   Peasant

Attribute	Roll	Modifiers
Strength	1D6	0
Dexterity	1D6	0
Stamina	1D6	0
Intellect	1D6	0
Charisma	1D6	0
Hit Points	1D8	+STA

The Enemy/Monster Classes

We can also create fantasy creatures and monsters described in Tables 14.6 to 14.9. These creatures are unprecedented because they have no equal on the "good side." But you will not want to make all of the bad guys too powerful—save that for the unusual monsters that are rarely encountered or the game will be way too hard to play. You will generally want to have at least one type of *bad guy* for each type of *character class* available to the player, and duplicate that character all over the game world. In addition, you must add weaker enemy characters that make good fodder for the player to help with leveling up. Another thing to remember is that monsters do not gain experience and level up, so they should start out with higher level stats than a typical level 1 player character. Since the human but otherwise *bad* characters share the same stats as the human *good guys*, we don't need to define them separately.

Remember, these are generic class types, or races, not individuals. Since we don't need to follow a modifier standard, you may get as creative as you want. Since these classes represent various level ranges, the attributes are calculated with die roll specifications *and* modifiers (both of which are supported in the character editor).

If you want to create a level 10 monster, then I recommend rolling 10D6 for its attributes. If the desired level is L, then each attribute roll is $LD6$. The modifiers may then be used to adjust the dice rolls to ensure minimum or maximum values are reached for the monster's intended abilities. For instance, if you want to create a zombie with a minimum of 20 STR while still using the attribute roll, then add 20 to the STR roll and the result will be 20 + STR. As long as the minimums are capped to zero, it's okay to add *negative* modifiers. If you want to specify a monster's level specifically in the editor data, go ahead and add it as a new property—I just prefer to get away from the numbers game and let the player learn each monster's abilities by fighting them (in the interest of improving the suspense of disbelief!).

As a final note, there is no reason to roll the charisma attribute for monsters so I have set CHA to 0 in these tables. If you have some purpose for this attribute in your own game, by all means go ahead and use it!

Skeleton Warrior

Skeleton warriors are the mainstay of the undead horde army, and as such, they can be found *almost everywhere* in the game world. At level 4, these guys are pretty tough for a new player but are soon dealt with handily once the player goes up a few levels. The skeleton warrior has high strength and stamina, and a lot of hit points!

Table 14.6 Level 4 Skeleton Warrior

Attribute	Roll	Modifiers
Strength	4D6	+10
Dexterity	4D6	+6
Stamina	4D6	+8
Intellect	4D6	0
Charisma	0	0
Hit Points	4D8	+STA

Skeleton Archer

Skeleton archers were once support units for the Viking army that became undead, so there aren't as many as the `warrior` class but they tend to be better trained and hit much harder—at range. They are crack shots with their arrows so be sure to close in fast and take them out before they get too many shots off.

Table 14.7 Level 8 Skeleton Archer

Attribute	Roll	Modifiers
Strength	8D6	+14
Dexterity	8D6	+20
Stamina	8D6	+16
Intellect	8D6	0
Charisma	0	0
Hit Points	8D8	+STA

Viking Guard

Viking guards are remnants of the Viking army who were not involved in the debacle that gave rise to the undead army, and they're lucky to have been spared! Normal Viking troops are somewhat like a traditional warrior but with training they have achieved a high hit rating as well as high strength, so not only can they hit, they hit *hard*!

Table 14.8 Level 12 Viking Guard

Attribute	Roll	Modifiers
Strength	12D6	+20
Dexterity	12D6	+18
Stamina	12D6	+16
Intellect	12D6	0
Charisma	0	0
Hit Points	12D8	+STA

Zombie

Zombies are also part of the undead horde of former Vikings, but due to some mishap they retained most of their original appearance and clothing, and did not get fully transformed into undead skeletons. As a result, zombies are confused about their existence and believe they still need to *feed*. They carry no weapons or armor because they were not in the army, but rather Viking citizens brought to colonize the land and further push out the native inhabitants. Despite having no weapons, zombies are extremely dangerous because they can take an extraordinary amount of damage before they fall.

Table 14.9 Level 16 Zombie

Attribute	Roll	Modifiers
Strength	16D6	+22
Dexterity	16D6	+12
Stamina	16D6	+28
Intellect	16D6	0
Charisma	0	0
Hit Points	16D8	+STA

THE CHARACTER EDITOR

The character editor is a VB program designed to create and edit game characters. Each character will be stored in its own file with an extension of .char, although this data is also just xml like the level editor data. Figure 14.1 shows the Character Editor program running.

I generally do not see the point of sharing source for a complex form-based application like this editor, because you can't create the editor from just this source code and it's too complex to list the properties for every control in an attempt to build it, tutorial style. As a compromise, I will go over the source code and explain each function clearly if it is not already self-explanatory.

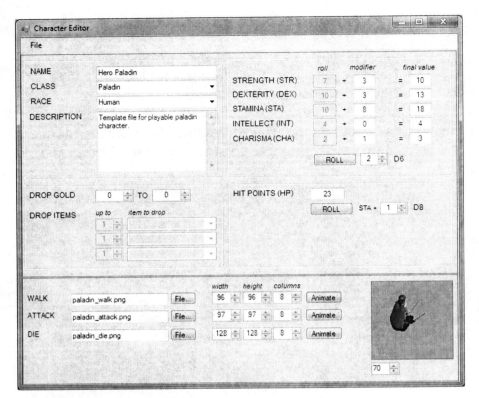

Figure 14.1
The Character Editor tool.

Hint

> The "DROP GOLD" and "DROP ITEMS" fields are not used yet, but reserved for Chapter 17, "Creating the Item Editor" and Chapter 18, "Looting Treasure and Drop Items." When we have the code to work with these data fields, then we can edit monster character files and specify what we want them to drop, but first we need an item editor. Furthermore, when quests are working, we'll want certain characters to drop certain items to satisfy quests!

This is not the complete source code for the character editor, just an explanation of the major functions in the code, in the interest of saving space. All of the user interface events (like button clicks) have been left out since they are just logistical and not vital to an understanding of the editor.

```
Public Class Form1
    Dim device As Graphics
    Dim surface As Bitmap
```

```
Dim animationImage As Bitmap
Dim sprite As Sprite
Dim rand As Random
Dim g_filename As String
Dim currentAnim As String

Private Sub Form1_Load(ByVal sender As System.Object, _
        ByVal e As System.EventArgs) Handles MyBase.Load
    surface = New Bitmap(Size.Width, Size.Height)
    PictureBox1.Image = surface
    device = Graphics.FromImage(surface)
    sprite = New Sprite(device)
    animationImage = Nothing
    rand = New Random()
End Sub
```

The btnWalkFile_Click() subroutine is called by the first "File..." button, next to the Walk animation filename field. This button is used to bring up the Open File dialog in order to choose a bitmap file to load for the walk animation.

```
Private Sub btnWalkFile_Click(ByVal sender As System.Object, _
        ByVal e As System.EventArgs) Handles btnWalkFile.Click
    Open1.DefaultExt = ".png"
    Open1.Filter = "Bitmap Files|*.png;*.png;*.jpg"
    Open1.Multiselect = False
    Open1.Title = "Load Bitmap File"
    Open1.InitialDirectory = Environment.CurrentDirectory
    Dim result As DialogResult
    result = Open1.ShowDialog(Me)
    If result <> DialogResult.OK Then Return
    txtWalkFile.Text = IO.Path.GetFileName(Open1.FileName)
    animationImage = LoadBitmap(txtWalkFile.Text)
End Sub
```

The btnAttackFile_Click() subroutine is called by the second "File..." button, next to the Attack animation filename field. This button is used to bring up the Open File dialog in order to choose a bitmap file to load for the attack animation.

```
Private Sub btnAttackFile_Click(ByVal sender As System.Object, _
        ByVal e As System.EventArgs) Handles btnAttackFile.Click
    Open1.DefaultExt = ".png"
    Open1.Filter = "Bitmap Files|*.png;*.png;*.jpg"
    Open1.Multiselect = False
    Open1.Title = "Load Bitmap File"
    Open1.InitialDirectory = Environment.CurrentDirectory
    Dim result As DialogResult
    result = Open1.ShowDialog(Me)
    If result <> DialogResult.OK Then Return
    txtAttackFile.Text = IO.Path.GetFileName(Open1.FileName)
    animationImage = LoadBitmap(txtAttackFile.Text)
End Sub
```

The btnDieFile_Click() subroutine is called by the third "File..." button, next
to the Die animation filename field. This button is used to bring up the Open
File dialog in order to choose a bitmap file to load for the die animation.

```
Private Sub btnDieFile_Click(ByVal sender As System.Object, _
        ByVal e As System.EventArgs) Handles btnDieFile.Click
    Open1.DefaultExt = ".png"
    Open1.Filter = "Bitmap Files|*.png;*.png;*.jpg"
    Open1.Multiselect = False
    Open1.Title = "Load Bitmap File"
    Open1.InitialDirectory = Environment.CurrentDirectory
    Dim result As DialogResult
    result = Open1.ShowDialog(Me)
    If result <> DialogResult.OK Then Return
    txtDieFile.Text = IO.Path.GetFileName(Open1.FileName)
    animationImage = LoadBitmap(txtDieFile.Text)
End Sub
```

The Timer1_Tick() subroutine performs animation using the specified sprite sheet
for either the walk, attack, or die animation files. A scratch sprite is used to animate
all three of the sprite sheets, depending on which "Animate" button was pressed.

```
Private Sub Timer1_Tick(ByVal sender As System.Object, _
        ByVal e As System.EventArgs) Handles Timer1.Tick
    If currentAnim = "walk" Then
        sprite.Width = numWidth.Value
        sprite.Height = numHeight.Value
        sprite.Columns = numColumns.Value
```

```
        ElseIf currentAnim = "attack" Then
            sprite.Width = numWidth2.Value
            sprite.Height = numHeight2.Value
            sprite.Columns = numColumns2.Value
        ElseIf currentAnim = "die" Then
            sprite.Width = numWidth3.Value
            sprite.Height = numHeight3.Value
            sprite.Columns = numColumns3.Value
        End If
        sprite.TotalFrames = sprite.Columns * 8
        sprite.Image = animationImage
        sprite.Animate(0, sprite.TotalFrames - 1)
        device.Clear(Color.DarkGray)
        sprite.Draw()
        PictureBox1.Image = surface
    End Sub
```

The btnRoll_Click() subroutine rolls the random "dice" calculations for the five main character attributes: STR, DEX, STA, INT, and CHA.

```
    Private Sub btnRoll_Click(ByVal sender As System.Object, _
            ByVal e As System.EventArgs) Handles btnRoll.Click
        txtRollStr.Text = rand.Next(1, 6 * numDCount.Value).ToString()
        txtRollDex.Text = rand.Next(1, 6 * numDCount.Value).ToString()
        txtRollSta.Text = rand.Next(1, 6 * numDCount.Value).ToString()
        txtRollInt.Text = rand.Next(1, 6 * numDCount.Value).ToString()
        txtRollCha.Text = rand.Next(1, 6 * numDCount.Value).ToString()
    End Sub
```

The loadFile() subroutine loads a .char file containing xml data for a character. The getElement() function assists with the loading of each field in the xml data with error handling in case of a load error. As each field is copied into the user interface TextBox and NumericUpDown controls, data type conversions are performed as needed.

```
    Private Function getElement(ByVal field As String, _
            ByRef element As XmlElement) As String
        Dim value As String = ""
        Try
            value = element.GetElementsByTagName(field)(0).InnerText
```

```vbnet
        Catch ex As Exception
            REM ignore error, just return empty
            Console.WriteLine(ex.Message)
        End Try
        Return value
    End Function
    Private Sub loadFile(ByVal filename As String)
        Try
            REM open the xml file
            Dim doc As New XmlDocument()
            doc.Load(filename)
            Dim list As XmlNodeList = doc.GetElementsByTagName("character")
            Dim element As XmlElement = list(0)
            REM read data fields
            txtName.Text = getElement("name", element)
            cboClass.Text = getElement("class", element)
            cboRace.Text = getElement("race", element)
            txtDesc.Text = getElement("desc", element)
            txtStr.Text = getElement("str", element)
            txtDex.Text = getElement("dex", element)
            txtSta.Text = getElement("sta", element)
            txtInt.Text = getElement("int", element)
            txtCha.Text = getElement("cha", element)
            txtHP.Text = getElement("hitpoints", element)
            txtWalkFile.Text = getElement("anim_walk_filename", element)
            numWidth.Value = Convert.ToInt32( _
                getElement("anim_walk_width", element))
            numHeight.Value = Convert.ToInt32( _
                getElement("anim_walk_height", element))
            numColumns.Value = Convert.ToInt32( _
                getElement("anim_walk_columns", element))
            txtAttackFile.Text = getElement( _
                "anim_attack_filename", element)
            numWidth2.Value = Convert.ToInt32( _
                getElement("anim_attack_width", element))
            numHeight2.Value = Convert.ToInt32( _
                getElement("anim_attack_height", element))
            numColumns2.Value = Convert.ToInt32( _
                getElement("anim_attack_columns", element))
```

```
        txtDieFile.Text = getElement( _
            "anim_die_filename", element)
        numWidth3.Value = Convert.ToInt32( _
            getElement("anim_die_width", element))
        numHeight3.Value = Convert.ToInt32( _
            getElement("anim_die_height", element))
        numColumns3.Value = Convert.ToInt32( _
            getElement("anim_die_columns", element))
        numGold1.Value = Convert.ToInt32( _
            getElement("dropgold1", element))
        numGold2.Value = Convert.ToInt32( _
            getElement("dropgold2", element))
    Catch ex As Exception
        MessageBox.Show(ex.Message)
    End Try
End Sub
```

The saveFile() subroutine has the job of building the xml schema as well as saving the character data to an xml file based on that schema.

```
Private Sub saveFile(ByVal filename As String)
    Try
        REM create xml schema
        Dim table As New DataTable("character")
        table.Columns.Add(New DataColumn("name", _
            System.Type.GetType("System.String")))
        table.Columns.Add(New DataColumn("class", _
            System.Type.GetType("System.String")))
        table.Columns.Add(New DataColumn("race", _
            System.Type.GetType("System.String")))
        table.Columns.Add(New DataColumn("desc", _
            System.Type.GetType("System.String")))
        table.Columns.Add(New DataColumn("str", _
            System.Type.GetType("System.Int32")))
        table.Columns.Add(New DataColumn("dex", _
            System.Type.GetType("System.Int32")))
        table.Columns.Add(New DataColumn("sta", _
            System.Type.GetType("System.Int32")))
        table.Columns.Add(New DataColumn("int", _
            System.Type.GetType("System.Int32")))
```

```
table.Columns.Add(New DataColumn("cha", _
    System.Type.GetType("System.Int32")))
table.Columns.Add(New DataColumn("hitpoints", _
    System.Type.GetType("System.Int32")))
table.Columns.Add(New DataColumn("anim_walk_filename", _
    System.Type.GetType("System.String")))
table.Columns.Add(New DataColumn("anim_walk_width", _
    System.Type.GetType("System.Int32")))
table.Columns.Add(New DataColumn("anim_walk_height", _
    System.Type.GetType("System.Int32")))
table.Columns.Add(New DataColumn("anim_walk_columns", _
    System.Type.GetType("System.Int32")))
table.Columns.Add(New DataColumn("anim_attack_filename", _
    System.Type.GetType("System.String")))
table.Columns.Add(New DataColumn("anim_attack_width", _
    System.Type.GetType("System.Int32")))
table.Columns.Add(New DataColumn("anim_attack_height", _
    System.Type.GetType("System.Int32")))
table.Columns.Add(New DataColumn("anim_attack_columns", _
    System.Type.GetType("System.Int32")))
table.Columns.Add(New DataColumn("anim_die_filename", _
    System.Type.GetType("System.String")))
table.Columns.Add(New DataColumn("anim_die_width", _
    System.Type.GetType("System.Int32")))
table.Columns.Add(New DataColumn("anim_die_height", _
    System.Type.GetType("System.Int32")))
table.Columns.Add(New DataColumn("anim_die_columns", _
    System.Type.GetType("System.Int32")))
table.Columns.Add(New DataColumn("dropgold1", _
    System.Type.GetType("System.Int32")))
table.Columns.Add(New DataColumn("dropgold2", _
    System.Type.GetType("System.Int32")))

REM copy character data into datatable
Dim row As DataRow = table.NewRow()
row("name") = txtName.Text
row("class") = cboClass.Text
row("race") = cboRace.Text
row("desc") = txtDesc.Text
row("str") = txtStr.Text
row("dex") = txtDex.Text
```

```
            row("sta") = txtSta.Text
            row("int") = txtInt.Text
            row("cha") = txtCha.Text
            row("hitpoints") = txtHP.Text
            row("anim_walk_filename") = txtWalkFile.Text
            row("anim_walk_width") = numWidth.Value
            row("anim_walk_height") = numHeight.Value
            row("anim_walk_columns") = numColumns.Value
            row("anim_attack_filename") = txtAttackFile.Text
            row("anim_attack_width") = numWidth2.Value
            row("anim_attack_height") = numHeight2.Value
            row("anim_attack_columns") = numColumns2.Value
            row("anim_die_filename") = txtDieFile.Text
            row("anim_die_width") = numWidth3.Value
            row("anim_die_height") = numHeight3.Value
            row("anim_die_columns") = numColumns3.Value
            row("dropgold1") = numGold1.Value
            row("dropgold2") = numGold2.Value
            table.Rows.Add(row)

            REM save xml file
            table.WriteXml(filename)
            table.Dispose()
        Catch es As Exception
            MessageBox.Show(es.Message)
        End Try
    End Sub
```

In addition to rolling for the character's five primary stats, we can also roll the hit points for a character using this button event. It's very simple: a random value from 1 to 8 (1D8) is added to the existing stamina value to come up with the character's hit points. Obviously you will want to roll the stats first before calling this.

```
    Private Sub btnRollHP_Click(ByVal sender As System.Object, _
            ByVal e As System.EventArgs) Handles btnRollHP.Click
        Dim stamina As Integer = Convert.ToInt32(txtSta.Text)
        Dim hp As Integer = stamina + rand.Next(1, 8)
        txtHP.Text = hp.ToString()
    End Sub
```

The three Animate buttons cause the specified animation to be rendered.

```
Private Sub btnAnimate3_Click(ByVal sender As System.Object, _
        ByVal e As System.EventArgs) Handles btnAnimate3.Click
    currentAnim = "die"
    animationImage = LoadBitmap(txtDieFile.Text)
    Timer1.Interval = numRate.Value
    Timer1.Enabled = Not Timer1.Enabled
End Sub
Private Sub btnAnimate2_Click(ByVal sender As System.Object, _
        ByVal e As System.EventArgs) Handles btnAnimate2.Click
    currentAnim = "attack"
    animationImage = LoadBitmap(txtAttackFile.Text)
    Timer1.Interval = numRate.Value
    Timer1.Enabled = Not Timer1.Enabled
End Sub
Private Sub btnAnimate1_Click(ByVal sender As System.Object, _
        ByVal e As System.EventArgs) Handles btnAnimate.Click
    currentAnim = "walk"
    animationImage = LoadBitmap(txtWalkFile.Text)
    Timer1.Interval = numRate.Value
    Timer1.Enabled = Not Timer1.Enabled
End Sub
Private Sub numRate_ValueChanged(ByVal sender As System.Object, _
        ByVal e As System.EventArgs) Handles numRate.ValueChanged
    Timer1.Interval = numRate.Value
End Sub
```

Now we come to the code responsible for applying the class-specific attribute modifiers discussed earlier. This is all manual code, which is not the best way to do it, but this approach keeps the code and user interface simpler. Otherwise, we're looking at a secondary form and additional data files to keep track of the stats. Since there are only a few actual classes shared by most characters and monsters in the game, this is the approach I have decided to take for now. Remember, you can always change the modifiers directly in the editor's fields as well as change the final value for each attribute manually.

```
Private Sub cboClass_SelectedIndexChanged( _
        ByVal sender As System.Object, ByVal e As System.EventArgs) _
        Handles cboClass.SelectedIndexChanged
```

```
                Dim cls As String = cboClass.Text.ToLower()
                If cls = "warrior" Then
                    txtModStr.Text = "8"
                    txtModDex.Text = "3"
                    txtModSta.Text = "4"
                    txtModInt.Text = "0"
                    txtModCha.Text = "0"
                ElseIf cls = "paladin" Then
                    txtModStr.Text = "3"
                    txtModDex.Text = "3"
                    txtModSta.Text = "8"
                    txtModInt.Text = "0"
                    txtModCha.Text = "1"
                ElseIf cls = "hunter" Then
                    txtModStr.Text = "2"
                    txtModDex.Text = "8"
                    txtModSta.Text = "4"
                    txtModInt.Text = "0"
                    txtModCha.Text = "1"
                ElseIf cls = "priest" Then
                    txtModStr.Text = "0"
                    txtModDex.Text = "6"
                    txtModSta.Text = "1"
                    txtModInt.Text = "8"
                    txtModCha.Text = "0"
                End If
            End Sub
```

LOADING CHARACTER FILES

You know what type of data you want to use in the game based on the descriptions of the various classes discussed so far, and that data is now editable with the new character editor tool. How, then, do you make use of these character files in the game? We already have a very convenient Level class that makes the game world scroll very easily with code like this:

```
Private level As Level
level = New Level(game, 25, 19, 32)
level.loadTilemap("sample.level")
level.loadPalette("palette.png", 5)
```

After loading the level, we can scroll and draw the level with simple properties based entirely on the data inside the .level file! I want the same kind of functionality for game characters as well! We have a great character editor available, but it uses a *lot* of data to define a character with unique properties, so we need a class to handle characters as well. I want to be able to load a .char file and have the class automatically load up the three sprite sheets (for walking, attacking, and dying). The class should also keep track of which "state" it's in, and draw the appropriate sprite animation automatically based on the animation state and all of the animation properties, completely wrapped up in a single Draw() routine. Here's an example:

```
hero = New Character(game)
hero.Load("paladin.char")
hero.Position = New Point(400 - 48, 300 - 48)
...
hero.Draw()
```

The Character Class

The Character class is the biggest class of the entire book so far, but that doesn't mean it's overly complex, it just has a lot of data to keep track of and makes use of a *lot* of convenient properties. This is a very user-friendly class, but that means there's a lot of code up front in the class. The end result is *much less* code in our game for dealing with characters. This class will necessarily require changes in the upcoming chapters to accommodate features that we haven't covered yet, like gaining experience and leveling (which are not found in the class yet!). Not to worry, our characters will gain experience and level up—and loot treasure and go on quests too! The properties in the class have been omitted to conserve space—so this is not a complete source code listing, just a reference.

```
Public Class Character
    Public Enum AnimationStates
        Walking
        Attacking
        Dying
    End Enum
    Private p_game As Game
    Private p_position As PointF
    Private p_direction As Integer
    Private p_state As AnimationStates
```

```
REM character file properties
Private p_name As String
Private p_class As String
Private p_race As String
Private p_desc As String
Private p_str As Integer
Private p_dex As Integer
Private p_sta As Integer
Private p_int As Integer
Private p_cha As Integer
Private p_hitpoints As Integer
Private p_dropGold1 As Integer
Private p_dropGold2 As Integer
Private p_walkFilename As String
Private p_walkSprite As Sprite
Private p_walkSize As Point
Private p_walkColumns As Integer
Private p_attackFilename As String
Private p_attackSprite As Sprite
Private p_attackSize As Point
Private p_attackColumns As Integer
Private p_dieFilename As String
Private p_dieSprite As Sprite
Private p_dieSize As Point
Private p_dieColumns As Integer

Public Sub New(ByRef game As Game)
    p_game = game
    p_position = New PointF(0, 0)
    p_direction = 1
    p_state = AnimationStates.Walking

    REM initialize loadable properties
    REM some code omitted due to space
End Sub

REM class properties omitted

Public ReadOnly Property GetSprite() As Sprite
    Get
```

```
            Select Case p_state
                Case AnimationStates.Walking
                    Return p_walkSprite
                Case AnimationStates.Attacking
                    Return p_attackSprite
                Case AnimationStates.Dying
                    Return p_dieSprite
                Case Else
                    Return p_walkSprite
            End Select
        End Get
    End Property

    REM This function animates and draws the character sprite
    REM based on the current state (walking, attacking, or dying)
    Public Sub Draw()
        Dim startFrame As Integer
        Dim endFrame As Integer
        Select Case p_state
            Case AnimationStates.Walking
                p_walkSprite.Position = p_position
                If p_direction > -1 Then
                    startFrame = p_direction * p_walkColumns
                    endFrame = startFrame + p_walkColumns - 1
                    p_walkSprite.AnimationRate = 30
                    p_walkSprite.Animate(startFrame, endFrame)
                End If
                p_walkSprite.Draw()
            Case AnimationStates.Attacking
                p_attackSprite.Position = p_position
                If p_direction > -1 Then
                    startFrame = p_direction * p_attackColumns
                    endFrame = startFrame + p_attackColumns - 1
                    p_attackSprite.AnimationRate = 30
                    p_attackSprite.Animate(startFrame, endFrame)
                End If
                p_attackSprite.Draw()
            Case AnimationStates.Dying
                p_dieSprite.Position = p_position
                If p_direction > -1 Then
```

```
                    startFrame = p_direction * p_dieColumns
                    endFrame = startFrame + p_dieColumns - 1
                    p_dieSprite.AnimationRate = 30
                    p_dieSprite.Animate(startFrame, endFrame)
                End If
                p_dieSprite.Draw()
        End Select
End Sub

REM Load a character .char file
Public Function Load(ByVal filename As String)
    Try
        REM open the xml file
        Dim doc As New XmlDocument()
        doc.Load(filename)
        Dim list As XmlNodeList = doc.GetElementsByTagName("character")
        Dim element As XmlElement = list(0)

        REM read data fields
        p_name = getElement("name", element)
        p_class = getElement("class", element)
        p_race = getElement("race", element)
        p_desc = getElement("desc", element)
        p_str = getElement("str", element)
        p_dex = getElement("dex", element)
        p_sta = getElement("sta", element)
        p_int = getElement("int", element)
        p_cha = getElement("cha", element)
        p_hitpoints = getElement("hitpoints", element)
        p_walkFilename = getElement("anim_walk_filename", element)
        p_walkSize.X = Convert.ToInt32( _
            getElement("anim_walk_width", element))
        p_walkSize.Y = Convert.ToInt32( _
            getElement("anim_walk_height", element))
        p_walkColumns = Convert.ToInt32( _
            getElement("anim_walk_columns", element))
        p_attackFilename = getElement( _
            "anim_attack_filename", element)
        p_attackSize.X = Convert.ToInt32( _
            getElement("anim_attack_width", element))
```

```
            p_attackSize.Y = Convert.ToInt32( _
                getElement("anim_attack_height", element))
            p_attackColumns = Convert.ToInt32( _
                getElement("anim_attack_columns", element))
            p_dieFilename = getElement( _
                "anim_die_filename", element)
            p_dieSize.X = Convert.ToInt32( _
                getElement("anim_die_width", element))
            p_dieSize.Y = Convert.ToInt32( _
                getElement("anim_die_height", element))
            p_dieColumns = Convert.ToInt32( _
                getElement("anim_die_columns", element))
            p_dropGold1 = Convert.ToInt32( _
                getElement("dropgold1", element))
            p_dropGold2 = Convert.ToInt32( _
                getElement("dropgold2", element))
        Catch ex As Exception
            MessageBox.Show(ex.Message)
            Return False
        End Try

        REM create character sprites (with error handling)
        Try
            If p_walkFilename <> "" Then
                p_walkSprite = New Sprite(p_game)
                p_walkSprite.Image = LoadBitmap(p_walkFilename)
                p_walkSprite.Size = p_walkSize
                p_walkSprite.Columns = p_walkColumns
                p_walkSprite.TotalFrames = p_walkColumns * 8
            End If
            If p_attackFilename <> "" Then
                p_attackSprite = New Sprite(p_game)
                p_attackSprite.Image = LoadBitmap(p_attackFilename)
                p_attackSprite.Size = p_attackSize
                p_attackSprite.Columns = p_attackColumns
                p_attackSprite.TotalFrames = p_attackColumns * 8
            End If
            If p_dieFilename <> "" Then
                p_dieSprite = New Sprite(p_game)
                p_dieSprite.Image = LoadBitmap(p_dieFilename)
```

```
                    p_dieSprite.Size = p_dieSize
                    p_dieSprite.Columns = p_dieColumns
                    p_dieSprite.TotalFrames = p_dieColumns * 8
                End If
            Catch ex As Exception
                MessageBox.Show(ex.Message)
                Return False
            End Try
            Return True
        End Function

        Private Function getElement(ByVal field As String, _
                ByRef element As XmlElement) As String
            Dim value As String = ""
            Try
                value = element.GetElementsByTagName(field)(0).InnerText
            Catch ex As Exception
                REM ignore error, just return empty
                Console.WriteLine(ex.Message)
            End Try
            Return value
        End Function

        REM note: portions of this source code have been omitted
        REM refer to the complete project in the chapter's resources

End Class
```

The Animated Character Artwork

Now I'd like to discuss how you can prepare a sprite for use in this game. Each sprite is somewhat different in the number of frames it uses for each type of animation, as well as the types of animation available. All of the character sprites that I'm using in Celtic Crusader have the full eight-direction walking animation sequences, as well as frames for attacking with a weapon. Some sprites have a death animation, and some have running and falling. Normally, to keep the game as uniform as possible, you would use character sprites that have the exact same number of animation frames for the key animation that takes place in the game so that it's easy to switch character classes without changing any source

Figure 14.2
Walking animation for the paladin sprite.

code. But since our editor stores the sprite data in the character data files, we don't need to worry about keeping the animations all uniform. Figure 14.2 shows the walking animation sprite sheet for the paladin class.

The source artwork from Reiner's Tilesets does not come in this format, but it comes with each frame of animation stored in a separate bitmap file. The easiest way to combine these frames into a sprite animation sheet is with Cosmigo's Pro Motion sprite animation program. Because Pro Motion works best with single animation strips, I decided to import each group of bitmaps for the character's walking animation in all eight directions. Using Pro Motion, I converted all 64 frames of animation into a single sprite sheet.

Nothing beats experimentation, so it is up to you to use the freely available sprites provided by Reiner's Tilesets (and other sources) to enhance Celtic

Crusader to suit your own needs. We can only accomplish so much in this book, so I want to give you as many tools, tips, and tricks as I can possibly squeeze in at this time. There are thousands of sprites and tiles available at www. reinerstilesets.de that you can use for your own games! There is a sprite for everything you can possibly imagine adding to an RPG!

All of the characters and monsters discussed in this chapter have been chosen very carefully because we have artwork available for them. Generally, when a game is being designed from the ground up, the game designer will not limit himself to what artwork is available, because none exists before the game goes into development. But in our case, we have all of this artwork provided by Reiner Prokein (www.reinerstileset.de). I strongly recommend that you start with artwork and design your game characters around that instead of designing first and looking for artwork later (unless you know a talented artist who can do the work!).

All of the sprite sheets used in Celtic Crusader were significantly manipulated from their original sources provided by Reiner Prokein. All of the sprites arranged in columns and rows in a sprite sheet and transparent regions have been converted to an alpha channel in each file, which is saved in the Portable Network Graphics (PNG) file format. When you visit Reiner's website, you will not find sprite sheets like these, as they are provided in individual bitmaps. Just be aware that additional work will be required on your part to add new characters or animations to your game. Figure 14.3 shows the three sheets used for the warrior character—note the different number of columns for each sheet, which is handled by the character editor and the Character class!

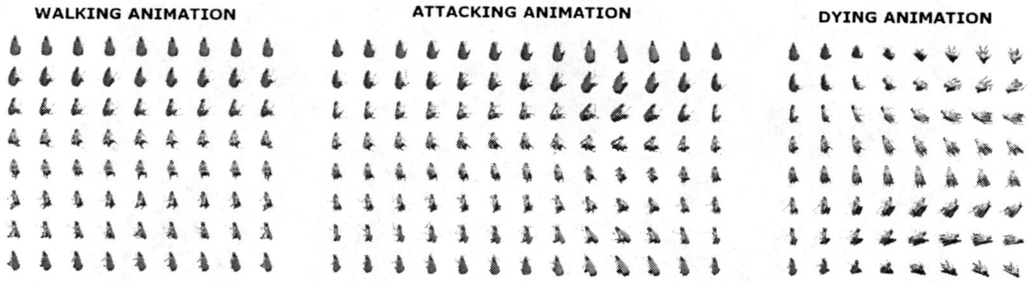

Figure 14.3
The warrior sprite sheets for walking, attacking, and dying.

Character Demo

Let's take the new Character class and artwork for a spin. The Character Demo program is not much different, functionally, from the Portal Demo in the previous chapter. However, *all* of the character code is now transferred over to the Character class, which knows how to load a .char file (created by the character editor tool), parse the xml fields, and create the three sprites needed for each character. In addition, the three animation states can be changed using the standard numeric keys 1, 2, and 3. The result is shown in Figure 14.4. The demo looks a little bit goofy since you have to move in order to show the attack and die animations, but that's okay, as those animations will not be used during normal walking, only when another action is triggered. The point is, the Character class works!

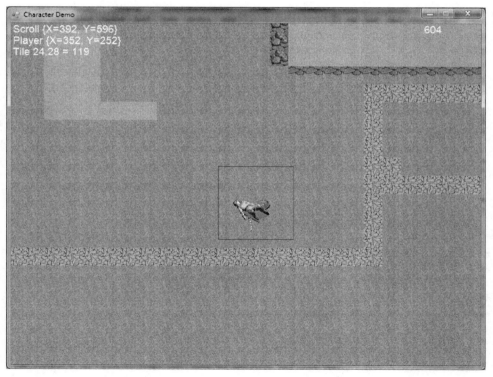

Figure 14.4
We can now kill the player character—wait, is that a good thing?

Since the code for the Character Demo is derived from the previous chapter's example, I will instead just show you the relevant sections of code related to the new Character class, and let you open the project to see the complete sources. Since the Character class mimics some of the Sprite class' properties and also makes available the current sprite object via the GetSprite() function, we can replace most of the Sprite-specific code in this demo with Character-based code without making significant changes.

First, we declare a new Character variable:

```
Private hero As Character
```

Next, we create the hero object and set its initial position.

```
hero = New Character(game)
hero.Load("paladin.char")
hero.Position = New Point(400 - 48, 300 - 48)
```

In the Form1_KeyUp() event, the AnimationState property is changed with the 1, 2, and 3 keys, to test the three different character states (which are Walking, Attacking, and Dying).

```
Private Sub Form1_KeyUp(ByVal sender As System.Object, _
        ByVal e As System.Windows.Forms.KeyEventArgs) _
        Handles MyBase.KeyUp
    Select Case (e.KeyCode)
        Case Keys.Escape : End
        Case Keys.Up, Keys.W : keyState.up = False
        Case Keys.Down, Keys.S : keyState.down = False
        Case Keys.Left, Keys.A : keyState.left = False
        Case Keys.Right, Keys.D : keyState.right = False
        Case Keys.Space
            If portalFlag Then
                level.GridPos = portalTarget
            End If
        Case Keys.D1
            hero.AnimationState = Character.AnimationStates.Walking
        Case Keys.D2
            hero.AnimationState = Character.AnimationStates.Attacking
        Case Keys.D3
            hero.AnimationState = Character.AnimationStates.Dying
    End Select
End Sub
```

In the main loop function, doUpdate(), we simply call hero.Draw(), which both animates *and* draws the character sprite. This Draw() function is so smart that it even figures out automatically which sprite to draw based on the AnimationState.

```
If ticks > drawLast + 16 Then
    drawLast = ticks

    REM draw the tilemap
    level.Draw(0, 0, 800, 600)

    REM draw the hero
    hero.Draw()
    . . .
End If
```

LEVEL UP!

The new character editor tool and the Character class that knows how to work with the new .char files have together dramatically improved our game's potential gameplay with even more data-driven features! It is now possible to design a totally new character or monster, edit the sprite sheet images, and save the new character to a data file, then load it up inside the Celtic Crusader game and have the new character moving around in a matter of minutes, with only a few lines of code! This is really getting exciting, because it means you aren't stuck with just what the designer has put into a game (at least, a game based on these tools). If you want to tweak a character, you won't have to edit any source code, you'll just open the file in the character editor, make the changes, save it, then try it out in the game again. That's the beautiful thing about game editor tools, and why this is such a hot topic in the game industry, with skilled tool programmers in high demand.

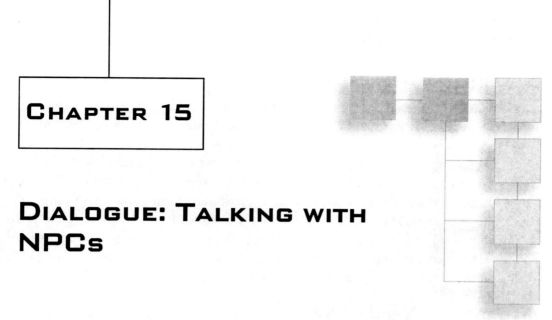

CHAPTER 15

DIALOGUE: TALKING WITH NPCs

The purpose of this chapter is to build a dialogue system for the game so that the player's character can talk with non-player characters (NPCs). This is important, because a dialogue system will allow the player to trade (buying and selling items), as well as allow the player to acquire and turn in quests to gain experience. The dialogue system developed in this chapter will be used to communicate with the player in many more ways beyond the single purpose of focus in this chapter.

Here's what we'll cover in this chapter:

- Creating the "Vendor" NPC
- Starting a conversation
- Dialogue choices
- Making eye contact
- Positioning the dialogue window
- Dialogue GUI
- Complete Dialogue class

TALKING WITH NPCS

For a dialogue system to work well in the game, the first step is to allow the player to get the attention of an NPC, who will either be walking around or staying in a certain location, usually in a town, in a shop, or on the street. Talking with NPCs usually involves walking up close to them and hitting a "talk" button. In console games, that is usually one of the non-combat buttons (like the X or Y button on an Xbox 360 controller, for instance). Until you are in range of the NPC, you cannot talk with them. So, we'll need to use the distance function to find out if we're close enough to an NPC. Interestingly enough, this distance code will be used for combat in the next chapter as well—you know, so that you can only hit an enemy if you're close enough to it.

Creating the "Vendor" NPC

Our example in this chapter has just one NPC—the vendor character. Normally, we would see many NPCs in a level file with a town in it, not just one character. But, this demo will be on the simple side so you can study the code and understand how this one NPC works. Adding more characters will then be no problem. We need to treat the NPCs like any other object in the game, and render it appropriately. Do you recall the Tree Demo from way back in Chapter 12, "Adding Objects to the World"? The same sort of code will be used now to draw the NPC, although we won't use an array or list this time because there's only one object. If you want to see a full-blown NPC system with many characters, scenery objects, and monsters, see the finished game in the last chapter!

We will use the character editor again to create the vendor character, which is shown in Figure 15.1. You'll note in the figure that the vendor has no real attributes worthy of note. That is because the vendor cannot fight, and cannot even be attacked. Note also that only one image is used for the vendor's so-called "animation" sheets, and the `columns` property is set to 1 for all three. This character doesn't need to animate or move, which keeps things simple in the art requirement!

Starting a Conversation

Since both the player and the NPC are based on the `Character` class, we know that they both have the same properties, including a `Position` property that

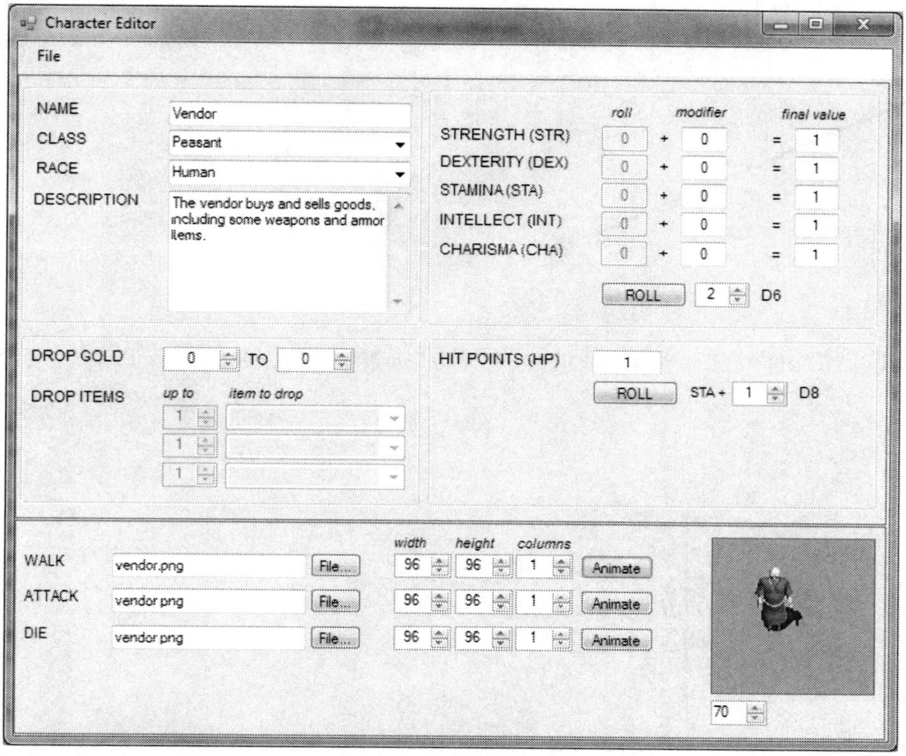

Figure 15.1
The Vendor character in the editor.

returns a PointF (which is like a regular Point structure but containing Singles instead of Integers). So, how do we use the position of the two characters to find the distance between them? First, we treat the position of each character as the endpoint of a line between them, as shown in Figure 15.2.

Hint

The properties were left out of the Character class in the previous chapter to save space. Some of the properties are mentioned in this chapter, which may be a surprise. Please open the project to see the complete source code (www.courseptr.com/downloads).

When using distance to determine whether two sprites are colliding, what we must do is calculate the center point of each sprite, calculate the radius of the sprite (from the center point to the edge), and then check the distance between

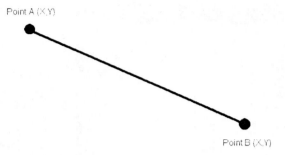

Figure 15.2
The center point of two sprites is used to calculate the distance between them.

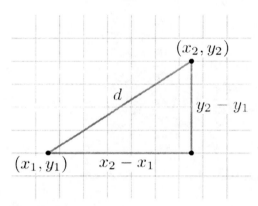

Figure 15.3
A triangle is used to calculate the distance between two points. Image courtesy of Wikipedia.

the two center points. If the distance is less than the two radii combined, then you know the sprites are overlapping. Why? The radius of each sprite, when added together, should be less than the distance between the two sprites.

To calculate the distance between any two points, we can use the classic distance formula. Any two points can be converted into a right triangle by treating them as the end points of the two sides of that triangle, as shown in Figure 15.3. Take the delta value of the X and Y of each point, square each delta value, add them together, then take the square root, and you have the distance between the two points.

```
delta_x = x2 - x1
delta_y = y2 - y1
```

```
delta_x_squared = delta_x * delta_x
delta_y_squared = delta_y * delta_y
distance = square root ( delta_x_squared + delta_y_squared)
```

Here is a function that will meet our needs for calculating distance. This Distance() function would be most helpful if added to the Game class along with some overloaded parameters. We may also need a more specific function suited for the player's standing position, so it might be helpful to add a helper function to the Character class that also calculates distance.

```
Function Distance(ByVal first As PointF, ByVal second As PointF) As Single
    Dim deltaX As Single = second.X - first.X
    Dim deltaY As Single = second.Y - first.Y
    Dim dist = Math.Sqrt(deltaX * deltaX + deltaY * deltaY)
    Return dist
End Function
```

But, we don't want to just use the player's raw X,Y position for the comparison. Remember back in Chapter 13, "Using Portals to Expand the World," we had to compare the player's *foot position* to see if he's walking on a portal or not? The raw position gives the upper-left corner of the player sprite's collision box. We need to use the same HeroFeet() function that returns an adjusted Point containing the coordinates of the player's feet, as if the sprite is really walking on the tiled ground.

```
Private Function HeroFeet() As Point
    Return New Point(hero.X + 32, hero.Y + 32 + 16)
End Function
```

After deciding whether the player is close enough to an NPC to talk with it, the next step is to trigger a new dialogue mode in the game. We will want the rest of the game to pause while talking so nothing happens that the player would be unable to respond to in the game (like being attacked). This pause mode can be handled with a flag that causes some parts of the game to stop updating, but we will want them to be drawn. While that is happening, we do want to allow dialogue to happen, so this probably calls for a Dialogue class. But what should the class do?

The first example for this chapter, Dialogue Demo 1, shows how to calculate the distance between the hero and an NPC, displays the distance, and draws a "talk radius" circle around the NPC so you can see when the character is in range. By

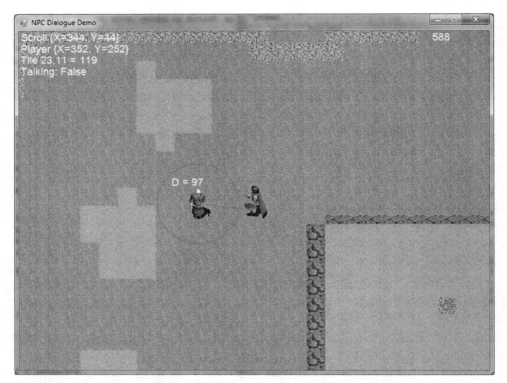

Figure 15.4
If the NPC is in range, then the player can begin a dialogue.

pressing the Space key when in range, a "talking" flag is triggered. Figure 15.4 shows the example. (The code to load the vendor and player characters will be shown in the second example later in this chapter.)

Without getting too deep into the complete source code listing, here is the key code from the first demo (there are three for this chapter). If the player is in range then the circle is drawn in blue to show that the player is in range. A line connecting both characters shows visually what the distance looks like from the precise locations from which it is calculated.

```
Private Sub doVendor()
    Dim relativePos As PointF
    REM draw the vendor sprite
    If vendor.X > level.ScrollPos.X _
```

```
    And vendor.X < level.ScrollPos.X + 23 * 32 _
    And vendor.Y > level.ScrollPos.Y _
    And vendor.Y < level.ScrollPos.Y + 17 * 32 Then
        relativePos.X = Math.Abs(level.ScrollPos.X - vendor.X)
        relativePos.Y = Math.Abs(level.ScrollPos.Y - vendor.Y)
        vendor.GetSprite.Draw(relativePos.X, relativePos.Y)
End If

Dim talkRadius As Integer = 70

REM get center of hero sprite
Dim heroCenter As PointF = HeroFeet()
heroCenter.X += 16
heroCenter.Y += 16
game.Device.DrawRectangle(Pens.Red, heroCenter.X - 2, heroCenter.Y - 2, 4, 4)

REM get center of NPC
Dim vendorCenter As PointF = relativePos
vendorCenter.X += vendor.GetSprite.Width / 2
vendorCenter.Y += vendor.GetSprite.Height / 2
game.Device.DrawRectangle(Pens.Red, vendorCenter.X - 2, vendorCenter.Y - 2, 4, 4)

REM draw line connecting player to vendor
Dim dist As Single = Distance(heroCenter, vendorCenter)
Dim color As Pen
If dist < talkRadius Then
    color = New Pen(Brushes.Blue, 2.0)
Else
    color = New Pen(Brushes.Red, 2.0)
End If
game.Device.DrawLine(color, heroCenter, vendorCenter)

REM print distance
game.Print(relativePos.X, relativePos.Y, _
    "D = " + dist.ToString("N0"), Brushes.White)

REM draw circle around vendor to show talk radius
Dim spriteSize As Single = vendor.GetSprite.Width / 2
Dim centerx As Single = relativePos.X + spriteSize
```

```
        Dim centery As Single = relativePos.Y + spriteSize
        Dim circleRect As New RectangleF( _
            centerx - talkRadius, _
            centery - talkRadius, _
            talkRadius * 2, talkRadius * 2)
        game.Device.DrawEllipse(color, circleRect)

        REM is playing trying to talk to this vendor?
        If dist < talkRadius Then
            If talkFlag Then
                talking = True
            End If
        Else
            talking = False
        End If
End Sub
```

Dialogue Choices

If our game had a mystery plot that required the player to interview dozens or perhaps hundreds of NPCs to find out "who dunnit," then we would absolutely need another game editor to handle all of the complex interactions with these NPCs, with branching dialogue trees and variables so that the NPCs remember past conversations—or at least *seem* to remember them. We don't want this level of complexity for Celtic Crusader. Basically, on each major area of the game, we want to have several NPCs that help the player: buying drop items, selling better gear, healing the player, and so on. These are pretty simple interactions. Since the inventory system and item editor won't be coming along for a couple more chapters, we can't offer up actual gear for the player to use, nor can we let the player sell drop items to the town vendors (yet). But we *can* get the framework in place so that these things *are* possible. In other words, we need a generic dialogue system with options that the player can select.

Continuing to think through the design considerations of our dialogue system, one assumption I'll make now is that we will not have any complex graphical controls like scrolling lists, drop-down lists, or even anything like a scrollbar. The level of complexity for our GUI will end with *buttons*, and there will be a limited number of them. However, with the use of a *state variable*, we can create multiple levels for the dialogue system. Let's say, first of all, there are two dialogue choices for a vendor:

- BUY
- SELL

If you choose the "BUY" option, then a variable is set so that a list of items for sale is displayed next. Then we just recycle the same dialogue with a different set of options (a limited list of items for sale).

- Dagger
- Short Sword
- Barbarian Hammer
- Leather Armor
- Chain Armor
- Plate Armor
- More. . .

There are some limitations to this system, but with creative use of state variables you could offer an unlimited number of items by making the last button a More button that brings up a second page, and so on. One design consideration that you might want to consider is abandoning any sort of Back button in the dialogue system. I know it seems reasonable to let the player go back one level or page, but that tends to complicate things. It is easy enough to just end the dialogue and start it up again with the character, and I have seen many games take this approach.

CREATING THE DIALOGUE SYSTEM

Now that we can determine whether the player is close enough to an NPC to talk with it, the next step is to bring up a dialog window and let the user interact with the NPC. First, we'll incorporate the new dialogue helper functions and properties into the classes to make more effective use of them.

Making Eye Contact

We can still use the distance function to find out when the player is close to an NPC, but Distance() is obviously so reusable that it *must* be moved into the Game class. I'll go a step further by adding an overload. Feel free to add any other variations of the core Game functions or properties that you would find useful. This new version works with individual coordinate values for the two points passed as parameters.

```
Public Function Distance(ByVal x1 As Single, ByVal y1 As Single, _
        ByVal x2 As Single, ByVal y2 As Single) As Single
    Dim first As New PointF(x1, y1)
    Dim second As New PointF(x2, y2)
    Return Distance(first, second)
End Function
```

The HeroFeet() function will work again, but it is becoming tiresome. Simple, yes, but it is not very reusable. I want a more generic version of this code actually built into the Character class. We have to make some more assumptions, about the tile size used in the game, but at this point we're set on 32 × 32 so I won't be concerned with that now. The HeroFeet() function has become the Character.FootPos property. This property is also now part of the Character class.

```
Public ReadOnly Property FootPos() As Point
    Get
        Return New Point(Me.X + 32, Me.Y + 32 + 16)
    End Get
End Property
```

Another helpful property that would greatly help to simplify our code is a CenterPos property for the Character class. The center of a character is its X,Y position plus its width and height, each divided by two.

```
Public ReadOnly Property CenterPos() As PointF
    Get
        Dim pos As PointF = Me.Position
        pos.X += Me.GetSprite.Width / 2
        pos.Y += Me.GetSprite.Height / 2
        Return pos
    End Get
End Property
```

Next, we'll incorporate the distance calculations right inside the `Character` class while taking into account both the foot position and the center position of the character.

```
Public Function FootDistance(ByRef other As Character) As Single
    Return p_game.Distance(Me.FootPos, other.FootPos)
End Function
Public Function FootDistance(ByVal pos As PointF) As Single
    Return p_game.Distance(Me.FootPos, pos)
End Function
Public Function CenterDistance(ByRef other As Character) As Single
    Return p_game.Distance(CenterPos, other.CenterPos)
End Function
Public Function CenterDistance(ByVal pos As PointF) As Single
    Return p_game.Distance(Me.CenterPos, pos)
End Function
```

I'm going to use the `CenterPos` property this time, rather than `FootPos`, to simplify the example code a bit and show that both techniques work equally well when you just want to know if the player is close enough to an NPC to talk to it. When the player character is within range of the NPC and the talk radius circle turns blue, then press the Space key to begin talking.

Dialogue GUI

What do we want this dialogue system to look like? It needs to be simple and positioned in such a way that it doesn't block out a large portion of the screen, but at the same time, it would be helpful to draw the dialogue interface as a window at a certain location every time. What about drawing the window at one of the four corners of the game window, depending on where the player character is located? It would be unfortunate to draw the dialogue window over the top of the player! That affects the user's suspension of disbelief. The player wants to *see* his character while talking with an NPC, not interact in some sort of disembodied way. Let's start by figuring out where the player is located and then drawing a box in an opposing corner—whichever corner is farthest from the player.

The `Dialogue` class will be reusable and serve many roles beyond just talking with NPCs. This will be our de facto way to communicate with the player, with either just simple messages requiring the click of an OK button to a more

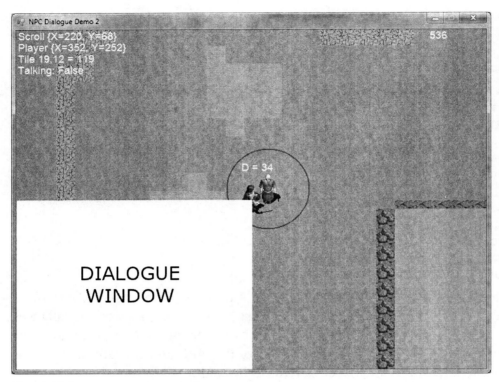

Figure 15.5
A possible dialogue window position.

complex message with many choices. The `Dialogue` class will be self-contained, requiring very little from other classes except for `Game.Device`, which is needed to draw. We're going to need to use a smaller font than the default font in the `Game` class. Although we have `Game.SetFont()` for changing that font, it will be too much of a pain to change the font back and forth after showing the dialogue text, so the dialogue system will use its own font. The dialogue window will be set up using properties and then drawn with a `Draw()` function, which will pause the game until the player chooses one of the options. Figure 15.5 shows a dialogue window positioned at the lower left with a size of one-quarter the screen (400 × 300).

Positioning the Dialogue Window

In my opinion, this window size is a bit too large, even if we give it some transparency with an alpha channel. While I would enjoy working on a resizable

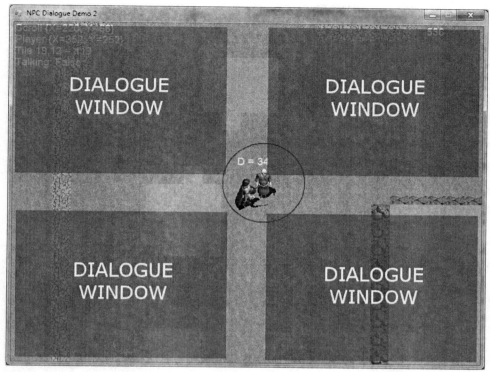

Figure 15.6
Positioning the dialogue window at any of the four corners.

dialogue window, I'm not willing to get into the complexity of drawing button controls onto a variable-sized window—no, we need to keep this simple and enhance it as needed for the needs of each game. Let's try a slightly smaller window with that alpha channel, shown in Figure 15.6. This screen mock-up shows the slightly smaller dialogue window (360 × 280) in the four corners. A border and shadow would certainly improve its appearance, but it already looks usable.

Hint

To create your own dialogue window with whatever level of transparency you want, use a graphic editor like GIMP, create a window with the resolution you want, and then use the Opacity slider or Layer, Mask menu option to change the alpha level of the image. An alpha level of 60% looks pretty good. However, we can also just draw a filled rectangle with whatever alpha level we want at runtime so that's probably the best solution (although it's a bit slower).

To automatically move the dialogue to one of the corners based on the player's position, we'll use an enumeration:

```
Public Enum Positions
    UpperLeft
    LowerLeft
    UpperRight
    LowerRight
End Enum
```

Now, based on the player's current position, the dialogue window will automatically reposition itself to one of the four corners farthest away from the player.

```
Select Case p_corner
    Case Positions.UpperLeft
        p_position = New PointF(10, 10)
    Case Positions.LowerLeft
        p_position = New PointF(10, 600 - p_size.Height - 10)
    Case Positions.UpperRight
        p_position = New PointF(800 - p_size.Width - 10, 10)
    Case Positions.LowerRight
        p_position = New PointF(800 - p_size.Width - 10, _
            600 - p_size.Height - 10)
End Select
```

In our main game code, the automatic positioning of the dialogue window is handled. This could easily be moved inside the Dialogue class itself if you prefer.

```
If hero.CenterPos.X < 400 Then
    If hero.CenterPos.Y < 300 Then
        dialogue.setCorner(Dialogue.Positions.LowerRight)
    Else
        dialogue.setCorner(Dialogue.Positions.UpperRight)
    End If
Else
    If hero.CenterPos.Y < 300 Then
        dialogue.setCorner(Dialogue.Positions.LowerLeft)
    Else
        dialogue.setCorner(Dialogue.Positions.UpperLeft)
    End If
End If
```

Drawing the window is done with a call to `Graphics.FillRectangle()`. The trick here is to create a color that contains an alpha channel at the percentage of transparency that we want. Since the color values fall in the range of 0 to 255, one easy way to calculate the alpha level is to just multiply 255 by the desired percentage like so:

```
Dim pen As New Pen(Color.FromArgb(255 * 0.6, 255, 255, 255))
p_game.Device.FillRectangle(pen.Brush, _
    p_position.X, p_position.Y, p_size.Width, p_size.Height)
```

The color manipulation code is a bit tricky, because `FillRectangle()` doesn't accept just a normal `Color` parameter, it must be a Brush. Since Pen can convert to a Brush, we can use a Pen with the desired Color components to arrive at a white rectangle with 60% alpha. The result is shown in Figure 15.7. See the example Dialogue Demo 2 to see the next step.

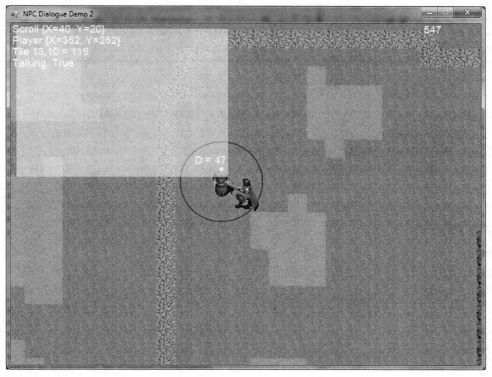

Figure 15.7
The dialogue automatically moves based on the player's location.

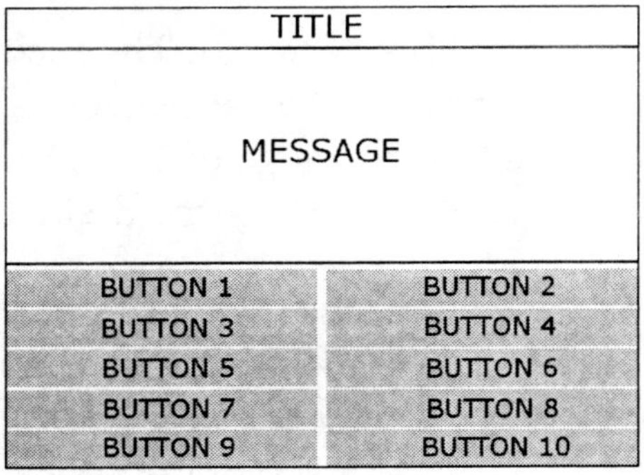

```
                    TITLE

                   MESSAGE



        BUTTON 1          BUTTON 2
        BUTTON 3          BUTTON 4
        BUTTON 5          BUTTON 6
        BUTTON 7          BUTTON 8
        BUTTON 9          BUTTON 10
```

Figure 15.8
A mock-up of the dialogue user interface.

Hint

If the window size is just way too small for your needs, you could make a much taller window and just cause it to stay in place or allow it to automatically move from left to right instead of jumping among the four corners. A window of this type could be used for the player's inventory system, for instance. For the dialogue system, I was thinking about keeping it smaller and using a small font.

Drawing the Dialogue Window

I think that's all we need to build the dialogue window at this point. All of the items on the window will be positioned relative to the window's position so that everything gets drawn in the right place even when the window moves. As for the interface, there will be a title, message text, and ten buttons, as shown in the design mock-up in Figure 15.8.

Drawing the Title

Let's begin with the title. It should display the name of the character with whom you're talking. The Title property, p_title, will be displayed in the Draw() function. To center the title on the dialogue window, we use a function called Graphics.MeasureString(), which returns the width and height of text according to the specified string and font. Using this information, we can get the width of the text and center it on the window.

```
Dim size As SizeF
size = p_game.Device.MeasureString(p_title, p_fontTitle)
```

```
Dim tx As Integer = p_position.X + p_size.Width / 2 - size.Width / 2
Dim ty As Integer = p_position.Y + 6
Print(tx, ty, p_title, Brushes.Gold)
```

Drawing the Message with Word Wrapping

Next up is the message text. This is the information an NPC wants to communicate to the player, be it for a quest or an introduction or any other purpose. We have quite a bit of room here for a lengthy message given the Arial-12 font. If you want to change the font for the title or the message, that could be done via properties. We again use `Graphics.MesaureString()`, but this time it is used to position multi-line text within a bounded region specified in the `SizeF` property `layoutArea`. Using the supplied dimensions, `MeasureString()` provides the minimum width and height needed to render the message with the specified font. It's a very cool function!

```
Dim layoutArea As New SizeF(p_size.Width, 80)
size = p_game.Device.MeasureString(p_message, p_fontMessage, _
    layoutArea, Nothing, p_message.Length(), 4)
Dim layoutRect As New RectangleF(p_position.X + 4, _
    p_position.Y + 34, size.Width, size.Height)
p_game.Device.DrawString(p_message, p_fontMessage, Brushes.White, _
    layoutRect)
```

Drawing the Buttons

Now we come to the buttons, and the most difficult aspect of the user interface. However, by making some assumptions we can keep the problem under control. First of all, let me state that there is a *huge* amount of variation in what you could potentially do with the dialogue buttons. With the right options in the form of enumeration values and some creative code, this could be an even more versatile dialogue system than planned. But, I don't want to go all out with it at this point—keep it functional and simple, with the knowledge that it can handle more at a later time if needed.

A helper structure is needed to manage and draw the buttons. We don't need to be concerned with the *position* of each button, because they are simply enumerated and drawn in order, based on the dialogue's properties. (A future enhancement to the user interface might require a position property for the buttons, though.) In fact, the `Dialogue.Button` structure doesn't really resemble a button at all! There is no positional or dimensional information in the structure, just a text property. What gives?!

The structure is in place for future needs (such as the aforementioned features). We don't need anything more than the `text` property, but putting it in a structure allows for much easier changes later.

For the *first time* we are actually going to use the mouse in our game code! That's quite a statement now that we're so heavily invested into 15 chapters, but until now we have not needed the mouse. The main form is covered up by the `PictureBox` that is created by the `Game` class and attached to the form, so we have to modify the `PictureBox` control in the `Game` class to support mouse input, oddly enough.

```
Private WithEvents p_pb As PictureBox
Private p_mousePos As Point
Private p_mouseBtn As MouseButtons
```

A new event handler is needed to support mouse input. This new function is added to the `Game` class and handles the events for `MouseMove` and `MouseDown`, which are both needed to get mouse movement and button clicks.

```
Private Sub p_pb_MouseInput(ByVal sender As Object, _
        ByVal e As System.Windows.Forms.MouseEventArgs) _
        Handles p_pb.MouseMove, p_pb.MouseDown
    p_mousePos.X = e.X
    p_mousePos.Y = e.Y
    p_mouseBtn = e.Button
End Sub
```

In support of the new mouse handler are these two properties in the `Game` class.

```
Public Property MousePos() As Point
    Get
        Return p_mousePos
    End Get
    Set(ByVal value As Point)
        p_mousePos = value
    End Set
End Property
Public Property MouseButton() As MouseButtons
    Get
        Return p_mouseBtn
```

```
        End Get
        Set(ByVal value As MouseButtons)
            p_mouseBtn = value
        End Set
End Property
```

Three private variables are needed to handle the buttons on the dialogue window.

```
Private p_buttons(10) As Dialogue.Button
Private p_numButtons As Integer
Private p_selection As Integer
```

The following code will cause the buttons to come to life when the mouse hovers over each button, and causes the Dialogue class to report which button was clicked.

```
Public Property NumButtons() As Integer
    Get
            Return p_numButtons
    End Get
    Set(ByVal value As Integer)
        p_numButtons = value
    End Set
End Property

Public Sub setButtonText(ByVal index As Integer, ByVal value As String)
    p_buttons(index).Text = value
End Sub

Public Function getButtonText(ByVal index) As String
    Return p_buttons(index).Text
End Function

Public Function getButtonRect(ByVal index As Integer) As Rectangle
    Dim i As Integer = index - 1
    Dim rect As New Rectangle(p_position.X, p_position.Y, 0, 0)
    rect.Width = p_size.Width / 2 - 4
    rect.Height = (p_size.Height * 0.4) / 5
    rect.Y += p_size.Height * 0.6 - 4
    Select Case index
        Case 1, 3, 5, 7, 9
```

```
                    rect.X += 4
                    rect.Y += Math.Floor(i / 2) * rect.Height
            Case 2, 4, 6, 8, 10
                    rect.X += 4 + rect.Width
                    rect.Y += Math.Floor(i / 2) * rect.Height
        End Select
        Return rect
End Function

Public Property Selection() As Integer
        Get
                Return p_selection
        End Get
        Set(ByVal value As Integer)
            p_selection = value
        End Set
End Property
```

Now we come to the Draw() function again. Previously, we have already added the code to draw the title and message onto the dialogue window. Now we need to write the code that draws the buttons and detects mouse movement and selection. This code is primarily based around the getButtonRect() function, which returns a Rectangle that represents the position and dimensions of the virtual button. This is then used to both draw the button and to look for mouse activity within its region.

```
REM draw the buttons
For n = 1 To p_numButtons
    Dim rect As Rectangle = getButtonRect(n)
    REM draw button background
    Dim color As Color
    If rect.Contains(p_mousePos) Then
        REM clicked on this button?
        If p_mouseBtn = MouseButtons.Left Then
            p_selection = n
        Else
            p_selection = 0
        End If
        color = color.FromArgb(200, 80, 100, 120)
        p_game.Device.FillRectangle(New Pen(color).Brush, rect)
    End If
```

```
      REM draw button border
      p_game.Device.DrawRectangle(Pens.Gray, rect)
      REM print button label
      size = p_game.Device.MeasureString(p_buttons(n).Text, p_fontButton)
      tx = rect.X + rect.Width / 2 - size.Width / 2
      ty = rect.Y + 2
      p_game.Device.DrawString(p_buttons(n).Text, p_fontButton, _
          Brushes.White, tx, ty)
Next
```

Final Example

I promised to go over the source code for a complete example before ending this chapter, so we'll do that now. There are three Dialogue Demo programs in this chapter's resource files (found at www.courseptr.com/downloads) that you can open and study one step at a time, from the initial code to calculate distance between the characters to the opening and positioning of the dialogue window to the full user interface. Figure 15.9 shows the final GUI for the dialogue window with all of the buttons filled with sample items for purchase, while Figure 15.10 shows that the game responds to the selection after the dialogue window is closed.

```
Public Class Form1
    Public Structure keyStates
        Public up, down, left, right As Boolean
    End Structure
    Private game As Game
    Private level As Level
    Private keyState As keyStates
    Private gameover As Boolean = False
    Private hero As Character
    Private vendor As Character
    Private talkFlag As Boolean = False
    Private talking As Boolean = False
    Private dialogue As Dialogue
    Private purchase As String = ""

    Private Sub Form1_Load(ByVal sender As System.Object, _
            ByVal e As System.EventArgs) Handles MyBase.Load
        Me.Text = "NPC Dialogue Demo 3"
```

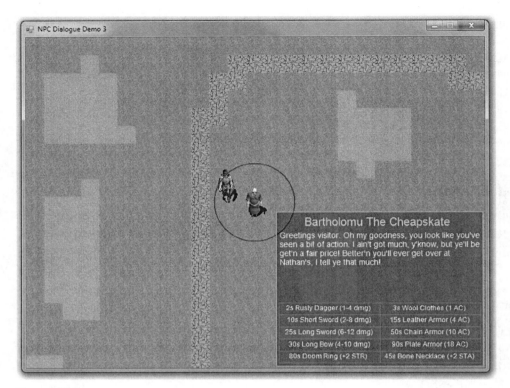

Figure 15.9
The final Dialogue Demo program responds to user choices.

Figure 15.10
Displaying the item selected in the dialogue.

```
REM create game object
game = New Game(Me, 800, 600)
REM create tilemap
level = New Level(game, 25, 19, 32)
level.loadTilemap("sample.level")
```

```
        level.loadPalette("palette.bmp", 5)
        REM load hero
        hero = New Character(game)
        hero.Load("paladin.char")
        hero.Position = New Point(300, 200)
        REM load vendor
        vendor = New Character(game)
        vendor.Load("vendor.char")
        vendor.Position = New Point(350, 250)

        REM create dialogue window
        dialogue = New Dialogue(game)

        While Not gameover
            doUpdate()
        End While
    End Sub

    Private Sub Form1_KeyDown(ByVal sender As Object, _
        ByVal e As System.Windows.Forms.KeyEventArgs) Handles Me.KeyDown
        Select Case (e.KeyCode)
            Case Keys.Up, Keys.W : keyState.up = True
            Case Keys.Down, Keys.S : keyState.down = True
            Case Keys.Left, Keys.A : keyState.left = True
            Case Keys.Right, Keys.D : keyState.right = True
            Case Keys.Space : talkFlag = True
        End Select
    End Sub

    Private Sub Form1_KeyUp(ByVal sender As System.Object, _
        ByVal e As System.Windows.Forms.KeyEventArgs) Handles MyBase.KeyUp
        Select Case (e.KeyCode)
            Case Keys.Escape : End
            Case Keys.Up, Keys.W : keyState.up = False
            Case Keys.Down, Keys.S : keyState.down = False
            Case Keys.Left, Keys.A : keyState.left = False
            Case Keys.Right, Keys.D : keyState.right = False
            Case Keys.Space : talkFlag = False
        End Select
    End Sub
```

```
Private Sub doUpdate()
    Dim frameRate As Integer = game.FrameRate()
    Dim ticks As Integer = Environment.TickCount()
    Static drawLast As Integer = 0
    If ticks > drawLast + 16 Then
        drawLast = ticks
        doScrolling()
        doHero()
        doVendor()
        doDialogue()
        If purchase <> "" Then
            game.Print(hero.Position.X, hero.Position.Y, purchase, _
                Brushes.White)
        End If
        game.Update()
        Application.DoEvents()
    Else
        Threading.Thread.Sleep(1)
    End If
End Sub

Private Sub doScrolling()
    REM move the tilemap scroll position
    Dim steps As Integer = 4
    Dim pos As PointF = level.ScrollPos
    REM up key movement
    If keyState.up Then
        If hero.Y > 300 - 48 Then
            hero.Y -= steps
        Else
            pos.Y -= steps
            If pos.Y <= 0 Then
                hero.Y -= steps
            End If
        End If
        REM down key movement
    ElseIf keyState.down Then
        If hero.Y < 300 - 48 Then
            hero.Y += steps
        Else
```

```
                    pos.Y += steps
                    If pos.Y >= (127 - 19) * 32 Then
                        hero.Y += steps
                    End If
                End If
            End If
        REM left key movement
        If keyState.left Then
            If hero.X > 400 - 48 Then
                hero.X -= steps
            Else
                pos.X -= steps
                If pos.X <= 0 Then
                    hero.X -= steps
                End If
            End If
            REM right key movement
        ElseIf keyState.right Then
            If hero.X < 400 - 48 Then
                hero.X += steps
            Else
                pos.X += steps
                If pos.X >= (127 - 25) * 32 Then
                    hero.X += steps
                End If
            End If
        End If
        REM update scroller position
        level.ScrollPos = pos
        level.Update()
        REM draw the tilemap
        level.Draw(0, 0, 800, 600)
End Sub

Private Sub doHero()
    REM limit player sprite to the screen boundary
    If hero.X < -32 Then
        hero.X = -32
    ElseIf hero.X > 800 - 65 Then
        hero.X = 800 - 65
```

```
            End If
            If hero.Y < -48 Then
                hero.Y = -48
            ElseIf hero.Y > 600 - 81 Then
                hero.Y = 600 - 81
            End If
            REM orient the player in the right direction
            If keyState.up And keyState.right Then
                hero.Direction = 1
            ElseIf keyState.right And keyState.down Then
                hero.Direction = 3
            ElseIf keyState.down And keyState.left Then
                hero.Direction = 5
            ElseIf keyState.left And keyState.up Then
                hero.Direction = 7
            ElseIf keyState.up Then
                hero.Direction = 0
            ElseIf keyState.right Then
                hero.Direction = 2
            ElseIf keyState.down Then
                hero.Direction = 4
            ElseIf keyState.left Then
                hero.Direction = 6
            Else
                hero.Direction = -1
            End If
            REM draw the hero
            hero.Draw()
        End Sub

        Private Sub doVendor()
            Dim relativePos As PointF
            REM draw the vendor sprite
            If vendor.X > level.ScrollPos.X _
            And vendor.X < level.ScrollPos.X + 23 * 32 _
            And vendor.Y > level.ScrollPos.Y _
            And vendor.Y < level.ScrollPos.Y + 17 * 32 Then
                relativePos.X = Math.Abs(level.ScrollPos.X - vendor.X)
                relativePos.Y = Math.Abs(level.ScrollPos.Y - vendor.Y)
                vendor.GetSprite.Draw(relativePos.X, relativePos.Y)
```

```
            End If
            Dim talkRadius As Integer = 70

            REM get center of hero sprite
            Dim heroCenter As PointF = hero.CenterPos

            REM get center of NPC
            Dim vendorCenter As PointF = relativePos
            vendorCenter.X += vendor.GetSprite.Width / 2
            vendorCenter.Y += vendor.GetSprite.Height / 2

            REM get distance to the NPC
            Dim dist As Single = hero.CenterDistance(vendorCenter)
            Dim color As Pen
            If dist < talkRadius Then
                color = New Pen(Brushes.Blue, 2.0)
            Else
                color = New Pen(Brushes.Red, 2.0)
            End If

            REM draw circle around vendor to show talk radius
            Dim spriteSize As Single = vendor.GetSprite.Width / 2
            Dim centerx As Single = relativePos.X + spriteSize
            Dim centery As Single = relativePos.Y + spriteSize
            Dim circleRect As New RectangleF( _
                centerx - talkRadius, _
                centery - talkRadius, _
                talkRadius * 2, talkRadius * 2)
            game.Device.DrawEllipse(color, circleRect)

            REM is playing trying to talk to this vendor?
            If dist < talkRadius Then
                If talkFlag Then
                    talking = True
                End If
            Else
                talking = False
            End If
        End Sub
```

```
Private Sub doDialogue()
    If Not talking Then Return
    REM prepare the dialogue
    dialogue.Title = "Bartholomu The Cheapskate"
    dialogue.Message = "Greetings visitor. Oh my goodness, " + _
        "you look like you've seen a bit of action. I ain't got " + _
        "much, y'know, but ye'll be get'n a fair price! Better'n " + _
        "you'll ever get over at Nathan's, I tell ye that much!"
    dialogue.setButtonText(1, "2s Rusty Dagger (1-4 dmg)")
    dialogue.setButtonText(2, "3s Wool Clothes (1 AC)")
    dialogue.setButtonText(3, "10s Short Sword (2-8 dmg)")
    dialogue.setButtonText(4, "15s Leather Armor (4 AC)")
    dialogue.setButtonText(5, "25s Long Sword (6-12 dmg)")
    dialogue.setButtonText(6, "50s Chain Armor (10 AC)")
    dialogue.setButtonText(7, "30s Long Bow (4-10 dmg)")
    dialogue.setButtonText(8, "90s Plate Armor (18 AC)")
    dialogue.setButtonText(9, "80s Doom Ring (+2 STR)")
    dialogue.setButtonText(10, "45s Bone Necklace (+2 STA)")

    REM reposition dialogue window
    If hero.CenterPos.X < 400 Then
        If hero.CenterPos.Y < 300 Then
            dialogue.setCorner(Dialogue.Positions.LowerRight)
        Else
            dialogue.setCorner(Dialogue.Positions.UpperRight)
        End If
    Else
        If hero.CenterPos.Y < 300 Then
            dialogue.setCorner(Dialogue.Positions.LowerLeft)
        Else
            dialogue.setCorner(Dialogue.Positions.UpperLeft)
        End If
    End If

    REM draw dialogue and look for selection
    dialogue.updateMouse(game.MousePos, game.MouseButton)
    dialogue.Draw()
    If dialogue.Selection > 0 Then
        talking = False
        purchase = "You bought " + _
```

```
            dialogue.getButtonText(dialogue.Selection)
         dialogue.Selection = 0
      Else
         purchase = ""
      End If
   End Sub
End Class
```

LEVEL UP!

This was a heavy-hitting chapter that covered some tough new material, but it was absolutely necessary and we ended up with a powerful new user interface class that can be used for many different parts of the Celtic Crusader game. Speaking of which, in the very next chapter, it will be time to learn about fighting, gaining experience, and leveling! We have a few minor things to fix by the time we get to the final game in the last chapter, such as character sprites jumping a bit as we near the edge of the level, but it's nothing that a little extra code won't fix.

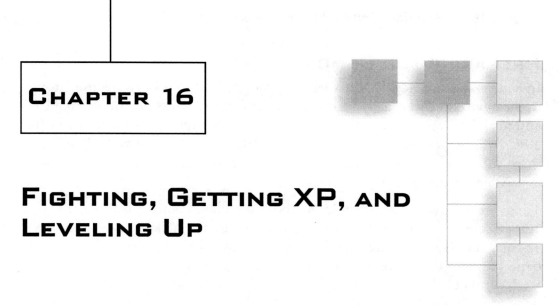

CHAPTER 16

FIGHTING, GETTING XP, AND LEVELING UP

This chapter explores the all-important topic of combat and how gaining experience affects the player's character. Chapter 15 gave us some tools that will be useful again now: to figure out when the player is close enough to an enemy combatant to engage him. This applies solely to melee fights, of course, and not to attacks at range, which will require a bit of extra effort. The simplest form of melee combat occurs when the player is close enough to an enemy and hits the attack button, similar to the way in which dialogue was engaged in Chapter 15. One additional requirement for combat is that we must ensure the player is facing toward his enemy in order to deal any damage. In this chapter, we will explore these techniques and the random attack dice rolls needed to make realistic combat that an RPG purist would find acceptable.

Here's what we'll cover in this chapter:

- Preparing for combat
- Character animation templates
- Creating the combat system
- Attack and damage rolls
- Facing your enemies
- State-based combat
- Dealing permanent damage

PREPARING FOR COMBAT

In a normal game, hostile NPCs will be guarding locations or wandering around in the environment, usually following a series of waypoints or just walking back and forth between two points. For our first few examples of combat, the hostile NPCs will be positioned in the level randomly and will *not move*. We will give them movement behavior later, but for now I just want to show you how to engage an enemy in order to attack them.

There are several ways we could go about handling combat in the game. In a 100% real-time game, there is never a pause in the action: when the player engages one enemy, there may be other nearby enemies who charge into the battle as well. A variation is a partial real-time game where the player can move freely through the game but each round of combat causes the game to pause while it is resolved.

A second type of combat is turn-based. Although our game allows the player to roam the world freely in real-time, I have decided to use a turn-based system with rounds to resolve combat. This choice comes after much play testing of a fully real-time combat system that just seemed to happen too quickly. With the player swinging his weapon and the hostile NPC swinging his, basically as fast as the attacks were allowed to go, the HP for each would slowly go down until one fell (or until the player ran away). This form of combat works great for a game like *Diablo* and *Baldur's Gate*, but those games are largely dungeon crawlers of the "hack-n-slash" variety rather than world-based RPGs. An example of a world-based RPG that pauses during combat is the *Might & Magic* series from New World Computing (Figure 16.1).

The gameplay for the *Might & Magic* series from the 1990s evolved with technology, with later games showing a full 3D world (software rendered at the time before GPUs were invented). Interestingly enough, the world looked a little bit like *World of Warcraft* (a soft/light RPG compared to *Might & Magic*). Hostile NPCs could be seen in the world, in dungeons, in rooms, and would only attack if you attacked them first or got too close to them. At that point, the game would go into a pseudo real-time mode where hostiles would basically stay in one place (if in range), allowing the player to attack the target of his choice. Opening a spell book or inventory would pause the combat, or the player could pause the game with a key press while choosing the appropriate attacks for each

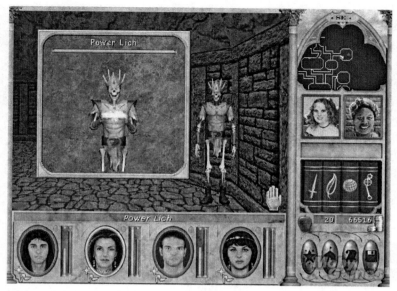

Figure 16.1
Might & Magic VI: The Mandate of Heaven. Image courtesy of MobyGames.

hostile. The earlier games in the *Might & Magic* series were entirely turn-based, while later ones were entirely real-time.

The combat system for Celtic Crusader will work with either real-time or turn-based with a few simple flags in the code. Normally, the player will walk around fighting monsters and going on quests, and the monsters should behave somewhat like they do in *Might & Magic*: if you attack them first or get too close, they'll attack you.

Starting an Attack

The code to draw the monsters is the same code used in previous chapters to draw objects with a global position within the scrolling level. Before drawing objects, we must get its relative position with respect to the scroll position and then draw it at the relative position.

```
If monsters(n).X > level.ScrollPos.X _
    And monsters(n).X < level.ScrollPos.X + 23 * 32 _
    And monsters(n).Y > level.ScrollPos.Y _
    And monsters(n).Y < level.ScrollPos.Y + 17 * 32 Then ...
```

If the object is within the viewport at the current scroll position, then we can figure out its relative position on the screen and draw it.

```
relativePos.X = Math.Abs(level.ScrollPos.X - monsters(n).X)
relativePos.Y = Math.Abs(level.ScrollPos.Y - monsters(n).Y)
monsterCenter = relativePos
monsterCenter.X += monsters(n).GetSprite.Width / 2
monsterCenter.Y += monsters(n).GetSprite.Height / 2
```

Distance is calculated from the center of the NPC's sprite to the center of the PC's sprite.

```
dist = hero.CenterDistance(monsterCenter)
If dist < attackRadius Then ...
```

As you can see, most of this code was developed previously. We first learned how to calculate relative position back in Chapter 12, "Adding Objects to the World," and then how to calculate distance to an NPC in Chapter 15. When the PC is within range of an NPC, its radius circle will change from red to blue, and then the Space key will trigger an attack. In this demo, nothing happens beyond printing out the attack flag status.

Combat Demo 1

The first Combat Demo project shows how to calculate the attack radius around each NPC and the logic to determine when the player is in range to attack. At this point, the NPCs do not move or react to the player and combat isn't working yet. We will build on this example while building a combat system. (See Figure 16.2.) In the truncated source code listing below, the sections related to the radius and combat are highlighted in bold.

```
Public Structure keyStates
    Public up, down, left, right As Boolean
End Structure

Private game As Game
Private level As Level
Private keyState As keyStates
Private gameover As Boolean = False
Private hero As Character
Private attackFlag As Boolean = False
Private attacking As Boolean = False
```

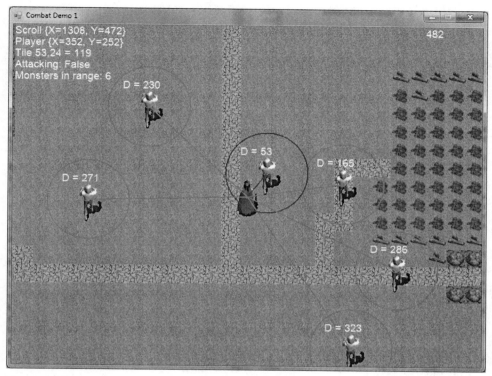

Figure 16.2
A circle around each hostile NPC shows its combat radius.

```
Private monstersInRange As Integer
Const NUM_ZOMBIES As Integer = 25
Private monsters(NUM_ZOMBIES) As Character

Private Sub Form1_Load(ByVal sender As System.Object, _
        ByVal e As System.EventArgs) Handles MyBase.Load
    Me.Text = "Combat Demo 1"
    game = New Game(Me, 800, 600)
    level = New Level(game, 25, 19, 32)
    level.loadTilemap("sample.level")
    level.loadPalette("palette.bmp", 5)

    REM load hero
    hero = New Character(game)
```

```
        hero.Load("hero axe.char")
        hero.Position = New Point(400 - 48, 300 - 48)

        REM create zombie sprites
        For n = 1 To NUM_ZOMBIES
            monsters(n) = New Character(game)
            monsters(n).Load("zombie.char")
            monsters(n).Position = New Point(game.Random(800, 2000), _
                game.Random(0, 1200))
        Next

        While Not gameover
            doUpdate()
        End While
    End Sub

    Private Sub doUpdate()
        Dim frameRate As Integer = game.FrameRate()
        Dim ticks As Integer = Environment.TickCount()
        Static drawLast As Integer = 0
        If ticks > drawLast + 16 Then
            drawLast = ticks
            doScrolling()
            doHero()
            doMonsters()
            game.Print(700, 0, frameRate.ToString())
            Dim y As Integer = 0
            game.Print(0, 0, "Scroll " + level.ScrollPos.ToString())
            game.Print(0, 20, "Player " + hero.Position.ToString())

            REM get position under player's feet
            Dim feet As PointF = hero.FootPos
            Dim tilex As Integer = (level.ScrollPos.X + feet.X) / 32
            Dim tiley As Integer = (level.ScrollPos.Y + feet.Y) / 32
            Dim ts As Level.tilemapStruct
            ts = level.getTile(tilex, tiley)
            game.Print(0, 40, "Tile " + tilex.ToString() + "," + _
                tiley.ToString() + " = " + ts.tilenum.ToString())
            game.Print(0, 60, "Attacking: " + attacking.ToString())
            game.Print(0, 80, "Monsters in range: " + _
                monstersInRange.ToString())
```

```
            game.Update()
            Application.DoEvents()
        Else
            Threading.Thread.Sleep(1)
        End If
End Sub


Private Sub doHero()
    REM limit player sprite to the screen boundary
    If hero.X < -32 Then
        hero.X = -32
    ElseIf hero.X > 800 - 65 Then
        hero.X = 800 - 65
    End If
    If hero.Y < -48 Then
        hero.Y = -48
    ElseIf hero.Y > 600 - 81 Then
        hero.Y = 600 - 81
    End If
    REM orient the player in the right direction
    If keyState.up And keyState.right Then
        hero.Direction = 1
    ElseIf keyState.right And keyState.down Then
        hero.Direction = 3
    ElseIf keyState.down And keyState.left Then
        hero.Direction = 5
    ElseIf keyState.left And keyState.up Then
        hero.Direction = 7
    ElseIf keyState.up Then
        hero.Direction = 0
    ElseIf keyState.right Then
        hero.Direction = 2
    ElseIf keyState.down Then
        hero.Direction = 4
    ElseIf keyState.left Then
        hero.Direction = 6
    Else
        hero.Direction = -1
    End If
    REM draw the hero
```

```
        hero.Draw()
End Sub

Private Sub doMonsters()
        Dim relativePos As PointF
        Const attackRadius As Integer = 70
        Dim color As Pen
        Dim heroCenter As PointF
        Dim monsterCenter As PointF
        Dim dist As Single
        Dim spriteSize As Single
        Dim center As Point
        Dim circleRect As RectangleF

        REM get center of hero sprite
        heroCenter = hero.CenterPos
        game.Device.DrawRectangle(Pens.Red, heroCenter.X - 2, _
            heroCenter.Y - 2, 4, 4)

        monstersInRange = 0
        For n = 1 To NUM_ZOMBIES
            REM is monster in view?
            If monsters(n).X > level.ScrollPos.X _
            And monsters(n).X < level.ScrollPos.X + 23 * 32 _
            And monsters(n).Y > level.ScrollPos.Y _
            And monsters(n).Y < level.ScrollPos.Y + 17 * 32 Then
                monstersInRange += 1
                relativePos.X = Math.Abs(level.ScrollPos.X - monsters(n).X)
                relativePos.Y = Math.Abs(level.ScrollPos.Y - monsters(n).Y)
                REM draw the monster sprite
                monsters(n).GetSprite.Draw(relativePos.X, relativePos.Y)
                REM get center of NPC
                monsterCenter = relativePos
                monsterCenter.X += monsters(n).GetSprite.Width / 2
                monsterCenter.Y += monsters(n).GetSprite.Height / 2
                game.Device.DrawRectangle(Pens.Red, monsterCenter.X - 2, _
                    monsterCenter.Y - 2, 4, 4)
                REM get distance to the NPC
                dist = hero.CenterDistance(monsterCenter)
                REM draw line to NPCs in view
```

```
                    If dist < attackRadius Then
                        color = New Pen(Brushes.Blue, 2.0)
                    Else
                        color = New Pen(Brushes.Red, 2.0)
                    End If
                    game.Device.DrawLine(color, heroCenter, monsterCenter)
                    REM print distance
                    game.Print(relativePos.X, relativePos.Y, _
                        "D = " + dist.ToString("N0"), Brushes.White)
                    REM draw circle around monster to show attack radius
                    spriteSize = monsters(n).GetSprite.Width / 2
                    center.X = relativePos.X + spriteSize
                    center.Y = relativePos.Y + spriteSize
                    circleRect = New RectangleF( _
                        center.X - attackRadius, center.Y - attackRadius, _
                        attackRadius * 2, attackRadius * 2)
                    game.Device.DrawEllipse(color, circleRect)
                End If

                REM is player trying to attack to this monster?
                If dist < attackRadius Then
                    If attackFlag Then
                        attacking = True
                    End If
                Else
                    attacking = False
                End If
            Next
        End Sub

        REM some code was omitted to conserve space
```

CHARACTER TEMPLATES

We have come to the point where additional artwork is needed to make any more progress with the Celtic Crusader game, so in this section we will look at most of the character art planned for the game, including sprites for the player character and NPCs. Real characters will be created out of these templates in the final chapter when the game is fully realized. So, you'll want to look at these character descriptions and animation artwork as mere templates of actual character classes, not characters themselves. Let's take a short break from working on the combat system to look at the artwork. As you continue into the combat system in this chapter, begin thinking about which of these sprites you plan to use in the game.

Animations : Player Characters (PCs)

For the last two chapters, we have been using the paladin character file generated back in Chapter 14, "Creating the Character Editor." That character has good animations and is representative of the PC for Celtic Crusader, but we have three additional sets of artwork available and need to bring them into the game world. Technically, we aren't supposed to pre-roll a player character. Part of the fun factor of playing an RPG—one might even argue that it's the *most important* part of the gameplay—is creating your own character. I don't want to take away that joy from players by pre-rolling them with the character editor. This tool is meant to be used to create NPCs, but we use it to manage the artwork for the PC classes. In Chapter 20, we will build an in-game character generator! Let's create random PC classes for use in this chapter. You have already seen the paladin, so we'll roll the other three classes.

I will provide animation sets so that it is easy for you to add new characters to the game without requiring much extra work. The hostile NPCs need attack animations, while the peasantry does not, so if the player attacks a peasant or any other nonfighting NPC, then you have to add behavior that causes the character to run away or die, depending on your style. (I recommend adding a state that causes civilians to flee.)

I won't focus on the player character classes here, but rather on what artwork is available for use in creating characters—because we have more artwork than we need for just the four classes (Warrior, Paladin, Hunter, and Priest). Feel free to use the animation sets specified in these template .char files for any unique classes of your own design. The purpose behind the .char file, at least for player characters, is to define the animation properties.

Hint

In the final game, these character templates will be used to create real game characters. The complete sets of animation and character editor data files are included for each one in this chapter's resource files (www.courseptr.com/downloads).

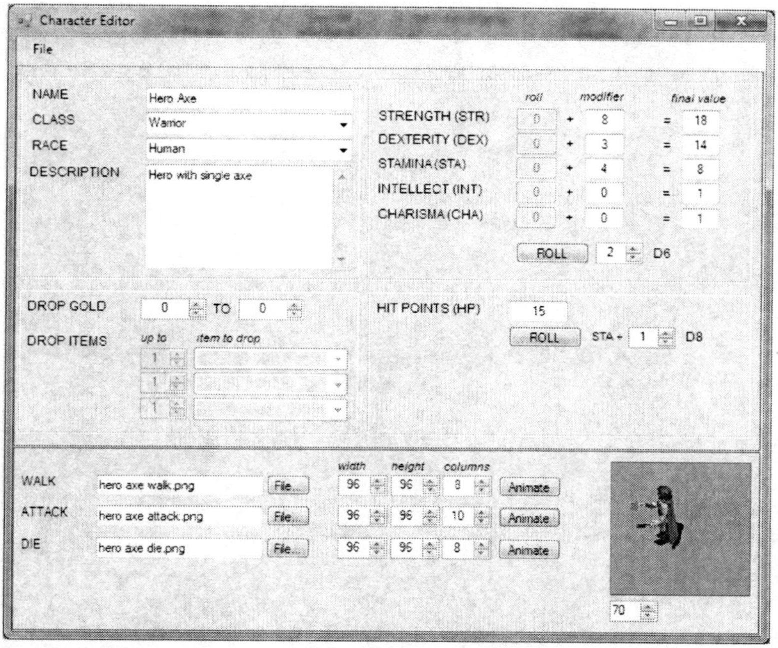

Figure 16.3
Hero sprite wielding a single axe.

Hero (Axe)

The hero sprite animations that show the character carrying an axe (Figure 16.3) are usually variations of the warrior, who may also carry a single sword, and is generally different from a paladin because he doesn't have a shield.

Hero (Sword)

This hero sprite has a single sword and is often a variation of the warrior class (along with the axe sprite) (Figure 16.4).

Hero (Axe & Shield)

We have already seen the paladin character back in Chapter 13, but the actual character is not all that important prior to the player actually creating a player character at the start of a new game.

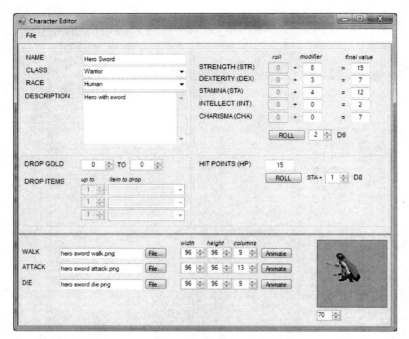

Figure 16.4
Hero sprite wielding a single sword.

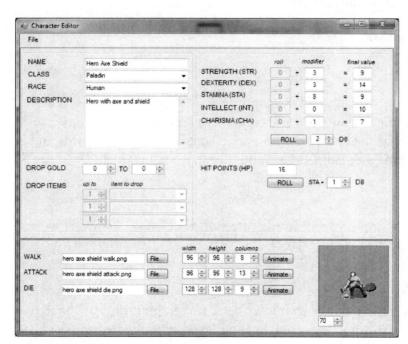

Figure 16.5
Hero sprite wielding an axe and shield.

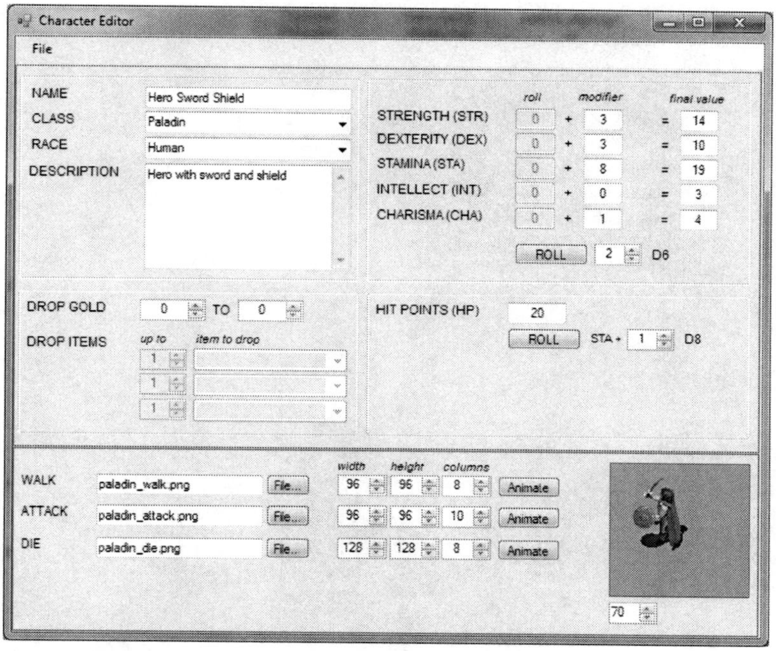

Figure 16.6
Hero sprite wielding a sword and shield.

Hero (Sword & Shield)

The hero sprite animation featuring both a sword and shield (Figure 16.6) is also usually associated with the paladin class, but this is a loose interpretation that you are welcome to change if you wish!

Hero (Bow)

The hero sprite with bow animations (Figure 16.7) is obviously associated with a hunter, archer, or scout class, but you may invent any name for the class using these animation sets.

Hero (Staff)

The staff-wielding hero character (Figure 16.8) usually represents a cloth wearing mage, wizard, or priest. To show how these animations are created,

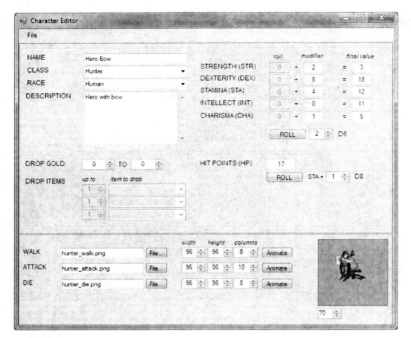

Figure 16.7
Hero sprite wielding a bow.

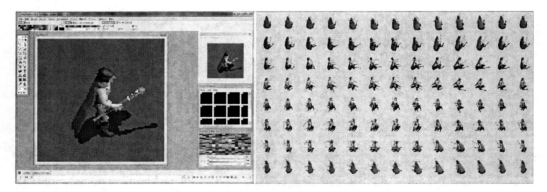

Figure 16.8
Hero sprite wielding a staff, shown here with animation assembled with Pro Motion.

I've included a screenshot of the priest sprite as it appeared in Pro Motion (the sprite animation software—see www.cosmigo.com for a trial copy). The sprite sheet produced by Pro Motion is shown next to it. Pro Motion saves the file as a .bmp file, so it must be converted to a .png with an alpha channel,

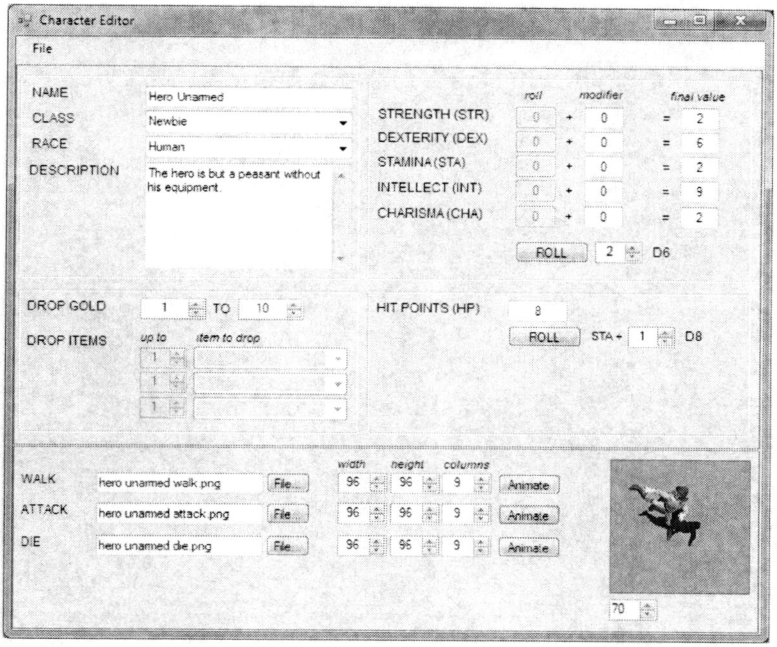

Figure 16.9
Hero sprite wielding only fists of fury!

and I prefer to use GIMP for that step. It's easy to use the Color Select tool to highlight the background color and convert it to a Layer Mask.

Hero (Unarmed)

The hero sprite animation with *no weapon or shield* (Figure 16.9) still has unarmed animations, with a kick attack, which might be fun to explore in a game. How about a Kung Fu character?

Female Hero (Axe & Shield)

I have to cheat a bit by suggesting this animation set as a potential female hero character (Figure 16.10), because this is a female Viking according to animator Reiner Prokein (www.reinerstileset.de). She has a permanent helmet, which poses problems for inventory and equipment. Since none of the male hero sprites have a helmet we would still equip an "armor set" (be it cloth, leather, chain, or plate), but not represent the character with the given

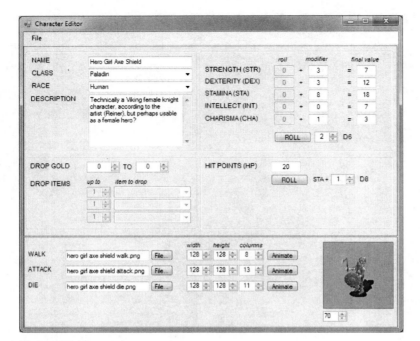

Figure 16.10
A heroic girl sprite?! Maybe, maybe not.

armor set, specifically. With this female sprite, that poses a problem, but she's compelling enough to work around the gearing up problems if you want to use her! The animation is quite good and she has discernible female physical attributes even for such a low-resolution animation. If not usable as a player character (PC), I was thinking she would make an interesting companion NPC that might follow or lead the player on a quest or two. Perhaps you can think of a good story arc around this sprite and incorporate her into your own game in a creative way? She's like Red Sonya to our Conan!

Animations : Hostile NPCs

The hostile NPC character sheets show just what is possible with these animation sets, but you are encouraged to create characters of your own design with the character editor using these template files as a starting point (with the animations already in place).

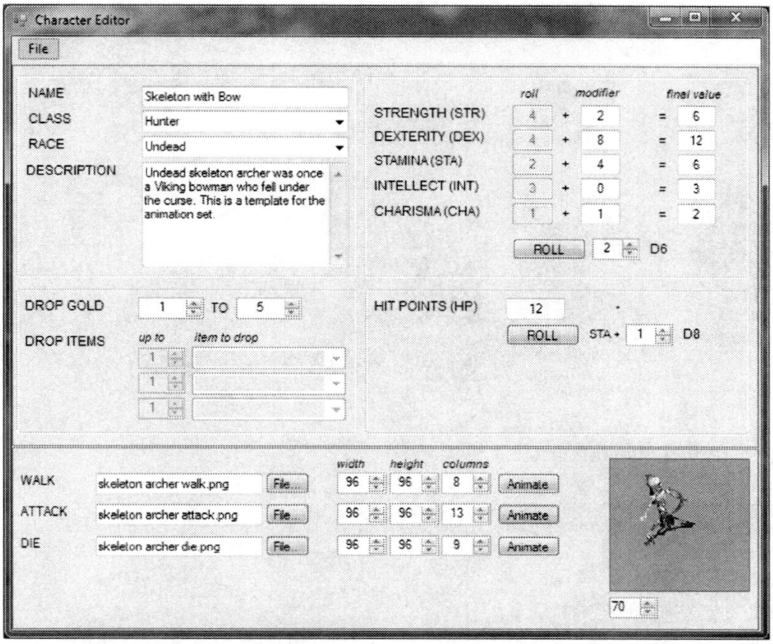

Figure 16.11
Undead skeleton sprite with bow.

Undead Skeleton (Bow)

The skeleton animation set with a bow (Figure 16.11) is obviously an archer or hunter class for the undead race, but these characters were once Viking bowmen who fell under the curse.

Undead Skeleton (Sword & Shield)

The sword & shield animation set for the undead skeleton (Figure 16.12) can be used for a typical *former* warrior or paladin turned undead, with any number of actual characters derived from it. Since there is no other variation of an undead melee character, this one will be reused. The image here shows the sprite animation as it appears in Pro Motion, along with the saved sprite sheet.

Undead Skeleton (Unarmed)

The unarmed undead skeleton sprite (Figure 16.13) is a good general-purpose template for lower-level enemy characters, which may be good for early leveling by player characters.

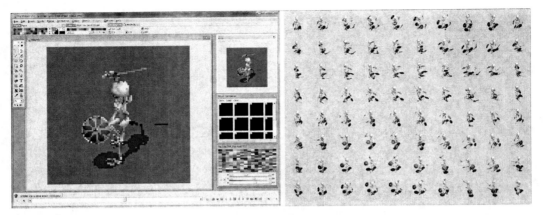

Figure 16.12
Undead skeleton sprite with sword & shield.

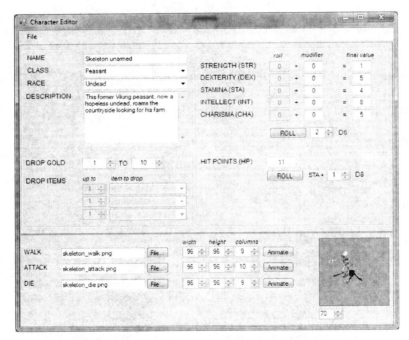

Figure 16.13
This undead skeleton sprite has no weapon.

Undead Zombie (Unarmed)

This undead zombie sprite (Figure 16.14) has no weapon, but that is traditionally accurate of zombies in popular culture (namely, zombie films). With

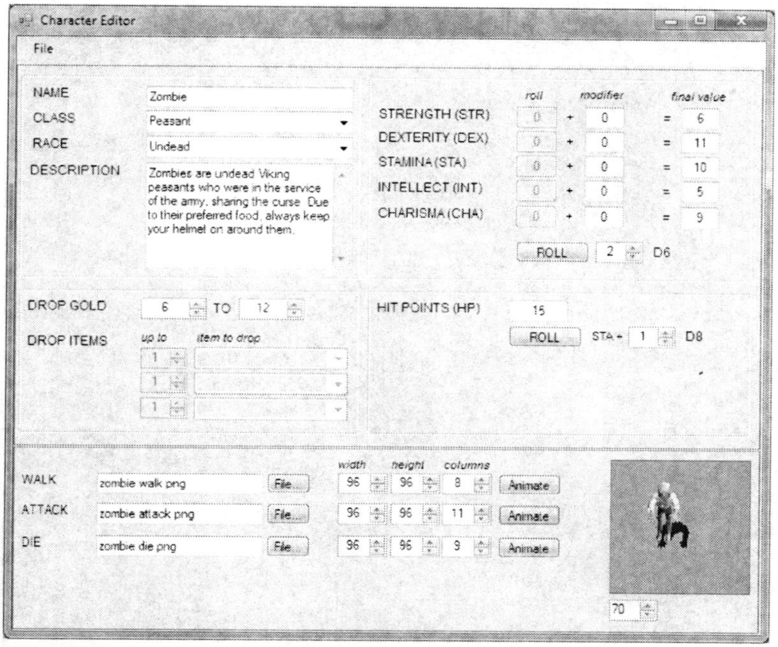

Figure 16.14
The zombie is undead—but what else could it be?

an appetite for gray matter, the player would do well to take them out at range!

Viking (Axe)

According to the game's story first presented in Chapter 9, there were some Viking soldiers who were not in the main army that was converted into undead by the curse. The Viking sprite shown here is wielding an axe (Figure 16.15), so he may be best classified as a warrior or barbarian, but that's up to the designer who will use this as a template for real game characters.

Viking (Sword & Shield)

Another soldier who escaped the undead curse is a full plate knight. This Viking template character is decked out in full battle plate with sword and shield (Figure 16.16), and might be used for a "dark knight" as suggested by the description.

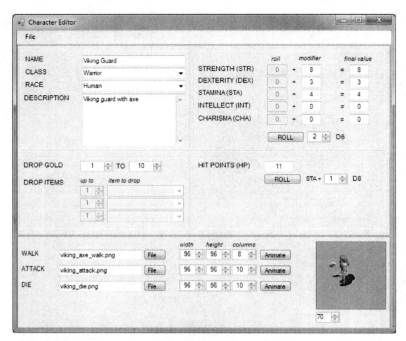

Figure 16.15
This Viking sprite is carrying a single axe.

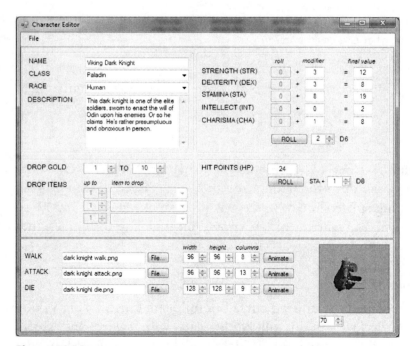

Figure 16.16
This heavily armored Viking sprite bears a sword & shield.

Animations : Friendly NPCs

I have prepared two complete friendly NPCs for any purpose you wish. In the finished game (see Chapter 20), they will be quest givers and random filler characters to make towns look more lively, but will otherwise not be interactive (although that's up to you—they could be given simple dialogue).

Anna the Peasant

There is only one animation set for Anna—walking. She is a good general-purpose NPC sprite. This would make a good character to show walking around a town as filler, or she could be used as a quest giver or any other purpose. (Figure 16.17.)

Joe the Farmer

Joe the farmer (Figure 16.18) is another friendly NPC that would be good to use for filler around towns. Unlike Anna, however, Joe comes with three complete

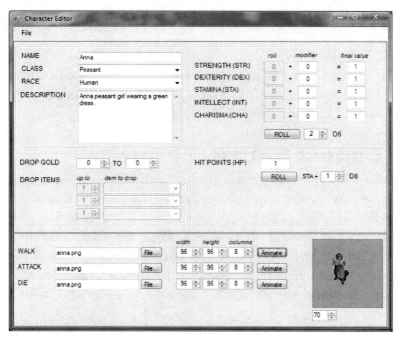

Figure 16.17
Anna the peasant girl.

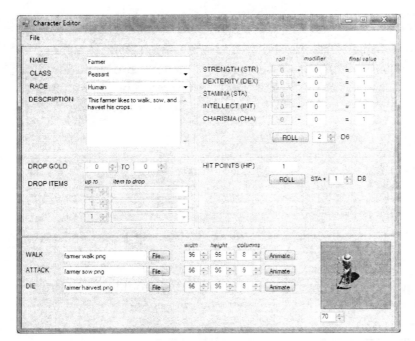

Figure 16.18
Joe the farmer.

sets of animation: walking, sowing seeds, and harvesting. The sowing animation is in the attack sprite, while the harvesting animation is using the die sprite (since friendly NPCs can't be attacked).

CREATING THE COMBAT SYSTEM

Melee combat occurs when opponents fight each other with hand-held weapons (while unarmed combat occurs when no weapons are used, as in a martial art). The game engine already has support for melee combat, but it is not yet implemented, so that is what we'll do in this chapter. First, we must determine when the player is near an enemy, then cause the enemy to turn toward the player, and then allow combat to ensue. Fortunately, the sprites available from Reiner's Tilesets (www.reinerstilesets.de) also include the attack and falling animations.

Combat requires another layer of logic added to the state engine that controls the characters. Although higher-level interaction with characters would make the game more realistic, we'll just be treating this like an old-style hack-and-slash game where the goal is not to follow some sort of complex storyline, but rather to gain experience and explore the world. A simple state-based system will be used to cause enemies to attack the player when in close range.

Making Up Our Own Rules

There are many role-playing game systems that we can emulate for our own games, or we can just borrow ideas from many different games and come up with totally unique gameplay and rules. I am not proposing following any particular franchise for the rules in Celtic Crusader, but some common rules will be familiar to an experienced RPG player.

The Celtic Crusader project, as of Chapter 15, is basically a template game that has most of the functionality you need to actually create an RPG, but is lacking most of the finer details. There is just an enormous amount of detail that must be put into even the simplest of RPGs. Although the size and scope of this book is insufficient to completely build the game, we can create a fun hack-and-slash game where the goal is to gain experience and go up levels, with the corresponding new abilities and skills.

Chapter 15 developed the ability for the player to have encounters with NPCs, which is an important first step in the game's NPC interaction. From this point, you can engage the NPCs in dialog or combat, and the game responds appropriately. A higher level of behavior over the NPCs is also needed to turn this skeleton game into a polished game, a system of behavior that causes NPCs to seek out and engage the player, rather than always *responding* to the player. At the very least, you can add the ability for NPCs to fight back.

Spawning Enemy NPCs

A non-player character (NPC) can be friendly or hostile—we might refer to them as "friendly NPCs" or "hostile NPCs"—but they are still grouped together as "not the player," for the sake of discussion. We're going to combine the work done back in Chapter 12 and in the previous chapter, to create random hostile NPCs that will react to the player with, well, *hostility*.

Hint

In the final game presented in Chapter 20, we will draw on all of the techniques of every chapter into a single game, and use all of the editors to make a compelling game world with a story and quests to complete. In that chapter, you will see how to position NPCs and objects in the game world using script code. For the sake of clarity, we will not be getting into the editor data in this chapter.

When you are fighting with an NPC and kill that character, there should be a death animation. These are not always possible in every case, due to a limited number of sprites. You are limited overall by the availability of artwork, without which you have to get creative with your sprites. Rather than dealing with a whole slew of death animations for each NPC, I have seen some games use the fade effect, where a character blinks out of existence or fades away. You might use the alpha color parameter in the sprite class to cause a character to fade out of existence after dying rather than using a death animation. The important thing is that you recycle your sprites in the game, which means recycling the NPCs. You don't want the NPCs to just respawn at the same place every time, because then the player can see the spawning taking place (which seriously ruins the realism of the game). In addition, if a player learns where some of the NPCs are respawning on the map, he or she will be able to spawn camp (which refers to hiding out near a spawn point and killing new players that appear) and rack up a ridiculous amount of experience, which also ruins the game.

Tip

The fully prepared sprite sheets (with all three animations) and the .char file for several hostile and friendly NPC characters are included in the chapter's resources (www.courseptr.com/downloads).

Attack Rolls

What really happens when you attack another character in the game? That is the basis of the game's combat system, and it has to do with each player's attributes, including weapon and armor class. Usually, the defender's defensive value is compared to the attacker's attack value, and a simulated "roll" of dice is made to determine if the attack succeeded (before calculating damage). All of the attributes are available already from the character editor files.

If the attack value is less than the defense value, then basically you can do no damage to your opponent! So, say you are a new warrior with an axe that does

Figure 16.19
Five different dice with 4, 6, 8, 10, 12, and 20 sides. Image courtesy of Wikipedia.

+10 damage, and you attack a level 10 zombie with 93 defense points. What happens in this situation? You can stand there and bang against this monster all day long with your pathetic little axe and do *no damage* to him! In a situation like this, you are helplessly outclassed by this character, who swiftly and easily kills you with a single blow.

This is called the "to-hit roll" and it adds a nice layer of realism to the game (as opposed to some games where just swinging your sword kills enemies nearby). Knowing that not every swing does damage requires you to use some tactics in your fighting method, and this gives players the ability to be somewhat creative in how they fight enemies. You can swing and run or swing several times in a row, hoping to get a hit. But in general, it's a hit-or-miss situation (sorry, bad pun). Figure 16.19 shows an example of several types of dice.

Many RPGs allow the player to equip modifiers such as rings and special weapons with bonuses for the to-hit value. These modifiers increase your chances of scoring a hit when you attack. Not only is it essential for a good RPG, but working with miscellaneous items as well as different types of swords, shields, armor, helmets, and so on, is an extremely fun part of the game! Our Character class will be modified over the next two chapters to add support for gear such as the weapon, armor, and other items that the player can equip, and you have an opportunity to use these special items to customize characters. You may even allow the player to pick up items found in the world and equip them.

Armor Class (AC)

A character's armor class determines whether an attack made against him will succeed or not. If the attack fails, then no damage is applied at all. Usually, regardless of the AC, an attack to-hit roll of 1 is an *epic fail* and does not hit. Here's one possible way to calculate AC:

```
AC = DEX + Armor Points + Shield Points
```

where `Armor Points` represent the sum total of all armor items and `Shield Points` represent the defense value of an equipped shield. I say *possible way* because this is not the *only way* to perform the calculation. Some game systems do not allow a DEX bonus for plate armor wearers because that represents a slow-moving character, whereas high DEX represents high agility. To keep the rules simple in Celtic Crusader, I just apply the full DEX and full AP to the calculation.

Based on the type of gear available in your game, you may want to add a modifier to the AC calculation to help balance the gameplay a bit if it seems that too many attack rolls are an instant hit. I would expect about half of all attacks to fail when rolled against a foe at the same level. If you find that significantly more than half of all attacks are succeeding, then that's a sign you need to add a modifier to the AC (such as +5).

Melee "Chance To-Hit" Rolls

The mechanics of combat for any game is entirely up to the designer. The important thing is not that your game works like many other RPGs out there, only that combat is balanced within your own game system. In other words, as long as the PC and hostile NPCs attack with the same set of rules, then the game is playable. One thing you really don't want to happen is for combat to end too quickly. It's generally necessary to artificially raise the hit points (HP) of monsters at the lower levels so they don't fall with one hit. You want the player to feel as if real combat is taking place, not that they're just walking around taking out enemies with a single blow as if they're using a lightsaber. We do want the player's attributes to play an important role in the to-hit roll as well as the damage done in an attack.

For Celtic Crusader, I'm going to use a D20 (a 20-sided die) as the basis for the to-hit roll. In RPG lingo, a D20 roll of 1 is an *epic fail* while a roll of 20 is a *critical hit*, which usually means a definite hit (ignoring the defender's AC).

`Melee Chance To-Hit = STR + D20`

Ranged "Chance To-Hit" Rolls

Ranged attacks with bow or spell are similar to melee with a D20 roll, but with DEX instead of STR as a modifier. The character's agility contributes to his ability to hit accurately at a distance, where his strength has little or no effect.

`Ranged Chance To-Hit = DEX + D20`

Rolling for Damage

If the To-Hit roll results in a hit, the next step is to roll again to determine how much damage was done to the target. This is where the weapon attributes come into play. If the game features real items that you can give your character to use in combat, then it makes a big difference in the gameplay. For one thing, you can scatter treasure chests around the game world that contain unique quest items (like magical swords, shields, and armor), as well as valuable jewels and gold. (These types of items are all modeled and available in the sprites provided in the Reiner's Tileset collection.)

Melee "Damage" Rolls

The melee damage value is calculated primarily from STR and weapon damage with a 1D8 roll added to the mix. This damage factor is then reduced by the defender's AC to come up with a total damage, which goes against the defender's HP.

`Melee Damage = D8 + STR + Weapon Damage - Defender's AC`

Some games apply a different die roll based on the type of weapon, such as a 2D6 for a two-handed sword, 2D8 for a two-handed mace, and 1D10 for a bow. You may use modifiers such as this if you want, but it adds an additional bit of information to the item database. I found it easier to use a base random die roll (D8) and the weapon damage as an *additional* die roll. The result is very nearly the same, but it results in more reasonable weapon damage factors. For instance, we wouldn't expect a rusty short sword to deal 12-16 damage where normally it should be 1-4. By using the D8 roll in addition to the weapon damage range, the damage factors will be more reasonable.

Ranged "Damage" Rolls

The ranged damage value is calculated primarily from DEX and weapon damage with a 1D8 roll added for some randomness. A range penalty is then subtracted from the total to arrive at a new attack value, which is further reduced by the defender's AC. The final value is the total damage dealt against the defender's HP.

```
Ranged Damage = D8 + DEX + weapon damage - range penalty - Defender's AC
```

Ranged damage differs slightly from melee due to the range penalty, but it's a reasonable subtraction, because without it the player would be nearly invincible, able to deal out full damage at long range where no monster would ever be able to catch him before being cut down.

Critical Hits ("Crit")

If the chance to-hit roll of the D20 results in a 20, then the attack is a *critical hit* and incurs additional damage! You may add whatever modifier you want to the attack damage factor, such as a 2x roll factor. So, if the damage was calculated with 1D8, then the critical damage will be 2D8. Optionally, you may just double the 1D8 damage roll. Remember, your system doesn't have to mimic the combat mechanic of any other system—be creative and unique!

Attack Roll Example

Let's simulate one half of an attack round where just one player attacks and the other defends, to see how the calculations are done and what results we get. First of all, we'll give the player these relevant attributes:

- STR: 18
- DEX: 12
- STA: 9
- Weapon: 2-8 dmg
- Armor: 10
- HP: 14

The monster will have these sample attributes:

- STR: 15
- DEX: 14
- STA: 16
- Weapon: 1-6 dmg
- Armor: 12
- HP: 16

Armor Class

First, we'll calculate the AC for the monster:

```
AC = DEX + Armor Points + Shield Points
AC = 14 + 12 + 0
AC = 26
```

Attack Roll

Now, we'll calculate the attacker's attack chance to-hit:

```
To-Hit = Attack Roll (STR + D20) - Defender's AC
Attack roll = STR + D20
Attack roll = 18 + 9 (roll) = 27
```

Did the attack succeed?

```
To-Hit = Attack Roll (27) - AC (26) = 1 (Hit!)
```

Damage Roll

Since our attack succeeded, but was not a critical hit, we calculate normal damage.

```
Damage = D8 + STR + Weapon Damage - Defender's AC
Damage = roll (1-8) + 18 + roll (2-8) - 26
Damage = roll (3) + 18 + roll (7) - 26
Damage = 3 + 18 + 7 - 26 = 2
```

Had the attack been a critical hit with an attack roll of 20, then critical damage would be calculated as follows:

```
Damage = D8 * 2 + STR + Weapon Damage - Defender's AC
```

```
Damage = roll (1-8) * 2 + 18 + roll (2-8) - 26
Damage = roll (3) * 2 + 18 + roll (7) - 26
Damage = 6 + 18 + 7 - 26 = 5
```

Hit Points

The monster's HP is reduced by the total damage until it reaches zero (which is death):

```
HP = 16 - 2 = 14 (normal damage)
HP = 16 - 5 = 11 (critical damage)
```

As you can see from these results, the die rolls are *crucial*! After all those many calculations, our hero only dealt 2 points of damage to the monster, and the monster then gets to strike back at the player. This continues round after round until one or the other loses all their HP or flees.

Dealing with the Player's Death

One drawback to combat is that you can die. It's a cold, hard, truth, I realize, but it can happen. What should you do, as the game's designer and programmer, when the *player's character (PC)* dies? That is a tough decision that requires some thought and should be based on the overall design of your game. You might let the player save and load the game, but that takes away from the suspension of disbelief. You want the player to be completely immersed in the game and unaware of a file system, an operating system, or even of the computer. You want your players to be mesmerized by the content on the screen, and something as cheesy as a load/save feature takes away from that. I'll admit, though, most players abuse the save/load game feature and complain if you don't have one. After all, you want the player to be able to quit at a moment's notice without going through any hassle. Let's face it: Sometimes the real world asserts itself into the reverie you are experiencing in the game, and you have to quit playing.

But just for the sake of gameplay, what is the best way to deal with the player character's death, aside from having a save/load feature? I recommend just re-spawning the PC at the starting point of a level file. The location of a re-spawn is up to you as the game's designer. Do you want to make it too easy for the player to die and come back too quickly, or do you want to make them work a little bit before resuming the fight they were in previously? Re-spawning too close to the last fight might make the game too easy, so a spawn point at a central hub town or other location might be better, and then the player must walk and portal to get back to the location where they were at prior to dying.

Combat Demo 2

The second Combat Demo shows how to make these calculations for an attack against an NPC (Figure 16.20). This demo uses the `Dialogue` class to show the results of attack rolls with each part of the calculation shown for you to study. This scene, for instance, shows a critical attack roll that dealt 14 damage to a target NPC. Most RPG purists will enjoy seeing this information, whereas casual RPG fans will prefer to just hurry up and kill the monster so they can loot its corpse for items and gold. It's up to you to decide how much information you want to share with the player.

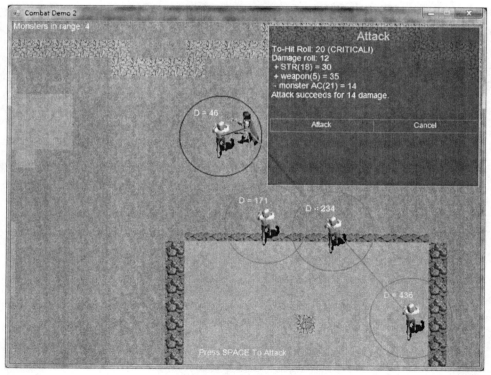

Figure 16.20
Demonstration of an attack roll against a hostile NPC.

On the one hand, it might be impressive to see what all is involved in an attack with the various rolls and calculations, since the casual player might just assume your combat system uses a simple attack roll versus defense roll system. If you don't show any information, and just show damage dealt (as in games like *Baldur's Gate*), the player might assume just a random attack roll is all there is to it. Every attribute is important and affects the outcome of combat, and every player knows this intuitively, but it's easy to forget if combat tends to happen very quickly. One advantage to turn-based combat is that it will reflect a pencil-and-paper game, which is at the root of every computer RPG. On the other hand, some players might get annoyed with the slow pace of combat and give up on your game. You have to decide on the best balance between information overload (TMI) and dumbed-down gameplay.

Turn-based Combat

When a turn-based combat system is the way to go, we need to make a few minor changes to the input system. In the previous example, we used the Space key to trigger a flag called attackFlag, which was set to False when the Space key was released. That works for a real-time combat system, but not for a turn-based one. For turn-based combat, we need to wait until the user *releases* the attack key. Otherwise, some sort of timing mechanism must be used and that can get messy. So, here is the new keyboard code—note how attackFlag is now handled.

```
Private Sub Form1_KeyDown(ByVal sender As Object, _
        ByVal e As System.Windows.Forms.KeyEventArgs) Handles Me.KeyDown
    Select Case (e.KeyCode)
        Case Keys.Up, Keys.W : keyState.up = True
        Case Keys.Down, Keys.S : keyState.down = True
        Case Keys.Left, Keys.A : keyState.left = True
        Case Keys.Right, Keys.D : keyState.right = True
    End Select
End Sub

Private Sub Form1_KeyUp(ByVal sender As System.Object, _
        ByVal e As System.Windows.Forms.KeyEventArgs) Handles MyBase.KeyUp
    Select Case (e.KeyCode)
        Case Keys.Escape : End
        Case Keys.Up, Keys.W : keyState.up = False
        Case Keys.Down, Keys.S : keyState.down = False
```

```
        Case Keys.Left, Keys.A : keyState.left = False
        Case Keys.Right, Keys.D : keyState.right = False
        Case Keys.Space : attackFlag = True
    End Select
End Sub
```

More Dialogue

We need the Dialogue class again to show the results of an attack. You can now see how useful Dialogue is beyond its original intended use as a way to talk with NPCs! Granted, the window is not very attractive yet. We will need to add some more configuration options to it so the buttons look better and the height is adjusted automatically to the number of buttons in use. But, the important thing is, we have a way to interact with the player. Before using it, we need to add some new features to the Dialogue class. See, I warned you in Chapter 15 that this was likely to happen! But, we can't possibly foresee in the future what new things we'll need to do with our code, so this is to be expected.

As you'll recall, the Dialogue class will display the dialogue window until a button is clicked, and then set the Selection property equal to the button number. Previously, the Dialogue class did not hide itself after a selection was made or reset any of its properties. The new feature we need to add is a Visible property.

```
Private p_visible As Boolean
Public Property Visible() As Boolean
    Get
        Return p_visible
    End Get
    Set(ByVal value As Boolean)
        p_visible = value
    End Set
End Property
```

The Draw() function will check p_visible before drawing anything. Now we will have the ability to continually update the Dialogue object and have it display whatever we want to the player, and selectively show it as needed.

```
Public Sub Draw()
    If Not p_visible Then Return
    ...
End Sub
```

Back to our main source code for Combat Demo 2. Here is the new doUpdate() function, which now handles scrolling, hero, monsters, attacking, and dialogue.

```
Private Sub doUpdate()
    Dim frameRate As Integer = game.FrameRate()
    Dim ticks As Integer = Environment.TickCount()
    Static drawLast As Integer = 0
    If ticks > drawLast + 16 Then
        drawLast = ticks
        doScrolling()
        doHero()
        doMonsters()
        doAttack()
        doDialogue()
        game.Print(0, 0, "Monsters in range: " + monstersInRange.ToString())
        game.Print(320, 570, "Press SPACE To Attack")
        game.Update()
        Application.DoEvents()
    Else
        Threading.Thread.Sleep(1)
    End If
End Sub
```

The doDialogue() function does not automatically move, but you may use that feature if you want (see Chapter 15 for details). I want the combat dialogue to stay in the same place.

```
Private Sub doDialogue()
    dialogue.updateMouse(game.MousePos, game.MouseButton)
    dialogue.setCorner(Dialogue.Positions.UpperRight)
    dialogue.Draw()
    If dialogue.Selection > 0 Then
        dialogue.Visible = False
        dialogue.Selection = 0
    End If
End Sub
```

The doDialogue() function is called continuously from the main loop, and properties determine what it should do. To trigger a dialogue to "pop up," we can call on this new showDialogue() function, which automatically formats the dialogue with two buttons:

```
Private Sub showDialogue(ByVal title As String, ByVal message As String, _
        ByVal button1 As String, ByVal button2 As String)
    dialogue.Title = title
    dialogue.Message = message
    dialogue.NumButtons = 2
    dialogue.setButtonText(1, button1)
    dialogue.setButtonText(2, button2)
    dialogue.Visible = True
End Sub
```

Attack!

The doAttack() function handles a single round of combat. Well, technically, it's just one-half of a round since the NPC doesn't fight back yet. Study the calculations in this function to learn more about how the armor class, attack roll, and damage roll are related.

```
Private Sub doAttack()
    Const DEF_ARMOR As Integer = 10
    Const DEF_SHIELD As Integer = 0
    Const WEAPON_DMG As Integer = 5
    Dim hit As Boolean = False
    Dim critical As Boolean = False
    Dim fail As Boolean = False
    Dim roll As Integer = 0
    Dim AC As Integer = 0
    Dim damage As Integer = 0
    Dim text As String

    If Not attacking Then Return

    REM calculate target's AC
    AC = monsters(target).DEX + DEF_ARMOR + DEF_SHIELD

    REM calculate chance to-hit for PC
    roll = game.Random(1, 20)
    text += "To-Hit Roll: " + roll.ToString()
    If roll = 20 Then
        REM critical hit!
        hit = True
        critical = True
```

```
            text += " (CRITICAL!)" + vbCrLf
        ElseIf roll = 1 Then
            fail = True
            text += " (EPIC FAIL!)" + vbCrLf
        Else
            REM normal hit
            roll += hero.STR
            If roll > AC Then hit = True
            text += " + STR(" + hero.STR.ToString() + ") = " + _
                roll.ToString() + vbCrLf
        End If

        REM did attack succeed?
        If hit Then
            REM calculate base damage
            damage = game.Random(1, 8)
            REM add critical
            If critical Then damage *= 2
            text += "Damage roll: " + damage.ToString() + vbCrLf
            REM add STR
            damage += hero.STR
            text += " + STR(" + hero.STR.ToString() + ") = " + _
                damage.ToString() + vbCrLf
            REM add weapon damage (usually a die roll)
            damage += WEAPON_DMG
            text += " + weapon(" + WEAPON_DMG.ToString() + ") = " + _
                damage.ToString() + vbCrLf
            REM subtract AC
            damage -= AC
            text += " - monster AC(" + AC.ToString() + ") = " + _
                damage.ToString() + vbCrLf
            REM minimal hit
            If damage < 1 Then damage = 1
            REM show result
            text += "Attack succeeds for " + damage.ToString() + " damage."
        Else
            text += "Attack failed." + vbCrLf
        End If
        showDialogue("Attack", text, "Attack", "Cancel")
End Sub
```

FACING YOUR ENEMIES

It goes without saying that attacking an enemy who is behind you is kind of silly. No, it's *ridiculous*. No one can swing a sword accurately behind them, let alone shoot an arrow backwards. So, the game shouldn't allow it either! What's worse, we can deal damage to a monster without even swinging *at it*. The code that figures out the direction to a target is like the code that sets the player's animation based on its direction. The getTargetDirection() function will "point" a character from its current angle toward a target. This is also useful for pitting NPCs against each other, or for having NPCs face the player when you talk to them. Figure 16.21 shows the Combat Demo 3 running with new code to cause sprites to face toward each other.

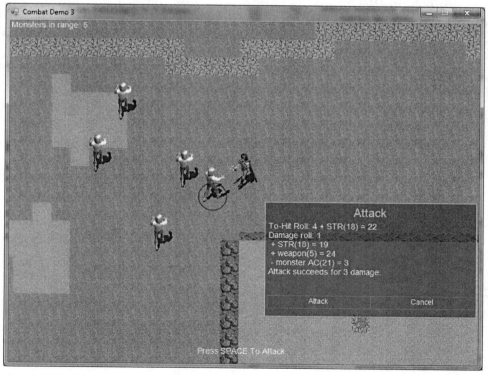

Figure 16.21
This demo shows how to cause sprites to face toward each other in order to fight.

Hint

Note: the code presented in these examples is not meant to be typed in to modify the first example in the chapter step by step, but only to show the most relevant code for each example (which share many unchanging functions). You will want to open the complete project for each example and observe it running as you study the text. These projects do show an evolution toward a final, working combat system, but the code is not all listed due to space considerations.

Which Way Did He Go?

The logic behind figuring out the direction from one point to another is really just about brute-force If statements. First, we look at the X position of both points to find out whether the target is left, right, or directly in line with the source. Then, it checks the Y position to figure out whether the target is above, below, or right in line with the source. Based on these conditions, we set the source in a direction that will most closely match the target's location (within the limits of the 8-way directions for our animations).

```
Private Function getTargetDirection(ByVal source As PointF, _
        ByVal target As PointF)
    Dim direction As Integer = 0
    If source.X < target.X - 16 Then
        If source.Y < target.Y - 8 Then
            direction = 3 'south east
        ElseIf source.Y > target.Y + 8 Then
            direction = 1 'north east
        Else
            direction = 2 'east
        End If
    ElseIf source.X > target.X + 16 Then
        If source.Y < target.Y - 8 Then
            direction = 5 'south west
        ElseIf source.Y > target.Y + 8 Then
            direction = 7 'north west
        Else
            direction = 6 'west
        End If
    Else
        If source.Y < target.Y - 8 Then
            direction = 4 'south
        ElseIf source.Y > target.Y + 8 Then
```

```
            direction = 0 'north
        End If
    End If
    Return direction
End Function
```

Using this function, we can modify doMonsters() and force the PC and NPC to face each other when the player triggers an attack! The result is much improved over the previous example.

```
REM is player trying to attack this monster?
If dist < attackRadius Then
    game.Device.DrawEllipse(New Pen(Brushes.Blue, 2.0), _
        monsterCenter.X - 24, monsterCenter.Y, 48, 48)
    If attackFlag Then
        attacking = True
        target = n
        attackFlag = False
        REM make PC and NPC face each other
        Dim dir As Integer
        dir = getTargetDirection(monsterCenter, hero.CenterPos)
        monsters(target).Direction = dir
        monsters(target).Draw()
        dir = getTargetDirection(hero.CenterPos, monsterCenter)
        hero.Direction = dir
        hero.Draw()
        Exit For
    End If
End If
```

A Change of Character

A minor change is required in the Character class to support the feature of forcing sprites to face toward each other. The original single Character.Draw() function is replaced with these three versions:

```
Public Sub Draw()
    Draw(p_position.X, p_position.Y)
End Sub

Public Sub Draw(ByVal pos As PointF)
    Draw(pos.X, pos.Y)
End Sub
```

```
Public Sub Draw(ByVal x As Integer, ByVal y As Integer)
    Dim startFrame As Integer
    Dim endFrame As Integer
    Select Case p_state
        Case AnimationStates.Walking
            p_walkSprite.Position = p_position
            If p_direction > -1 Then
                startFrame = p_direction * p_walkColumns
                endFrame = startFrame + p_walkColumns - 1
                p_walkSprite.AnimationRate = 30
                p_walkSprite.Animate(startFrame, endFrame)
            End If
            p_walkSprite.Draw(x, y)
        Case AnimationStates.Attacking
            p_attackSprite.Position = p_position
            If p_direction > -1 Then
                startFrame = p_direction * p_attackColumns
                endFrame = startFrame + p_attackColumns - 1
                p_attackSprite.AnimationRate = 30
                p_attackSprite.Animate(startFrame, endFrame)
            End If
            p_attackSprite.Draw(x, y)
        Case AnimationStates.Dying
            p_dieSprite.Position = p_position
            If p_direction > -1 Then
                startFrame = p_direction * p_dieColumns
                endFrame = startFrame + p_dieColumns - 1
                p_dieSprite.AnimationRate = 30
                p_dieSprite.Animate(startFrame, endFrame)
            End If
            p_dieSprite.Draw(x, y)
    End Select
End Sub
```

STATE-BASED COMBAT

The combat system is now complex enough to require a state variable. Previously, a Boolean variable, attacking, kept track of just whether combat was supposed to happen. Now, we need to involve several steps for combat:

1. Player triggers an attack

2. Attack introduction

3. Attack commences

4. Report the attack results

This enumeration will handle the four states in the combat system:

```
Public Enum AttackStates
    ATTACK_NONE
    ATTACK_TRIGGER
    ATTACK_ATTACK
    ATTACK_RESULT
End Enum
```

This is the variable we will be using to keep track of the current state of the combat system:

```
Private attackState As AttackStates
```

By the time we're done adding state to the combat engine for this Combat Demo 4 project, shown in Figure 16.22, the game will allow you to make distinct, individual attacks against an enemy with a click of the Attack button.

Dialogue Improvements

Now that we're using a state-based system for combat, we need to modify other parts of the game code to also work correctly: namely, the Dialogue class. Previously, we just looked for a mouse click to trigger a button selection event. Now, that will not work because the dialogue will be repeatedly updated so a mouse click will be seen as *many clicks* while the button is being held. No matter how fast you press and release the mouse button, it will pick up several events because the loop is running at 60 fps. What we need to do is look for a button *release* event instead. This change has been made to the Dialogue.Draw() function:

```
REM clicked on this button?
If p_mouseBtn = MouseButtons.None And p_oldMouseBtn = MouseButtons.Left Then
    p_selection = n
Else
    p_selection = 0
End If
```

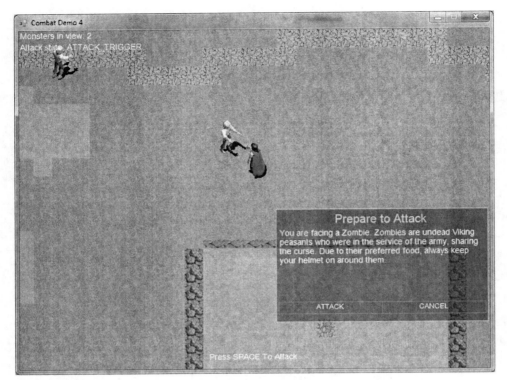

Figure 16.22
The new state-based combat system slows down and improves the gameplay.

Plugging in Attack State

I will not go over every line of the next example, but suffice it to say there were a lot of changes made to move the combat system over to a state-based system. The most important changes were made to doMonsters() and doCombat(), which mainly involved just checking the current state and acting appropriately. For instance, in doMonsters(), rather than simply setting the target to whatever monster the player is close to without regard for any previously targeted monster, the code now checks to see if the player isn't already in a fight.

```
If attackState = AttackStates.ATTACK_NONE Then
    If attackFlag Then
        attackState = AttackStates.ATTACK_TRIGGER
        target = n
        attackFlag = False
```

```
            dialogue.Visible = True
            REM make PC and NPC face each other
            Dim dir As Integer
            dir = getTargetDirection(monsterCenter, hero.CenterPos)
            monsters(target).Direction = dir
            monsters(n).Draw(relativePos)
            dir = getTargetDirection(hero.CenterPos, monsterCenter)
            hero.Direction = dir
            hero.Draw()
            Exit For
        End If
    End If
End If
```

Also, after all of the monsters have been processed in the loop, then we need to reset combat if the player has walked away or cancelled combat.

```
If monstersInRange = 0 Then
    target = 0
    attackText = ""
    dialogue.Visible = False
    attackState = AttackStates.ATTACK_NONE
End If
```

Likewise, some serious changes have been made to doAttack() to support the new state-based combat system. Here is the new code for the function. All of the previous code in doAttack() is now contained solely inside the ATTACK_ATTACK state condition.

```
Private Sub doAttack()
    Const DEF_ARMOR As Integer = 10
    Const DEF_SHIELD As Integer = 0
    Const WEAPON_DMG As Integer = 5
    Dim hit As Boolean = False
    Dim critical As Boolean = False
    Dim fail As Boolean = False
    Dim roll As Integer = 0
    Dim AC As Integer = 0
    Dim damage As Integer = 0
    Dim text As String = ""

    If dialogue.Selection = 2 Then
        attackState = AttackStates.ATTACK_NONE
```

```
            Return
        End If
        Select Case attackState
            Case AttackStates.ATTACK_NONE
                Return
            Case AttackStates.ATTACK_TRIGGER
                If target > 0 Then
                    text = "You are facing a " + monsters(target).Name + _
                        ". " + monsters(target).Description
                    showDialogue("Prepare to Attack", text, "ATTACK", "CANCEL")
                End If
                If dialogue.Selection = 1 Then
                    attackState = AttackStates.ATTACK_ATTACK
                End If
            Case AttackStates.ATTACK_ATTACK
                REM calculate target's AC
                AC = monsters(target).DEX + DEF_ARMOR + DEF_SHIELD
                REM calculate chance to-hit for PC
                roll = game.Random(1, 20)
                text += "To-Hit Roll: " + roll.ToString()
                If roll = 20 Then
                    REM critical hit!
                    hit = True
                    critical = True
                    text += " (CRITICAL!)" + vbCrLf
                ElseIf roll = 1 Then
                    fail = True
                    text += " (EPIC FAIL!)" + vbCrLf
                Else
                    REM normal hit
                    roll += hero.STR
                    If roll > AC Then hit = True
                    text += " + STR(" + hero.STR.ToString() + ") = " + _
                        roll.ToString() + vbCrLf
                End If
                REM did attack succeed?
                If hit Then
                    REM calculate base damage
                    damage = game.Random(1, 8)
                    REM add critical
```

```
                If critical Then damage *= 2
                text += "Damage roll: " + damage.ToString() + vbCrLf
                REM add STR
                damage += hero.STR
                text += " + STR(" + hero.STR.ToString() + ") = " + _
                    damage.ToString() + vbCrLf
                REM add weapon damage (usually a die roll)
                damage += WEAPON_DMG
                text += " + weapon(" + WEAPON_DMG.ToString() + ") = " + _
                    damage.ToString() + vbCrLf
                REM subtract AC
                damage -= AC
                text += " - monster AC(" + AC.ToString() + ") = " + _
                    damage.ToString() + vbCrLf
                REM minimal hit
                If damage < 1 Then damage = 1
                REM show result
                text += "Attack succeeds for " + damage.ToString() + _
                    " damage."
            Else
                text += "Attack failed." + vbCrLf
            End If
            attackText = text
            attackState = AttackStates.ATTACK_RESULT
        Case AttackStates.ATTACK_RESULT
            showDialogue("Attack Roll", attackText, "ATTACK AGAIN", _
                "CANCEL")
            If dialogue.Selection = 1 Then
                attackState = AttackStates.ATTACK_ATTACK
            End If
    End Select
End Sub
```

DEALING PERMANENT DAMAGE

The final step to complete the combat system is to give the player experience after defeating a monster. This will require some new fields in the Character class since we did not account for experience or leveling when originally designing the class. Some additional code will be required in this final example, Combat Demo 5, to allow the animation for the killed monsters to stay on the

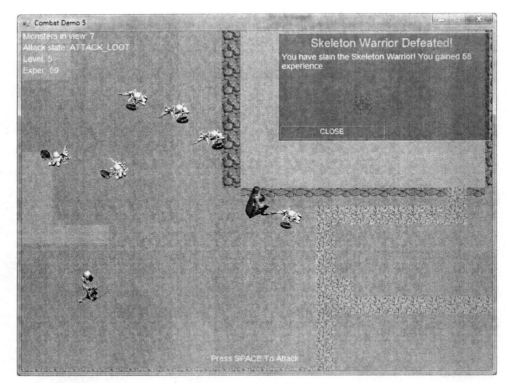

Figure 16.23
The skeletons don't get a free ride any more!

screen after they fall. Figure 16.23 shows the result. The amount of experience awarded is a random value from 50 to 100, which is just an arbitrary range that I made up as filler. How should we award experience in the real game? It should be a factor that involves the monster's level, which is not something we're currently using in the character editor files. What would you do with this design decision: add a level field, or a pair of fields that define how much experience the player receives? Something to ponder between now and the final chapter.

These few changes are needed in the doAttack() function to add the ability to kill monsters, gain experience, and level up. Portions of the code that have not changed that we have already recently covered are omitted. There are two states involved when a battle is concluded: ATTACK_RESULT and ATTACK_LOOT. The former tallies the experience, kills the monster, and displays the dialogue message. The latter is simply used to hold the dialogue window up until the player has acknowledged the information by clicking the "CLOSE" button.

Note: some variables in this code will be new; refer to the source code in the finished project to see the variable declarations.

```
Select Case attackState
    Case AttackStates.ATTACK_NONE
        hero.AnimationState = Character.AnimationStates.Walking
        dialogue.Visible = False
        Return
    Case AttackStates.ATTACK_TRIGGER
        If target > 0 Then
            text = "You are facing a " + monsters(target).Name + ". " + _
                monsters(target).Description
            showDialogue("Prepare to Attack", text, "ATTACK", "CANCEL")
        End If
        If dialogue.Selection = 1 Then
            attackState = AttackStates.ATTACK_ATTACK
        End If
    Case AttackStates.ATTACK_ATTACK
        hero.AnimationState = Character.AnimationStates.Attacking
        monsters(target).AnimationState = _
            Character.AnimationStates.Attacking
        REM calculate target's AC
        ...
        REM calculate chance to-hit for PC
        ...
        REM did attack succeed?
        ...
        attackText = text
        monsters(target).HitPoints -= attackDamage
        attackState = AttackStates.ATTACK_RESULT
    Case AttackStates.ATTACK_RESULT
        hero.AnimationState = Character.AnimationStates.Walking
        REM is monster dead?
        If monsters(target).HitPoints <= 0 Then
            monsters(target).Alive = False
            Dim xp As Integer = game.Random(50, 100)
            addExperience(xp)
            text = monsters(target).Name + " Defeated!"
```

```
            attackText = "You have slain the " + monsters(target).Name + _
                "! You gained " + xp.ToString() + " experience."
            showDialogue(text, attackText, "CLOSE")
            attackState = AttackStates.ATTACK_LOOT
        Else
            showDialogue("Attack Roll", attackText, _
                "ATTACK AGAIN", "CANCEL")
            If dialogue.Selection = 1 Then
                attackState = AttackStates.ATTACK_ATTACK
            End If
        End If
    Case AttackStates.ATTACK_LOOT
        hero.AnimationState = Character.AnimationStates.Walking
        If dialogue.Selection = 1 Then
            attackState = AttackStates.ATTACK_NONE
            target = 0
        End If
End Select
```

Gaining Experience

A helper function called addExperience() will take care of granting the player experience and leveling up. At this early stage of development, leveling up is a trivial affair meant only to demonstrate that it can be done. In the finished game, we will want to grant the player new attribute points (to STR, DEX, etc.) to reflect the fact that their new level makes them stronger. This function is just a stopgap for the time being to demonstrate experience and leveling, while a more permanent solution will be offered in the final chapter.

```
Private Sub addExperience(ByVal xp As Integer)
    hero.Experience += xp
    If hero.Experience > 200 Then
        hero.Level += 1
        hero.Experience -= 200
    End If
End Sub
```

The Character class needs some new features to accommodate the requirements for gaining experience and leveling up the character.

```
Private p_experience As Integer
Public Property Experience() As Integer
```

```
        Get
                Return p_experience
        End Get
        Set(ByVal value As Integer)
                p_experience = value
        End Set
End Property

Private p_level As Integer
Public Property Level() As Integer
        Get
                Return p_level
        End Get
        Set(ByVal value As Integer)
                p_level = value
        End Set
End Property
```

We will also add a new `Character.Alive` property to make it easier to flag monsters as they are killed and prevent the code from updating those characters.

```
Private p_alive As Boolean
Public Property Alive() As Boolean
        Get
                Return p_alive
        End Get
        Set(ByVal value As Boolean)
                p_alive = value
        End Set
End Property
```

The death animation will require a new item in the `Character.AnimationStates` enumeration so that when the animation finishes one cycle, the sprite will remain on the ground, showing the final frame of the death animation for good.

```
Public Enum AnimationStates
        Walking
        Attacking
        Dying
        Dead
End Enum
```

LEVEL UP!

After play testing the Combat Demo 5 project a few times, I'm extremely pleased with the decision to use a turn-based combat system instead of real-time. This slows down the game, gives it more character, and allows the player to become more involved in the gameplay. Combat in a traditional pen-and-paper RPG is not a quick "hack-n-slash" affair that ends in seconds—the players must calculate the results of each attack, roll the dice for their attack roll and damage roll, while the defender often has "succeed or fail" rolls to block the attack, based on their abilities. It is this interaction that makes the game fun. Simply swinging the weapon as fast as the game will let you and mopping up the loot afterward takes away a huge amount of the fun factor. However, there most certainly is a balance to be found: you don't want to bore your player with micro managing his character. One type of combat we did not address in this already lengthy chapter is ranged attacks (of the bow and spell variety). As it turns out, these types of attacks tend to get handled very much like melee attacks but with a little bit more range, so all we need to do is increase the attack radius around each monster to allow for ranged weapons. Perhaps that is an attribute best handled by the weapon's stats? Ironically, that is the very subject we're covering in the next chapter.

CHAPTER 17

CREATING THE ITEM EDITOR

This chapter focuses on the development of an item editor to make creating and managing game items (such as swords, armor pieces, rings, and other gear found in a typical RPG) easier for a designer. If you have ever tried to create an RPG without an editor like this, I'm sure you ran into the same roadblock that I have when it comes to working with items. Just giving the player a sword tends to be a hard-coded, manual process, with less than favorable results. Even just storing items in a text file and reading them in is better than manually creating arrays of items in code, unless your game is on the extremely simple side with just "hack & slash" gameplay without much depth. Since our goal is to send the player on quests before we finish this book, having items that satisfy the quests is essential! For an example of how the item data is used, we'll put that on hold until the next chapter and just focus on editing in this one.

Here's what we'll cover in this chapter:

- Item images
- Looking up items
- The Item class
- Item editor source code

Item Editor Design

The item editor is a bit different from the character editor that we developed back in Chapter 14. While characters are stored one per .char file, many items are stored in a .item file. The editor has a File menu, which allows you to start a new item database, load an existing file, or save the current file to a new file. The item editor is shown in Figure 17.1.

The editor was designed to work with groups of items in a file. The example shown here contains some weapons and armor items, but it would be better to organize the items into separate groups (weapons, armor, rings, etc.) so that it's easier to manage and search for specific items. Another approach is to just store everything in a single item database, which is perfectly okay but it's just harder to find and edit items when there are so many in a single file.

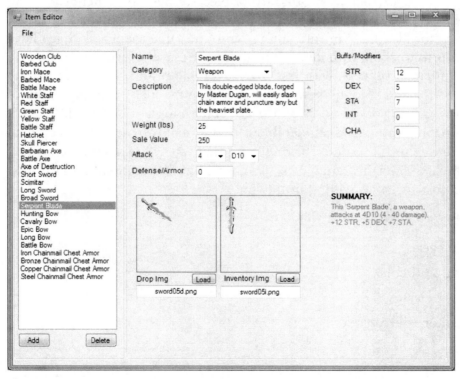

Figure 17.1
The item editor works with an entire list of items at a time.

This editor does make it possible for players to cheat on your game. By giving the filenames a different extension besides .xml, we can at least hide the data from casual wanna-be hackers, but anyone with bare minimum skills will try opening the .item file in a text editor and immediately see that it is an editable text file containing .xml tables. There are ways to get around this problem, but that subject is beyond the scope of this book. Experience has shown me that for players who want to hack a game file, whether it's a core database or a saved game, no effort short of hard encryption will prevent them from doing so. If someone wants to hack your game that badly, take it as a compliment.

Item Images

The item editor works with just single-frame bitmaps, with support for two versions for each item: a *drop* image and an *inventory* image. The drop image is usually smaller and oriented with the ground tiles, while the inventory image is often oriented straight-on so it looks better in an inventory screen (the player's equipment). Neither image is suitable for both purposes. If you try to use the inventory image as a drop item, it will look funny on the ground at the wrong angle. However, one alternative is to bring up a "loot window" showing the contents of an item rather than dropping items directly onto the ground. A loot window does eliminate quite a bit of work since we do not need to keep track of two different images *in addition* to the added code to allow the player to pick up items on the ground.

An advantage to the ground image is that you can place individual items anywhere in the game world for the player to find. But, due to the extra work required, I think most designers would rather have their artists working on new gameplay art rather than extra *drop* images. This is why in most games you'll most often find crates and boxes rather than usable items in the game world. Since we have both versions of the artwork for every item from Reiner, we can use them with the item editor. Just note that both are not absolutely necessary and it's acceptable to just use the inventory version, as long as you have a loot window come up in the game whenever the player opens a container. I kind of like the realism added when items drop to the ground when an NPC falls in combat (maybe even add the dramatic effect of having the items scatter around the body randomly). Since it's fairly common to "loot the corpse" in most computer RPGs, use whichever method you want in your own game since the artwork is available.

What if we were to add multiple image frame support to the item editor, so that batches of item artwork could be stored on a sprite sheet? That's a distinct possibility. At the very least, we could store both the drop and inventory image together in a two-frame image. The problem is, the artwork is not all uniform in size, with the drop items being somewhat smaller (in Reiner's). Sure, you could enlarge the images to a fixed size all around, but will that save time in the long run versus just adding both image filenames into the item editor fields?

There is the additional problem of having literally hundreds of asset files in the game's folder. The limited set of item images used so far already accounts for a large number of files cluttering the game's main folder. A definite improvement would be to store the images in a sub-folder like .\assets under the main folder, and then prefix all of the image filenames stored in the item editor database with .\assets. So, a filename field such as "drop plate 1.png" would become ".\assets\drop plate 1.png." You can do any such manipulation in the game code while loading these assets.

Looking Up Items

I wanted to use an auto-increment identifier for each item in the item editor database and then use the ID in quests and in the player's inventory. But, though an identifier-based database is required for a professional project, it's not the best choice for an amateur game with multi-purpose tools like what we have for Celtic Crusader. Instead of using an ID, the `Item.Name` property will be used to look up the data for an item. All that is required to make this work effectively is to ensure that your items each have a unique name. If you want to have three rings called "Magic Ring," be sure to add a qualifier to the name like "Magic Ring +1" or something to uniquely identify each item. Since the name is the lookup field, the first item matching the name will be used in a lookup.

Item Class

As with the previous level editor and character editor, the new item editor includes a class (called `Item`) that makes the data available to our game. The `Item` class is meant to handle a single item from the editor database (which is stored in an XML file). In our game code, we will need to load the .item file with additional code and then use the `Item` class for each item that is loaded. In other words, there is no overall "Items" class that loads an entire .item file, is saved by the editor, and makes those items available to the game. Perhaps there should be?

```
Public Class Item
    Private p_name As String
    Private p_desc As String
    Private p_dropfile As String
    Private p_invfile As String
    Private p_category As String
    Private p_weight As Single
    Private p_value As Single
    Private p_attacknumdice As Integer
    Private p_attackdie As Integer
    Private p_defense As Integer
    Private p_buffStr As Integer
    Private p_buffDex As Integer
    Private p_buffSta As Integer
    Private p_buffInt As Integer
    Private p_buffCha As Integer

    Public Sub New()
        p_name = "new item"
        p_desc = ""
        p_dropfile = ""
        p_invfile = ""
        p_category = ""
        p_weight = 0.0
        p_value = 0.0
        p_attacknumdice = 0
        p_attackdie = 0
        p_defense = 0
        p_buffStr = 0
        p_buffDex = 0
        p_buffSta = 0
        p_buffInt = 0
        p_buffCha = 0
    End Sub

    Public Property Name() As String
        Get
            Return p_name
```

```vbnet
        End Get
        Set(ByVal value As String)
            p_name = value
        End Set
    End Property

    Public Property Description() As String
        Get
            Return p_desc
        End Get
        Set(ByVal value As String)
            p_desc = value
        End Set
    End Property

    Public Property DropImageFilename() As String
        Get
            Return p_dropfile
        End Get
        Set(ByVal value As String)
            p_dropfile = value
        End Set
    End Property

    Public Property InvImageFilename() As String
        Get
            Return p_invfile
        End Get
        Set(ByVal value As String)
            p_invfile = value
        End Set
    End Property

    Public Property Category() As String
        Get
            Return p_category
        End Get
        Set(ByVal value As String)
            p_category = value
        End Set
    End Property
```

```
Public Property Weight() As Single
    Get
         Return p_weight
    End Get
    Set(ByVal value As Single)
        p_weight = value
    End Set
End Property

Public Property Value() As Single
    Get
         Return p_value
    End Get
    Set(ByVal value As Single)
        p_value = value
    End Set
End Property

Public Property AttackNumDice() As Integer
    Get
         Return p_attacknumdice
    End Get
    Set(ByVal value As Integer)
        p_attacknumdice = value
    End Set
End Property

Public Property AttackDie() As Integer
    Get
         Return p_attackdie
    End Get
    Set(ByVal value As Integer)
        p_attackdie = value
    End Set
End Property

Public Property Defense() As Integer
    Get
```

```
            Return p_defense
        End Get
        Set(ByVal value As Integer)
            p_defense = value
        End Set
    End Property

    Public Property STR() As Integer
        Get
            Return p_buffStr
        End Get
        Set(ByVal value As Integer)
            p_buffStr = value
        End Set
    End Property

    Public Property DEX() As Integer
        Get
            Return p_buffDex
        End Get
        Set(ByVal value As Integer)
            p_buffDex = value
        End Set
    End Property

    Public Property STA() As Integer
        Get
            Return p_buffSta
        End Get
        Set(ByVal value As Integer)
            p_buffSta = value
        End Set
    End Property

    Public Property INT() As Integer
        Get
            Return p_buffInt
        End Get
        Set(ByVal value As Integer)
            p_buffInt = value
```

```vb
        End Set
    End Property

    Public Property CHA() As Integer
        Get
            Return p_buffCha
        End Get
        Set(ByVal value As Integer)
            p_buffCha = value
        End Set
    End Property

    Public ReadOnly Property Summary() As String
        Get
            Dim text As String
            text = "This '" + p_name + "', "

            Dim weight As String = ""
            Select Case p_weight
                Case Is > 50 : weight = "a very heavy "
                Case Is > 25 : weight = "a heavy "
                Case Is > 15 : weight = "a "
                Case Is > 7 : weight = "a light "
                Case Is > 0 : weight = "a very light "
            End Select
            text += weight

            Select Case p_category
                Case "Weapon" : text += "weapon"
                Case "Armor" : text += "armor item"
                Case "Necklace" : text += "necklace"
                Case "Ring" : text += "ring"
                Case Else : text += p_category.ToLower() + " item"
            End Select

            If p_attacknumdice <> 0 Then
                text += ", attacks at " + p_attacknumdice.ToString() _
                    + "D" + p_attackdie.ToString() _
                    + " (" + p_attacknumdice.ToString() + " - " _
```

```
                        + (p_attackdie * p_attacknumdice).ToString() _
                        + " damage)"
            End If

            If p_defense <> 0 Then
                text += ", adds " + p_defense.ToString() + " armor points"
            End If

            Dim fmt As String = "+#;-#"
            If p_buffStr <> 0 Then
                text += ", " + p_buffStr.ToString(fmt) + " STR"
            End If
            If p_buffDex <> 0 Then
                text += ", " + p_buffDex.ToString(fmt) + " DEX"
            End If
            If p_buffSta <> 0 Then
                text += ", " + p_buffSta.ToString(fmt) + " STA"
            End If
            If p_buffInt <> 0 Then
                text += ", " + p_buffInt.ToString(fmt) + " INT"
            End If
            If p_buffCha <> 0 Then
                text += ", " + p_buffCha.ToString(fmt) + " CHA"
            End If

            Return text + "."
        End Get
    End Property

    Public Overrides Function ToString() As String
        Return p_name
    End Function
End Class
```

Item Editor Source Code

Like the character editor from a few chapters back, the item editor is all Visual Basic source code (the only editor written in C# is the level editor). The item editor is completely self-contained and it can create new item files from scratch as well as edit existing files. One nice feature is auto-save: while editing items, if you click on a different item in the list or close the editor, the current item is automatically saved. This takes out some of the tedium from editing a large number of items—just point, click, and edit, without concern for saving at every step.

Obviously, there is a form filled with controls that are not listed here, because the user interface is too complex to build from scratch (as in a tutorial-style walkthrough). The sources here are familiar because the XML code is similar to the code in the other editors. Some of the source code for the editor has been omitted to save space. To see the complete source code listing, please open the project (www.courseptr.com/downloads).

```
Public Class Form1
    Dim device As Graphics
    Dim surface As Bitmap
    Dim g_filename As String = "items.item"
    Dim currentIndex As Integer

    Private Sub Form1_Load(ByVal sender As System.Object, _
            ByVal e As System.EventArgs) Handles MyBase.Load
        surface = New Bitmap(Size.Width, Size.Height)
        picDrop.Image = surface
        device = Graphics.FromImage(surface)
        clearFields()
        loadFile(g_filename)
    End Sub

    Private Sub showItem(ByVal index As Integer)
        clearFields()
        Dim item As Item = lstItems.Items(index)
        txtName.Text = item.Name
        txtDesc.Text = item.Description
        txtDropImageFilename.Text = item.DropImageFilename
        txtInventoryImageFilename.Text = item.InvImageFilename
        cboCategory.Text = item.Category
        txtWeight.Text = item.Weight.ToString()
        txtValue.Text = item.Value.ToString()
        cboAttackNumDice.Text = item.AttackNumDice.ToString()
        cboAttackDie.Text = "D" + item.AttackDie.ToString()
        txtDefense.Text = item.Defense.ToString()
        txtSTR.Text = item.STR.ToString()
```

```vb
        txtDEX.Text = item.DEX.ToString()
        txtSTA.Text = item.STA.ToString()
        txtINT.Text = item.INT.ToString()
        txtCHA.Text = item.CHA.ToString()
        txtSummary.Text = item.Summary
End Sub

Private Function getElement(ByVal field As String, _
        ByRef element As XmlElement) As String
    Dim value As String = ""
    Try
        value = element.GetElementsByTagName(field)(0).InnerText
    Catch ex As Exception
        REM ignore error, just return empty
        Console.WriteLine(ex.Message)
    End Try
    Return value
End Function

Private Sub loadFile(ByVal filename As String)
    Try
        REM open the xml file
        Dim doc As New XmlDocument()
        doc.Load(filename)
        Dim list As XmlNodeList = doc.GetElementsByTagName("item")
        For Each node As XmlNode In list
            Dim element As XmlElement = node
            Dim item As New Item()
            item.Name = getElement("name", element)
            item.Description = getElement("description", element)
            item.DropImageFilename = getElement("dropimagefilename", _
                element)
            item.InvImageFilename = getElement("invimagefilename", _
                element)
            item.Category = getElement("category", element)
            item.Weight = Convert.ToSingle(getElement("weight", element))
            item.Value = Convert.ToSingle(getElement("value", element))
            item.AttackNumDice = Convert.ToInt32( _
                getElement("attacknumdice", element))
```

```
            item.AttackDie = Convert.ToInt32( _
                getElement("attackdie", element))
            item.Defense = Convert.ToInt32(getElement("defense", _
                element))
            item.STR = Convert.ToInt32(getElement("STR", element))
            item.DEX = Convert.ToInt32(getElement("DEX", element))
            item.STA = Convert.ToInt32(getElement("STA", element))
            item.INT = Convert.ToInt32(getElement("INT", element))
            item.CHA = Convert.ToInt32(getElement("CHA", element))
            lstItems.Items.Add(item)
        Next
    Catch ex As Exception
        MessageBox.Show(ex.Message)
        Return
    End Try
End Sub


Private Sub saveFile(ByVal filename As String)
    Try
        REM create data type templates
        Dim typeInt As System.Type
        Dim typeSingle As System.Type
        Dim typeStr As System.Type
        typeInt = System.Type.GetType("System.Int32")
        typeStr = System.Type.GetType("System.String")
        typeSingle = System.Type.GetType("System.Single")


        REM create xml schema
        Dim table As New DataTable("item")
        table.Columns.Add(New DataColumn("name", typeStr))
        table.Columns.Add(New DataColumn("description", typeStr))
        table.Columns.Add(New DataColumn("dropimagefilename", typeStr))
        table.Columns.Add(New DataColumn("invimagefilename", typeStr))
        table.Columns.Add(New DataColumn("category", typeStr))
        table.Columns.Add(New DataColumn("weight", typeSingle))
        table.Columns.Add(New DataColumn("value", typeSingle))
        table.Columns.Add(New DataColumn("attacknumdice", typeInt))
        table.Columns.Add(New DataColumn("attackdie", typeInt))
        table.Columns.Add(New DataColumn("defense", typeInt))
        table.Columns.Add(New DataColumn("STR", typeInt))
```

```
            table.Columns.Add(New DataColumn("DEX", typeInt))
            table.Columns.Add(New DataColumn("STA", typeInt))
            table.Columns.Add(New DataColumn("INT", typeInt))
            table.Columns.Add(New DataColumn("CHA", typeInt))

            REM copy character data into datatable
            For Each item As Item In lstItems.Items
                Dim row As DataRow = table.NewRow()
                row("name") = item.Name
                row("description") = item.Description
                row("dropimagefilename") = item.DropImageFilename
                row("invimagefilename") = item.InvImageFilename
                row("category") = item.Category
                row("weight") = item.Weight
                row("value") = item.Value
                row("attacknumdice") = item.AttackNumDice
                row("attackdie") = item.AttackDie
                row("defense") = item.Defense
                row("STR") = item.STR
                row("DEX") = item.DEX
                row("STA") = item.STA
                row("INT") = item.INT
                row("CHA") = item.CHA
                table.Rows.Add(row)
            Next

            REM save xml file
            table.WriteXml(filename)
            table.Dispose()

        Catch es As Exception
            MessageBox.Show(es.Message)
        End Try
    End Sub

    Private Sub saveCurrentItem()
        Dim item As Item
        If currentIndex < 0 Or txtName.Text = "" Then
            Return
        End If
```

```
    Try
        item = lstItems.Items(currentIndex)
        item.Name = txtName.Text
        item.Description = txtDesc.Text
        item.DropImageFilename = txtDropImageFilename.Text
        item.InvImageFilename = txtInventoryImageFilename.Text
        item.Category = cboCategory.Text
        item.Weight = Convert.ToSingle(txtWeight.Text)
        item.Value = Convert.ToSingle(txtValue.Text)
        item.AttackNumDice = Convert.ToInt32(cboAttackNumDice.Text)
        item.AttackDie = Convert.ToInt32(cboAttackDie.Text.Substring(1))
        item.Defense = Convert.ToInt32(txtDefense.Text)
        item.STR = Convert.ToInt32(txtSTR.Text)
        item.DEX = Convert.ToInt32(txtDEX.Text)
        item.STA = Convert.ToInt32(txtSTA.Text)
        item.INT = Convert.ToInt32(txtINT.Text)
        item.CHA = Convert.ToInt32(txtCHA.Text)
        lstItems.Items(currentIndex) = item
    Catch ex As Exception
        MessageBox.Show(ex.Message)
    End Try
End Sub

REM portions of this code have been omitted to conserve space
```

LEVEL UP!

That concludes our work on the item editor. This editor has been developed with slightly different goals than the other editors we've seen so far, in that many items are stored in a single xml file rather than one item per file. This makes it quite easy to edit many items quickly by simply clicking each item in the list and making changes to it. Since the editor automatically saves changes made to items, this works quite well. Just be sure to save the file when you're done editing.

CHAPTER 18

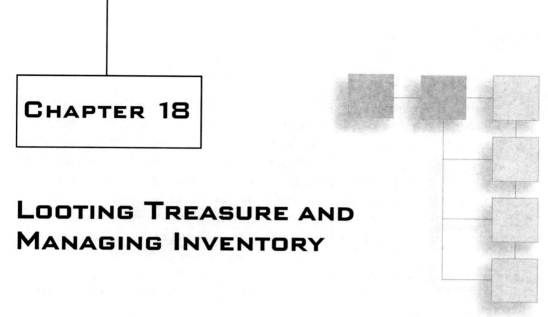

LOOTING TREASURE AND MANAGING INVENTORY

Some role-playing games are so focused on inventory micro-management that they lose track of the fun factor and replace real gameplay with an almost never-ending job of sorting and dealing with stuff (also called "loot"). I've seen some RPGs allow the player to carry around *tons* of stuff (I mean literally *thousands* of pounds of items)! This is, of course, completely ridiculous. But some players like micro-management. I guess there's room for those types of games, as long as there are players for them. I've always been a fan of the simpler approach—giving the player simple weapon, armor, and modifier items. Why should the player spend hours of game time swapping armor items when a single suit of armor would be easier to deal with? (Some games allow you to configure chest, leggings, helmet, bracers, and so on, individually.) There's certainly some realism in this, but does it make a game more *fun*? In this chapter, we will build a looting system so that monsters will drop gold and gear items at random when they fall, and a simple inventory screen that allows the player to equip items and move items around in their "bag of loot."

Here's what we'll cover in this chapter:

- Looting treasure
- Managing inventory

LOOTING TREASURE

There are two ways to handle looting: by dropping items directly on the ground, or by opening up a loot window from a dead monster or container (such as a treasure chest). Since we're already heavily invested in code for the inventory manager (coming up later in the chapter), I will forego the loot window and instead just drop items directly on the ground for pickup. We can treat drop items in the game code like monsters as far as range and targeting are concerned—when an item is in range, we can highlight it with a colored circle. Yes, there is a slight conflict when there are many items on top of each other or when a monster is in the way, but we can assume the player will clear out any bad guys from the immediate vicinity before looting. Both attacking and looting will use the Space key so it's just a matter of whether a loot item or a monster is closer in range.

For the loot demo, I have removed all living monsters and just dropped items randomly near the player's start position to speed up the demo a bit. In the finished game coming up two chapters from now, we will use this code to drop random items directly on the ground when a monster dies. The code *already* does this, but in the interest of speeding up testing of the inventory system, as the monsters are created, they are immediately killed so that the loot can be dropped (which is unfair, I know, but necessary for the sake of this important research!).

Hint

There are quite a few reusable functions in the Form1 code of the Looting Demo in this chapter that can be moved inside the Game class once we're confident that they're working correctly. It is sometimes better to keep uncertain code close at hand while working on it for quick editing without searching through your project's classes. Remember, we aren't going over *every line of code*, so consider this chapter an overview, not a tutorial.

Preparing to Loot

We need four variables to get started. As you can see, the item database is handled by a single class, Items, which we'll go over shortly. DrawableItem is a simple structure that extends Item in order to make it drawable. You could easily make the argument that this should be a class that inherits from Item, and I might agree with you—this is just one of those times where a structure seemed easier, and it works just as well in the end.

```
Public Structure DrawableItem
    Public item As Item
    Public sprite As Sprite
End Structure

Private lootFlag As Boolean = False
Private treasure As List(Of DrawableItem)
Private lootTarget As Integer
```

The `treasure` object is created as a linked list of `DrawableItem` structures. A linked list is an advanced container that we can go through with the `ForEach` looping statement, and it's more convenient than an array because we can add as many items to it as we want.

```
treasure = New List(Of DrawableItem)
```

The `items` variable is created and initialized in the main program startup code as well.

```
Private items As Items
items = New Items()
If Not items.Load("items.item") Then
    MessageBox.Show("Error loading file items.item")
    End
End If
```

The `Inventory` variable is actually found inside `Game` and is declared with public scope so it's visible anywhere in the game. We need to access the player's inventory easily so that is why I put it in the `Game` class.

```
Public Inven As Inventory
```

Despite being found in `Game`, the `Inven` variable is initialized in our main program, not in the `Game` constructor. This is also where default items can be added to the player's inventory, such as the items listed here. Perhaps in the final game, when the player creates a new character, some items will be added based on their class? Another common approach is to make the player earn gear from the start, and give him basically just a dagger and rags to wear. I gave the player these four items for testing purposes, but it demonstrates the power of the `Items` class, because sure enough, these four items show up in the inventory screen.

```
game.Inven = New Inventory(game, New Point((800 - 532) / 2, 50))
```

```
game.Inven.AddItem(items.getItem("Iron Chainmail"))
game.Inven.AddItem(items.getItem("Long Sword"))
game.Inven.AddItem(items.getItem("Small Shield"))
game.Inven.AddItem(items.getItem("Cape of Stamina"))
```

To add sample piles of loot for testing the inventory system, I just use a real .char file with the `loot` properties set and then immediately kill the monster that would have been visible in the game world. There are a pair of functions that make this all possible (and fairly automatic too, thanks to the `Items` class). The number of loot piles is not that important; I just used 20 and positioned them all within close range of the player's starting location.

```
For n = 1 To 20
    Dim monster As New Character(game)
    monster.Load("skeleton sword shield.char")
    monster.Position = New Point(game.Random(100, 1200), _
        game.Random(100, 1200))
    monster.AnimationState = Character.AnimationStates.Dead
    monster.Alive = False
    REM add some loot
    DropLoot(monster)
Next
```

Stumbling Upon Loot

The `doTreasure()` function in the Looting Demo project should look very familiar! It's essentially the same as the `doMonsters()` function from the previous chapter! There are a few differences, of course, because we don't actually *fight* with treasure, we pick it up. So, instead of a variable called `fightRadius`, we have `lootRadius`, and instead of `monsterCenter`, we have `itemCenter`. The logic is somewhat complex, though. I didn't want to make it overly complex, but it just turned out that way, mainly because of the way in which dialogue works. We usually can't just say, "Show this message to the player" and then forget about it—we have to wait for the player to click a button and then hide the dialogue window. Figure 18.1 shows a bunch of gold on the ground with one highlighted under the player's feet. An interesting side effect of this code is that you can loot many items without having to close the window (with the OK button), and it will just display the name of the next item looted.

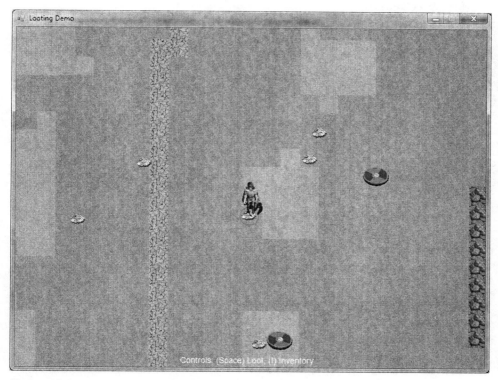

Figure 18.1
Dropped items are highlighted as the player walks over them.

Figure 18.2 is the message displayed (via the `Dialogue` class) when the player picks up gold. Gold is a special case that must be handled differently than regular items because it is not added to inventory, just to the `Player.Gold` property.

The second condition in `doTreasure()` occurs when the player is standing over a real item that can be picked up. When that is the case (rather than gold), a message displays information about the item. Do you recall the `Item.Summary` property from Chapter 17? We use it to display a quick tidbit of information about the item with any buffs it provides the player and any attack or defense values. This handy property works great here as well, telling the player at a glance what the item can do for him. Figure 18.3 shows the message after picking up an item. Note that this is the item shown in the character editor file as a drop item!

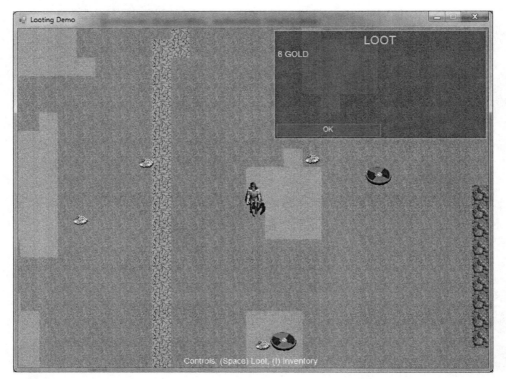

Figure 18.2
The amount of gold looted is specified in the character editor.

Here is the doTreasure() function. Fortunately, there are a lot of code comments so you should be able to make out what each section of code does. Just remember that this function looks at *all* of the items in the treasure container (funny variable names, don't you think?). Another interesting aspect of this code is that it prevents the player from picking up any more items if inventory is full! How cool is that? And we're still at the prototype stage for this inventory thing.

```
Private Sub doTreasure()
    Dim relativePos As PointF
    Const lootRadius As Integer = 40
    Dim heroCenter As PointF = game.Hero.CenterPos
    Dim itemCenter As PointF
    Dim dist As Single
    For Each it In treasure
```

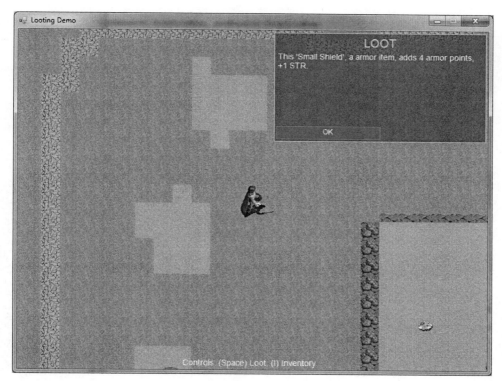

Figure 18.3
This dropped item corresponds to the "Small Shield" selected in the character editor.

```
REM is item in view?
If it.sprite.X > level.ScrollPos.X - 64 _
And it.sprite.X < level.ScrollPos.X + 23 * 32 + 64 _
And it.sprite.Y > level.ScrollPos.Y - 64 _
And it.sprite.Y < level.ScrollPos.Y + 17 * 32 + 64 Then
    REM get relative position of item on screen
    relativePos.X = it.sprite.X - level.ScrollPos.X
    relativePos.Y = it.sprite.Y - level.ScrollPos.Y
    REM get center of item
    itemCenter = relativePos
    itemCenter.X += it.sprite.Width / 2
    itemCenter.Y += it.sprite.Height / 2
    REM get distance to the item
    dist = game.Hero.CenterDistance(itemCenter)
    REM is player trying to pick up this loot?
```

```
            If dist < lootRadius Then
                game.Device.DrawEllipse(New Pen(Color.Magenta, 2.0), _
                    itemCenter.X - it.sprite.Width \ 2, _
                    itemCenter.Y - it.sprite.Height \ 2, _
                    it.sprite.Width, it.sprite.Height)
            If lootFlag Then
                REM collect gold or item
                If it.item.Name = "gold" And it.item.Value > 0 Then
                    game.Hero.Gold += it.item.Value
                    treasure.Remove(it)
                    showDialogue("LOOT", it.item.Value.ToString() + _
                        " GOLD", "OK")
                Else
                    If game.Inven.AddItem(it.item) Then
                        treasure.Remove(it)
                        showDialogue("LOOT", it.item.Summary, "OK")
                    Else
                        showDialogue("OVERLOADED!", _
                        "You are overloaded with too much stuff!", "OK")
                    End If
                End If
                REM wait for user
                If dialogue.Selection = 1 Then
                    lootFlag = False
                    dialogue.Selection = 0
                End If
                Exit For
            End If
        End If
        REM draw the monster sprite
        it.sprite.Draw(relativePos.X, relativePos.Y)
    End If
    Next
End Sub
```

Items Class

The Items class is a helper class to handle the items database (which was mentioned as a need in Chapter 17). The Items class reads in the entire .item file and is used to drop items when a monster is killed, as well as to show items in the player's inventory. So, this class is very important—it keeps our main code tidy by providing a very useful helper function called getItem(). When creating an object using this class during program initialization, be sure to use Load() to load the .item file needed by the game. This should be the same .item file you used to specify drop items in the character editor.

```
Public Class Items
    REM keep public for easy access
    Public items As List(Of Item)
    Public Sub New()
        items = New List(Of Item)
    End Sub

    Private Function getElement(ByVal field As String, _
            ByRef element As XmlElement) As String
        Dim value As String = ""
        Try
            value = element.GetElementsByTagName(field)(0).InnerText
        Catch ex As Exception
            REM ignore error, just return empty
            Console.WriteLine(ex.Message)
        End Try
        Return value
    End Function

    Public Function Load(ByVal filename As String) As Boolean
        Try
            REM open the xml file
            Dim doc As New XmlDocument()
            doc.Load(filename)
            Dim list As XmlNodeList = doc.GetElementsByTagName("item")
            For Each node As XmlNode In list
                REM get next item in table
                Dim element As XmlElement = node
                Dim item As New Item()
                REM store fields in new Item
                item.Name = getElement("name", element)
                item.Description = getElement("description", element)
                item.DropImageFilename = getElement("dropimagefilename", _
                    element)
```

```
                item.InvImageFilename = getElement("invimagefilename", _
                    element)
                item.Category = getElement("category", element)
                item.Weight = Convert.ToSingle(getElement("weight", _
                    element))
                item.Value = Convert.ToSingle(getElement("value", element))
                item.AttackNumDice = Convert.ToInt32( _
                    getElement("attacknumdice", element))
                item.AttackDie = Convert.ToInt32(getElement("attackdie", _
                    element))
                item.Defense = Convert.ToInt32(getElement("defense", _
                    element))
                item.STR = Convert.ToInt32(getElement("STR", element))
                item.DEX = Convert.ToInt32(getElement("DEX", element))
                item.STA = Convert.ToInt32(getElement("STA", element))
                item.INT = Convert.ToInt32(getElement("INT", element))
                item.CHA = Convert.ToInt32(getElement("CHA", element))
                REM add new item to list
                items.Add(item)
            Next
        Catch ex As Exception
            Return False
        End Try
        Return True
    End Function

    Public Function getItem(ByVal name As String) As Item
        For Each it As Item In items
            If it.Name = name Then
                Return it
            End If
        Next
        Return Nothing
    End Function
End Class
```

Character Class

A slightly improved character editor is included in this chapter's resource files (found at www.courseptr.com/downloads). We won't be going over the

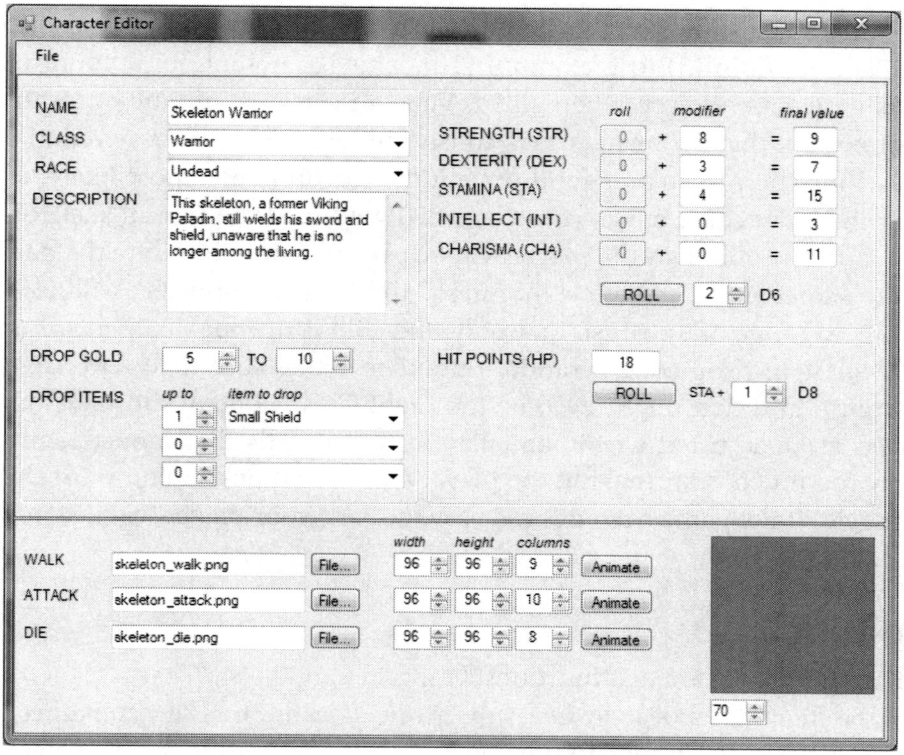

Figure 18.4
Setting the gold and drop items in the character editor.

code here, because the changes are rather trivial. Do you remember the three drop-item fields that have gone unused so far? Now we can finally enable those three drop-down combo list controls and fill them with items from the item database. This is where things start to get *very* interesting! I'll show you the results in a bit. Some changes have been made to the Character class to support the three drop-item fields that are now functional. Check Character. vb to note the changes. Because of these changes, .char files saved with the old version of the character editor will generate an error. Please use the new character editor to save any characters you have created into the new format. Figure 18.4 shows the new character editor. Well, it's the same old editor, but with the three item-drop fields now working! Take a look at the item name and quantity: one "Small Shield."

Take note of this, as I'll show you this item in the game shortly. Take note also of the gold fields: minimum (5) to maximum (10). This is the random amount of gold that this monster will drop when killed. You can use any amount you want here, but just be sure that dropped gold is consistent with item prices at vendors that will be selling the player gear (and buying their drop items, most likely, as well). If your most awesome epic sword costs 250 gold, and the typical skeleton warrior drops 10-20 gold, then the player will be earning enough to buy the best weapon in the game within just a few minutes! I think many monsters will need to be set to a gold range of 0 to 1, so that only one gold is dropped 25 percent of the time. (In the item-drop code, a random number makes sure that items only drop at this rate—and that might even be too high! This is one of those factors that may need to be adjusted when gameplay testing reveals that monsters are dropping way too much gear, making the player rich very quickly. You want the player to struggle! If the game becomes too easy too fast, your player will become bored with it.)

Dropping Loot

In the main program code are two functions: DropLoot() and DropTreasureItem(), which cause the items to appear in the game world (via the treasure container). The code to draw items is similar to the code for drawing trees found way back in Chapter 12, "Adding Objects to the World," and similar to drawing monsters in the previous few chapters. We just need to figure out whether the item is within the scrolling viewport and then draw it at the relative position. We have already seen examples of picking up loot, so I wanted to share an interesting thing that my 12-year-old son, Jeremiah, did with it. I was surprised because I wouldn't have tried this myself! He "maxxed out" the number of drop items in the character editor for a total of 300 items. Now, mind you, there is still only a 25 percent chance that any one of those will drop, but on average we will see about 25 of each item out of that maximum setting of 100. Figure 18.5 shows the data in the character editor.

I have to admit, I was a little surprised that the game was able to handle this large number of item drops so easily. It works like a charm even with scores of items piled on top of each other. The inventory fills up before you can even loot it all. Because of this, the code accounts for gold first, so when you go to a pile of loot the gold is picked up first (as shown in Figure 18.6).

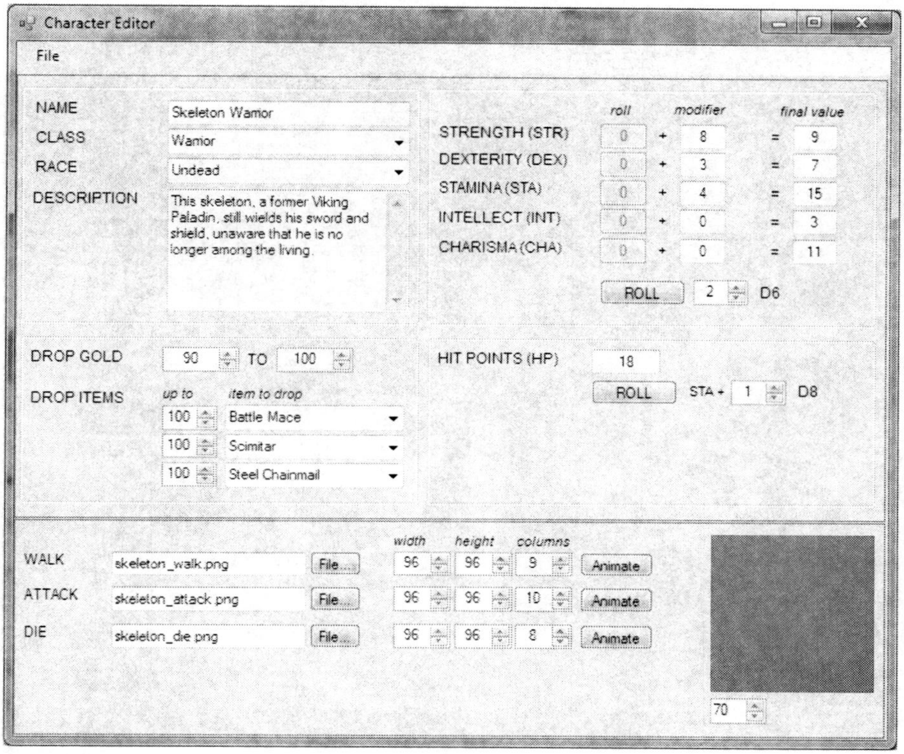

Figure 18.5
This skeleton character has a ridiculous number of drops!

The DropLoot() function is listed next. Gold is handled with custom code that requires the gold.png image, so be sure to include that among the many images now required for inventory. A helper function called DropTreasureItem() keeps the code tidy.

```
REM drop loot specified in the monster's character data file
Public Sub DropLoot(ByRef srcMonster As Character)
    Dim itm As Item
    Dim p As Point
    Dim count As Integer
    Dim rad As Integer = 64

    REM any gold to drop?
    itm = New Item()
```

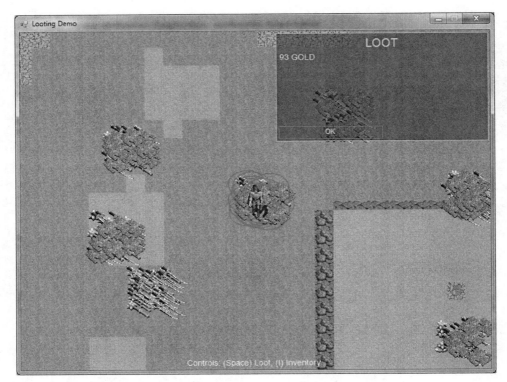

Figure 18.6
The gold is picked up first when there's a huge pile of dropped items.

```
Dim gold As Integer
gold = game.Random(srcMonster.DropGoldMin, srcMonster.DropGoldMax)
itm.Name = "gold"
itm.DropImageFilename = "gold.png"
itm.InvImageFilename = "gold.png"
itm.Value = gold
p.X = srcMonster.X + game.Random(rad) - rad / 2
p.Y = srcMonster.Y + game.Random(rad) - rad / 2
DropTreasureItem(itm, p.X, p.Y)

REM any items to drop?
If srcMonster.DropNum1 > 0 And srcMonster.DropItem1 <> "" Then
    count = game.Random(1, srcMonster.DropNum1)
    For n = 1 To count
        REM 25% chance for drop
```

```
                If game.Random(100) < 25 Then
                    itm = items.getItem(srcMonster.DropItem1)
                    p.X = srcMonster.X + game.Random(rad) - rad / 2
                    p.Y = srcMonster.Y + game.Random(rad) - rad / 2
                    DropTreasureItem(itm, p.X, p.Y)
                End If
            Next
        End If
        If srcMonster.DropNum2 > 0 And srcMonster.DropItem2 <> "" Then
            count = game.Random(1, srcMonster.DropNum2)
            For n = 1 To count
                REM 25% chance for drop
                If game.Random(100) < 25 Then
                    itm = items.getItem(srcMonster.DropItem2)
                    p.X = srcMonster.X + game.Random(rad) - rad / 2
                    p.Y = srcMonster.Y + game.Random(rad) - rad / 2
                    DropTreasureItem(itm, p.X, p.Y)
                End If
            Next
        End If
        If srcMonster.DropNum3 > 0 And srcMonster.DropItem3 <> "" Then
            count = game.Random(1, srcMonster.DropNum3)
            For n = 1 To count
                REM 25% chance for drop
                If game.Random(100) < 25 Then
                    itm = items.getItem(srcMonster.DropItem3)
                    p.X = srcMonster.X + game.Random(rad) - rad / 2
                    p.Y = srcMonster.Y + game.Random(rad) - rad / 2
                    DropTreasureItem(itm, p.X, p.Y)
                End If
            Next
        End If
End Sub
```

The helper function, DropTreasureItem(), verifies that the Item.DropImageFilename property contains a valid filename, then adds a new sprite to the treasure container. The game code looks for sprites to draw and interact with in the game world—not Items—so that is why we need the DrawableItem structure. It's a relatively trivial amount of code, wherein the Item and Sprite are each initialized here and added to the list container that handles all drop items in the game.

```
Public Sub DropTreasureItem(ByRef itm As Item, ByVal x As Integer, ByVal y As
Integer)
    Dim drit As DrawableItem
    drit.item = itm
    drit.sprite = New Sprite(game)
    drit.sprite.Position = New Point(x, y)
    If drit.item.DropImageFilename = "" Then
        MessageBox.Show("Error: Item '" + drit.item.Name + "' image file is i-
nvalid.")
        End
    End If
    drit.sprite.Image = game.LoadBitmap(drit.item.DropImageFilename)
    drit.sprite.Size = drit.sprite.Image.Size
    treasure.Add(drit)
End Sub,
```

MANAGING INVENTORY

Isn't it great that the game engine has been developed up to the point where we can begin discussing higher level topics like inventory? It feels as if all the hard work getting to this point was justified. Now what I'm going to do is explain the approach I've decided to take with Celtic Crusader when it comes to managing inventory. There are many different approaches or possible directions we could take with an inventory system. One possibility is to give the player a "backpack" in which all inventory items are stored (this is used in a lot of games). Another approach is to display a list of inventory items by name (popular in online MUDs (multi-user dungeons). We could limit the player to a fixed number of inventory items, or base the limit on weight, in which case every item in the game would need to have a weight property.

Another approach is to follow more of an arcade-style inventory system where the player only possesses what he needs. In other words, the player has a weapon, armor, and modifiers like rings and amulets. The player wields a single weapon, based on the character's class (i.e., axe, sword, bow, or staff), wears a complete suit of armor (i.e., leather, studded, scale, or chain), and then has the option of wearing rings or amulets. Those *modifiers* or *buffs* help to boost the player's stats (such as strength or intelligence). The Inventory class keeps track of 30 items total—that's 9 worn items plus 21 items being carried.

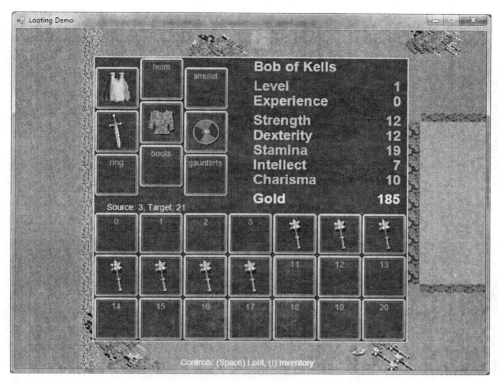

Figure 18.7
Items can be moved around in the inventory system!

Figure 18.7 shows the inventory window after the player has picked up a bunch of sample items from the Looting Demo. If you fight the same hostile NPCs, odds are you will end up with several of the same drop items after a while. This Inventory class is *awesome!* You can move stuff around in the "bag," equip items, remove items. The same inventory window also shows the player's basic stats—level, experience, strength, gold, etc. If you want to have a separate screen for that, you are welcome to duplicate the Inventory class and then make the necessary changes. I wanted to keep it simple for this game, to keep the code on the shorter side.

Inventory Class

The Inventory class does double duty as a container for the player's inventory *and* it produces the rendered output of the inventory screen that the player uses to manage his stuff. This is by far the largest class we've seen with quite a few lines of code! The inventory system has to keep track of the mouse position, highlighting buttons when the mouse moves over them, drawing the inventory and equipped items, and the player's stats. Whew, this class does a lot! The great thing about it is that all of the inventory buttons are positioned in code as rectangles, so if you want to redo the inventory/character screen, you can move the gear buttons around if you want.

```
Public Class Inventory
    Public Structure Button
    Public rect As Rectangle
        Public text As String
        Public image As Bitmap
        Public imagefile As String
    End Structure
    Private BTN_HEAD As Integer
    Private BTN_CHEST As Integer
    Private BTN_LEGS As Integer
    Private BTN_RTHAND As Integer
    Private BTN_LTHAND As Integer
    Private BTN_RTFINGER As Integer
    Private BTN_LTFINGER As Integer
    Private p_game As Game
    Private p_font As Font
    Private p_font2 As Font
    Private p_position As PointF
    Private p_buttons(30) As Button
    Private p_selection As Integer
    Private p_sourceIndex As Integer
    Private p_targetIndex As Integer
    Private p_mousePos As Point
    Private p_mouseBtn As MouseButtons
    Private p_lastButton As Integer
    Private p_oldMouseBtn As MouseButtons
    Private p_visible As Boolean
    Private p_bg As Bitmap
    Private p_inventory(30) As Item

    Public Sub New(ByRef game As Game, ByVal pos As Point)
        p_game = game
```

```
        p_position = pos
        p_bg = game.LoadBitmap("char_bg3.png")
        p_font = New Font("Arial", 24, FontStyle.Bold, GraphicsUnit.Pixel)
        p_font2 = New Font("Arial", 14, FontStyle.Regular, _
            GraphicsUnit.Pixel)
        p_selection = 0
        p_mouseBtn = MouseButtons.None
        p_oldMouseBtn = p_mouseBtn
        p_mousePos = New Point(0, 0)
        p_visible = False
        p_lastButton = -1
        CreateInventory()
        CreateButtons()
    End Sub

    Public Sub CreateInventory()
        For n = 0 To p_inventory.Length - 1
            p_inventory(n) = New Item()
            p_inventory(n).Name = ""
        Next
    End Sub

    Public Function AddItem(ByVal itm As Item) As Boolean
        For n = 0 To 20
            If p_inventory(n).Name = "" Then
                CopyInventoryItem(itm, p_inventory(n))
                Return True
            End If
        Next
        Return False
    End Function

    Public Sub CreateButtons()
        Dim rx, ry, rw, rh As Integer
        Dim index As Integer = 0
        REM create inventory buttons
        For y = 0 To 2
            For x = 0 To 6
                rx = p_position.X + 6 + x * 76
                ry = p_position.Y + 278 + y * 76
                rw = 64
```

```
            rh = 64
            p_buttons(index).rect = New Rectangle(rx, ry, rw, rh)
            p_buttons(index).text = index.ToString()
            index += 1
      Next
Next
REM create left gear buttons
rx = p_position.X + 6
ry = p_position.Y + 22
p_buttons(index).rect = New Rectangle(rx, ry, rw, rh)
p_buttons(index).text = "cape"
index += 1

ry += 76
p_buttons(index).rect = New Rectangle(rx, ry, rw, rh)
p_buttons(index).text = "weapon 1"
BTN_RTHAND = index
index += 1

ry += 76
p_buttons(index).rect = New Rectangle(rx, ry, rw, rh)
p_buttons(index).text = "ring"
index += 1

REM create center gear buttons
rx = p_position.X + 82
ry = p_position.Y + 6
p_buttons(index).rect = New Rectangle(rx, ry, rw, rh)
p_buttons(index).text = "helm"
BTN_HEAD = index
index += 1

ry += 76
p_buttons(index).rect = New Rectangle(rx, ry, rw, rh)
p_buttons(index).text = "chest"
BTN_CHEST = index
index += 1

ry += 76
p_buttons(index).rect = New Rectangle(rx, ry, rw, rh)
```

```
        p_buttons(index).text = "boots"
        BTN_LEGS = index
        index += 1

        REM create right gear buttons
        rx = p_position.X + 158
        ry = p_position.Y + 22
        p_buttons(index).rect = New Rectangle(rx, ry, rw, rh)
        p_buttons(index).text = "amulet"
        index += 1

        ry += 76
        p_buttons(index).rect = New Rectangle(rx, ry, rw, rh)
        p_buttons(index).text = "weapon 2"
        BTN_LTHAND = index
        index += 1

        ry += 76
        p_buttons(index).rect = New Rectangle(rx, ry, rw, rh)
        p_buttons(index).text = "gauntlets"
        index += 1
End Sub

Public Property Visible() As Boolean
    Get
         Return p_visible
    End Get
    Set(ByVal value As Boolean)
        p_visible = value
    End Set
End Property

Public Property Selection() As Integer
    Get
         Return p_selection
    End Get
    Set(ByVal value As Integer)
        p_selection = value
    End Set
End Property
```

```vbnet
        Public Property Position() As PointF
            Get
                Return p_position
            End Get
            Set(ByVal value As PointF)
                p_position = value
            End Set
        End Property

        Public Property LastButton() As Integer
            Get
                Return p_lastButton
            End Get
            Set(ByVal value As Integer)
                p_lastButton = value
            End Set
        End Property

        Private Sub Print(ByVal x As Integer, ByVal y As Integer, _
                ByVal text As String)
            Print(x, y, text, Brushes.White)
        End Sub

        Private Sub Print(ByVal x As Integer, ByVal y As Integer, _
                ByVal text As String, ByVal color As Brush)
            p_game.Device.DrawString(text, p_font, color, x, y)
        End Sub

        REM print text right-justified from top-right x,y
        Private Sub PrintRight(ByVal x As Integer, ByVal y As Integer, _
                ByVal text As String, ByVal color As Brush)
            Dim rsize As SizeF
            rsize = p_game.Device.MeasureString(text, p_font)
            p_game.Device.DrawString(text, p_font, color, x - rsize.Width, y)
        End Sub

        Public Sub updateMouse(ByVal mousePos As Point, _
                ByVal mouseBtn As MouseButtons)
            p_mousePos = mousePos
            p_oldMouseBtn = p_mouseBtn
```

```
        p_mouseBtn = mouseBtn
End Sub

Public Sub Draw()
    If Not p_visible Then Return
    Dim tx, ty As Integer

    REM draw background
    p_game.DrawBitmap(p_bg, p_position.X, p_position.Y)
    p_game.Device.DrawRectangle(New Pen(Color.Gold, 2.0), _
        p_position.X - 1, p_position.Y - 1, p_bg.Width + 2, _
        p_bg.Height + 2)

    REM print player stats
    Dim x As Integer = 400
    Dim y As Integer = p_position.Y
    Dim ht As Integer = 26
    Print(x, y, p_game.Hero.Name, Brushes.Gold) : y += ht + 8
    PrintRight(660, y, p_game.Hero.Level.ToString(), _
        Brushes.LightGreen)
    Print(x, y, "Level", Brushes.LightGreen) : y += ht
    PrintRight(660, y, p_game.Hero.Experience.ToString(), _
        Brushes.LightBlue)
    Print(x, y, "Experience", Brushes.LightBlue) : y += ht + 8
    PrintRight(660, y, p_game.Hero.STR.ToString(), Brushes.LightGreen)
    Print(x, y, "Strength", Brushes.LightGreen) : y += ht
    PrintRight(660, y, p_game.Hero.DEX.ToString(), Brushes.LightBlue)
    Print(x, y, "Dexterity", Brushes.LightBlue) : y += ht
    PrintRight(660, y, p_game.Hero.STA.ToString(), Brushes.LightGreen)
    Print(x, y, "Stamina", Brushes.LightGreen) : y += ht
    PrintRight(660, y, p_game.Hero.INT.ToString(), Brushes.LightBlue)
    Print(x, y, "Intellect", Brushes.LightBlue) : y += ht
    PrintRight(660, y, p_game.Hero.CHA.ToString(), Brushes.LightGreen)
    Print(x, y, "Charisma", Brushes.LightGreen) : y += ht + 8
    PrintRight(660, y, p_game.Hero.Gold.ToString(), _
        Brushes.LightGoldenrodYellow)
    Print(x, y, "Gold", Brushes.LightGoldenrodYellow) : y += ht

    REM draw the buttons
    For n = 0 To p_buttons.Length - 1
```

```
        Dim rect As Rectangle = p_buttons(n).rect
        REM draw button border
        p_game.Device.DrawRectangle(Pens.Gray, rect)
        REM print button label
        If p_buttons(n).image Is Nothing Then
            Dim rsize As SizeF
            rsize = p_game.Device.MeasureString(p_buttons(n).text, _
                p_font2)
            tx = rect.X + rect.Width / 2 - rsize.Width / 2
            ty = rect.Y + 2
            p_game.Device.DrawString(p_buttons(n).text, p_font2, _
                Brushes.DarkGray, tx, ty)
        End If
    Next

    REM check for button click
    For n = 0 To p_buttons.Length - 1
        Dim rect As Rectangle = p_buttons(n).rect
        If rect.Contains(p_mousePos) Then
            If p_mouseBtn = MouseButtons.None And _
                p_oldMouseBtn = MouseButtons.Left Then
                p_selection = n
                If p_sourceIndex = -1 Then
                    p_sourceIndex = p_selection
                ElseIf p_targetIndex = -1 Then
                    p_targetIndex = p_selection
                Else
                    p_sourceIndex = p_selection
                    p_targetIndex = -1
                End If
                Exit For
            End If
            p_game.Device.DrawRectangle(New Pen(Color.Red, 2.0), rect)
        End If
    Next

    Dim text As String = "Source: " + p_sourceIndex.ToString() + _
        ", Target: " + p_targetIndex.ToString()
    If p_sourceIndex = p_targetIndex Then
        text += " : same item"
    End If
```

```
        If p_selection <> -1 And p_sourceIndex <> -1 _
                And p_targetIndex <> -1 Then
            If p_buttons(p_sourceIndex).image Is Nothing Then
                text += " : source is empty"
            ElseIf p_buttons(p_targetIndex).image IsNot Nothing Then
                text += " : target is in use"
            Else
                text += " : good to move!"
                MoveInventoryItem(p_sourceIndex, p_targetIndex)
                p_selection = -1
            End If
        End If
    End If
    p_game.Device.DrawString(text, _
        p_font2, Brushes.White, p_position.X + 20, p_position.Y + 255)

    REM draw equipment
    For n = 0 To p_inventory.Length - 1
        DrawInventoryItem(n)
    Next
End Sub

Private Sub DrawInventoryItem(ByVal index As Integer)
    Dim filename As String
    filename = p_inventory(index).InvImageFilename
    If filename.Length > 0 Then
        REM try to avoid repeatedly loading image
        If p_buttons(index).image Is Nothing Or _
                p_buttons(index).imagefile <> filename Then
            p_buttons(index).imagefile = filename
            p_buttons(index).image = p_game.LoadBitmap(filename)
        End If
        Dim srcRect As RectangleF = p_buttons(index).image.GetBounds( _
            GraphicsUnit.Pixel)
        Dim dstRect As RectangleF = p_buttons(index).rect
        p_game.Device.DrawImage(p_buttons(index).image, dstRect, _
            srcRect, GraphicsUnit.Pixel)
    End If
End Sub

Private Sub MoveInventoryItem(ByVal source As Integer, _
```

```
                ByVal dest As Integer)
        CopyInventoryItem(p_inventory(source), p_inventory(dest))
        p_inventory(source).Name = ""
        p_inventory(source).InvImageFilename = ""
        p_buttons(source).imagefile = ""
        p_buttons(source).image = Nothing
    End Sub

    Public Sub CopyInventoryItem(ByVal source As Integer, _
            ByVal dest As Integer)
        CopyInventoryItem(p_inventory(source), p_inventory(dest))
    End Sub

    Public Sub CopyInventoryItem(ByRef srcItem As Item, _
            ByRef dstItem As Item)
        dstItem.Name = srcItem.Name
        dstItem.Description = srcItem.Description
        dstItem.AttackDie = srcItem.AttackDie
        dstItem.AttackNumDice = srcItem.AttackNumDice
        dstItem.Category = srcItem.Category
        dstItem.Defense = srcItem.Defense
        dstItem.DropImageFilename = srcItem.DropImageFilename
        dstItem.InvImageFilename = srcItem.InvImageFilename
        dstItem.Value = srcItem.Value
        dstItem.Weight = srcItem.Weight
        dstItem.STR = srcItem.STR
        dstItem.DEX = srcItem.DEX
        dstItem.CHA = srcItem.CHA
        dstItem.STA = srcItem.STA
        dstItem.INT = srcItem.INT
    End Sub
End Class
```

Player Class

The Player class is a bit of a pushover at this point, because we're getting a bit ahead of ourselves delving into the player's game state data for just the Looting Demo project, but I wanted to at least show you what's in the class at this early stage since it's in the project. The only thing here is the Gold property. In the final chapter, this class will be responsible for keeping track of all the player's information, and for saving and loading the game.

```
Imports System.Xml
Public Class Player
    Inherits Character
    Private p_gold As Integer
    Public Sub New(ByRef game As Game)
        MyBase.New(game)
    End Sub
    Public Property Gold() As Integer
        Get
            Return p_gold
        End Get
        Set(ByVal value As Integer)
            p_gold = value
        End Set
    End Property
    Public Overrides Function ToString() As String
        Return MyBase.Name
    End Function
End Class
```

LEVEL UP!

And that successfully finishes off the inventory system! I'm pleased with how it turned out. When I look at the inventory screen, I'm really pleased with it because there isn't a whole lot of code there and it works so well. But you know what's still missing? You can equip items to *any* gear slot, and they don't actually do anything for the player yet. That will be made functional soon; the focus in this chapter was just getting the inventory system to display the right items, pick up loot, and let the player move stuff around. The good news is, the code is already in place to make that happen, and we'll be able to apply inventory item modifiers to the player's stats.

CHAPTER 19

CREATING THE QUEST EDITOR

We arrive at the final development chapter for the Celtic Crusader toolset before embarking on the final project in the next chapter. While an RPG *can* be devoted entirely to fighting as a means to give the player experience, there isn't much of a story behind a game devoted solely to combat without a goal for the player to achieve. "Defeat the dragon, save the princess" is an age-old theme that still works today, and that might very well be the goal you will give the player in your own game. Quite simply, it works to motivate the player! But, if you're looking for *steps* along the way, then smaller quests are important. The goal of this chapter is to build a quest editor tool. Our game will handle just *one quest* at a time, with the editor supplying the specific details of each quest, such as the quest giver, conditions that must be met, rewards for success, and so on. Completing a quest might result in gold and/or loot, so we can draw on code developed in Chapter 18 when granting the player his reward for successfully completing each quest. Since the quest system will be linear, the player must finish each quest in order to proceed to the next one. Therefore, it's important to design the "quest chain" in such a way that it gradually brings the player up to speed so that he or she is eventually able to complete more challenging quests late in the game. Completing the final quest, "saving the girl," so to speak, should end the game with fanfare.

Here's what we'll cover in this chapter:

- Quests as data
- Quests as story driver

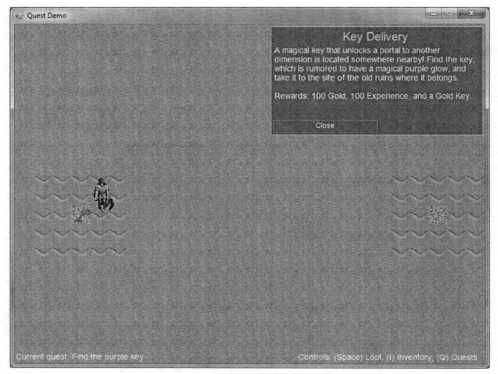

Figure 19.1
The quest window displays information about the current quest.

Quests as Data

There are two ways to handle quest delivery to the player: by pushing the quest data out via a defined representative (as a character in the quest record), or by pulling the quest data out of the database and presenting it however we want. The "push" approach is attractive because it makes the quest system more self reliant, with the quest giver, conditions, and rewards handled internally. The "pull" approach is more flexible, just data waiting to be used without any other built-in resources. Both forms are appealing in the benefits they afford, with the only drawback to one over another being the amount of game code needed to make quests work. Figure 19.1 shows the quest details displayed by the Quests class while the game is running. We will build this later in the chapter.

Pushing or Pulling?

The Inventory class in Chapter 18 used the push approach, handling the player's gear and carry items as well as the inventory screen seen in the game. Similarly, a "push" quest system would read fields in a quest record and assemble whatever is necessary to show the quest to the player, to test for its completion, and give the player a specified reward. The Items class uses more of a "pull" mechanism, supplying data to the program as needed, but doing no extra work such as a user interface. It goes without saying that we need a system to give the player a quest, and then remind the player of the quest conditions needed to complete it. This data needs to be shown in the game somewhere, somehow. So, should it be push or pull? If this were a theoretical chapter about gameplay concepts, I might expound on this thread by citing examples in recent games that used each approach. But this is an *applied* chapter, with the expectation that we have a working quest system by the end—no "cliffhanger" allowed.

As it turns out, we will be using a combination of both for quests in the game, with a Quests class that loads and supplies quest data through a user interface via a helper Quest class, much like the Inventory class in Chapter 18 used the Item and Items classes. It might have been intriguing to specify the actual quest giver in the editor, by choosing the sprite and so forth, but that restricts the quest system too much. What happens if you use one sprite for a series of quests, and then decide to change that character to better fit the storyline? Then every record that uses the sprite must be edited! Even if there are only a few quests that use a particular sprite for a character as the quest giver, the limitation is there. We want to develop a robust game with versatile tools and classes that *support* the designer's vision for a game, not to make the source code easier to write. In order of priority, the player comes first, followed by the designer, and then the engineer. Software should not be designed for the convenience of the programmer, but for the user. Besides, a more generic quest database might be useful for projects using another programming language!

Quest Condition Types

Many games require the player to talk with an NPC in order to get and turn in quests. We can do that also, but in a slightly different manner: instead of *talking* with an NPC, we need merely walk up to them. The quest system will not be linked to any character, only to *drop items* and *locations* on the map. Through

some creative design and programming, we can use these two basic requirements to meet almost any conceivable need. For instance, even though a quest
turn-in condition is a location on the map, we can make it seem like the turn-in
is actually a character by putting a sprite there! The Quests class will display the
status of the current quest, so going to the correct location on the map as
specified will trigger a "Quest Complete" to be displayed. To receive the reward,
acquire the item and/or go to the target location on the map (measured in *tiles*,
not pixels, and for reference there are 128×128 tiles in a map). The two
conditions are as follows:

- Get Item
- Go to Location

But, what if you don't want to deliver an item to some location? What if you
want to just have the player pick up an item and that's it, no requirement to turn
it in anywhere? That's fine, just select "Get item" condition and choose the item
from the list.

Hint

If you do not check at least one quest condition, then it will be impossible to complete the quest!

What about a quest where you have to go kill like 10 zombies or something like
that, where the condition isn't an item or a location? That's also possible, but
requires a slight workaround. Instead of keeping track of how many zombies the
player kills, we can instead check the player's inventory for 10 "zombie ears" or
some similar item. You would have to add that item to the item database, of
course, and then make it a drop item for the zombie character. But then when
you kill a zombie, there's a 25 percent chance that it will drop a "zombie ear,"
and there's your quest solution.

However, that raises another issue: what if the player doesn't have enough free
slots in his inventory to pick up 10 zombie ears? Our inventory system doesn't
handle "item stacks" like some games do. It's a great feature, for sure, but not
something we can support right now. What's the workaround? Again, this is a
matter of game design: if you know the features of the game, then you must
work within those known features and account for all the possible scenarios the

player is likely to get into (such as the problem of inventory space). Do we want to just go ahead and require 10 zombie ears, or would 5 get the job done just as well? The "inventory bag" can hold 21 items—an odd number that comes from three rows of seven each in the small inventory screen. If that's not enough for your taste, you could redesign the inventory system to use smaller item slots (say, 32 × 32 or 48 × 48), and then scale the images when drawing them in the slots; `Graphics.DrawImage()` can do this easily. Since the `Inventory` class treats the buttons as an array of 30, you would need to enlarge the array. Note also that the gear items share this array, but they are defined *after* the regular inventory items, so as long as the array size is enlarged the class can handle more items. I'm just not sure this is necessary, though! Why not design the game so that *gobs of stuff* isn't needed? Remember my premise over the last two chapters, that gear micro-management tends to ruin the suspense of disbelief for a game, and that's usually the best measure of a game's fun factor—its *funativity*? Consider the enormous popularity of Nintendo's *Zelda* series, which somehow manages to get by without "gigantique bags." But, hey, if you love loot, who am I to deny you your fun?

Quest Rewards

The reward is what the player receives upon completing a quest. The reward can be any one or all of the following: Experience, Gold, or an Item. If you don't want to use one or two of the reward types, just leave them blank and the game will ignore them. You could, for instance, grant 500 experience, 50 gold, and a "Battle Axe" item as the rewards for one quest, or any one of the three. Choose the reward item from the drop-down list, which is read directly from the .item file.

It goes without saying that completing a quest should give the player experience— that's the motivation driving most players to complete a quest. If you have a quest, though, that simply rewards the player with gold or an item, consider granting at least a token amount of experience to make the game seem more realistic: going through the effort to complete the quest did require some persistence, however great or small, and that should be reflected with experience as well as reward items. Just be sure to keep the amount in balance with your preferred leveling up algorithm—don't make it too easy for the player to level, or he may very well get bored with the game. Keep the challenge high, but not frustrating. It's a fine line to balance on but worth it in the end if the gameplay works well. Generally, you want your players to have achieved enough experience and gear to succeed in new challenges without it being so difficult that they just die over and over again. If that happens, then you have failed to balance the gameplay effectively!

Quest Class

The Quest class is a support class used by Quests and by the main program for any purpose related to reading information about a quest. The Quest class is very similar to the Item class developed over the previous two chapters, which worked closely with Items and Inventory.

```
Public Class Quest
    Private p_title As String
    Private p_summary As String
    Private p_desc As String
    Private p_RequiredItemFlag As Boolean
    Private p_RequiredItemCount As Integer
    Private p_RequiredItem As String
    Private p_RequiredLocFlag As Boolean
    Private p_RequiredLocX As Integer
    Private p_RequiredLocY As Integer
    Private p_RewardXP As Integer
    Private p_RewardGold As Integer
    Private p_RewardItem As String

    Public Sub New()
        p_title = "new quest"
        p_summary = ""
        p_desc = ""
        p_RequiredItemFlag = False
        p_RequiredItemCount = 0
        p_RequiredItem = ""
        p_RequiredLocFlag = False
        p_RequiredLocX = 0
        p_RequiredLocY = 0
        p_RewardXP = 0
        p_RewardGold = 0
        p_RewardItem = ""
    End Sub
```

```
Public Overrides Function ToString() As String
    Return p_title
End Function


Public Property Title() As String
    Get
        Return p_title
    End Get
    Set(ByVal value As String)
        p_title = value
    End Set
End Property


Public Property Summary() As String
    Get
        Return p_summary
    End Get
    Set(ByVal value As String)
        p_summary = value
    End Set
End Property


Public Property Description() As String
    Get
        Return p_desc
    End Get
    Set(ByVal value As String)
        p_desc = value
    End Set
End Property


Public Property RequiredItemFlag() As Boolean
    Get
        Return p_RequiredItemFlag
    End Get
    Set(ByVal value As Boolean)
        p_RequiredItemFlag = value
    End Set
End Property
```

```
    Public Property RequiredItemCount() As Integer
        Get
            Return p_RequiredItemCount
        End Get
        Set(ByVal value As Integer)
            p_RequiredItemCount = value
        End Set
    End Property

    Public Property RequiredItem() As String
        Get
            Return p_RequiredItem
        End Get
        Set(ByVal value As String)
            p_RequiredItem = value
        End Set
    End Property

    Public Property RequiredLocFlag() As Boolean
        Get
            Return p_RequiredLocFlag
        End Get
        Set(ByVal value As Boolean)
            p_RequiredLocFlag = value
        End Set
    End Property

    Public Property RequiredLocX() As Integer
        Get
            Return p_RequiredLocX
        End Get
        Set(ByVal value As Integer)
            p_RequiredLocX = value
        End Set
    End Property

    Public Property RequiredLocY() As Integer
        Get
            Return p_RequiredLocY
        End Get
```

```
            Set(ByVal value As Integer)
                p_RequiredLocY = value
            End Set
        End Property

        Public Property RewardXP() As Integer
            Get
                Return p_RewardXP
            End Get
            Set(ByVal value As Integer)
                p_RewardXP = value
            End Set
        End Property

        Public Property RewardGold() As Integer
            Get
                Return p_RewardGold
            End Get
            Set(ByVal value As Integer)
                p_RewardGold = value
            End Set
        End Property

        Public Property RewardItem() As String
            Get
                Return p_RewardItem
            End Get
            Set(ByVal value As String)
                p_RewardItem = value
            End Set
        End Property

End Class
```

Quest Editor

The quest editor is our fourth and final game development tool. It's been quite exciting to watch as each new tool (and its supporting classes) was built and added to the Celtic Crusader toolbox. This editor is fairly simple and works on the same user interface principle as the item editor, with a list of quests along

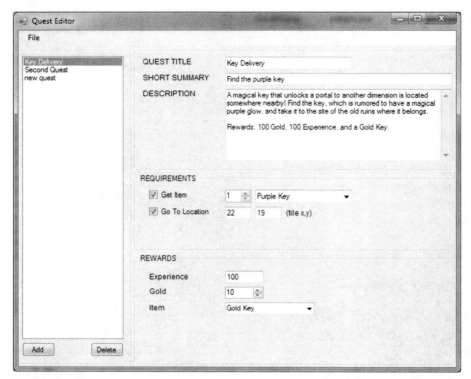

Figure 19.2
The quest editor is our fourth and final tool.

the left side and simple list item selection and auto-saving of edited fields. Figure 19.2 shows the quest editor.

The only thing I want to share with you from the sources are the loadFile() and saveFile() functions, which will show you what all of the XML fields are called for this editor data. The source code is otherwise almost identical to that of the item editor, so we'll save some paper.

```
Private Sub loadFile(ByVal filename As String)
    Try
        REM open the xml file
        Dim doc As New XmlDocument()
        doc.Load(filename)
        Dim list As XmlNodeList = doc.GetElementsByTagName("quest")
        For Each node As XmlNode In list
```

```
            Dim element As XmlElement = node
            Dim q As New Quest()
            q.Title = getElement("title", element)
            q.Summary = getElement("summary", element)
            q.Description = getElement("description", element)
            q.RequiredItem = getElement("req_item", element)
            q.RequiredItemCount = getElement("req_item_count", element)
            q.RequiredItemFlag = getElement("req_item_flag", element)
            q.RequiredLocFlag = getElement("req_loc_flag", element)
            q.RequiredLocX = getElement("req_loc_x", element)
            q.RequiredLocY = getElement("req_loc_y", element)
            q.RewardGold = getElement("reward_gold", element)
            q.RewardItem = getElement("reward_item", element)
            q.RewardXP = getElement("reward_xp", element)
            lstQuests.Items.Add(q)
        Next
    Catch ex As Exception
        MessageBox.Show(ex.Message)
        Return
    End Try
End Sub


Private Sub saveFile(ByVal filename As String)
    Try
        REM create data type templates
        Dim typeInt As System.Type
        Dim typeBool As System.Type
        Dim typeStr As System.Type
        typeInt = System.Type.GetType("System.Int32")
        typeStr = System.Type.GetType("System.String")
        typeBool = System.Type.GetType("System.Boolean")
        REM create xml schema
        Dim table As New DataTable("quest")
        table.Columns.Add(New DataColumn("title", typeStr))
        table.Columns.Add(New DataColumn("summary", typeStr))
        table.Columns.Add(New DataColumn("description", typeStr))
        table.Columns.Add(New DataColumn("req_item", typeStr))
        table.Columns.Add(New DataColumn("req_item_count", typeInt))
        table.Columns.Add(New DataColumn("req_item_flag", typebool))
        table.Columns.Add(New DataColumn("req_loc_flag", typeBool))
```

```
            table.Columns.Add(New DataColumn("req_loc_x", typeInt))
            table.Columns.Add(New DataColumn("req_loc_y", typeInt))
            table.Columns.Add(New DataColumn("reward_gold", typeInt))
            table.Columns.Add(New DataColumn("reward_item", typeStr))
            table.Columns.Add(New DataColumn("reward_xp", typeInt))
            REM copy data into datatable
            For Each q As Quest In lstQuests.Items
                Dim row As DataRow = table.NewRow()
                row("title") = q.Title
                row("summary") = q.Summary
                row("description") = q.Description
                row("req_item") = q.RequiredItem
                row("req_item_count") = q.RequiredItemCount
                row("req_item_flag") = q.RequiredItemFlag
                row("req_loc_flag") = q.RequiredLocFlag
                row("req_loc_x") = q.RequiredLocX
                row("req_loc_y") = q.RequiredLocY
                row("reward_gold") = q.RewardGold
                row("reward_item") = q.RewardItem
                row("reward_xp") = q.RewardXP
                table.Rows.Add(row)
            Next
            REM save xml file
            table.WriteXml(filename)
            table.Dispose()
        Catch es As Exception
            MessageBox.Show(es.Message)
        End Try
    End Sub
End Sub
```

Quests as Story Driver

Now that we have a quest editor—which is admittedly in an early stage but quite usable already—we can begin working with quest data. First, we will need a new Quests class that reads a supplied .quest file to pull in all of the quest data, which will then be made available to the game. Not merely a database like the Items class, our new Quests class will actually maintain the current quest number and return the properties for the current quest, which will be handled internally. We can't limit the ability to control this process, but we can automate it a bit. A function will allow us to jump to any quest number and then retrieve the current properties at any time without any further lookup function calls. This approach treats the Quests class like a database class *and* gameplay class combined (where we have two classes, Item and Items, for working with the item database, for instance).

The Quest Demo project in this chapter is a stripped down example that does not include combat, but *does* still have the inventory system because that is an integral part of completing quests. As a simplified demo, we will not be able to test how quests will work based on monster drop items, but based on the examples we've gone over in recent chapters, there's no reason to worry about that right now; we'll see that working in the final game coming up in the next chapter.

Quests Class

The Quests (plural) class differs from the Quest (singular) class previously covered in that it handles all of the quests and also draws the quest window in the game. The Quest (singular) class handles the properties and functions for a single quest read in from the quest editor data file. The Quests class begins like so:

```
Private p_current As Integer
Private p_quest As Quest
Private p_dialog As Dialogue
Private p_game As Game
Private p_enable As Boolean
Public quests As List(Of Quest)

Public Sub New(ByRef game As Game)
    quests = New List(Of Quest)
    p_current = -1
    p_quest = New Quest()
    p_game = game
    p_dialog = New Dialogue(p_game)
    p_enable = False
End Sub
```

The Quests class is responsible for loading the .quest file passed to its Load() function:

```
Private Function getElement(ByVal field As String, _
        ByRef element As XmlElement) As String
    Dim value As String = ""
```

```
    Try
        value = element.GetElementsByTagName(field)(0).InnerText
    Catch ex As Exception
        REM ignore error, just return empty
        Console.WriteLine(ex.Message)
    End Try
    Return value
End Function


Public Function Load(ByVal filename As String) As Boolean
    Try
        REM open the xml file
        Dim doc As New XmlDocument()
        doc.Load(filename)
        Dim list As XmlNodeList = doc.GetElementsByTagName("quest")
        For Each node As XmlNode In list
            REM get next record in table
            Dim element As XmlElement = node
            Dim q As New Quest()
            REM store fields
            q.Title = getElement("title", element)
            q.Summary = getElement("summary", element)
            q.Description = getElement("description", element)
            q.RequiredItem = getElement("req_item", element)
            q.RequiredItemCount = getElement("req_item_count", element)
            q.RequiredItemFlag = getElement("req_item_flag", element)
            q.RequiredLocFlag = getElement("req_loc_flag", element)
            q.RequiredLocX = getElement("req_loc_x", element)
            q.RequiredLocY = getElement("req_loc_y", element)
            q.RewardGold = getElement("reward_gold", element)
            q.RewardItem = getElement("reward_item", element)
            q.RewardXP = getElement("reward_xp", element)
            REM add new item to list
            quests.Add(q)
        Next
    Catch ex As Exception
        Return False
    End Try
    Return True
End Function
```

Starting a Quest

We now have the quest data (via our quest editor tool and the two support classes), a way to display quest information in the game, a function that tests whether the conditions have been met, and a way to give rewards to the player. There's just one problem: when the game starts up, the first quest is already available. We need to use a flag to selectively enable a quest. That flag is called Quests.Enabled, and is set to True for the Quest Demo. Since this is a global property, it can be set from *anywhere* in the game's code. It's up to the quest writer to make sure the player has enough information to complete it! In this simple example, all you have to do is pick up the key nearby and go to the obvious tile on the right. Obviously, real quests will be more involved than this, but it was necessary to keep it simple while testing the QuestComplete() function.

```
Public Property Enabled() As Boolean
    Get
        Return p_enable
    End Get
    Set(ByVal value As Boolean)
        p_enable = value
    End Set
End Property
```

The QuestNumber and QuestItem properties keep the current quest at the forefront so we don't have to mess with that in the game code.

```
Public Property QuestNumber() As Integer
    Get
        Return p_current
    End Get
    Set(ByVal value As Integer)
        REM update position
        p_current = value
        If p_current < 0 Then
            p_current = 0
        ElseIf p_current > quests.Count - 1 Then
            p_current = quests.Count - 1
        End If
        REM update active quest
        p_quest = GetQuest(p_current)
```

```
        End Set
End Property
Public ReadOnly Property QuestItem() As Quest
    Get
        Return p_quest
    End Get
End Property
```

Quest Window

The quest window comes up with the 'Q' key. This class is using its own Dialogue rather than sharing the global one in the main program. This has a number of advantages, not least of which is getting rid of conflicts with other parts of the game that are vying for the dialogue window. When updating the Quests class, we need to pass it the mouse state like usual, to cause the buttons to highlight and respond to click events. The code to draw the quest window is tasked with setting the properties for the Dialogue object so it displays the desired quest properties.

```
Public Sub updateMouse(ByVal pos As Point, ByVal btn As MouseButtons)
    p_dialog.updateMouse(pos, btn)
End Sub

Public Sub Draw()
    If Not p_enable Then
        p_dialog.Title = "No Current Quest"
        p_dialog.Message = "You do not have a quest at this time."
        p_dialog.NumButtons = 1
        p_dialog.setButtonText(1, "Close")
    Else
        p_dialog.Title = p_quest.Title
        If QuestComplete() Then
            p_dialog.Title += " (COMPLETE)"
        End If
        p_dialog.Message = p_quest.Description
        p_dialog.NumButtons = 2
        p_dialog.setButtonText(1, "OK")
        p_dialog.setButtonText(2, "Cancel")
    End If
    p_dialog.Draw()
End Sub
```

Completing a Quest

In order to tell when a quest's conditions have been met, we need to add a new feature to the Inventory class that was not foreseen in the previous chapter. Inventory is self-contained and works well, but until now it has not needed to expose any of its items. Now, in order to figure out whether an item quest condition was met, we have to ask Inventory whether it has a certain item (and return the number of items held). These two new functions must be added to the Inventory class:

```
Public Function HasItem(ByVal name As String) As Boolean
    Dim count As Integer = ItemCount(name)
    If count = 0 Then
        Return False
    Else
        Return True
    End If
End Function
Public Function ItemCount(ByVal name As String) As Integer
    Dim count As Integer = 0
    For Each it As Item In p_inventory
        If name = it.Name Then count += 1
    Next
    Return count
End Function
```

Hint

The map file is not taken into account when testing the "Go To Location" field. This might be a required field in the quest editor due to the distinct possibility that a portal might take the player into a new map.

Another piece of information we need in order to test for quest conditions is the player's current location on the map. This has been handled in the Form1 code in all of our demos up to this point, but now the time has come to move that code into the Game class so it can be used for purposes such as this. The Level class has been used with a simple level variable like so:

```
Private level As Level
```

But now we need to move this into Game. Let's call it World, which seems appropriate.

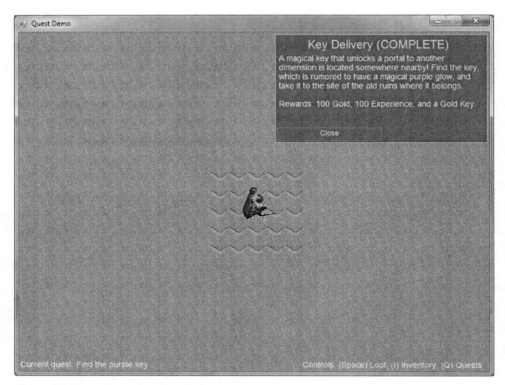

Figure 19.3
The quest's conditions have been met—and the reward is waiting.

```
Public World As Level
```

Now, in the `Form1_Load` startup function, the level-loading code needs to be modified like so:

```
game.World = New Level(game, 25, 19, 32)
game.World.loadTilemap("quest demo.level")
game.World.loadPalette("palette.bmp", 5)
```

There are other areas in the program code that refer to the old `level` variable; they have all been changed to `game.World`. When a quest's conditions have been met, the window displays a "COMPLETE" message, as you can see in Figure 19.3.

```
Public Function QuestComplete() As Boolean
    Dim itemcount As Integer
    Dim itemname As String
    Dim sitex, sitey As Integer
```

```
    Dim absX, absY As Integer
    Dim tileX, tileY As Integer
    REM look for required quest items
    If p_quest.RequiredItemFlag Then
        itemcount = p_quest.RequiredItemCount
        itemname = p_quest.RequiredItem
        REM check inventory for item
        Dim count = p_game.Inven.ItemCount(itemname)
        If count < itemcount Then Return False
    End If
    REM look for required location
    If p_quest.RequiredLocFlag Then
        sitex = p_quest.RequiredLocX
        sitey = p_quest.RequiredLocY
        absX = p_game.World.ScrollPos.X + p_game.Hero.X + 48
        absY = p_game.World.ScrollPos.Y + p_game.Hero.Y + 48 + 24
        tileX = absX \ 32
        tileY = absY \ 32
        If tileX <> sitex Or tileY <> sitey Then Return False
    End If
    Return True
End Function
```

There are a few more helper functions and properties to round out the Quests class, but I'll let you review the code in the Quests class yourself since it's pretty basic stuff. One more thing about completing quests: we will need to remove the required quest item from the player's inventory after the quest is complete. Figure 19.4 shows the reward message.

Over in our main program code, we handle quests with the doQuests() function:

```
Public Sub doQuests()
    quests.updateMouse(game.MousePos, game.MouseButton)
    quests.Draw()
    If quests.Selection > 0 Then
        quests.Visible = False
        quests.Selection = -1
        If quests.QuestComplete() Then
            Dim q As Quest = quests.QuestItem()
            reward = "You have received "
            If q.RewardXP > 0 Then
```

Figure 19.4
The quest reward message notifies the player what has been awarded.

```
        game.Hero.Experience += q.RewardXP
        reward += q.RewardXP.ToString() + " experience"
        If q.RewardGold > 0 Then reward += ", "
    End If
    If q.RewardGold > 0 Then
        game.Hero.Gold += q.RewardGold
        reward += q.RewardGold.ToString() + " gold"
        If q.RewardItem <> "" Then reward += ", "
    End If
    If q.RewardItem <> "" Then
        game.Inven.AddItem(items.getItem(q.RewardItem))
        If q.RewardXP > 0 Or q.RewardGold > 0 Then
            reward += " and "
        End If
```

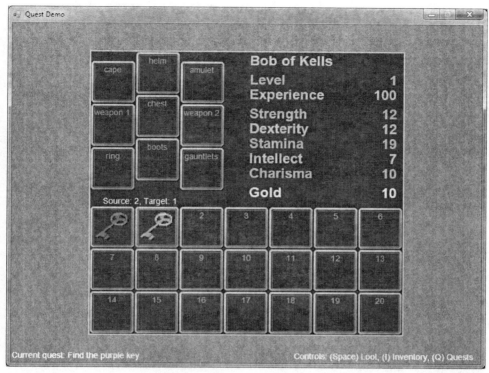

Figure 19.5
Inventory shows that the experience, gold, and item have been received.

```
            reward += "a " + q.RewardItem
        End If
        reward += "."
        showDialogue("QUEST REWARD", reward, "Close")
    End If
  End If
End Sub
```

The end result after all of this data editing and source code? When the quest has been completed and the reward message is displayed, the reward items are also credited to the player's assets in the form of experience, gold, and/or an item. The proof is shown in Figure 19.5. It will be unusual to grant all three as the reward for a single quest but this does show that all three reward types are working.

LEVEL UP!

That concludes the quest system for Celtic Crusader. Thanks to the features already in the game, it was a piece of cake to get this up and running quickly using mainly the Dialogue class (which still looks decent but could definitely use a face-lift). A data-driven quest system is a powerful feature in a game. Although our little example didn't explore a complete quest chain, the foundation has been laid for the example coming up in the next and final chapter.

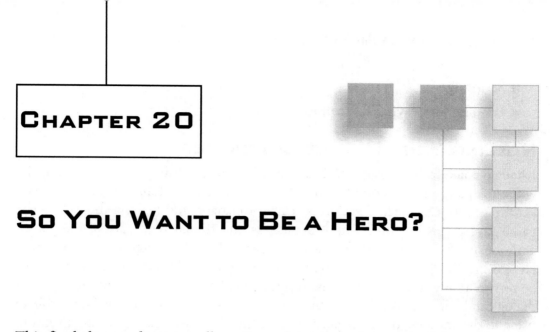

CHAPTER 20

SO YOU WANT TO BE A HERO?

This final chapter draws on all previous chapters to demonstrate a sample game using the tools and source code developed up to this point, with special attention paid to Lua script programming. My goal is to make it as easy as possible for you to create your own RPG, by giving just enough information in the example to show how things work, but without going so far into the gameplay that it's difficult to understand how the sample game works. We will build a character creation screen and learn how to save the game, and then use script code to create a simple scenario with a few quests. If questing is your thing, then you can create your own set of quests for your own game. If "hack & slash" is your thing, then you can use simple quests to direct the player toward a goal while primarily just throwing hordes of monsters at them! Along the way, many small but significant improvements have been made to the classes (especially the Game class) to accommodate the requirements of a complete game. We have to pull the sample code from all of the prior chapters into a single project that required these changes—using a custom Dialogue for each component (treasure, combat, quests, etc.), among the usual improvements made to code while a game is being developed. All of the editors are in the run-time folder for the game in this chapter's resource files (www.courseptr.com/downloads) for easy access, so if you want to make changes to the game just fire up the editors and start editing!

Here's what we'll cover in this chapter:

- Rolling your player character

- Scripting

- Loading and saving the game

ROLLING YOUR PLAYER CHARACTER

I had to make a few design decisions in order to get this game finished, again, without making it too complex (at which point, it is no longer very useful as a learning tool). One such decision is related to saving and loading the game. The game save revolves around the Player class and the current state of the player, without much concern for the rest of the game data (NPC states, treasure drops, etc.). Basically, the levels are pretty much self-contained modules that can simply be re-run at any time, based on the script code of course. Getting into a load/save dialog can be messy. We do have the Dialogue class, and it is absolutely possible to use it to display a list of saved game files for the player to load, but I didn't want to get into all the code needed to do that (reading the directory for existing savegame files, for example). So, in the interest of time and brevity, only one savegame file will be used. This game is simple enough that I do not feel this detracts at all from the experience. You can use the load/save code to implement your own load/save system. Figure 20.1 shows the character generator for the game.

SCRIPTING

The great thing about the source code for Celtic Crusader is that all of the "big pieces" are in classes that are initialized in Form1_Load. Furthermore, all of the real work is being done in the doUpdate() function, which calls doScrolling(), doMonsters(), doHero(), etc. This is a very clean way to build a game, because it is easy to add new things to it, and we can see easily what's happening in this game at a glance without wading through hundreds of lines of code muddying up these main functions. The way this code is structured *also* makes it possible to *script* much of it with Lua! We haven't touched Lua since way back in Chapter 13, "Using Portals to Expand the World." Now we'll dig up that Lua code again and add it to the final game project so we can script portions of the game, such as loading levels.

Hint

Refer back to Chapter 13 if you need help adding the LuaInterface library to the project, which dll files are needed, etc.

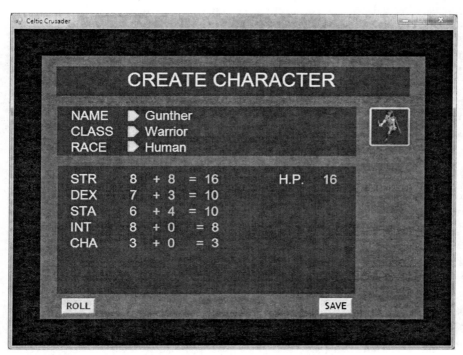

Figure 20.1
Rolling the stats for a new character.

Binding Basic Functions

In order to give the script something to *work on*, we have to call a function in the script file. When a script is opened, if there is no function, then it is simply parsed and no more processing takes place. You can continue to use the script global variables but no work takes place in the script unless you tell it to do something from the Basic game code. In our Form1 source code, we have a function called doUpdate() which does timing, calls all of the update functions, displays info on the screen, etc.—in other words, this is our workhorse function, the core loop of the game. We're going to plug the Lua update into Game.Update(), which is already functioning. It is called from doUpdate():

```
game.Update()
```

Hint

The script.lua file *must* be in the folder Celtic Crusader\Project\bin\Debug or else the LuaInterface library won't be able to find it. If you add the .lua file to the project with "Add Existing Item," unfortunately, Visual Studio will *copy* the file to the project folder which is the wrong location, so that won't work. It's probably best to just open the .lua file with Notepad or another text editor outside of Visual Studio.

The loop in `Form1.doUpdate()` calls a function to update Lua. The only thing `Game.Update()` really does is refresh the game window (technically, the `PictureBox` *on* the form), so it doesn't matter whether we update Lua before or after `Game.Update()`, it will work either way. I've added a new function call to a `ScriptUpdate()` function which we will write.

```
Private Sub doUpdate()
    Dim frameRate As Integer = game.FrameRate()
    Dim ticks As Integer = Environment.TickCount()
    Static drawLast As Integer = 0
    If ticks > drawLast + 16 Then
        drawLast = ticks
        doScrolling()
        doMonsters()
        doTreasure()
        doHero()
        doDialogue()
        doInventory()
        doQuests()
        doCombat()
        game.ScriptUpdate()
        game.Update()
        Application.DoEvents()
    Else
        REM throttle the cpu
        Threading.Thread.Sleep(1)
    End If
End Sub
```

Binding Lua Functions

Below is a sample Lua script for the final game demo in this chapter. All of the major components of the game can be selectively loaded with script functions, and almost total control is given to the script to override what happens in the default Basic code (in `Form1_Load()` and `doUpdate()`). Let's briefly review the properties available. Note that most are all read-only properties. Making changes to them does not affect the game, as they are just intended to supply information to the script. The exception is ScrollX and ScrollY, which are both sent to the script and *back* to Basic, so you can change the player's current location in the world with these properties.

- WindowTitle
- ScrollX
- ScrollY
- PortalFlag
- CollidableFlag
- Health
- HP
- QuestNumber
- QuestSummary
- QuestCompleteFlag
- MessageResult

Here are the functions available to our Lua script, which are tied in to the Basic code.

- LoadLevel()
- LoadItems()
- LoadQuests()
- LoadHero()
- DropGold()
- AddCharacter()
- Write()
- Message()

Hint

This code assumes the reader has a basic understanding of the Lua language, since we aren't learning the language in this book. Lua is not difficult, but it is more "C-like" than Basic, so it may come as a bit of a surprise. Just study the example and modify it to see what happens in the game.

```lua
--Celtic Crusader Lua Script
state = 0

--called once when game starts up
function startup()
    WindowTitle = "Celtic Crusader"
    ScrollX = 1000
    ScrollY = 100
    LoadLevel("kildare.level")
    LoadItems("default.item")
    LoadQuests("default.quest")
    LoadHero("default.char")
    DropGold(2, 900, 420)
    DropGold(4, 940, 440)
    DropGold(3, 920, 430)
    DropGold(1, 910, 420)
    DropGold(5, 930, 420)
    DropItem("Silver Key", 700, 450)
    AddCharacter("skeleton unarmed.char", 880, 400, 380, 150)
    for n = 1,20 do
        AddCharacter("skeleton unarmed.char", 1750, 100, 2000, 800)
    end
end


--called regularly every frame
function update()
    Write(480, 580, "Controls: (Space) Action, (I) Inventory, (Q) Quests")
    Write(0, 540, "Portal: " .. tostring(PortalFlag))
    Write(0, 560, "Collidable: " .. tostring(CollidableFlag))
    Write(650, 0, tostring(Health) .. "/" .. tostring(HP) .. " HP")
    text = "Current quest: " .. tostring(QuestNumber) .. ": " .. QuestSummary
    if QuestCompleteFlag == true then
        text = text .. " (COMPLETE)"
    else
        text = text .. " (incomplete)"
```

```
    end
    Write(0, 580, text)
    if state == 0 then
        Message("Welcome!", "Welcome to the land of Celtic Crusader, "
            .. "brave adventurer! "
            .. "Make your way to the room nearby and search for a key."
            ,"Continue")
    end
    if MessageResult == 1 then
        state = state + 1
    end
end
```

With this script code working, we can see in Figure 20.2 that the 20 skeleton NPCs have been added and are roaming within the specified range.

Figure 20.2
Attacking enemy characters that were added to the level with script code.

LOADING AND SAVING THE GAME

The *only* thing that is saved is the player character, not the game state. Think of the player's stats, inventory, gold, experience, level, and so on, as the persistent data, while the game levels are replayable with simple goals and repeatable logic.

Saving

Here is the `Player.SaveGame()` function. This is an expandable function that can handle future needs for player data. Presently, all of the player's stats, gold, inventory items, current world position, and current quest are saved. Just remember, the levels are intended to be stateless, meaning they reset when they are loaded, so treat the levels as replayable when designing your game. An alternative is to save all of the data for a game level, such as which items have been picked up, which monsters have been killed, etc.—a daunting amount of information to keep track of! And not to mention, that messes up the data-driven nature of the game, making it difficult to change anything in the editors when some things are stored in the save file and others are not.

```
Public Sub SaveGame(ByVal filename As String)
    Try
        REM create data type templates
        Dim typeInt As System.Type = System.Type.GetType("System.Int32")
        Dim typeBool As System.Type = System.Type.GetType("System.Boolean")
        Dim typeStr As System.Type = System.Type.GetType("System.String")

        REM create xml schema
        Dim table As New DataTable("gamestate")
        table.Columns.Add(New DataColumn("name", typeStr))
        table.Columns.Add(New DataColumn("class", typeStr))
        table.Columns.Add(New DataColumn("race", typeStr))
        table.Columns.Add(New DataColumn("level", typeInt))
        table.Columns.Add(New DataColumn("xp", typeInt))
        table.Columns.Add(New DataColumn("hp", typeInt))
        table.Columns.Add(New DataColumn("str", typeInt))
        table.Columns.Add(New DataColumn("dex", typeInt))
        table.Columns.Add(New DataColumn("sta", typeInt))
        table.Columns.Add(New DataColumn("int", typeInt))
        table.Columns.Add(New DataColumn("cha", typeInt))
```

```
table.Columns.Add(New DataColumn("quest", typeInt))
table.Columns.Add(New DataColumn("scrollx", typeInt))
table.Columns.Add(New DataColumn("scrolly", typeInt))

For n = 1 To 9
    table.Columns.Add(New DataColumn("item0" + n.ToString(),
      typeStr))
Next
For n = 10 To 30
    table.Columns.Add(New DataColumn("item" + n.ToString(),
      typeStr))
Next

REM copy data into datatable
Dim row As DataRow = table.NewRow()
row("name") = Name
row("class") = PlayerClass
row("race") = Race
row("level") = Level
row("xp") = Experience
row("hp") = HitPoints
row("str") = STR
row("dex") = DEX
row("sta") = STA
row("int") = INT
row("cha") = CHA
row("quest") = p_game.quests.QuestNumber
row("scrollx") = p_game.world.ScrollPos.X
row("scrolly") = p_game.world.ScrollPos.Y

Dim itm As Item
For n = 1 To 9
    itm = p_game.inven.GetItem(n)
    row("item0" + n.ToString()) = itm.Name
Next
For n = 10 To 30
    itm = p_game.inven.GetItem(n)
    row("item" + n.ToString()) = itm.Name
Next
table.Rows.Add(row)
```

```
            REM save xml file
            table.WriteXml(filename)
            table.Dispose()

        Catch es As Exception
            MessageBox.Show(es.Message)
        End Try
    End Sub
```

Loading

Loading a game with `Player.LoadGame()` involves a minor workaround regarding the character artwork. First, the "class" property is read from the save file, and then an appropriate animation set is loaded based on the class (remember, the .char files for the player are templates, not actual characters). Here are the files loaded for the four classes:

Warrior	hero sword.char
Paladin	hero axe shield.char
Hunter	hero bow.char
Priest	hero staff.char

After one of the four .char files have been loaded—just to get the animations going—then the save file data is loaded over the top of the template data that was just loaded. So, fields like Name, Race, STR, and so on, replace the template values stored in the .char file. These properties are stored in the .save file, and will override the defaults.

```
Public Sub LoadGame(ByVal filename As String)
    Try
        REM open the xml file
        Dim doc As New XmlDocument()
        doc.Load(filename)
        Dim list As XmlNodeList = doc.GetElementsByTagName("gamestate")
        Dim element As XmlElement = list(0)

        REM load default animations based on class
        p_game.hero.PlayerClass = GetElement("class", element)
        Select Case p_game.hero.PlayerClass
```

```
        Case "Warrior"
            p_game.hero.Load("hero sword.char")
        Case "Paladin"
            p_game.hero.Load("hero axe shield.char")
        Case "Hunter"
            p_game.hero.Load("hero bow.char")
        Case "Priest"
            p_game.hero.Load("hero staff.char")
End Select

REM read data fields
p_game.hero.Name = getElement("name", element)
p_game.hero.PlayerClass = getElement("class", element)
p_game.hero.Race = getElement("race", element)
p_game.hero.Level = Convert.ToInt32(GetElement("level",
    element))
p_game.hero.Experience = Convert.ToInt32(GetElement("xp",
    element))
p_game.hero.HitPoints = Convert.ToInt32(GetElement("hp",
    element))
p_game.hero.STR = Convert.ToInt32(GetElement("str", element))
p_game.hero.DEX = Convert.ToInt32(GetElement("dex", element))
p_game.hero.STA = Convert.ToInt32(GetElement("sta", element))
p_game.hero.INT = Convert.ToInt32(GetElement("int", element))
p_game.hero.CHA = Convert.ToInt32(GetElement("cha", element))
p_game.quests.QuestNumber = Convert.ToInt32(GetElement("quest",
    element))
p_game.world.X = Convert.ToInt32(GetElement("scrollx", element))
p_game.world.Y = Convert.ToInt32(GetElement("scrolly", element))

Dim itm As Item
For n = 1 To 9
    itm = p_game.items.GetItem(GetElement("item0" + _
        n.ToString(), element))
    If itm IsNot Nothing Then
        p_game.inven.SetItem(itm, n)
    End If
Next
For n = 10 To 30
    itm = p_game.items.GetItem(GetElement("item" + _
```

```
                    n.ToString(), element))
            If itm IsNot Nothing Then
                p_game.inven.SetItem(itm, n)
            End If
        Next

    Catch ex As Exception
        MessageBox.Show(ex.Message)
    End Try
End Sub
```

Level Up!

Unfortunately, we're out of time and space to go any further with the game within the pages of this book. So, despite there being much more we could do with the game, this will have to conclude the Celtic Crusader game and the book. The adventure will continue in *Visual C# Game Programming for Teens*, which delves into dungeon-based RPGs! I hope you have enjoyed the journey we have taken together while learning how to build a custom role-playing game. It has been enjoyable for me to share my thoughts about RPG programming. I would welcome your comments and game ideas as well! Be sure to stop by my forum to say hello at http://www.jharbour.com/forum. Safe journeys ahead.

INDEX

SYMBOLS

* (multiplication), 48
\+ (plus sign), 35, 47–48
− (minus sign), 47–48
/ (division), 48
= (equal to) operator, 54

A

absolute paths, 116
accessing bitmap pixels, 104–106
ActiveX, 25
actors, 114
addExperience() function, 402
adding
    Lua source code, 281–287
    objects, 237
    real-time game loops, 135–136
    resource files, 156–158
    scenery, 238–253
    Timer controls, 37
    trees, 247–253
    Windows Media Player control, 165
addition, 47–48
adventure games, 18
aligning tiles, 228–229
allocation, memory, 33
alpha blending, 115–116
ambient light, 154
ambient sound, 154
Animate() function, 126, 247
animation
    characters, 319–321
    death, 399–403
    frames, calculating, 127
    friendly NPCs (non-player characters), 375–376
    hostile NPCs (non-player characters), 370–374
    player characters (PCs), 364–370
    real-time, 113
    sprites, 117–128
Anna the Peasant, 375
applying
    If...Then statements, 41
    Media Player control, 163–166
    variables, 32–35
Aquaphobia: Mutant Brain Sponge Madness, 13
archers, skeletons, 301–302
architecture, 134
    .NET Framework, 23
armor, NPCs (non-player characters), 190–191
armor class (AC), 380
arrays, 57–58
artwork, 14
attacks
    rolls, 378–384
    starting, 357–358
    state, 396–399
attributes
    characters, 180–181, 292–303
    Charisma (CHA), 293
    Dexterity (DEX), 292
    hit points (HPs), 293–294
    Intellect (INT), 293
    Stamina (STA), 293
    Strength (STR), 292
    variables, 34. *See also* data types
audio, programming, 153–162. *See also* sound
Audio Demo program, 158–162
automatically moving dialogue, 338

axes
    female heroes, 369–370
    heroes, 365
    Vikings, 373

B

backgrounds, bitmaps, 214–215
Baldur's Gate, 17, 171, 356
base character classes, 294–299
Basic, 22–24
basic functions, binding, 473–474
Battlefield, 13
Beginning Game Programming, Third Edition, 10
behavior, sprites, 117
binding
    basic functions, 473–474
    Lua functions, 474–477
bins, 116
bit block transfers, 115
Bitmap Drawing Demo, 104
Bitmap.GetPixel() function, 104
Bitmap.RotateFlip() function, 103
bitmaps, 99–111
    accessing, 104–106
    backgrounds, 214–215
    drawing, 99–103
    exporting, 201
    flipping, 103–104
    loading, 100–102
    rotating, 103–104
    scaling, 103
    storing, 68
Bitmap.SetPixel() function, 105

483

CPSIA information can be obtained
at www.ICGtesting.com
Printed in the USA
FFOW02n0846050614
5770FF